samsara

david abramczyk

for Gerard

The old man likes his whiskey. I bring it to him as muted shadows expand across the square. A gust of wind bites my face. Digging my chin into my coat, I hopscotch past the beggars on the cathedral steps.

"Vous avez de la monnaie?" A nappy-headed beggar holds out his hand.

You've got to be joking. I'm only a half a step from your dejected state, my man. No, no *monnaie* for...

He lunges at my bag. Paper bursts into the air as I rip the bottle back.

"Hey!"

Tossing his bum half of the wishbone to the wind, he darts off, cursing. The poor robbing the poor: god, I love socialism.

I tuck the bottle into my pants like a loaded gun. 'Yankee Go Home' is scrawled angrily in marker across the door. Home, sweet home. I press the button without a name.

The buzzer whirrs, a lock clicks. A door slams. The lights are broken...they're always broken. Hands stake out a cigarette. Gauloise soft pack, corner pocket: a cigarette for people serious about dying. *For that freshly paved taste.* I spark the warped butt between my lips.

"Christ." I chuck it against the wall – wrong end. My hand meets the cold rail-four floors, all the way to the top. Steam sneaks through a transom. Something falls; a child shrieks, a mother scolds. My footsteps echo off the tiles: *forty-seven, forty-eight, forty-nine...*

Silhouettes morph on a frozen sea of stucco as I near the glow seeping from the door.

"What's up, doc?" creaks a voice from the bedroom.

"Same shit, different day," I say.

The sofa rots quietly at the far end of the room. Antennae mangled, a dusty television hums erratically against the wall opposite like a mutated insect. Inside, a perfect woman stands before a map manipulating clouds with her arms. I look away, trying to recall better days, better beds.

I slump into a chair and stare down at the chipped place mat of *Tintin et Milou*. A clump of sage hangs over crusty burners. A fly fitzes lazily over a coagulated pot of stew. I sigh, lift myself up, and enter his room. *His lair.* It's always dark in there. I hate going in but I have to. A mouse slinking past a snoozing viper.

Dirty shagpile carpet crawls between my toes. I pick up his steady wheeze from the bed. There he is, biding his time as I near: waiting to make the kill.

My eyes adjust. The table, a glass-and-chrome deal, brims over with twisted cigarette packets, tattered copies of *Liberté* and half-burnt sticks of incense. A crack runs along its length, expanding invisibly like the fault line beneath some sleepy California town. Some day the table will shatter, sucking all existence into its chasm.

Maybe the Buddha will save us. So happy, so serene, yet fat. Enthroned on a tattered wicker chair in the far corner, one leg raised slightly, he beams towards the heavens as if he just won the lottery, flakes of golden paint curling off his belly like autumn leaves: a benevolent Jabba the Hut.

I glance in the other direction at an entirely different picture. The scores on his face run deep, suggesting vice. He duffs a butt into the ashtray, rasps. Two polished stones – one green, the other red – sag from a hole in his left ear like an ancient talisman. His entire body sags. Once, you might have called him lanky, but gravity has taken hold and is winning. He is one of the survivors: a resilient spore that slipped through the cracks.

Gerard used to roll the dice, back in his day, with some good ol' boys from Paris, Texas. A couple of roughnecks: genuine, corn-fed, cattle-rustling rednecks. "Gonna go see the other Paris," the story went. Next thing they knew, they were trucking through Central Asia with a bunch of heroin junkies from *Quartier Nord,* running VW busloads of opiates from Calcutta to Cannes. The way he tells it, he put the French in *French Connection.*

Gerard has hung onto a mixed bag of hippie expressions from those days, tainted with a Parisian accent and stressing every fifth to seventh word. The overall effect falls somewhere between that of a fire-and-brimstone backwoods preacher and Charlie Manson.

"It's getting pretty lame down here, Gerard," I say. "Those Algerians or Tunisians, or whoever the fuck they are, shake me down every time I come within a hundred yards of the beach. Arab bastards."

"Keep taking their shit like a good boy and some day they're gonna make you their bitch...*enculé!*" Gerard spits.

"It's going to snow tonight, isn't it? That's what the weather lady was just talking about..."

"Why don't you ask *him*?" he says, rolling his eyes at the Buddha. "He knows when it's going to *snow* or rain; he knows when you're *happy* or sad..."

Why can't he just answer the question?

Somewhere in the back of my head, 'Santa Claus is Coming to Town' starts up.

"...he knows when you're *gonna* get some nice fresh *cunt*, when you're gonna..."

"Fuck off."

I hate when he talks about women like that.

"Hey man, *relaaax.*"

"Give me a Valium and I'll think about it. This whole scene blows. Flat pints of *Kronenbourg*, stale *sandwiches aux crabes*, those little fluffed-up rats tethered to disasters in plastic surgery. Why the fuck don't they call them *sandwiches faux crabes*? Seven euros for a fake crab sandwich...what a joke."

"Life is *sooo hard!*"

"I've had smoother rides."

"...Maybe it's time to go," he sighs. "Maybe it is not such a good life for you here."

"You think those dickheads who wrote my eviction notice on the door could hook me up with a discounted airfare? It's either that or join the circus."

"The circus. *Cool, man.*"

"Yeah, right."

A smirk lurks within his wiry nest, yellowed from a million un-filtered cigarettes. He's ready to pounce but he's not going to kill the mouse yet: what would be the fun of that? Just bat it around for now, play with it a while.

"You see anything good today?"

His cheekbones rise. "I saw nice *chica*...she had on a tight little *jupe*. Mmmm..." Fluttering his eyelids, he tilts his chin against the backside of his hand. "Just like Betty *boop-oop-a-doop!*"

Then he wheels round, the stones in his ear clicking like abacus beads, and smiles up at a glossy poster of Betty Boop, tacked on the wall above.

"...Boop-oop-a..." He coughs up a gob of phlegm – I spotted it in the street, fanned between Jimmy Dean and Peter Tosh.

He was always going on about her...Betty. Before he became a total prick. Besides, I still owe him rent and it might hold him off for another few weeks.

I had turned up in these parts four months back with twenty euros and a sassy French girlfriend I'd met down in Tangiers. The euros ran out the next day; the girl didn't last much longer.

Gerard had found me curled up on a bench like a lost kitten. I was an easy mark. Must have looked like one of those bubbly Midwestern farm girls stepping off a bus in Hollywood who wound up in a cheap porno getting fucked beside someone's pool a week later.

Promised to take me in until I got back on my feet...for a price. A few weeks here, a few weeks there – at the moment, my marker roughly stands at about 1,800 euros, no easy feat in a socialist country. Unless, of course, you're dealing.

Square face, sultry pout, feather boa floating round her twiggy frame, framed in a big juicy red heart... Betty Boop: she was his girl. The kind of girl who'd fuck your brains out and leave you believing she was still a virgin in the morning. Maybe she reminded him of the waitress at the corner restaurant, or the skittish Arab whores who loitered near the harbor like tattered gulls waiting for chunks of stale bread. Still, it was almost as if he respected her, as if she meant something to him. Probably the only girl he ever cared about. Or maybe she didn't exist...ask me if I give a shit.

I focus on the bed, running my eyes down the bony frame. The woolen blanket hugs the mattress below his trunk. It hugs his leg, or lack of one. Amputated from the hip. Only a stump remains. I only asked once. "An accident," he'd said.

Most young guys have roommates their own age to go out with on weekends – hit the bars and meet some girls, maybe get lucky. I've got a repugnant, smelly, chain-smoking amputee who only leaves the apartment for hookers, liquor and drugs. Most of the time he suckers me into being his delivery bitch.

He holds out some pistachios; I push his hand away.

"Come on. How you gonna fly away from here if you don't eat?" he says.

"I don't want any. They taste like ass."

"*Oh man.* You're too much! What have you got to worry about? You're young, you got a place to crash...all you need is *la* and *la* and *la*!"

With each syllable, his hands slice wildly through the air, discharging nuts as they carve out the figure of a woman. A wave of blood surges through my head, breaks, ebbs...

Fucking letch.

"Did you talk to that dude?" I mutter.

"Yeah, man. He's gonna drop by the fountain later tonight with maybe six, seven ounces. The *best* shit in town. And then we'll split down to Crillon."

"I'm not going out; I'm kind of low on cash."

"You pay me back if you want to come...if not, *ça va.*"

That's what he wants. Keep up the tab, keep me on my knees. I'm already into him for nearly two large. And at the rate I'm going, it's only going to get worse.

I hoist myself onto the edge of the bed, twisting a pocketful of paraphernalia from my jeans: cigarettes, lighter, OCBs, a small chunk of hash...all the necessary components. I hold the hash over the flame, sprinkling the table with tiny black flecks.

'*I smoked, but didn't inhale.*' Non-demurral answers on cocaine use...yeah, right. Who do you guys think you're kidding? If you're going to do drugs, at least be up front about it.

I'll give Gerard that...him and Charlie Sheen. That's about all I'll give him. And he's definitely not 'winning.'

My tongue slides along a cigarette. I gut it like a fish.

"So I'll smoke my joint, too."

Reaching for a cigarette, he shifts in the dying light. A salvo of smoke rings curl round his natty beard, expanding, dissipating over a sun-dried pate that resembles the topside of a sea turtle's shell. I rip off a corner of the rolling paper packet, curl up a filter on my thumb.

I don't know why I smoke hash anymore. I don't particularly like the high. It annoys me when I get so stoned that it inhibits simple things – doing laundry or cooking Mac and Cheese. I think I do it mostly to pass the time. Isn't that why most people do drugs – to pass the time, spackle in the gaps between point A and B? The perfect filler: the Ikea furniture for all those empty caverns and corridors of your mind.

There's something about making something with your hands, too. The construction of a well-designed joint requires a certain degree of skill…like sculpting.

Each time I roll one, I try to make it a little tighter (but not too tight), a little smoother, edging closer and closer to the perfect unblemished cone, the perfect *mélange* of tobacco and hash, complete with hand-spun filter meticulously selected from the fresh packet of cigarettes…

Sounds like I'm talking about a bottle of chardonnay now, doesn't it? The impermanence of it all could be likened to that of a Tibetan sand *mandala*, a transient geometric representation of the universe… but that's reaching a bit, isn't it? Who am I kidding? I've been reading too many of these Buddhist books Gerard has lying around. Like I said, it's mostly to pass the time.

Gerard rifles through a stack of CDs. A sharp lick of Buddy Guy cuts through the room.

"Asked my baby for a dollar, and she gave me a twenty-dollar bill."

I reach for the light switch but he checks me.

"Leave it, man."

Flicking his wrist, metallic click, he sparks his Zippo, lights the candle atop a rainbow-speckled mound of wax fused to the table. Gerard hates light almost as much as a vampire. He battles all day to keep it out of his room, constantly realigning his veteran soldiers – the faded batiks and tapestries that guard the edges of the windows.

Chill air wafts in, rustling the troops.

I slide my tongue along the gum and snatch his lighter off the table. Not my best work, but an honorable mention. The guitar wavers, spitting sorrow.

"*Asked my baby for a little drink of liquor…and she gave me a whiskey still…*"

Gerard and his country-music eyes. Sometimes I almost feel sorry for him. Almost. But after a second, those eyes are full of *schadenfreud*, secrets and lies.

I pull the pint out from the back of my pants and place it on the table.

"Oh yeah!" he exalts. "Now we're gonna get down to *business*!"

Suddenly, they spark: a lifer getting a hand job from the prison whore on Christmas Day. The fix is in. He takes a swig, passes me the bottle.

A stream of wax spills down the candle, joining, running over previous paths…paths already frozen, already sealed.

"First we're gonna get *drunk*, then we're gonna get the *shit*, and *then* we're gonna get some *nice little bitches!*"

"…Whatever."

Gerard raises the candle to his cigarette.

"Goddamnit, Gerard! Why do always have to do that? You've got a lighter – use it!"

Call me superstitious, but I do not like it when people light cigarettes or cigars or crack pipes or *anything* off of a candle. They say it kills a sailor. My father was a sailor…so was I.

"Oh, *mon dieu*! Did I *kill* your *daddy*? Who's your *daddy*?"

Grinning malevolently, he spews a cloud of smoke in my face. My adrenal gates open; blood pulses through my temples…that *motherfucker*!

"You want to fuck some tight Arab pussy tonight? You can shit on them if –"

Clenching the neck of the whiskey bottle, I hurl it across the room. It clips the candle, ricochets off the Buddha's head and flies out the window, smashing in the street three floors down.

"*Shit*, man, mellow out."

Angry voices surge upwards.

"Fuck you, Gerard! Every time I bring a girl here, you spook them… every goddamn time! You know why? 'Cos you're twisted old bastard who can't look at a women without mentally fucking them in the ass, you sick fuck! And why do you always pull that shit with the candle, huh? Just *laisse tomber*, all right?"

Gerard peers out from behind his bifocals, gloating like a hyena.

"Man, if I was your age, I would be fucking women every day, every hour. That's all they want to do is fuck: they *pray* to get fucked! I've got to go out and pay for it – you can still get the shit for free, but you wanna be mister *strangers in the night, lalala dahdah, patati patata...*"

He's gyrating to his own melody.

"It's not about *fucking*, Gerard. Besides, you always end up paying one way or the other."

"Yeah, but at least they *leave* when you pay them up front! They're all whores – my mother, *your* mother…"

Shouts erupt from the street.

"Shut the fuck up about my mother!"

Suddenly, Gerard hops off the bed and onto his crutch.

"*Merde alors! Putain de bougie!*"

I shake my head, chuckling, as he stamps his good leg against the flaming blob of paraffin on the carpet. Good thing he doesn't have a wooden peg. Digging his crutch into the tiles, he hobbles over to the window.

"Hey, *soorry, maan!*" he shouts.

Irate voices holler back.

"*Oh putain, vas t'faire foutre!* All your mothers are whores, you fucking French fascists!"

He cranks up the volume on the radio, immersing the room in distortion. Three loud, thuds sound against the bedroom wall. The stout, silver-haired woman across the way materializes in her window, waving a broom.

Gerard hoists himself up with his crutch and disappears into the kitchen, stomping back in with a large pot. Lurching toward the window, he upends the contents over the railing. The stew splatters; glass shatters; someone screams. A piece of fruit blurs past the window, exploding in a wet thud. Swinging his fist in the air, Gerard roars down, a maddened dictator whipping up his masses.

"We want the world and we want it now!

We want the world and we want it now!

We want the world and we want it now!"

The lights in the kitchen blaze to life. I check my watch – 3:13am. Feminine voices chirp in the stairwell like crickets. Two silhouettes, whispering to one another in abrupt, hushed tones.

Arab girls: no more than thirty years between the two of them. Caramel faces smudged with rouge like a sloppy color-by-numbers picture; bodies clad in tight mini-skirts and tops, hugging underdeveloped bodies.

I prop myself up, rub my eyes. One of the girls forces an uncertain smile.

Gerard staggers over, tosses a solid clump of cellophane on my lap and slumps over his crutch like a weathered pirate. What booty have you brought me, Long John Silver? Pieces of eight? I unravel the twisted plastic. Hash…thick, dark chocolate, worth just as much in weight.

"This shit smells *good*. Definitely not that pollen bullshit I've been picking up off the Arabs."

"Yeah, not bad, *mais c'est pas donne* – a thousand euros. You still want it?"

One thousand euros…it sounds even worse when you convert it into dollars, but definitely better than what I could scratch off the Algerians...and it was fronted.

The trick is to move it quick, not to stretch it out. I've got my regulars – mostly yachties – but who knows how many will stick it out through the winter? Shops get boarded up, money and boats shift to warmer climes. It will be a hard push to dump it before the last of them flutter away.

"Here's four hundred now. I'll get you the rest by next week."

Four hundred euros: that could have been a plane ticket home. Something tells me it's going to be a hard winter for this grasshopper. Now that it's upon us, there's nothing stored up for the lean months. Between the rent and the exorbitant hash rates, Gerard is making a killing off of me.

Looking over his shoulder, he stashes the crumpled bills in his waistband.

I light a cigarette. I've been smoking a lot lately – too much. My lungs can't keep up. I can feel the insides of the walls searing with every toke: tiny alveoli screaming out for help like lost kittens. Maybe when I work my way out of this Oliver Twist, I'll stop. Get out in the wilderness; get away from all this bullshit and quit.

Selling hash by the gram in the south of France wasn't exactly the get-rich-quick scheme I had in mind to get me out of debt, but it beat the 'Raise Alpaca!' and 'Be a Locksmith!' ads I'd read in the back of my grandpa's hunting magazines when I was a kid. Even at five or six years old, I had enough sense to know that there were better ways to make money than raising alpaca on repossessed farmland or legally picking people's locks, but there aren't many job opportunities for aloof Americans on the Côte d'Azur.

I'm not very good at it, either. Always giving out discounts and IOUs as if they were doing *me* a favor. Always to the girls, like a sucker. Now they only send the girls. At least I get to work my own hours.

Gerard loves it. A steady, non-taxable form of income via price gouging: the perfect pension plan for a retired heroin smuggler.

"You wanna fuck – I mean, *make love* to one of these angels? *Forty* for an hour, one *hundred* for the night..."

I look away. He knows my answer. He knows damn well I don't

want any part of this, but he asks anyway.

"*Comme tu veux*...more for me!"

Ushering the girls into his room, he pauses, smacking his lips like Midas over a pile of gold.

"*Hallelujah!*"

The door shuts, sealing me off. What a bastard. Reaching under the sofa, I fumble for my earplugs, twist them, shove them deep inside. I don't want to hear the children crying tonight.

A shriek...or was I dreaming? Gerard's door swings open; two shadows dart out. I bolt upright. An earplug dribbles down my shoulder. Stifled laughter oozes out of the bedroom, fades to silence. Funny they should leave in such a hurry. For the night, wasn't it?

I really don't want to talk to his ass but I'm starving. That stew was my dinner. Maybe he's asleep. Wrapping a blanket around myself, I shuffle across the red tiles towards the kitchen. I bend over the spigot, slurp a mouthful of water. Another spurt of laughter.

"Got your rocks off, huh?"

I push open the cracked bedroom door and flip on the lights. Hog-tied and gagged, Gerard lies curled on the floor in nothing but a T-shirt, wrinkly dilapidated ass facing me.

Not a good look.

"Jesus, what's with the S & M? You really are a sick fucker, you know that?"

Dropping the blanket, I bend down and roll him over. Entrails loll out of his blood-smeared T-shirt like Doberman tongues. I recoil.

"Gerard, *what* the *hell*?"

A rancid stench hits me. I loosen the 'gag': a slinky pair of women's underwear. A rivulet of spittle runs off his cheek. His face is milky, wet.

"*Les salopes m'ont bien coupé!* I guess they don't like it up the ass, eh? *Enculé!*"

I sprint to the bathroom, returning with a hot-water-soaked towel to cover his disgorging stomach.

"Oh man. You're really fucked, Gerard."

"As long as I don't come back as a donkey, everything will be cool. Not a...*goddamn donkey!*

He coughs violently, spraying my legs with blood. What's wrong with a donkey? With being a beast of burden? I can see the reasoning, but if you reincarnated as a little girl's pet on a plush farm in the Shenandoah Valley, you'd have it made. You could only wish to be so lucky, Gerard: you'll be lucky to make it back as a slug on a Monsanto farm.

"Don't let Betty see me like this...she can't see me like this, man!"

Jumping onto the bed, I rip the poster of Betty Boop from the wall. A strange wish, not to be seen by an animated character, but a dying wish all the same.

"She can't see you now."

"Cool, cool...but..."

"What?"

"...Can you...cook me up some shit?"

"You need a doctor, not another hole in your body. I'm gonna call..."

"No! No doctors!" Lifting his head slightly, he stares at me. "Look at me – no
goddamn doctors!"

"Alright, no doctors. But where am I gonna find shit at five in the morning?"

It's not my scene but I know that heroin is an a.m. game. Junkies score first thing in the morning, just after they wake up, around nine or ten...but not this early. At five in the morning, I'll only find meth-heads or a lingering drunk.

"...And you snaked all my cash. I've only got about five euros left on me."

"Don't worry, you'll get your money, *mais...*"

"Give it to me. Give it to me *now*."

"*C'est dans la poche de mon froc.* But listen…"

I reach for his pants, fish out the money.

"That's right, bitch!" I yell as he looks on helplessly. "This is *my* money now, Gerard." I wave it over him. "You've been feeding off me too long – now you're back on the ground where you belong, you dirty French carp!"

I make for the door, but his hand latches onto my ankle, pulling me off balance.

"Get off of me!" I jerk my leg away.

"Goddamnit, listen to me." he says. "Promise me something…will you go to her?"

Poor, pathetic fuck…I can't do it: I can't leave him like this.

"Listen, Gerard, you need help fast. You're lucky I'm still here – most people would leave you to die. We're not going anywhere right now except to a hospital."

"I said no *goddamn doctors.* Go to her. I need you to give her… *quelque chose.*"

"Who? Give who *quelque chose,* Gerard? The girl down at Saint Antoine, the one who gives us free *pastise?*"

"Jack will bring you to her…but watch out, *C'est un salopard comme moi!*" He's spitting up blood now. "Just get on a plane and split. It's the best way…fly away, *papillon.*"

"Go where, Gerard – *Paris?* What are you talking about? What the fuck is a *salopard?* Goddamnit, speak English!"

"The address is on…the letters…he's the last one. Just go to him, *baabu.* He will tell you everything."

"What letters? Where are the letters, Gerard?"

"…La tête…la tête…du Buddha…"

His bloodshot eyes arc towards the golden statue. I stand over it, running my fingers carefully over its contours.

"Dans la tête…la tête."

Sanguine tendrils now radiate from under his body, tracing the grout between the tiles.

I grab the statue by the head and pull, nearly dragging it off the chair. The Buddha's not giving up his secrets easily. I wrench at it again: with a twist, the head snaps to the left and pops off.

Nestled in the Buddha's belly is a box. Intricate carvings score its sides. I open it: on top rests a syringe, a strap of leather, and a tiny folded square of newspaper. The only thing missing is a little glass box with an axe next to it and the words, 'In Case of Emergency, Break Glass.' I lay the tourniquet across Gerard's side and unfold the paper, revealing a tightly packed lump of brown powder.

"Damn! I didn't know you had it. I thought you wanted me to go hunt some down."

"Just a little *cadeux*...I..."

He coughs spastically. Sputum froths from his mouth like sea foam.

"*Jesus!* Isn't there someone I can call, someone who can patch you up? *You're gonna die, Gerard.* Am I getting through – or does this junk matter more?"

"Nobody left, man...I...just...give me my fix."

Not one to get between a dying man and his wish, I scoop a bit of powder onto a tablespoon.

"Now what? Do I mix it with water?"

I replay *Drugstore Cowboy* in my head, trying to remember the sequence...only hats on beds come to mind.

"Just...cook."

Gulping air, he twitches: a tadpole suffocating at a pond's edge.

I grab a lighter. Some powder spills as I shift the spoon.

"Shit!"

OK: still some left. I set the flame under the spoon, transforming powder into liquid. A wisp of smoke trails off the handle. Stirring with the needle, I draw back the syringe slowly. A shiver skips up my spine. Dangerous stuff. Too pure and you OD. Not pure enough and you could be left with a strychnine smile. A balancing act of additives and alkaloids that would challenge even the most agile tightrope walker.

"This is fucking ridiculous, Gerard. Look, this isn't right. There are air bubbles in the liquid. You can't have bubbles. If I inject this into your bloodstream, you could..."

Wide-eyed, curled up and bloody, he quivers.

"Gerard?"

I nudge him with my foot.

-Fin-

I've never seen this before: death, front row center. I saw a raccoon die once. Fell off a barn roof and curled up into a ball...but nothing like this. He looks like the victim of a famed mass murderer in Madame Tussaud's wax museum, a prop on a horror film set...but not real. I've seen people die on the inside, though. Slowly losing their incentive to live as their eyes cool, their hearts hollow. Not a sudden event, but fatal all the same.

In your head you always think death is scary – that you'll want to run off before your blood runs cold. But I want to do exactly the opposite now: I want to hang out a bit, see the old boy off. It's not so bad now he's not ranting or raving or harassing me. Like the town drunk who everyone misses, suddenly, after he careens his car into a semi late one Friday night.

Tossing the syringe, I flick off the light and drop onto the bed, staring at the dead lump of meat on the floor. Cowboys aren't supposed to go out like this. Where's the shoot-out, the last stand at the border, guns a'blazing? Sliced up by a couple of whores...that's not right, that's a different film.

Soft hues permeate the room, sketching shadows. The wine-dark puddle lies still, his stump nuzzled against his thigh. A lone sparrow chirps...then another.

Gradually, the room begins to brighten. Gerard's eyes are glazed tarns tricked by an early frost, slowly crusting over with death.

A ray of sunlight pierces the window, instigating motion. I retrieve the box from the kitchen and, crawling between the table and the bed, spill its contents onto the tiles.

A couple of forty-five-caliber bullets, a piece of turquoise, a clump of braided hair from an animal, some brightly colored flags covered with inscriptions. I dig further, uncovering a packet of letters and postcards tightly bound with hemp string. Addresses, some in strange scripts, from Iran, Pakistan, India, Nepal. A roadmap across the Orient…dusty border towns, late-night drops, Kalashnikov-toting soldiers. Nepal. Most addressed to Nepal. Some returned to sender.

A paper trail. These letters, these addresses: they must be from the ring. 'The Four Horsemen of the Apocalypse,' as Gerard liked to call them. Or what's left of them.

I thumb through the letters until I reach the last of them. A thick brown envelope. Slicing it open, I dump the contents on the table – a set of beads, wads of one-hundred and five-hundred euro notes tightly wound with rubber bands. Some five-hundred franc notes as well… can't change those anymore.

Just like Salvador and Gala, saving up for some rainy day.

Shit, there must be at least five grand here in euros! I shake the envelope; fragments of raw amber and coral sputter out. A tattered piece of rice-paper clings to the inside. It reads:

John Bigby, Box 108, Katmandu, Nepal.

This must be Jack. Gerard had never mentioned a Jack before yesterday. Tex and Dusty, yes, but never Jack. Some guru Gerard had started dishing money off to in his twilight years, attempting to ward off bad karma? Doubt it: Gerard followed no-one. A real dark horse. Jack will bring me to her, that's what he said…but who's *her*? Betty?"

The shiny Betty Boop poster lies before me on the bed. A jaded lover? Love *Gerard*? Who in their right mind could love *him*? Not likely. A daughter? Nah. I'm gonna go with masochistic hooker addicted to men who treat her like toilet paper.

I unroll the wads of cash and count. When I'm finished, three neat stacks of bills rest smugly the table: four thousand, eight hundred and two euros. Fuel for travel. For nearly a year now, I've been trying to scratch together a couple grand. Now, here it is and then some. Gerard's retirement package, no longer needed by him.

I pick up the beads. Strung on a tattered piece of leather, they snap together like magnets. Finely polished red spheres, like the one in Gerard's ear, flank a center bead that's oblong in shape. Milky-white patterns meander over a rich black center. Sounds like a chocolate bar commercial, doesn't it? Gingerly, I bite it: a stone of some sort.

I grab Gerard's Zippo off the table. The etching of a nude woman arches over the words 'Easy Rider'. I roll it in my palm, watching it catch the early morning light. I always wanted a Zippo.

The cries of vendors rise from the morning market.

A shiny card pokes out from between the letters...a photo, cracked and yellowed. On it are two men – one blond, the other not – on either side of... Is that Gerard... with hair? That must have been at least forty years ago. Look at that fucker, still with that beard! They are all smoking cigars; they seem very pleased with themselves. In the corner of the picture, in long cursive strokes:

The World is Our Oyster!!!

Obviously, whoever wrote this was referring to a different time. I flip it over. Taped to the back is a piece of paper, with more writing:

Ring us anytime you're up against it.

+977 1 4414588.

Hmmm...looks like the same handwriting, whoever wrote it. Us, us, us...is that a reference to the other two in the picture? Doesn't sound right. Sounds like a gay couple. *'Don't forget to include us in your masquerade ball, Nigel.'* No, these guys look a little too rough around the edges to be gay. Militant fags? I fling the picture onto the table.

There's still some heroin in the paper. Not my usual song and dance, but given the circumstances... I slip an OCB from the sleeve. Lining it with tobacco, I sprinkle on the powder, light it...*spin, spin sugar*...nice and easy. One second becomes three as my mind downshifts to neutral.

I only smoked it once before...back home at a Grateful Dead show in Vegas. I was already flying on mushrooms and beer, but there was no mistaking the fuzzy feel of opiates: a thick shag-carpet ride, the feel of honey running through your veins. Not bad to hop aboard every once in a while, but it can turn on you if you're not used to it. Remember how sick I felt the next day, puking up bile behind the Hare Krishna mobile church unit? And yet... a little couldn't hurt, especially in a situation like this. A little puff never hurt anyone. I could never shoot it, though. I've got a phobia of needles. Needles and blood. I'd pass out before the needle even pricked my vein...and I thank god for that.

I look again at Gerard. Cooling, settling, solidifying...he's toast.

I'm going to miss you, old buddy...like I miss a cold toilet seat on a crisp February morning. I wonder if he's still here, hovering over me like a cloud. Probably pissed off that I'm smoking his stash. A few more tokes of this mix and I'll be right up there with him.

My gaze drops to his beard, the corners of his mouth tucked inside…the bastard's still smiling!

What's with the smile, Gerard? Is it because you're free at last – free from that stump of a leg, that decrepit, failing excuse for a body that didn't do you any favors? Maybe you've traded it in already for a better model. Maybe you've been downgraded to the donkey…that would serve you right! I would take the donkey over Gerard's old body any day. Not so sure about the slug, though.

…Man, this shit is really strong. I'm dropping down deep and haven't even cleared half of the joint. I look down at the Buddha's head on the floor, grinning serenely. Smiles everyone, smiles…why the fuck is everyone so happy around here? I take another drag. The corners of the room are rounding out nicely now.

I lay the roach in a tray, move to the bathroom. My hair is slippery with grease. I've lost weight…heavy circles under my eyes. Not a glowing picture of health. Straight out of a Calvin Klein ad.

Heroin? How do you get to heroin? That's the end of the road, isn't it? Skid row…next thing you know, I'll be bumming change on the beach, chasing down half-burnt butts, stealing…just like the bum who tried to rip me off. You've really got to work at it, put some serious effort in to get to heroin, don't you? Burroughs was right. *And what do you want to be when you grow up, Jay, an astronaut or a fireman? No, Miss Crabtree, I want to be a heroin junkie like my Uncle Gerard!*

How the fuck do you end up here?

I splash water on my face…it's not helping. Opening the cabinet, I examine the plethora of prescriptions. Nothing like rummaging through someone's drug cabinet, especially if there are goodies to be found. I'm sure Gerard left behind some juicy pharmaceuticals. Being the son of a doctor, I'm also quite well versed.*Prenez-en une à deux avant de vous coucher.*

Two before bed…I don't need to go to bed, not yet. Red, yellow, blue…all the colors of the rainbow. I know Gerard was downing some pretty serious painkillers for his hip. Sleeping pills as well…are these Seconal? I scoop up a few of the amber containers and enter the bedroom.

Dzzzzz!

The door buzzer chimes and I jolt as if electrocuted, the vials of pills bouncing off the tiles. Stepping over Gerard, I rip the collage of batiks, tapestries and sarongs from their pins, calling an end to the battle. *Light floods in, liberating the room…victory is ours!*

I open the window, look down into the street. A milk chocolate face with a neatly trimmed goatee smiles up at me. *Shit* – Armando! What am I going to do with him? He's got a girl on his sleeve, too.

"Howzit, my Tjommie?" he bellows. "Beam me up!"

Shit. I wish I could beam him right out of this universe right about now. Why does he always have to be so loud?

"He's sleeping. Come back a little later," I shout back down.

"…Listen, bru, ring me up. I must speak to Gerard…Come on bru, I've got this hot chick here who's dying for a *pom* and I've got to piss like a thoroughbred."

"*Shhhh!*" I hiss, putting my finger to my lips. "People are still asleep!"

"Don't shoosh me or I'll come straight up and slap you 'cross the face, bru! Now open up this damn door!"

Curtains part in the room across the street. *Shit, shit, shit!* The madam flashes me a haughty look, then vanishes. Fuck – did she see Gerard?

"Stop toying with me, china!" he shouts. "Come on, bru, my dick is going to explode!"

I jut my head out the window. I wish it would, cocksucker! Of all the times to show up…

Dzzzzz, dzzzz, dzzz! The bell chimes like an asthmatic alarm clock.

…Alright, he's not leaving. He will only get exponentially louder until either a) He will cause a general disturbance that will inevitably lead police to a crime scene reeking of homicide, or b) I let him in.

"Give me one second!" I yell.

I drag the bloody corpse onto the bed, prop his head up and throw a blanket over his abdomen. *Phew – rancid.* I jab a fresh stick of incense into the holder and light it, then spray Gerard down with a quick coat of air freshener from the bathroom, giving the room one more blast as I close the door behind me.

Dzzz, dzzz, dzzzzzzz!

Fuck, the cash. I scoop up piles of notes with both hands and shovel them under the sofa cushion.

Dzzzzzzzzzzzzzzzzzzzz!

Defeated, I walk over and buzz him up…here we go.

Armando is from South Africa…and it shows. He claims to have been raised by his uncle in the bush but I think it much more likely that he spent his childhood roaming Krueger National Park with a pride of lions. He calls me 'bru' and 'china' constantly. 'China' is slang for 'friend' in Afrikaans but if I were to rub him the wrong way, I have no doubt that this good 'friend' of mine would bash and bloody my face without thinking twice. Moreover, I have no recollection of ever befriending Armando…I am now and will remain an acquaintance, even under duress, an indentured friend if you will. My tactic? Don't fight it: let electricity flow down the path of least resistance and try not to get zapped.

He is not your typical blond, blue-eyed Dutch/English hybrid. His father, he claims, was a Portuguese merchant marine; his mother was black. He came out looking something like a rough-sodden Harry Belafonte…a real smooth-talking son-of-a-bitch.

"…Hey, china!"

Armando throws the door open so hard it slams against the wall… always a grand entrance. He has wavy black hair, combed back, just long enough to have a curl. He is wearing a tan duster that falls below his knees. Good-looking guy, but still looks as though he's been up all night. Maybe he played right through to forty-eight straight. The girl looks to be asleep and is practically falling off his arm. He plops her down on the sofa like a sack of onions.

"Hey, bru!" He chucks his hand into mine. He's breathing hard from the steps.

It's not bro, it's bru, bru.

"Hey, I almost forgot! Jay, this is…what is your name again, woman?"

No response. She clutches his side instinctively like a baby koala.

"*Hey!* Anybody home in there?" He slaps her face roughly.

No signal coming through.

"Ah, fuck it! Fuck bru, you should have been there last night – it was fucking hectic! All kinds of cherries on the beach last night! Everyone had a fucking bankie on them and then this okie pulls out the charlie! Man, you should have been…what are you up to, bru?"

"Smoking heroin, want some?"

"Heroin? *Damn, bru!* That is some heavy duty TNT! His fingers snap as he flicks his wrist. "Where did you get that shit from?"

"…Gerard. He gave me a little."

"*Shiiit,* china! You don't want to be messing with that junk! Fuck, I must tell Gerard to keep that kind of shit away from you. He's a professional, but that will hurt you, bru. Knock you down and never let you get up. Fuck, where is Gerard? I must speak to him about this."

That's the trouble with Armando: always so imperative. He 'must' do this and 'must' do that, not a second to spare.

"Where is that old devil? Gerard, get your *fokken* ass out of bed!"

He springs off the sofa. The girl's head spills onto my lap. I shove her away, trying to pull him back, but only catch a fringe of his jacket.

"*No.* Don't go in there! Gerard is…"

He slams the door open. The girl groans.

"…sleeping."

Armando's jaw is on the floor. He scans the room, then looks back again at me. Had to attend to the matter immediately, didn't you? Couldn't wait to be appraised of the situation. Well, there you have it. If I only had time to get to the bomb shelter before…

"*Jiingaaaz!*" He runs his hand through his hair. "This is not on, not on at all, my china. What are we going to do about this?"

"*We* are not going to do anything about this. This doesn't concern you and, secondly, don't you fucking realize that I know this is *not on*? Just let me handle it."

The anonymous girl lifts herself up in slow motion, scratches her head. Armando lurches towards me and squeezes his fingers into my face.

"You tell me what happened here, china, and then I'll let you know if I'm involved or not. You might be my friend, but Gerard was my china as well! *Faaack!* And if you fucked him, I swear on my pop's soul I'll kick your teeth in *right fucking now.*"

See, what did I tell you about my good friend Armando? Bru to tooth-kicker in sixty seconds flat. I'm inches away from being laid into a coma.

I jerk backwards, releasing my face from his grip.

"Armando, I had nothing, absolutely *nothing,* to do with this. I swear this wasn't me! When I woke up…"

"Oh, putain!"

The comatose-up-until-seconds-ago girl is standing in Gerard's doorway, a hand over her mouth. How did she sneak off the couch without me noticing? She was right fucking next to me a second ago.

The girl, now wide awake, starts screaming loud and high-pitched, the sound a cross between that of a smoke detector and a chimpanzee. Louder and louder, like an approaching ambulance. I never met a girl who could scream that loud.

"Merde alor! C'est pas vrai! C'est pas vrai!"

"Armando, you've got to get her out of here now. You've got to believe me."

He jumps to his feet and wraps one hand around her waist, the other around her mouth, tucking her under his arm like a bundle of wood. She kicks and flails but he doesn't let go. She bites his hand. He smacks her briskly across the face.

"Stop it, you *fokken teef!*" Then, turning to me, "I'll be back, china, and when I do, I want some fucking answers!"

"I swear it wasn't me," I plead as he rushes his lost baggage out the door.

I slam it behind him. *Damn* – when it rains, it pours. I feel as if I've just staved off Attila the Hun…for now. What a buzz-kill.

Pinching the heroin roach from the ashtray between my fingers, I spark it up. A few long drags will help me put this whole mess into perspective.

The smell…it's getting worse. They must have cut through his colon. I stretch out my legs, lazily weaving a pen through the congealed puddle, etch-a-sketching it between the tiles. How long before he starts reeking? He's a little malodorous already – just a whiff every now and then, but I'm talking liquefaction.

When will he really begin to rot? When will the flies and maggots show up and start to break things down? When will the stench begin to radiate out, float up to next landing, the madam's window? How long will it be before they locate this stench, before the landlord shows up with his ring of keys…a couple hours? Maybe they already smell it. Interpol would eat this one up, wouldn't they?

'Well, I believe he upset a few underage prostitutes when he attempted to sodomize them. Yes, officer, I realize that my visa expired several months ago, but the rotting shell you see before you was actually trying to help expedite my departure by fronting me large quantities of hashish, and, of course, fleecing me in the process. Traces of heroin? What do you mean, trafficking?'

Not good. I'd love to stick around and help usher you into the afterworld, Gerard, but it might be best if I got out of Dodge before the rigor mortis sets in. And Attila might come back with reinforcements… no, he *will* show up, and by the time he's finished with me, there will probably be two dead bodies on the floor.

I pick up the photo from the table.

'Ring us anytime you're up against it.'…I can't think of a time that I've been more up against it. A good friend of Gerard's is…a good friend of mine? Maybe it's Tex, or Dusty. I could call them, tell them of the calamity that has befallen their old comrade…or maybe I'd just tell them I was a friend of Gerard's. That would be enough. That Gerard gave me this number in case I was ever 'up against it.' They would invite me over to…977? What country code is that? Anyway, they would invite me over and we'd sit up late into the night, burning joints and the midnight oil over stories of the good old days in Asia, when men were men and the drugs were clean.

I grab the phone off Gerard's bed, glance over at him.

"What have I got to lose, right?"

I dial…wait, this must be international: too many numbers. OK, here we go.

…*Bbbbbring, bbbring…bbbring, bbbring…bbbring, bbbring…* *click!*

A slight crackle in the line, a gruff clearing of the throat.

"…Yes, hello? Hello? Is anyone there?"

Sounds painfully British.

"Hello?"

"…Yeah," I stammer. "I'm here."

"This is counselor Gunn. May I ask with whom I am speaking?"

"…This – this is a friend…a friend of Gerard's."

Silence.

"…Gerard told me to call…we need a favor."

"Gerard? *Who is this? Who put you up to this?*" asks the counselor.

"Listen, Gunn," I swagger. "Don't get huffy with me."

"I'm through dealing with Gerard, do you hear me? *Absolutely finished.*"

"Gerard is in a jam…we're in a jam and we need your help, OK? You told us you could help. *You owe us*…and we're calling in our marker."

"I…I don't know what you're talking about."

I'm winding him up now…got him running scared. I launch into my best Sam Spade impression.

"You know *exactly* what I'm talking about, Gunn. Don't try and weasel out of it. I've got the photo in my hand…in my hand, do you understand?"

"…Listen, my good man, let's be reasonable! That was ages ago. I can't fathom what Gerard would want of me now."

"We're calling in our marker," I murmur. "It's payback time, Gunn, and you know it. If you don't, I'm sure the authorities would be more than interested in hearing of your past exploits. I don't think that heroin smuggling would be taken lightly in a man of your stature."

"…Well," his voice drops low, "if it is, as you say, payback time, I'm certain the money can be arranged. What kind of figure did you have in mind?"

"A hundred grand…in US dollars."

"That's quite a bit of money. May I speak with Gerard?"

"He's…detained at the moment."

"This is preposterous! I have absolutely no idea what…"

"Listen to me. Unless you cough up the money, Gerard is going to fuck you so hard your ass is going to bleed. You'll feel like you've spent your whole life inside a Turkish prison. I'm his agent now. You'll be dealing with me directly."

Gunn clears his throat. "Well then, I would need to know who I'm paying back…may I ask your name, good sir?"

"…Jupiter…Jupiter King," I say. Like the sun and the moon and the stars, I'm up there in the sky, always watching. And I'll be watching over you, Gunn, you better believe it."

"So you're coming for a visit then?" he asks.

"You could say that, Gunn, you could say that. Get the money together and wait for our instruction. We'll give you a week."

"A *week*? Unheard of!"

"There's a lot more than money at stake here, Gunn. Think about your family, your job…your *reputation*. Don't even think about contacting the authorities or your name will be splashed all across the tabloids in a second. We'll be watching your every move!"

I slam down the phone. The receiver emits a dull clang, signaling each fighter back to his corner.

Well, that…didn't go as planned. Always phone *before* smoking opiates. Wasn't I supposed to form some sort of rapport with this guy? Instead, I've just blackmailed him for a hundred large by launching into a lost episode of *Mission Impossible*. But…that's a lot of dough. Enough to work with for a while. That kind of cash could get me back on my feet, help me sort things out back home.

Shit! I didn't even figure out where I was calling. Was it Nepal? There's got to be a British consulate in Nepal, but British consulates are everywhere, infiltrating every diplomatic nook and cranny of the world.

Gunn...counselor Gunn... Sounds intriguing, international. Sounds like someone who might be able to come up with that kind of money. I definitely had the right guy. And he knew Gerard, alright...didn't sound happy to hear his name, though.

Maybe I should call him back, try to explain instead of derange. *But what if he can come up with the money?* It's worth a try. No, let's keep him guessing for now, quivering in his boots. He's probably shakily pouring himself a glass of sherry right now, trying to make sense of what just transpired.

I've got to take charge of this situation before it takes charge of me. I look again at the letters, beads, flags and money strewn across the table, then over towards Gerard.

Nepal...sounds like the name of a rare gem, doesn't it? Didn't the country's royal family get mowed down in some sort of conspiratorial plot? There was some serious shit going down there a few years back, something to do with Maoists. Civil war, half the country in the hands of guerillas...

Nepal...could be interesting.

Her hands flip deftly through the bills like those of a croupier dealing a fresh hand of cards...bullets, baby. Enough of those and you can go to the moon.

"*...quatre...cinq...six...*seven thousand."

Stacking them against the counter, she slides a pile of notes through the metal trough. Play it safe and go with greenbacks, just in case.

"*Merci, madame.*"

"*Mademoiselle,*" she replies, fluttering her lashes. Sorry, sweetheart, flight's already booked...maybe next time.

I take a seat in a smoky lounge. The same lounge in every airport across the world. The same sullen bartender, the same stoned businessman in the corner, the same sad muzak evoking childhood dreams of what might have been. People going everywhere, people going no-where…people always, always never there.

"Un rum et coca, s'il-vous-plaît."

I stare into the mirror behind the bottles…heroin eyes, still riding out the wave. On the way to the airport, I've dumped most of my stash on the Scouser for eighty euros an ounce. I would have gotten a better price from Algerians – but with them, you always run the risk of getting elbowed in face. With Armando I might have gotten more than an elbow.

I practically gave the shit away, but you can't take it with you…well, you shouldn't, anyway. The rest is taped against my waist. Not much, just a little *sum'n sum'n*. Risky, but a decent, god-fearing young white boy like myself doesn't have much to worry about in places where the National Front gets more than twenty percent of the vote. If you breathe slow enough, you practically forget it's there.

Shit! I left my phone back at Gerard's. That's not good. They could trace the SIM back to me. The police here are fairly efficient, too. They might already be checking flight manifests. All the more reason to get out of here quick.

"Voulez-vous boire un autre?"

Yes, I would like another drink – in fact, make it a double. It's not every day I throw the next ten to fifteen years of my life on the line like a wet sock. Customs doesn't like drunks, no matter the country. But the drunk, he's nothing compared to that pasty face slinking in the corner with the nervous twitch. He's the one they're scanning for, weighing, preying on. I am neither. I am the lighthearted backpacker, full of life, who has taken a drink or two before his harrowing flight…*j'espère*.

I slam another double…one last thing.

Unraveling my last fifty euro note on the bar, I slide off my stool.

A row of phones stares me down from across the lounge. I've got to do this. I dial the number…it's not too early, is it? Five, no six hours difference. She'll probably be asleep, anyway. Sleeps most the time these days.

Bbbrringh…bbrringh…bbringh…bbrringh…

My heartbeat quickens with each ring.

Click!

I try to think of something to say – something light and springy, like a salad.

"Hello? Hello, anyone there?" she says, in a voice tainted with self-pity and Valium. Talk about the weather, the neighbors, the Cubs for Christ's sake! Say something, anything. I take a deep breath, am afraid to exhale.

"*Helloo?* Anyone there?"

Where do I start? Start with the basics. Let her know I'm alive; let her know I'm all right. Tell her that I…

"Hello? Can I help you?"

It's…not …fair!

I drop the receiver, leave it dangling from its cord. Not yet, not today…when I get to Nepal I'll call again and tell them I'm OK; that I need to get a little more traveling under my belt before I come home.

Home…funny I still call it that. It sounds like a distant era, locked in the annals of history: a golden period when the world was prosperous and peaceful…it seems so long ago. I won't find any peace there, only a thick film of guilt that will permeate my soul.

Maybe I'll just shoot her an e-mail. What am I talking about? She barely knows how to fire up a computer. It probably hasn't even been turned on since…I'm such a coward.

I walk down the velvet carpet that I wish led into a nightclub but actually leads towards customs…*step right up, roll the dice*. The officer motions me forward. I cross the yellow line, the point of no return, place my passport on his desk. I should have left the hash back in the bathroom. That was my last chance.

He thumbs through the warped pages, then flips back to my photo, clocking me hard.

Why do I do these things to myself, wind up in these predicaments? Why push the envelope? I've got enough cash for now. One has choices, one –

"…How long have you been in France?"

"Just a couple of weeks."

"And what about your visa? Do you know that it expired over four months ago?"

"Oh no, that was *last* time I visited. They didn't stamp my passport when I flew in this time."

"*Monsieur*, you must have a valid visa."

"But they didn't –"

"Please step to the side."

He waves me off, signaling another officer.

Fuck! How stupid am I? You really needed to bring along that little something for smoking immediately on arrival, didn't you? Stupid stoner. Couldn't wait, need your crutch pressed up against your side at all times. *Dumb ass.*

Adrenal glands fire up, pores dilate…snake eyes.

I am ushered through a door. The officer says something but sounds far off, drowned out by the thudding of my heart.

A pudgy man assaults me with pig eyes from behind a spotless desk…nice comb-over, dude. He gestures for me to sit; I do, smiling obsequiously. OK, what's this going to cost me? My passport slides across the desk…*can I have that back, please?* The man leans back; his chair groans.

I'd groan, too, if I was stuck in this sterile room reeking of bureaucracy, forced to support his fat, pimply, sweaty ass.

"So, *monsieur*," he starts in a heavy accent, "you have overstayed your welcome in France. Is this true?"

Nothing I tell you will be true and you know it.

"…Actually, I just arrived a few weeks ago."

"But your entry stamp is from last April. Is there another visa that has escaped my eye?"

Ah, Inspector Clouseau! Nothing can escape your cunning wit! This must be the French version of Homeland Security – Tom Ridge would be proud. Sweat accumulates under the tape, heating the malignant lump against my belly. What the fuck was I thinking?

Don't be a smart-ass: just humor him. ·

"…Well, they didn't stamp my passport when I came in. I thought the rules had changed."

"No *monsieur*, nothing has changed."

What a load of bullshit! This is the EU. They don't give a shit about visas anymore. Maybe for a Columbian or a Nigerian, but not for an American. This guy is trying to play me but I'm in no position to revert to brinkmanship.

"And your passport, do you realize that it will expire in three months?"

Fuck…I forgot about that. Ten years: it's been that long? We had to get them for the family outing down to the Caymans…*shit.*"No sir, I didn't realize…"

"I doubt that any country will issue you an entry visa with this passport. Do you still have your ticket receipt?"

"Um…no."

It's in the garbage can back at the check-in counter but if he sees that I only bought it with cash an hour ago, it might look a little suspicious.

"It was actually a one-way ticket. I thought I would be staying longer, but..."

"Yes, of course you don't. Now listen carefully, this is a –"

"But I –"

He draws a hand from under the desk, demanding silence.

Heat wave fast approaching, visible perspiration likely. The hash around my waist is really starting to cook now…please don't smell! Where's that Right Guard confidence when you need it? Weather the storm, young lad, weather the storm. Reduce sail area and fall off! If I make it just this once, I promise never to tape…

"This is a very serious offence. We can even put you in prison – but I don't think you want that, do you?"

Why is this happening to me? A hundred other notorious criminals and terrorists must sift past here every day with expired visas and soon-to-expire passports, most of them fake. I'm white, for god's sake! All these Tunisians and Algerians and Moroccans roaming about, wreaking havoc on the fabric of your society, and you're worried about me? One bumbling, wayward American? I've committed only petty crimes (other than the one taped to my stomach) and want nothing more than to leave your country…can't I just go?

"…No sir," I answer.

What kind of question is that? Actually, the more I think about it, the more I realize I would *love* to kick it for a few years and see what France's penal system has to offer. Something along the Seine, preferably, with one of those quaint little flower boxes at the window. Finally find that insatiable French lover I always dreamed of. How long before I can get bumped up to the Foreign Legion for good behavior?

He strums his fingers on the desk.

"…And I don't want to sit here filling out paperwork for the rest of the day because of your silly mistakes, so I will give you a choice. You can pay a fine of one thousand euros right now and catch your flight immediately."

Your wife, she's banging someone else, isn't she? Someone with a full head of hair and forty pounds thinner. You haven't fucked her properly in years, have you? You found his gloves on the nightstand. They were nice, too…Louis Vuitton, suede…he must be rich as well. She didn't even care that you find out. She *wanted* you to find out. You haven't confronted her, don't have the balls. But here, *well!* This is *your* domain! Here is where justice is served, where wrongs are righted. By you and you alone, *monsieur* Clouseau!

"Will you take dollars?"

"Oui."

(How about MasterCard, motherfucker?)

"One to one point three?"

"I am afraid not, *monsieur.* One to one point five is the rate *ici.*"

One point five? Are you fucking kidding? So much for cashing in my euros, but I'm in no position to argue.

I pull fifteen crisp C-notes out of my jacket and slide them across the table, letting French diplomacy run its course. There goes my return ticket back…home. As I do, my hand catches my shirt, exposing an edge of my secret care package. An eager bead of sweat meanders down my temple; I swipe it away with my sleeve. *Shit.* Did he see?

All he sees are those fucking green bills fluttering across his path. I don't suppose I get a receipt, do I? Cracking his desk drawer, he brushes the bills nonchalantly into his coffer and flings my passport across the desk. I grab it, turn and reach for the doorknob.

"Just a moment."

Yelping dogs, strip search, possession with intent to…

"Where exactly are you going, *monsieur*?"

"Nepal."

"Be careful: I hear there is trouble in that country. They may not be as understanding as we are here in France." He smiles smugly.

"No, they probably aren't."

I exit stage left, take a deep breath. Close shave, no nicks; steady drip from my pits.

…Phew.

I will never tape contraband to my waist ever again, I swear…but I only promised around the waist, right? Alright, I'll never tape contraband anywhere on my person…or swallow it in condoms. There's no sense in piddling around with a few grams of hash. If you're going to do it, you've got to go big: kilos of uncut Bolivian coke…did I say never?

I saunter down the corridor to the departure gate. Climate control is turning the excessive perspiration from my near-mishap into chills. Damn, everyone's already here. I feel like a conductor approaching his orchestra…what shall we play now?

I shove my pack into the overhead, producing an audible snap somewhere from within the luggage already stashed. Ooops, I hope that wasn't a gift for Aunt Margaret.

There's something incredibly abrupt about traveling on a plane. Yank the plug from the wall and step aboard – links neatly severed with a crisp greeting at the boarding gate. No turning back, destination locked, figure out the rest upon arrival.

I flag down a waxy stewardess, well past her prime, in the aisle. Foundation is caked onto her face, a slapdash Bondo job to cover up the dents.

"Could I get a Bloody Mary?"

"We're not allowed to serve drinks until after take-off, sir," she says, her English tinged with French disdain.

"The doctor said it's important I take my medicine before flying."

Oxygen mask in hand, she stations herself in the aisle, lethargically pointing out the aircraft's 'safety features.' Call me a pessimist but if thousands of tons of steel suddenly decide to plummet from 35,000 feet into anything, whether it's mountain or ocean or feather bed, I doubt that a circa-1950s seatbelt and an oxygen mask with a rubber band around it are going to keep me out of harm's way. Every time I board a jet and the cabin steward or stewardess goes through the routine, I want to rise from my seat and shout, "*It's no use!* If this plane goes down, we're all done for, no questions asked. The seat is going to turn into a flotation device my ass! Don't you see?"

But what's the point? Why fight it? I'd only end up in a jail cell with maximum fines and minimal press coverage on the other end.

I defer and press play on my iPod. There's a gentle tap on my shoulder.

"I'm sorry, sir, but you are not allowed to use electronic equipment during take-off."

"*Pardon.* How about that Bloody Mary?"

"Not until after –"

"Oh, stop with the party line crap."

That pisses her off. I grab her wrist in desperation.

"You know, you look a lot like Bridgette Bardot."

She turns away but I maintain my grip. She doesn't know whether to take that as a compliment or an insult. It's like deciding whether to remember the fat or the skinny Elvis.

"Sir, would you please *release* me!" she stammers.

"Alright, I'm sorry. I'll tell you what." Slowly, I lower my headphones around my neck. "You give me that Bloody Mary and I promise to turn off my tunes, OK?"

"Sir, this is not *Let's Make a Deal*!"

Let's Make a Deal? I didn't know they got Bob Barker over here. A sad, yet humorous consequence of globalization.

"Mais madame, je suis gravement malade," I whisper, trying to force a cough. *"Voici mon médicament habituel."*

"...I will see," she counters stiffly, with her best compulsory smile. Just one more inch and she would have called for back-up. I can finally say that those *Learn French!* disks are paying off.

I slip my headphones back on as she clears first class. I know it's wrong, I know she's just doing her job, but I can't help it. How the fuck is a Global Underground track going to hamper flight patterns anyway?

I dig through a small stuff-sack, clasp a tiny vial. Flipping the top, I smack it against my palm...a salvo of pills dribbles out. Some look like Xanax. Are the red ones Darvies? Yellows could be Valium, but where's the V? Color-coding them with emotion, I decide that red is up, blue down, and yellow must be optimum for cruising altitude.

I yank off my headphones as the stewardess approaches...with my drink. No celery: just canned tomato juice and a hint of vodka.

"Just keep 'em coming."

I pop three yellow and a blue for good measure, swilling them down with my *sans*-celery Bloody Mary. Can a Bloody Mary without a celery stick actually be classified a Bloody Mary? Might as well have given me a V8.

The jets rev as we lumber away from the terminal. The plane pauses momentarily, then rushes towards the sea, and we're off.

Au revoir.

A sharp tug at my shoulder urges me from my slumber...tugging... tugging...go away. *Tug-tug-tug.* I twist to no avail...*tug-tug-tug.*

I lift an eyelid. A bearded *sheik* is harassing me, annoyed that I've invaded his air space. My eye screams out for reprieve...I can't hold it open.

Just...lemme...*sleep.*

Voices drift past. I am the drunk passed out under the pool table at closing time; the narcoleptic nodded off in the street, holding up traffic. *Don't have to go home but you can't stay here...*sinking deeper now, sinking deeper...

...*Tug-tug-tug...tug-tug-tug-tug...tug-tug-tug...*

"Whaaatt the fuck, mmmaaaan!"

"Fuck me? Fuck *me*? Fuck you, *kefir*!" he counters.

"Easy, Sinbad...I can't...wwwhha-?"

I squint, trying to make sense of his face as it kaleidoscopes around me. *Fucking terrorists, anyway.* A string of cryptic curses issues from his mouth.

"Jeez, taake a...chill piiilllll," I burble, drowning in my words.

Those pills have floored me...looped. I yawn, nuzzle my pillow... *So...tired.* My mouth tastes like charcoal; something scrunches between my legs. Fuck, my legs are wet...blanket's wet, too. I fish out a cracked plastic cup, drop it to the floor...Bloody Mary...finger's bleeding. I bring it close to my face; stare at the blood trickling down my wrist. My finger's bleeding!

"Sir? Sir?"

A figure hovers over me.

"We're about to land...Please faaaasten...brrrring your chair... uuupright position."

Land? I just took off – and it seems I'm not coming down for a while.

"Do you hhhavee...Baaand-Aid?" I slur.

"We'll be touching dowwwn innnn jjjjjjust...a few minutes. It might also be....ggggood idea for you to fill out your immigration card before...aaarriivallll. There's one in the seat pocket in fffffffroonntttttt ooooff yyyyyyyyouuuuu."

Slithering through the vortex, sweating hard now.

She stretches, elongates, her face smearing into a candy-coated swirl. Something pinches at my neck....damn mosquitoes! My hand wraps round a small warm ball. Feels…nice. I rub it against my skin… soooo fuzzzzy. Another mosquito bites me under my chin. There shouldn't be any mosquitoes up this high! I swat at it – *snap*! A severed headphone dangles limply in my hand. I grope at the seat pocket in front of me, trying to find…what? Wasn't I supposed to do something in there? What did I…the *sheik* looks on disdainfully. Fuck, I've got to chill…to the bathroom. *That's it, the bathroom. Where salvation lies!*

I dig my elbows into the armrests, writhing upwards, but my knees refuse to obey.

"Faaaaccckk!"

I slouch back into my seat, fling up the armrest, and curl up…soft, fuzzy seats. Soft, fuzzy, *mmm*…no! Got to *get…up. Get uuuup!*

I drop the wounded headphone, undo my seatbelt and muscle past Sinbad on my exodus to the rear of the plane. The aisle parts expectantly before me. Turbulence hits…or is that just me? I reach for the seats on either side to catch my fall. More turbulence. I lunge forward; someone gasps. Sinbad's turban is in my left hand, blood everywhere. I drop into a seat across the aisle, take a deep breath.

My finger's bleeding. How the hell did that hhhaappen? Got to take care of that…let's see here. Looks like a big, bloody tampon…oh, that's your turban…sorry about that. Sinbad rips it from my grasp and begins charging for the bathroom…the bathroom, that's where I'm going! Man, I've got to take care of this bloody blood situation. Don't like the blood, you know. Don't like it one bit.

I pull a case from its pillow and wrap it tightly around my hand… done!

My foot…something's pulling at my foot. I kick it.

"Sir…sir! Arre yyyyooouuu alllllllrrrrighhhht?"

"Fffine."

"Sir, you can't…"

Tapping. More shaking. *Stop with the shaking, for Christ's sake!*

"Jjust." I jerk my shoulder. "Jusssth…"

…I'm being lifted; arms grapple my torso. Awwrighhhtt, goddamnit…lezgo.

"Sir, sir!" A slap to the face. "Sir!"

"Cccan yyou heearuh mmme?"

Someone keeps messing with the volume in my head, turning the dial up and down with reckless abandon. Please think before acting, as objects in your overhead compartment may have shifted during the flight.

"Alright, lezgo."

"Arrre you alllrright?"   .

"...Just...little turbulence, but...fine." I blow a kiss to her...*kiss the sky.*

I hoist myself up, determined. People are watching now – speculating, scrutinizing the connection between me and the rampant *sheik*... Fuck them. I wipe my brow...so much sweat. *Steady there, partner.* Fuck it. Mellow yellow...Jell-O, here we go!

I stumble down the aisle, bracing myself against the seats. Lots of turbulence...at least for me. Lunging for a seat, I miss, thrusting into someone's head by mistake. *Synapses...not...firing.*

"Ssssoorry!" I slur.

The pillowcase falls off my hand. Someone squeals...OK, this is getting messy. Quickening my gait, I push forward, banging into armrests, arms and legs with alarming frequency. I get to the back and lean in close to the door for a better look...VACANT.

"Yyyeeesss!" I cheer.

A stewardess looks up from her magazine.

"Sssssirr! You haaave...rreturrn...yyyyooour sseat!"

"Bbbback offff!"

I lean back against the wall, sweating bullets. A man is staring at me. Black suit, black tie, staring.

"Whuduyawont?" I ask.

He keeps staring, unwavering...gazing right through me, that thousand-mile stare...*he knows something!*

"Yyyou wit Gunn? Yyyou tellll Gunn to jjjst bbback offfff!"

I swing the door open and lock it behind me: OCCUPIED, BUT VACANT.

That was close! Gunn must have traced my call and sent his agents out to tail me. I rubbed him wrong and now he's going to rub me out. I wipe the sweat from my brow. Shit, this is serious. Get a grip.

I slap myself across the face, nearly missing.

They know what happened to Gerard; they want information. The black suit might bust in and pat me down at any second. Or tail me off the jumbo and hustle me past the taxi stand with a hidden pistol in my back. Take me down to Gunn's headquarters, where they can tie me up and have some real fun with electricity and power tools. Gunn's not messing around this time…he'll stop at nothing!

Frantically, I scan the bathroom for something, anything that might serve as a weapon. Toilet paper, paper towels, sanitary napkins…all the paper in the world can't save me now! I'd be better off trying to scrounge up a weapon in a high-security prison.

Wait, what's…an air freshener! I rip the square chunk off the wall. Solid, but not much more than a bar of soap. It must be toxic, though. My last-ditch cyanide pill. *Don't come any closer or I'll eat this air freshener! Then you'll have nothing, hear me? Nothing!*

No…no, that's not going to work. I'll just be doing their dirty work for them. Damn, where the hell is a box-cutter when you need one?

…Knock, knock, knock!

Shit, this is it. They're going to take me down right here, right now.

Knock, knock, knock, knock, knock!

"Sssssirrr, we are about to land. *PPPPlleasssse* return to your seat *immmmmediatellly*!

I'm not falling into your crony's hands that easy, Gunn! I know you're out there. *Make a move, make a move, bitch!*

Swinging open the door, I reach out and wrestle Gunn's man in-side…*gotcha!* Squeezing my arm around his neck, I stick the air fresh-ener up to his mouth.

"SSssir!" he squeals.

"Ssshhut up!" I say. "Yyyou think I'mmm gonna fall into yyyour handsss tttthat easy? Jjusssst shut up and listennn! Yyyou let me walk off thisss plane or I'mmm gonna ram this stick-up down yyyour tthhhroat!"

"Sssssirrr! I don't knnoooow what you're talking about. I'm jjjuust a flight aaattendantttt!"

"Oh, you thhhink I'm that ssstupid?"

The plane bounces against the tarmac. *Whoa! Eaasy,* Trigger. My unfortunate opponent's head jolts forward against the faucet head. Damn, that got him pretty good. Never cross a faucet! Gonna need some stitches on that one.

I check out his reddening face in the mirror, a trickle of blood rolling off his brow…he *is* a flight attendant. I've got the wrong man! Slipped through my fingers, Gunn, but we will meet again!

"Sssssshit!" I loosen my grip on his neck. "I thought yyyou were…"

He slugs me in the face.

"Vous êtes fou!" He swings again. I throw my hands up in defense.

"Hhhey. Ya donn' haave tah hiii…" My vision begins to blur. Synapses…not…

Suddenly the door flies open and hands are prodding me.

I slip and my chin bounces off a large, opaque figure. Something wraps around my head, morphs into a snake, then coils round my neck, constricting. I rip at it, bite into it…screams erupt. Locked together, we bowl downwards. A sharp object stabs into the back of my neck… Fade to black.

Urine. Stale urine. Something flits across my face. Blood pulses against my skull, popping capillaries, threatening veins. Ringing, incessant mind-numbing gunshot ringing. I turn; a dull, excruciating pain rips through my neck. Nausea surge…*big swell, big swell*…and down. I groan. Don't move.

I crack a lid; I am in an oversized lava lamp. Thick whorls of red, green and blue melt into one another…separate…merge. I am the broken, limp glob eternally stuck to the bottom. I shut my eye but cannot escape...*sleep*...*try to sleep*. I inhale, exhale, inhale...exhale...*don't move!* My stomach convulses – vomit spurts across the cot. Whimpering, I curl into a ball.

I open my eyes again, wiping away tears. Colors shift, swirl, subside, fading into bland yellow blotches of paint, peeling off the ceiling.

Light...up in the corner. Rotating in minute, near-undetectable increments, I shift like a sunflower, fixate on it. *Focus...focus.* Soft light filters in through a small window on the far wall where the ceiling meets the wall. There are bars on it. Hushed, conspiratorial voices, an echoing shout...footsteps, rapidly approaching.

Chink-clink-chink...clank! A heavy door swings open and a taut-faced man edges forward, depositing a steaming plate of rice and lentils near my head.

"Hey – where am I?" I croak.

He slinks away.

"Wait...*yo!* Where am I?"

Reds and blues skip through my head.

"Hey, buddy!"

The door clangs shut. Not the answer I was looking for. My head churns...*deep breaths, deep breaths*. I brace myself against the wall and sidle up to the window. A pile of rotting vegetables is pressed against the bars.

My stomach convulses. I look over at the steaming rice...when was the last time I ate? A huge centipede meanders out from under the rice. Oh my god, I'm going to be sick again!

...Before the...plane, I was on a plane. The black suit and tie, *he* was after me. Is this his pre-torture holding cell? Something tells me he'd already have my nipples hooked up to a car battery if I was in his care.

Then things got real mushy and the guy jumped me in the bathroom...no wait, *I* jumped him! He was a flight attendant, wasn't he? What was I thinking? Ass-kicked by a male flight attendant, there's a story for the grandchildren. I didn't want to hurt him. First the heavy in the suit, then the flight attendant...was that the same guy? He barged in on me…didn't he? They were after me, *right?*

I was so spun out on Gerard's pain pills that's it's hard to be sure what went down. I'd pulled off a performance that had rivaled that of a severely disturbed schizophrenic. Maybe they'll make a new regulation in Air France's rulebook as a consequence of my behavior. Get a lawyer; wait for him to tell me the details. How much could they actually give me for assault? It *was* on a plane, though. The FAA won't be happy about that. Assault on a plane is not a matter to be taken lightly…it's like a magnified charge. But they got me pretty good, too, didn't they? Maybe I can use aerophobia as my defense. Couple that with drug-induced temporary insanity and I might be able to sneak past justice.

I run my hand over the scratches on my cheek…those are pretty deep. My nose doesn't feel right, either. I touch the blood caked around each nostril gingerly. It must look pretty bad. I should get somebody in here to take pictures, a court photographer or something, bang my head against the bars a few times right before they come to freshen me up. With the right lawyer and a little luck, I might be able to play the abuse card. I could countersue. Maybe they'll just call it a wash. Then I'll be Scott free!

Wait a minute…

I lift up my shirt, revealing residual tape marks.

"…Oh fuck! Fuck, *fuck, fuck*… Faaaack!"

I shout up at the ceiling, slamming a fist against the wall. The room begins to spin – my stomach twists. I drop down onto the cot. *Go to a happy place, happy place…slow breaths…happy place.* A cockroach flits across the mattress, disappears. This is not a happy place.

Midnight Express: overfed, oily apathetic lawyers who don't give two shits, never had any intention of – no, *no, NO*…Think, damn it.

Let's see: I had about eight ounces to begin with, dropped six ounces to the Scouser, smoked a little before I left, maybe lost a couple grams in the wash…so I still had at least an ounce or two on me…but where does that leave me? *Doesn't look good, Billy*…new trials, sentence extensions – no, not me. *Not me!*

…Mom – she can't know. It would kill her. She's already maxed out on antidepressants. I'll get myself out of this, find a way. Tell her I'm doing some volunteer…sodomy. *They want to make an example of you, Billy.*

A light voice slices through my darkening scenario.

"...So, how are you feeling, Captain America?" I raise my head, searching for the source. Has my guardian angel finally arrived? I hope she knows how to litigate.

"Hello?" I mumble.

"Up here."

British accent – or is it Australian?

A scuffed Doc Martens boot kicks a brown-leafed cabbage away from the barred window. "For fuck's sake, this place is an absolute tip."

British. Definitely British.

Scrunching down, a slight, twenty-something strawberry blonde pokes her head in the window, smirks.

"Hello," she says.

"Hey," I croak. I can still taste puke at the back of my throat.

Her voice: high-class with a tinge of *East Enders*, like slightly over-cooked *foie gras*.

"Alright?"

"It feels like a badger just tunneled through my head." I say and run a hand through my hair, wincing as my fingers trace the lump at the back of my skull. "...Still a bit noopy but I'll survive. I've slept in better places, though."

"Yes, well, Nepali prisons don't afford much in terms of accommodation, do they? Actually, this is just a holding cell; the prisons are even more miserable. Here, I thought you might be hungry so I brought you a bite to eat."

She snakes a plastic bag and an opened bottle of Coke through the bars. I slide to the end of the cot and take them, chugging down half the soda. Black aspirin: flat, warm and syrupy...never tasted so good.

"Thanks. My rice seems to be inhabited."

"Don't touch it. Even the best *daal bhaat* can send your stomach churning and I imagine the stuff they serve here is highly suspect. There are some *momos* in the bag in case you get hungry later."

"Some what?"

"*Momos*. It's a Tibetan dish – fried spinach and cheese dumplings, basically."

Coke and fried cheese…I couldn't think of a better hangover combo cure.

"Here's a blanket as well. It cools down quite a bit at night."

She squeezes a folded woolen blanket through the bars.

What else is she going to pull out…a white rabbit?

"Do you need anything else?" she asks.

"You wouldn't happen to have a key to fit the lock on this door, would you? That's what I really need."

She smiles.

"You had quite an escapade today, didn't you?"

"Yeah, yeah, I did…but how did you –"

"I was at the airport when you came stumbling off a plane. Tell me, do you always make such grand entrances?"

"No – that would be a first."

"Assaulting a male flight attendant with air-freshener? Shocking! I heard he got the better of you as well."

"Hey, I didn't mean to hurt anybody. I took a few too many sedatives."

"Among other things…"

"Oh, you mean the hash? Yeah, major fuck-up, huh?"

My head throbs. *Go to a happy place, happy place.*

"You should've waited: it's much cheaper here."

"Curiosity killed the..." I close my eyes; the pain subsides.

"Don't worry – capital punishment isn't an option here," she says.

"Any clue on what they're going to do with me?"

"Well, as I understand it, Air France wants to press full charges for assaulting the flight attendant and is pushing to extradite you back to France and try you there."

"Extradition? Don't they only do that for murderers and rapists? That's trumped up – it was only…"

"But since Nepalese authorities found the hash on you in their custody, they want to hold you and try you here for smuggling before handing you over to the French…you are a very hot commodity right now."

"Smuggling? You're joking, right?"

"My guess is that Nepal is going to have their way with you first, which could involve a fair amount of time and money. I wouldn't worry too much about the assault charges until you're in the clear with the smuggling."

"Isn't there some sort of personal-use clause? I thought smoking weed was a national pastime in Nepal."

"Only with tourists. Next time, pick up a guidebook before you travel. They've always got snippets of law and tips on what and what not to bring – though I can't imagine hashish being on any 'to bring' lists."

"I'll be sure to do that…it isn't legal, then?"

"About forty years ago, yes, it was – until hippies started coming in droves and went overboard. There were loads of them down on Freak Street, completely caned out of their minds, pratting about in saris and loincloths. Until one day, finally, the police packed them all into buses, shipped them off to India and changed the rules overnight. I heard the CIA had something to do with it."

"That doesn't surprise me. They've got their paws in everything."

"As for your case, I honestly don't know. I've never heard of anyone trying to smuggle hash *into* Nepal."

"But it was personal use!" I exclaim.

She rolls her eyes ever so slightly.

"There was a Belgian bloke a few months back who turned up at the airport with a guitar amplifier. When they questioned him, he went on about being a traveling musician. So they asked him to plug it in. They found over ten kilos inside – I think he got five years."

"*Five years!* That's fucked up. Well, I must have only had an ounce on me."

"You had enough. They aren't too keen on drug trafficking around here. There are several loopholes in Nepali law but if you happen to fall between the holes, they might end up making an example of you. The Nepali court system is a corrupt mess. A judge just got his head blown off in midday traffic and no-one knows why. And they don't differentiate between Class As and soft drugs, either.

"Fortunately, you're American. The US Embassy will probably make some effort to keep your neck above water, though they tend to shy away from such cases. Even so, it wouldn't be a bad idea to pursue other channels...backhanders are as much as part of Nepali culture as lentils and rice."

"Like bribery?"

"Exactly. We can't do much at the moment but once you get to the courts, we can find out who'll be presiding over your case – and, more importantly, whose pockets we can line. Sorry, but I've really got to be going now. I'll try to pop by sometime tomorrow morning, alright?"

"...Just one more question. Why are you here? I mean, you don't even know me."

"Look, the important thing is to get you out of here. Let's just concentrate on that right now."

"OK."

"I'm Maya, by the way."

"Nice to meet you, Maya. I'm Jupiter."

"I know."

Pitching me a quick smile, she straightens her legs, turns and disappears from view. I grin broadly at her back as she goes, this unexpected lifeline of hope.

The room is growing dark now, only residual grays. I crawl to the end of the cot, flip the distended switch that dangles from the wall. The glare from an obnoxious bare bulb bleaches the yellowed walls.

What was that all about? Was she with some amnesty group or something? She'd said she was at the airport: does she spend her days waiting around for sorry-asses like myself to come toppling off of planes? Far too much arbitrary benevolence for my liking – and yet she didn't strike me as the angelic, ne'er-do-bad type.

She *did* bring food and a blanket. That was pretty damn nice of her.

I dig into the plastic bag, fingering the warm, greasy lumps. I pull one out, take a bite... oh my god, when was the last time I ate? One by one, I devour the *momos*, each one more quickly than the last. At the bottom, festering in coagulated grease, is a clump of colored papers. I peel them apart, fan them out on the cot. Green, red, blue and orange... rupees.

I study them, trying to envision this land of temples, rhinoceroses, mountains and tigers, elephants and kings.

The light flickers, then suddenly sizzles out, shrouding me in darkness. My pupils dilate, catching the glowing filament as it fades. Drops of water resonate faintly through a tiny peephole in the door. *Drip... drip...drip...* All alone now, kid. *Drip...drip...drip...* Months...years, caged like an animal. Can you hack it? *Drip...drip... drip...* Wasting away from dysentery in some third-world shithole of a prison.

Drip...drip...drip... There's a problem, Billy... Drip...drip...they want to make an example of you, Billy. Can you hack it, punk?

Minutes...or is it hours...go by. After a while, I realize that my hands are clawing into the stained edges of the cot, ripping out chunks of filler. Tears stream from my cheeks, and my sobs infuse the darkness.

High mountains surround me. Jagged rocks pepper frozen earth. The corner of an animal-skin tent flaps wildly in the distance. I move towards it. Smoke is spilling into the wind from a hole in the tent's top. I lift back the flap and enter. Thick white smoke envelops me, obstructing my view.

Slowly, I discern a fire glowing dimly at the far end. Three figures materialize from the haze around it. One motions for me to join them; I take a place near the center. The fire is blazing. I shoot glances at the figures, searching desperately for a face, but their heads are shrouded in cloaks. I sense danger but am not afraid.

Suddenly one extends a hand, offering a bowl. I pull back. The figure draws the hood away from its face: it's Maya. Again, she gestures for me to take the bowl. Then I see fear in her eyes. Something, someone is coming for us. We cannot run from it...the fire blazes, spitting embers onto my legs.

I bolt upright; something darts across my legs. *Rats?!*

Recoiling, I kick violently at the scurrying shadows. One foot squashes down onto warm fur: a demonic shriek echoes through the cell. I jump to my feet, screaming.

"Motherfucker fuck! Fuuuccck!"

I crumple back onto the cot, whimpering. *Drip...drip...drip...* I shiver, cold air clinging to my body. A bead of sweat drips off my brow.

Why, why, why? Why?

...Drip...drip.........drip... Can you hack it, punk?

I awake to people whispering...a key scrapes in the lock, clicks over. I swallow, wiping the crust off my lips.

"Good morning, Jupiter. I hope you slept well?"

My cheek twitches. "Yes...no, I..."

A sterile man in a tweed suit offers his outstretched hand.

"Please, call me Jay."

"Allow me to introduce *myself*: my name is Bill Richardson. I am one of the US consular agents here in Kathmandu. Now, let me get this straight..."

He flips open a folder, ruffles through the pages. "You assaulted a male flight attendant on Air France flight number 108 from Nice to Kathmandu?"

"Yeah," I sigh. "It was a misunderstanding...I –"

"I have been informed that the attendant sustained some moderate facial injuries, including a broken nose, but from the looks of it he got the better of you," He laughs.

Who is this fucking joker? That's right, Dick, laugh it up!

"...Yeah, speaking of that, can I get someone to take some pictures of my face? If you're not going to help me, I guess I'll have to help myself."

Dick clears his throat.

"In addition…you were caught smuggling approximately one and a half ounces of hashish into Tribhuvan International Airport yesterday afternoon – is that correct?"

"It wasn't smuggling; it was for personal use."

"I was informed that amphetamines and barbiturates were found on your person as well, but they've decided not to press charges and will consider *those* only from a personal use standpoint."

"Wow, what a break," I say. "Will they drop the whole thing if I can convince them I'm suffering from glaucoma?"

"I do not have time to go into the details of your case, Mr King. It would best if you discuss such matters with your lawyer."

Who am I kidding? This guy has never gotten high in his life. No, let me guess: that one time back in prep school. Things got a little out of hand, didn't they? Your homoerotic fantasy, Seth, yanked a joint out of his blazer pocket out on the green at the homecoming dance and before you knew it you had more than spiked eggnog to contend with. Seth was so handsome in his blue blazer, his chiseled jaw reflecting the autumn moonlight. If only you could leave those silly girls behind and just *be* with him. Maybe the joint would somehow bridge the gap, make him *understand*…

You didn't enjoy one minute of it, did you? Couldn't ride the wave, right? Probably got paranoid and went back to the dorm early, stared in the bathroom mirror at your receding hairline and up-and-coming jowls, then cried yourself to sleep knowing your love would forever be unrequited.

"…What I can tell you is this: Air France wishes to press charges and is currently going forward with extradition procedures, but when the Nepalese authorities discovered the hashish on your person, they moved to put you on trial here before considering extradition. At this point it's hard to say whether they will push for extradition after your trial here…they may favor an international court hearing at that juncture."

"What, like the fucking Hague?" I ask.

"Please, Mr King, contain yourself," cautions Dick.

"That's easy for you to say from the other side of the bars. I'm not a war criminal, for Christ's sake."

"...Therefore..." He straightens himself. "It is in your best interest to first consider the smuggling charges. We will do everything we can in terms of providing legal information, but we can offer no other form of intervention."

Is he reading from a goddamn script? I'm surprised he got my name right. 'Meet Bill Richardson, your virtual consular agent. For lost or stolen passports, please press 1. For immigration requirements, please press 2. For all other enquiries, please stay on the line. Please listen carefully as our options have changed...'"...We deal with quite a few cases of this nature every year but I must say that the Nepalese government does not take this kind of thing lightly. From my experience, I can honestly say that you face the strong possibility of being imprisoned for a considerable amount of time. It would be wise to get yourself a good lawyer. Here's a list we provide for all US citizens finding themselves in predicaments such as yours."

A list...they've got a list. He must have done this a hundred times, probably more. Heeding the path well-trodden, toeing the party line. Thanks for dropping by, 'Bill, son of Dick' or whatever the hell your name is.

Sliding a neat packet of papers from his briefcase, he hands it to me and sits on the edge of the cot...watch that puke, Dick. Don't want to stain that trophy pair of pleated khakis you've got rocking there.

"Now the good news. I'm happy to learn that you have a close friend here in Nepal – close enough to be willing to provide the 200,000-rupee bail that has been set for your release."

A slight, mustachioed Nepali man enters, shoving his sweaty palm into mine.

"Hello, Mr Jupiter, my good friend! How are you doing now? I hope you are well."

Pleading eyes, desperate with deception.

"I'm, uh...yeah, how you doing?"

Who is this guy? What the hell is going on? They're actually going to let me walk out of here...with him? Why the hell did he post bail for *me?*

"You two can have the opportunity to catch up once we get through the formalities. If you'll just sign these papers here, we'll be able to release you."

Pulling a chair out from the corner of the room, he places the papers on it. "Please understand that you are now being placed under house arrest and that during this time, you are forbidden to leave the Kathmandu valley. Is this clear?"

"Um, OK."

Did they mix me up with someone else? Harry Tuttle, perhaps? *Just sign the damn papers before they change their minds.*

"The high-level security measures the government has adopted recently to deal with Maoist resurgence would make it virtually impossible for you to leave the valley without a passport, which will be kept in the possession of the Ministry of Immigration until the outcome of the trial."

Dick extracts a pen from his breast pocket and hands it to me. I scribble my name on the documents in haste and pass the pen to my mustachioed friend, who does the same. I haven't the slightest clue what is going on. Is this really happening? *Just roll with it.*

"Fine. Follow me," he says.

We rise and exit into a series of dusky concrete hallways. A plump man donning a black, flat-topped cap emerges from behind his desk, briskly shaking hands with Dick(head). Behind the desk are stacks and stacks of yellowed, dying papers – I'm guessing two to three decades of backlog.

"Your court date will officially be set within the next week and any information regarding your case will be relayed to this office," continues Dick. "As I mentioned, they'll be holding your passport as well, as a preventative measure against you leaving the valley. You must check into this exact office daily with Mr Raj Thapa here, at say, three pm?" Mr Thapa jiggles his head from side to side like a hula doll on a dashboard. I look down at my watch.

"What time is it here, now?"

"Exactly three thirty-seven."

"Three thirty-seven pm?"

"Correct."

I unscrew the knob, synchronize. Everyone has a quick look to make sure we're on the same page. I feel so special.

"Although you are free to travel within the valley, you will still be considered a flight risk. If you fail to check in with Mr Thapa on a daily basis, he will alert the authorities. Well, I guess that's all for now," sighs Dick. "I assume you'll be staying with Mr Shresta. Is that correct?"

Shresta and I nod in agreement, both knowing it's not true. *Anywhere but here!*

"Uh…yeah, sure."

"Good. Now here's my card. Give me a call if anything pertinent comes up, but please understand that we've got our hands full at the moment with an expedition that was lost up in Gokyo last week. Your lawyer will have more time to answer specific questions concerning your case. Be careful…and Jupiter," he says, holding up my pack, "the authorities found quite a large sum of cash in this pack. Four thousand dollars, to be exact."

"There should be over five thousand in there!"

"That's not my problem, Jupiter. You'll have to take that up with the Nepalese authorities if you wish. Consider yourself lucky that they didn't confiscate it all as evidence. What *is* my problem is that you might have plans to do something with that cash – something illicit, something rash, like run away. My advice to you is this: save it for your lawyers because you are going to need it. Are we clear on that, Jupiter?"

I yank my pack from his grasp.

"I don't need any more of your advice. Now I think it's best that you get back to that government-funded gated community of yours before they start missing their milk toast."

"Well, I guess we're done here!" he says. "Don't bother calling unless absolutely necessary."

"Bye, *Dick.*"

His face spasms into a snarl as he brushes past me.

"Hey! You might want to give those Dockers a scrub. Looks like you sat in something nasty." I point to his pants.

He swipes ineffectually at the puke stain, *my* puke stain, on the back of his khakis. *You've been served!*

"And it's Jay, not Jupiter, Dick!"

Two men in blue uniforms usher me through a hallway. A door swings opens. Damn, it's bright outside. I squint in the intense sunlight.

Free at last, free at last! Imprisonment is a nasty feeling, worse than any disease or shortcomings you may possess. You might be crippled but with a crutch, you can walk out that door. You might be bedridden with dengue fever, but at least you *know* that chances are good you'll be walking out that door soon. In prison, there are no incentives, just time to pass, which is why sleeping is a favorite pastime. Incarceration is death – or a suspension of death, to be exact. Purgatory, with the option to die. When you're locked up, you're not really living. Your heart is pumping, blood is flowing, but you are not alive. One day feels like twenty and is one too many…I am *not* going back.

An arm grabs me from behind. It's Shresta, the dude who'd posted my bail.

"Do I know you?" I stammer.

"No sir, you do not, but we share a friend," he says. "Please take this."

He stabs a folded piece of rice paper into my hands. I unfold it.

Thank the gods for loopholes! Meet me at Pashupatinath at five pm and don't be late!

-Maya

Maya. I should have known my angel would come through! How did she scrape that money together? Two hundred thousand rupees… what is that in dollars? Sounds like a lot of moolah. She must be loaded. She's pretty cute as well. Dangerous combination.

Pashupatinath, five o'clock…let's go see what she has to say.

I turn around – my 'friend' is gone. Where the hell did he go? A whorl of dust wafts up from the street. Where the fuck is Pashupatinath? Clouds of dust curtain the buildings. A bead of sweat spills off my chin. Across the street, I spot a figure tucked into the shadows: an old woman wrapped in a headscarf. Huddled against a brick wall, she puffs on a cigarette protruding from her fist.

A cycle whizzes past. I cross the street and crouch next to the crone. Her face is gaunt, scored by deep wrinkles; a cigarette protrudes from her fist. More cigarettes, in boxes and loosies, are stacked neatly on a bamboo mat in front of her. People hustle past, nearly stepping on them.

She pulls one from a pile, offers it to me.

"Light?"

I jiggle my thumb, mimicking the universal symbol for a lighter.

She holds out a cord of smoldering hemp…that will do. I take a long drag, coughing violently. *Rough.* I didn't think it was possible to beat a Gauloise in harshness, but *voila!* The next step down must be bark. My eyes water. Ungluing a pasty hundred-rupee note from the clump in my pocket, I hand it over. Chuckling, she gives me back my change. Five rupees a pop? I could smoke myself silly here! Suddenly, I realize why Nepal appeals to the counter-culture crowd. You could roll in here with a couple grand and live like a king for three or four months, milk it into six if you had to.

I pass a line of hat hawkers and hang a right onto a shaded street. Warped by time, crumbling brick buildings lean drunkenly against one another, waiting for a tremor to send them all to their knees. I duck inside one. I have to crouch down to avoid banging my head on the ceiling. I'm a veritable giant in this strange land, a Gulliver among Lilliputians.

A slight man in a brightly checkered hat sits amid a clutter of spice bins, a scale at his feet. A conductor summoning symphonic scores, he flicks his wrist to and fro as he argues with a buyer. Curry and sewage season the air.

A man in baggy trousers trolls from a stool.

"*Hello!* Carpet? Change money?"

Goats' heads garnish a wooden table. Greasy yellow carcasses hang above; flies orbit them like angry planets. I grab a head by the horn; stare at my reflection in the pupil. Returning it to the table, I notice a man in a bloodstained apron eyeing me from behind the carcasses and move along.

I enter a huge square filled with temples. Bells chime. A flock of pigeons melts into the sun. A pudgy woman in a colorful *sari* with a red streak running through her hair passes by, bearing trays of fruit and butter lamps. A dreadlocked ascetic moves toward me, a glob of red ink on his thumb. Smearing it across my forehead, he smiles like a miracle-pumping televangelist. *Foreigners can be Hindus, too!*

"Good luck," he intones, tilting his bowl expectantly.

Not feeling any salvation. Sorry, bank's closed, my friend.

Over his shoulder, I spot…is that Shresta?

"Hey," I yell. "Hey, Shresta!" He evaporates into the crowd.

What the hell? Is he watching me? That was *him*. That had to be him. Maybe Maya's making sure I don't get lost. But why not just take me there himself?

The checkered hats are everywhere, bobbing up and down in the crowd. A dark-skinned, lanky man hustles up to my side, hawking a large curved knife wrapped in a cloth. I have become a communal salt lick from which all the deer want a taste.

"…Hello, friend! You buy *gurkha* knife?"

He pulls the bent-bladed weapon from its sheath, holds it to my face. I brush his arm to the side. Suddenly, another man is strumming what looks to be a crude wooden violin against his chest. I've been flanked! What would Sun Tzu's strategy be in this situation?

"Ris um phri di di, ris um phri di di!"

"Hello! Trade?" He points to my wrist. "Trade watch?"

He feasts his eyes on my wristwatch…*fuck* – ten to five.

The driver reluctantly palms a hundred.

"Sorry, my man, I'm all tapped out on rupees…Pashupatinath?" I ask, holding up my hands.

He points down a long slope. I head down the path: a dirt track smoothed hard with use. What the hell is Pashupatinath…a restaurant…a mall? I look around for a sign, preferably in English; the taxi driver points from his beat-up Corolla. *OK* – I read you, loud and clear.

Eucalyptus trunks catch the lingering rays, carving long bars across the packed earth. A band of monkeys scurries past, fleeing gypsies, a pair of wiry boys tailing them with sticks.

Farther on, a scrum of people clusters around a large flat stone that protrudes from the corner of a building. On the stone sit a child and a monkey. The child wears a bonnet; the monkey has a manky strip of plastic round his neck. I half expect them to start up a comic routine. Or is this a ventriloquist act? The monkey's pink hands pluck up a peanut, deftly shuck the shell, hand it to the child. The child slips it in its mouth. A roar of laughter emanates from the crowd...Nepali vaudeville.

Without warning, a bearded man jerks towards the monkey. It leaps over the child, kicking off the bonnet, and shimmies up the side of the building. The infant is scratched – two fine cherry lines ooze from its cheek. Got you pretty good, didn't he? Not as bad as mine, though. After a ten-second infantile delay, the kid frowns, begins to wail. Disgruntled, the mother snatches up her offspring, unsure of the exhibition's outcome. The sidekick needs a little more work on his delivery. Chill him out and glue a bellhop's cap to his head and you might be onto something.

"Pashupatinath?" I ask.

Fingers point down the hillside to a bridge. Stone edifices, bleached and pitted with time, line the steps. Red-eyed, ashen ascetics stare from some of them like stoned koalas. Below, the bridge is thronged with people. Plastic wrappers and Styrofoam swirl in the blackened water below. Brandishing a shiny figurine, a street vendor makes a beeline for me.

"Hello – friend!"

"No, no, *no*."

I hurdle a few steps, take a seat on a terrace and look out across the river. Smoke billows into the sky, coating the area in a gauzy haze.

Holy shit, they're burning bodies.

Funeral pyres jut out from the bank on stone platforms...launch pads to the other side. Each is rectangular, fitted together like a big set of Lincoln logs. Behind them, a stream of people trickles in and out of a pagoda-style building, its gold-plated roof glinting in the evening sun. One pyre smolders as another is being built...this never stops, does it? This is a non-stop, full-service cremation factory. They've been doing this since the days of Siddhartha. The same ancient ritual since the beginning of time.

Another dreadlocked ascetic breaks through the haze. Smiling obsequiously, he raises his bowl to my face. How can you be happy when your hair is so nappy? No more red blotches on my forehead, please!

"Maagnelai taato bhaat!" A high-pitched voice from behind stops the ascetic in his tracks. He retreats down the steps like a dog that's just been scolded. I turn around. Maya.

"Sorry I'm late – the traffic was horrendous."

"No big…Hey, thanks for getting your friend to bail me out. I don't think I would have lasted much longer in that rat-infested prison."

"They don't make the best bedmates, do they?"

"No, they don't. Looks like you got *tika-ed*!"

"What?"

She points to my forehead.

"Oh yeah," Gently, I finger the caked-on concoction above my brow. "A holy man was dead-set on giving it to me. I think he wanted a little cash for it."

"Blessed by a s*addhu.* It's good luck."

"…So, I've got to know, how did you spring me? Are you tennis partners with the prince or what?"

"No, the prince isn't playing much tennis these days, let alone anything else," she says, smiling.

I look at her askance.

"Never mind; it's a long story. I do some work for the embassy here."

"The US Embassy?" I ask.

"Um, yes."

"So you know that dickhead consular guy who came to see me this morning? What was his name – Bill, Bill Richardson?"

"No, I'm afraid I don't." She frowns. "I'm not directly involved with most of the people at the embassy."

"But you're British, anyway, aren't you? How can a non-US citizen work for the American embassy?"

"Dual citizenship: my mother is American…another long story. But yes, I am loosely affiliated with the American embassy. It took some time convincing them to hire me, but they came around."

Bullshit. She's about as loosely affiliated with the embassy as spelunking is to skydiving. I've been here a day and I know more people that work there than her. That's strange, isn't it? It's an embassy, not a major university. Everybody knows everybody.

"…What about Shresta? Is he with the embassy?"

"Who?"

"Shresta – the dude who posted my bail."

"Oh…oh no, he's just an old friend."

"So…the embassy didn't post my bail?"

"No, I did…through Mr Shresta. As a foreigner, I couldn't do it directly."

Either I'm missing something really huge or this whole equation isn't adding up.

"…Why did you have him tail me?"

"I beg your pardon?"

"Tail me. Why did you send him after me?"

"I don't know what you're talking about."

"I saw him in the market just before I hopped in the taxi to come here. He was definitely watching me. I called to him and he disappeared. Hey, it's no big deal. I just want to know who's keeping score."

"Are you sure it was him? You've gone through quite a lot in the last few days. Maybe you mistook him for someone else."

"Maybe."

I know it was him; I'd bet every dollar I have on it. I'll let it slide… for now.

"So many questions!" she says. "Anyway, what do you think of Nepal now you've finally got a glimpse of it?"

Good transition game, Maya. Keep the ball rolling, keep the mind moving...well executed.

"I feel as if I've spent the entire afternoon stuck in someone's garage with the car running, but it's a fantastic garage...and I dig the monopoly money."

"It is amazing, isn't it? The pollution's completely out of hand and the population's gone through the roof since the war, but the magic's still here."

I look up at her on the step, poised in the gentle light: tall and slender, a red tank top and a pair of faded blue jeans hang loosely off her body, faint freckles dappling oddly feline cheeks. She moves like a cat, too – in quick, calculated movements.

"I loved to come here as a child, to watch the bodies burn," she says. "I guess it's a bit morbid when you think about it, but this place is always bustling...so much energy. But what about you? First off, you must tell me how your parents came up with the name Jupiter."

"Hippie parents," I tell her. "They're not hippies anymore, but I was conceived during their Aquarian phase of enlightenment...just call me Jay."

The most asked, least desired question of my life. Not what do you do for a living or where are you from, but where the hell did you get that name? I've reverted to Jay, as in the letter J, but the passport keeps fucking me up. Passports don't lie. Maybe I should change it by deed poll...the novelty wore off long ago. Thanks, mom and dad.

"...What kind of name is Maya, anyway? That sounds pretty hippie-esque to me," I counter.

"My parents were nothing of the sort. Yeah, they were outgoing, but only in the old-fashioned, British- colonial sense: you know, khakis and tiger hunts and tea and biscuits in the jungle and all that. I suppose naming me was one of the most creative things my father did...it means 'love' in Nepali.'"So your parents must have spent some time here, having tea and biscuits between tiger hunts?"

"Yes, they did...but that was ages ago."

"I like the way your name sounds. Maya...Maya." I roll the name over in my mouth like a gumdrop.

"...It also means 'illusion.' That was probably what my father had in mind when he chose it. I was more like an apparition than a child to him…a pleasant image to watch skipping through the yard on Sunday afternoons at teatime."

Touched a nerve there, did I? All not well with daddy dearest? I've got no room to talk about family issues.

"I'm sure he had the former in mind." I feel an uncharacteristic urge to reassure her.

"So…why did you come to Nepal? Searching for enlightenment as well?"

She runs a hand through blonde-streaked hair, hair that drapes over delicate shoulders. A gold stud pokes defiantly out of her button nose. She's slender, but you wouldn't call her fragile – more ocelot than housecat. She would do just fine in the wild. "Uh…well, I guess you could say I'm on a bit of a mission."

"A *mission*," she says. "Sounds exciting."

She likes missions, likes danger. Prim and proper schoolgirl gone bad…I love it. All she needs now is a tight-fitting uniform with those knee-high socks to…*stop it* or you're going to get a hard-on.

Drawing her legs up to her stomach, she brushes a wayward lock of hair back over her ear and locks her gaze on mine. Her eyes are fiery green, splendid green, almost jade.

"…Yeah, well, I was staying with this burnt-out hippie in France. It's a long story, but he ended up on the wrong end of a knife. He wanted me to bring something back here for him…it was his final wish."

"So, this French hippie – he's dead?"

"Yeah, he's done."

"And you're returning something for him?"

"Partly for him, partly for me. He set me on a trail and I want to see what's at the end of it."

"So you're working for him?"

"How can you work for a dead guy?"

"And what is it you're supposed to return?"

I sift through my rucksack and pluck out the beads, letting them dangle from my hand.

"There's nothing else? Nothing else this Frenchman wanted you to do?" she asks.

"Nope, that's it."

"I see," she sighs. "Well, mostly Tibetans and Sherpas wear this type of necklace. The two stones on the side are coral, probably from India, and the stone in the center is called a *dzi*. This is quite a nice piece. I've never seen one like this before. And who are you supposed to return it to?"

"Hard to say…he didn't have time to tell me much more. I think I'll figure out the rest once I'm able to contact this guy."

Digging further into my pack, I extract the torn piece of paper and slip it between her shins. She unfolds it.

"This is an address for a post box down at the post office on New Road. Do you know this man?"

"Only in name."

"And he works for the Frenchman?"

"Like I said, Gerard is dead. *Nobody* is working for Gerard. Why are you so worried about him, anyway? You've asked me ten questions about him the last thirty seconds."

"They're just questions, Jupiter. I got you out of jail. You owe me at least that much."

I look her in the eyes; she holds my stare. *Something's not right here.* Maya. She's after something.

"…Right," she says. "It's going to be rather difficult to find him if this is all you've got to go on, but we might be able to help you out."

Who is she talking about when she says we? Brits say that though, don't they? Always with 'let us have a look' or 'give us a look,' referring to themselves as if they were a goddamn committee.

"…It won't be the end of the world if I don't find him. I didn't really care too much for Gerard. To tell the truth, he was a complete bastard."

"So what is it you do exactly? Are you just another trustafarian starved for adventure or what?"

"Trustafarian? I don't take handouts from my parents, if that's what you're asking. I wasn't born into poverty, either, but don't tell me you were weaned in some mountain hovel. Where did you come up with the money to spring me out of jail, anyway?"

"I've got connections," she says. "And just so you know, it took a lot more than money to get you out."

"Connections. I guess they go a long way in a place like this."

"...So, that's your story? That's the whole reason you're here? To carry out a dead Frenchman's final wishes?"

"I figured things could get interesting."

"Well, it appears you have a knack for that. But if we don't sort out your case soon, you could be spending the next five years of your life wishing you'd married a succubus and taken a job in accounting."

"I'd rather be dead than an accountant."

"You say that now."

"...We'll see what happens. Oh, I almost forgot: I need to meet up with this guy from the British Embassy as well. His name is Gunn. Any chance you know him?"

"Not offhand. What's his first name?"

"I, um, forgot. Anyway, he should have something for me in about a week or so."

"What's that?"

"Some...help."

"Maybe you should concentrate on contacting this other bloke first. I'll check down at the embassy and see what I can find out about him."

A bell clangs through the twilight, signaling the heavens. All that remains of the sun is a mild glow. The smoldering pyres illuminate their surroundings like photosensitive streetlights. To the left of the pyres, a group of men, some clad in white loincloths, maneuvers a fresh corpse wrapped in orange cloth onto a bamboo frame, which they proceed to carry down to the riverbank. They lay the frame on the stone steps, perpendicular to the shore, so that the body's feet dip slightly into the water.

"Is that how everyone goes? I mean, by cremation?"

"For the most part, but other ethnic groups use other methods. If they can afford it, Hindus get a proper burning…what remains is tossed into the rivers. But some Buddhists, especially Tibetans, go a different way. They call it sky burial."

A puff of wind catches a plastic bag on the river, transforming it into a man-o-war.

"So how do they do it, this sky burial? Blast corpses up to the heavens?"

I'm picturing a huge cannon, packed chock-full of bodies. That could be messy.

"Not exactly. After it's determined that the person's spirit has departed, a group of shamans, and usually a relative or two, carry the body up to a holy site and dismember it into small chunks. They sacrifice it to the vultures as a gesture of selflessness. It's considered one of the highest acts of altruism, giving up one's body for the life of others. I've never seen one – they're extremely secretive about the whole ordeal. It has to do with the cyclic flow, returning to the earth and all."

"Sounds pretty gory," I say, then, "So, Maya, are you up for getting a sandwich or something?"

"Yeah. Why not? I'm famished."

She springs up, jerking me to my feet with her hand. Twilight has vanished. The pyres glow like oil refinery stacks, glimmering hypnotically on the flaccid water below. I spot a freshly lit corpse, its head propped slightly. He was alive yesterday…in another hour, he'll be ash. Flames lap against the wooden frame of the pyre, encroaching slowly on the center. Burn, baby, burn. The unmistakable odor of burning flesh swims through my nostrils. Gerard would have liked it this way…in a blaze of glory.

People flutter through swatches of light like moths: appearing suddenly, then melting into the darkness. Maya leads me up a flight of concrete steps into a restaurant.

A woman in a colorful apron shoots out from the back, smiling…an

Asian Aunt Jemimah.

"Tashi delek!"

"Tashi delek," Maya replies.

She seats us in a curtained stall towards the back. A gas flame sputters hysterically in the kitchen.

"Smells good," I say. "So, do you bring all of your freshly sprung friends here?"

Maya smiles. "I haven't been here in ages – ever since…yes, it's been some time."

"So you're not with some amnesty organization or something?" I ask.

"…I never said that, did I?"

"No. I just never thought people who worked for governments had much interest in human rights, that's all."

"Like I said, most the work I do is behind the scenes."

The woman returns with two fat bamboo mugs brimming with a brown, pasty liquid. "Drink up. It's *tongba:* millet beer."

I take a hit off the straw. Warm and yeasty. It coats my mouth with a rancid, sticky film…just like her story. Call me paranoid, but I don't trust this girl for shit. *American embassy my ass!* From the looks of it, she should just be getting her Bachelor's degree about now – maybe twenty-four, twenty-five tops. You've got to put some serious time in to work your way out of the mailroom. If she was employed by the US Embassy, she'd be licking stamps, not out in the field on covert ops.

She might not be dangerous but then again, she might. She *is* pretty, though…and that's all the more reason not to trust her. Every pretty woman I ever trusted took my money and ran. She's no fucking angel, I can tell you that. There's something else keeping her here…I just can't put my finger on it. Too much interest in a dead Frenchman half a world away for my liking. I swear she said Gerard's name first. What's your angle, angel?

I suck down some more millet beer.

"Tastes like a bad experiment in fermentation."

"Don't care for it?"

"I've had enough cultural experiences for one day. What I need is a Coke…and an explanation. Listen, Maya. I really appreciate everything you've done for me…but why?"

"You ask quite a lot of questions, do you know that?"

"What do you have to gain by getting me out of jail? The personal satisfaction of having saved one more sorry soul from the third-world injustice system? Come on, Maya, give me a break! You just said yourself that you aren't with any amnesty organizations – and I'm a high risk-factor. I could bail on you tonight and you'd be out a few hundred thousand rupees…"

"I wouldn't do that if I was you," she snaps.

"What, are you going to stop me?"

"There's no need for that. Nepal is a small place, smaller than you think. You wouldn't make it very far, not with the curfews, *bandhs* and checkpoints. It would only be a matter of time before we found you."

"Who's this 'we'?" I ask. "You're always saying things in the plural, like 'before *we* found you' or '*we* might be able to help you.' Let me ask *you* a question. Who are *you* working for, Maya? What's *your* motive?"

"Does there always have to be a motive?"

"You ask quite a few questions yourself, Maya. Every time you open your mouth, you're asking me something about Gerard like I'm part of some secret operation."

"You're so paranoid!" she counters. "First you pull a John Nash stunt on the plane and go off on a flight attendant and now you think I'm after you…really?"

"If you can't tell me why you're doing this, how can I trust you?"

"The question is can I trust *you,* Jupiter. I'm putting everything on the line with a bloke I don't know from Bob."

"I never asked you to, did I? I didn't ask for any of this. You just popped your pretty face between those cell bars a few days back and next thing I know, I'm out. I'm grateful, but don't try and spin this back on me, girl."

The curtain flies back and the smiling woman slides two steaming plates of dough balls onto the table.

Maya reaches over and grabs my hand.

"Jupiter, calm down," she reassures. "I'm here to help you. Things might seem a bit strange right now but you can trust me, I assure you."

"Can you please call me Jay?" I say sulkily.

I know Shresta was following me; I *saw* him. He wouldn't have disappeared when I called if it wasn't. I'm not buying her stock, but she's right about one thing. She did put a lot of money on the line for me. I pick up a dumpling, bite in. A hot lava flow of grease explodes in my mouth.

"Whaaa!" I spit it back into my hand.

"Not so fast!"

Maya laughs, hands me a diminutive napkin. "One thing you'll have plenty of in Nepal is time."

"Yeah. Probably a lot more than I'd ever want."

"What I mean is that the locals always take their time so things often end up taking longer than expected. They say Nepali time is elastic – it can be stretched."

She pulls a strand of chewing gum from her mouth, slowly reeling it back in with her tongue. "The woman who served us, is she Nepali?" I ask. "She seems different."

"No, she's Tibetan. There are more than two hundred thousand Tibetans in Nepal. Most of them came in the fifties and sixties during Mao's experiments in brutality. It's been an ongoing exodus since. You still get a few these days, staggering half-starved into monasteries and villages on this side of the border. The Chinese government has really clamped down, though, since they got caught on film in 2006 gunning down innocent refugees at Nangpa Pass."

"Brutal. The Chinese never were very big on human rights."

"Absolutely atrocious."

I pop another dough ball into my mouth…a distant cousin of a pierogie. Mom cooked a mean pierogie. I liked the cheese ones best. She always made extra for me…well, she used to.

"What are these things called again?"

"*Momos*. Delicious, aren't they?"

"Good filler, but I don't suppose you could get a pizza around here?"

"That's all down in Thamel, the tourist district. I'm not very keen on it myself. But don't worry, you can still cop your daily intake of Coca-Cola here." Her mouth corkscrews into a smirk.

"Great. I think I just fried the roof of my mouth with those *momos*."

"Eutaa Coke wahaalai dinos," she shouts back to the kitchen.

She tops off my mug with hot water from a Thermos flask.

"I'll stick with the Coke for now…anyway, it was just like you said. They're going to try me here first for the smuggling, then ship me back to France for the other mess once I'm in the clear. It sounds like I could be in for a long haul, though. Dick from the US Embassy said I might be looking at some jail time. He wasn't very helpful…and kind of a dickhead."

"He's telling it to you by the book. It's his job to tell it to you by the book. Like I said, Nepali law is strict on smuggling. If they found it on your person walking around Kathmandu, it would be different story, but not at the airport. What we've got to prove is that you weren't smuggling: that you intended only to use it yourself. If that fails, then we'll try and find out whose pockets to line. Remember what I said about pursuing other channels?"

"Yeah, that's right. Listen, I've a fair amount of cash on me. Unfortunately, there was a service charge for handling my baggage at the prison. They took a good chunk out for themselves, but I got most of it back."

"That doesn't surprise me. You're lucky you got any back at all."

"…Well, I could give it to you to put towards the lawyers. It's all I have, but if it keeps me out of jail…"

"All in good time," she says.

She could care less about my money. If I posted bail for a complete stranger – something I would never dream of doing in the first place – I would need some kind of guarantee, some collateral. I'm offering to throw down hard cash, the best guarantee there is, and she doesn't want it. What does she want from me?

"…What do you say we get out of here?" I say, licking my fingers.

The proprietor waves, a glimmer of gold in her smile.

Outside, a chill breeze sweeps up against me. An aluminum door slams across the way. The street is empty. Drivers lie curled inside their rickshaws like ferrets, children stoking ashes at their feet. One jumps up and jabs a smoldering postcard into my hand. On it, a half-burnt child, fingers in mouth, stares back.

"*Paisaa, paisaa!*" shrieks the child, groping at my pockets.

"*Maagna hundaina. Bhaag!*" Maya stamps her foot on the ground.

"...*Paisaa, paisaa, paisaa!*"

They scuttle into the shadows like fiddler crabs.

A small group of soldiers in blue fatigues and M16s marches out of the darkness. One casts a glance in our direction.

"*Namaste.*"

I watch them pass in quiet determination.

"What's with the heavy-duty military presence?" I ask Maya. "That's the second time I've seen soldiers in the street today. And it seems like the police are everywhere."

"That would be due to the Maoists.""As in Mao Zedong."

A vision of little red books, populist slogans and blue cadre jackets flashes through my mind.

"They are guerilla fighters. Insurgents who fought a nasty ten-year civil war against the government and monarchy – or should I say, what's left of it. A thorn that neither of them could tweeze loose. They've grown steadily in numbers since the mid '90s, mostly in the western districts and small pockets of the plains. Slowly but surely, they built up troops and an arsenal of weapons. They really upped the ante when the prince mowed down the Nepali royal family back in 2001. Guess they thought the time was ripe for regime change."

"That's right. I remember reading something about that."

"There were heavy casualties on both sides and economically speaking, it was disastrous, given that Nepal's economy is so dependent on tourism. King Gyanendra finally capitulated and gave power back to parliament in 2006. But after the Maoists won elections as the United Communist Party and became a political entity, they dissolved the monarchy altogether, pending a new constitution. The new constitution never materialized and the remnants of the royal family are now out of a job, but there are still hardcore loyalists who want to see them back in power."

She takes a sip of her millet beer. She's really into all this political shit. Smart cookie. I'm impressed. Like a hip, hot history teacher. *Do you want to see me for an after-school, detention, Ms Maya?*"After they booted the king," she continues, "it seemed like they were finally going to get what they wanted. A peace agreement was struck up in parliament a while back to disarm their army – the PLA – but all sides reneged on the deal. Several thousand PLA soldiers have been in limbo for years waiting to get integrated into the government army.

"Then, in 2008, a constituent assembly was assigned to draft a new constitution over four years, but they missed the deadline last spring and the assembly was dissolved. That was a move many considered illegal.

"New elections were promised for this November but it looks like the people are running out of patience. They're fed up with delays. Many of the PLA have rearmed themselves by raiding the weapons stores they'd handed over as part of the peace process. Now they've splintered into several factions and everything's in disarray again. Meanwhile, loyalists to the monarchy are trying to get back into the fray.

"It's crazy out there: Maoist groups are not only fighting the army, which is controlled by the somewhat politically credible Maoists, but each other. There's strong division among members of the UCP, which looks headed for a vertical split if they don't get this bloody constitution written. One side has made repeated demands for the Prime Minister to leave office, and a bomb went off last week in one of the ministry buildings. All the while, Chairman Prachanda seems to be losing his grip on power. It's all very confusing and extremely difficult to keep track of."

Maya pauses, takes a breath.

"Sounds like a communist soap opera," I say.

"Recently, it's got much bloodier, and there seems to be no end in sight. The army has sent several thousand troops up into the hills to quash the opposing factions, but it doesn't appear to be helping. I read about a police station or a military garrison getting attacked at least once a week."

"So…the civil war never ended?"

"Officially, yes, but most days it seems like we're still in the throes.

One major Maoist sect controls most of the hill country west of Pokhara and some other isolated areas to the east and south – roughly a third of the country, if you add it all up. On top of that, there are smaller camps that I've lost track of.

"Until recently, they left tourists and trekkers out of it, but there are rumors of skirmishes in the Annapurna circuit and farther west. Forcibly stealing cameras and gear, stuff like that. I heard that they even commandeered some rafts from a whitewater river expedition. They've been extorting money for their own trekking permits, too. There was an incident a few months ago. Seems some bloke didn't want to pay twice for trekking in the same region, so they beat him pretty badly. And now these other parties are starting to bring their struggle back to the valley, setting off bombs and threatening violence to those who don't adhere to their *bhandhs*."

"*Bhandhs?*"

"General strikes. It seems like there are more strikes these days than festivals, which is saying a lot. Actually, there's one tomorrow. They locked up an official near Chitwan and a rival political gang overran the prison and literally ripped him apart."

"…Are those M16s they're carrying?"

"Yes, Uncle Sam has his hand in the pot as well, if that's what you're wondering. The US made some rather large arms deals with Nepal's military before the UCP was voted into office and categorized them as 'terrorists.' Now the 'terrorists' are using the weapons that were initially sent to kill them to kill the other 'terrorists.' To top it off, your government recently blacklisted Nepal again as a high risk for travel and re-recalled the Peace Corps, which I'm certain will dissuade a substantial number of dollars from flowing into Rastra Bank's coffers this year. There is quite a bit of anti-American sentiment here as a result."

"Not a good time to be an American," I mumble.

"Is there ever?" she grins.

I glare sullenly.

"What are you talking about? I thought you were half American."

"That doesn't necessarily make it favorable."

A man in a tightly clamped scarf hustles past. A dog skitters off, a rat dangling from its mouth…late-night snack. We bundle through a narrow alley. Solitary lights cut halos in the night. A group of men laughing loudly intersects our path…one giddily shouts out 'hello' as we pass.

"Not much for nightlife, is it?"

"Curfews have their drawbacks, but they usually leave foreigners alone. Are you up for something, then?"

A few drinks back at your place…perfect!

"Sure, what did you have in mind?"

"Do you like music?"

"Anything but country."

She takes my hand.

"Come on, then. I've got something I want to show you."

An after-hours club…she can't be serious. Now *that* would be a nice surprise. Take my mind off all of last night's ratscapades and my impending doom. Too bad they snagged all my drugs on the plane. Maybe I can sniff out some at the club.

A crescendo of aluminum roller-doors punctuates the night as shopkeepers lock up their wares. "Everything seems to be shutting down," I say.

"Things are still going on. You just have to know where to find them."

Hand in hand. I like this! It verges on romantic. Just me and her and this big, empty, ancient city. *She's so sexy.*

Just play it cool.

A lone motorcycle rattles past as we enter a courtyard. Springing up a series of steps, we climb towards a medieval-era pagoda. Struts of wood teem with carved deities contorted into various sexual positions, stretching upward to the eaves…a prelude, perhaps…

A beggar coughs in the shadows. Prowling serpents, drumbeats undulate through the cool night air. A flurry of moths aggressively circles the dim bulb that glows above.

She leads me to a narrow wooden door. The drumbeats increase in volume, intertwining with steady chanting. Dipping our heads to enter, we crouch down into a small, sparse room in which a half-dozen men are crammed, cross-legged in a circle. Incense smoke pours out of a reddish clay pot, weaves between the men as they play. Some thump steadily at drums resting on their knees. One cajoles melodies from a flute; another claps small brass cymbals.

I feel like I've just entered a National Geographic special. *Rhythms of Ancient Cultures,* with your host, Jay King. I jerk my hand from Maya's. Are we interrupting? These people, with their rich garb and graceful movements, are like a flock of rare, delicate birds existing in some pocket of untainted jungle. I don't want to scare them. I want to be very still, very quiet, lest they disappear into the canopy.

One grins, motioning for us to sit on a bamboo mat off to the side. I move cautiously as if in church. *Buum-da-daap, buum-da-daap, buum-da-daap* go the drumbeats, pulsing through the air like an ancient incantation. *Buum-da-daap...buum-da-daap...buum...da...daap.* The rhythm grinds sluggishly to a halt, punctuated by shuddering cymbals. One of the men lifts a bleached conch shell to his lips, emitting an eerie high-pitched howl.

The hair on my neck stands on end. How long has this been going on? Even they couldn't tell me – only that their grandfathers did it, and the grandfathers before them. How old does a tradition have to be before it becomes lost in time?

"Pretty funky," I whisper.

I stare at an oblong-shaped drum. One of the men follows my gaze. Deftly unhooking the instrument from around his legs, he hands it to me. The other musicians begin to talk in excited, expectant tones. I cast Maya a dubious look.

"Go on, then."

Taking it from my hands, she positions the drum on top of my knees; I cross my legs.

"Use the palms of your hands to hit the center – like this."

"Yeah, but I can't sit like this!"

"You just have to learn to..." She pushes down on my thigh. "Stretch a bit."

"My body doesn't go that way."

"Just takes a little time, that's all." She tucks her feet under her thighs.

"You can try, but it's not going to happen. I've been like this since birth – or at least since Indian Guides."

Indian Guides…those were the days. Huddled around campfires telling ghost stories, roasting marshmallows. Dad and I had made our own vests out of some crappy brown fabric from Kmart. 'Big Bear' and 'Little Bear', pasted on the backs in hastily cut golden felt: 'Team Bear!' I was so damn proud of that vest, I wore it to school every other day (every day would have been a fashion *faux pas*). Mom had to wrestle it off of me to get it in the wash.

We used to be so close back then. Then suddenly it ended, a vase shattered carelessly on the floor.

Maya pushes down on my thigh again, this time more hesitantly.

"I'm telling you, I cannot sit cross-legged," I snap.

I hate trying to sit like this. Every time I try to, people point and stare like I'm a carnival attraction. *Come see the unbendable man! A young man trapped inside the body of a ninety-year-old! Absolutely no flexibility whatsoever! Step right up and see for yourself this rigid freak of nature!* I must be missing a gene or something.

"I tried yoga once, but even though everyone was very Zen, I felt like they were about to point and snicker. There didn't seem much point in paying for derision – I'm not a fucking masochist."

"That's all in your head – no-one would ever do that sort of thing in a yoga class," she says.

"Well, it felt like they were about to."

"…You're right, your legs aren't bending, are they?" Maya seems mildly surprised.

I kick my feet out from under me.

"Let's just go."

"Stop pouting and play." She grabs my feet, pushes them to the side. "Just don't point the soles of your feet at them – it's very disrespectful."

"Maybe we should just go."

"Maybe you should stop pouting and start playing!" she says.

I bang my palm against the drum, discharging a hollow thud.

OK, Maya, I'll play the damn thing, but I wasn't expecting a hands-on cultural experience on my first day out. They've stopped their show for me and I can't play a drum for shit. Who did they expect, Tito Fuentes? I feel like the kid at band practice in the last chair who's been fucking up so badly that the leader's stopped practice to publicly ridicule him. Wasn't the cross-legged attempt enough?

"Why don't *you* play it, Maya?"

"Here, like this," she counters. Her hand pops off the leather face – *tha-thump.* I try again: *clunk.* One of the men beams. I hand the drum back.

"Tell him I need to brush up on my bongos before I crash another jam session."

"I can't. He doesn't speak Nepali. He's Newari."

"Where is he from?" I ask.

"Here, Kathmandu. They were some of the original inhabitants of the Kathmandu valley. They ruled the valley long before the Shahs and Ranas started turning up."

"So why can't he speak Nepali?"

"They have their own language, their own script. Most of them can speak Nepali even though it's not their mother tongue, but a few of these blokes are strictly old-school…a dying breed. You know there are more than a hundred languages spoken in Nepal?"

"I've got enough trouble with one."

She really knows her shit about Nepal, knows the ins-and-outs. Shit, she got me out of jail, didn't she? Maybe she does work for the embassy and got an early promotion.

Something's still not right, though.

"In a few generations, I doubt if half their mother tongues will be spoken," she says. "This whole place is like a museum that's been exposed to the elements and is crumbling away."

A bearded man, noticeably older than the rest, circumambulates the others, holding the pot of incense to each of their faces in turn. Each cups the smoke with his hands, spreading it around his face. Bearded dude lifts the pot to Maya's face; she follows suit. My turn: like the others, I spill a handful of the smoke over my face, inhaling its thick scent.

"So how long before I hit nirvana?" I ask.

"I think you're still a few lifetimes off."

The drums beat on, lulling me. I close my eyes, swaying back and forth. *Buum-da-daap, buum-da-daap, buum-da-daap...buum-da-daap...* I nod forward.

"Come on," she says then. "You've probably had enough for one day."

As we exit, the men clasp their hands together.

"*Namaste.*"

Outside, the streets are devoid of people. Sacred street cleaners, a cow and her calf graze on a damp pile of cardboard. The stench of rotten vegetables wafts past my nose. Rats chatter and squeal incessantly from all directions.

"Damn, it's nippy out here! Listen to those rats: it sounds like they're conspiring against us, doesn't it?"

"You really are paranoid!" she says. "Sounds to me like you've got far too many Orwellian schemes running around your head."

"I guess prison does that to you."

"You were only in there for a day. Are you planning on writing the next *Shantaram* with all that material?"

"What?"

"Nothing," she giggles. "Keep moving, old man!"

She darts past me and disappears into the shadows. Two men in blue army fatigues emerge, tapping long sticks against the ground...the dissident patrol. Hustling past them, I find Maya standing in front of a massive black stone figure brandishing a sword.

Its expression livid, on the brink of psychosis, the grotesque demon-face snarls down at me. A goat lies tethered at his feet.

"Who's this dude? He looks like a bad-ass."

"It's *Kaalo Bhairab*, an extremely angry form of Shiva, the destroyer. You'd like him. He's a bit crass and likes to smoke loads of *ganga*."

"He sounds like my kind of guy. Did they lock him up as well?"

"He's a *god,* and not one to cross at that. He's a real hothead, apt to go off at any moment. He even chopped off his own son's head; fortunately, he was able to replace it with that of an elephant, creating *Ganesh,* god of luck and wisdom."

"Harsh. What's with the goat…another fortunate son?"

"He's not so fortunate, I'm afraid."

"So…am I going to crash at Shresta's place tonight or what?"

"Oh, I'd forgotten about that. What time is it?"

"Coming up on midnight…"

"He'll be asleep by now. Bloody hell, it slipped my mind completely!"

"Don't worry about it. I could get still get a room if you want," I say.

"No, no…it would better if we looked after you. Right…you can stay at my flat tonight. That might work better for the time being."

There she goes with the 'we' again. What does she mean 'work better?' Who *is* she working for? The embassy, supposedly, but wouldn't Dickhead Richardson be in the know? And why wasn't she there when Shresta bailed me out?

It might work better for me, too: I haven't been laid in months. Even if she's not on my team…007's best action always came from his hot-chick enemies, didn't it? *Get it on, then get the hell out!*

Maya's not my enemy, though – not yet. I'll refrain from categorizing her until further notice.

"Yeah, cool," I say. "That sounds great…thank you." Try not to sound overenthusiastic, now. This could be easy money.

"No problem at all. Let's go!" She's already tugging at my palm.

Rusted-out Corollas line the intersection. Maya taps on a window.

It creaks downwards, and out pops a ruffled head. *"Kahaa jaane ho?"*

"Budhanilkantha."

The head shakes, and drops back into its nest. Another taxi is quick to fill the void.

"Hello! Hello, taxi?"

We veer into a bumpy alley, bouncing in and out of potholes. Maya raps against a corrugated tin gate; nearby, a dog barks. Then the gate creaks open and a small, somewhat scruffy urchin appears. Maya's words follow him as he shuffles back into the compound.

"Who was that?" I ask.

"One of our servants," she replies.

There she goes with the plurals again. Don't jump the gun, 007; let's see where this is going.

"...Servants, eh? How many servants do you have?"

"Bim is the only one left now. We had to let the others go."

She must be loaded. Or are servants a fringe benefit of embassy employment? This could be fun, having this little tike bring me drinks and snacks as I read the morning papers poolside. Maybe I should get a white linen suit, start smoking a pipe. *Tea and tiger hunts, I say!*

We enter a spacious room lined with paintings and photographs, select pieces of ornate wooden furniture punctuating large interior voids.

"This is quite a spread you've got here."

"It's not mine," she explains. "It's my father's. It's a bit of a tip at the moment."

"I thought your parents didn't live in Nepal anymore?"

"They don't. What I meant to say is that both of them don't. My father still does. He took a smaller place after mother...moved away."

"Oh...I'm sorry.""No, it's been years – I was just a little girl when it happened."

The boy reappears with a stack of pillows and blankets and sets them neatly on the floor. "I can't offer you a proper bed," she says, apologetic. "They've sold off almost all of the other furniture since the move; I'm afraid you'll have to make do on the couch."

"I'm sure I'll sleep better than last night."

"*Bonne nuit.*"

"I, uh…"

She disappears into a back room, shutting the door behind her.

What happened to our night of passion? I thought we had some kind of connection here, Maya.

Fuck it, I'm exhausted.

"…Good night," I yawn.

The boy darts down a hallway.

She's still not adding up. Her mom's been out of the picture for years, but they've only sold the furniture recently? Where is her dad, and what's he still doing here? Does *he* work for the embassy? That might explain her meteoric rise from the mailroom, and it definitely accounts for her choice of plural pronouns. Maybe I'm a little paranoid, like she said…maybe I'm too fucking tired to care right now.

I crawl underneath the blankets and pull them tight around me.

Mmmm. Beats a urine-stained prison cot. This is more like it! What shall I have for breakfast in the morning? Fruit salad? No, I'll have the bacon and eggs, little Bim, some French toast, lots of syrup…with a side of…

A soft clattering awakes me. The boy hovers over me, a cup of tea jittering on a small plate in his hands. He places it delicately next to my pillow.

"Hey there, Bim!"

"*Hajur.*" Smiling, he scurries away.

I take a sip: sweet and hot, with a touch of cinnamon. This place is enormous! I wander into a room at the end of a hallway. A large black trunk rests in the center; photos are scattered across the top. I run my fingers across the pile, fanning them out. Sunny beaches, palm trees, waterfalls…a close-up of a tanned guy with short dark hair. He is smiling…not bad looking…older, maybe mid-forties. Mirrored sunglasses hide his eyes.

"Sleep well?"

Maya stands in the doorway, hand against the frame.

I release the picture; it flutters to the floor. Her eyes flit downwards to the trunk.

"I'm sorry…I didn't…"

"What are you *like*?"

A lost puppy? A wayward traveler in need of lodging? An obnoxious American who loves to meddle in the lives of others? I'm not sure I'm supposed to answer that question.

"…Right – we've got to sort you out with a room then, haven't we?"

What happened to my stay at the luxurious Maya Resort & Spa? Bim hasn't even brought me my fruit salad and bathing salt selection yet. I blew it…*persona non grata.*

"You've got to check in at the Immigration Office today as well, haven't you?"

"Yeah. At two o'clock. But I don't really remember how to get there."

"Which is why I wrote 'Immigration Office' in Nepali on this piece of paper. Show it to any driver and he will get you there. Let's sort this before there are any more intrusions."

"Hey, Maya, I'm sorry. I didn't mean to pry. They were just lying there…I always pick up pictures. It's an awful rude habit of mine…"

A small framed picture in the opposite corner of the room catches my eye.

"Well, then," says Maya. "There's not a second to spare."

"No, there is," I say, pushing past her to the picture. In it, a man and a woman are dressed to the nines…they could be dressed for a ball. They certainly look as though they have something to celebrate.

"Jupiter, haven't you seen enough pictures for now?"

I know that face. Where did I see…? *From the picture* – the picture with Gerard!

I swing around.

"Well, it looks like we've got some explaining to do!" I say.

"I have no idea what you're on about."

She makes a move for the picture.

Oh no you don't, you sly little bitch.

"Not so fast, missy!" I grab Maya by the arms, shove her up against the wall.

That's right, Miss Mysterious, now it's your turn.

"I'm paranoid, huh? What embassy was it you said you worked for? The American Embassy? Funny how they didn't mention you, and how you didn't seem to know anything about them...Are you sure it's not the *British* embassy you're working for? How's counselor *Gunn* doing these days?"

My fingers squeeze into her flesh.

"Please...stop."

"You stop, Maya – stop fucking with me! Do you think I'm that stupid? You're in on it with Gunn, aren't you? You were in on it from the start. *He* sent you, didn't he? *Didn't he?*"

"Jupiter – please...I can't..."

Oh shit, I'm lifting her off the ground. I release my grip; Maya slumps against the wall and coughs.

"I'm sorry, I...what the *fuck* is going on, Maya? Tell me who the fuck is in the picture or I swear I'll slam you back up against that wall."

Gasping, she gets to her feet.

"Goddamnit, Maya – tell me!"

"OK!" she capitulates. "Anthony...Anthony Gunn...is my father."

Well, well, well...

"Seriously? Your father?" I ask.

"I don't know – I mean, I'm not sure exactly...who *you* are." she falters. "He wasn't sure, either. He thinks you're after him."

"*After him?* Why would *I* be after him? I don't even know your father!" I lie.

"You rang *him*. And how dare you!"

She smacks me across the face. Warm blood pulses through my cheek. I guess I deserved that.

"...Yeah, I called him." I run a grimy hand through my hair. "How in the hell did he know I was coming? There's got to be thousands of people pouring in here every day...He tailed me, didn't he? He had taps on Gerard and men waiting to move on me. The man on the plane – your old man sent him. He sent him to kill me!"

"What *are* you on about?" she says. "He hadn't spoken to Gerard in well over thirty years and had no idea where he was. That's why my father considered him – and you – so dangerous. You were the one trying to extort money. A hundred thousand, if I'm not mistaken. How dare *you*!"

She slaps me again. This time it feels kind of good. Can we transfer this to the bedroom?

"OK, how about we stop assaulting each other and work this out?" I say, rubbing my cheek. "I'm not going to take any cash from your dad, I promise. But how the hell did he know who I was?"

"You told him your name on the phone!" she says. "How many Jupiters do you think there are running around the world? My father has connections at the airport. He checked all the incoming flight manifests. And when you make such a grand entrance, how could he miss you?

"Tell me," she adds, straightening. "If you got a sinister call in the middle of the night from a stranger threatening to destroy your livelihood, wouldn't it put you off a bit? Wouldn't you want to figure out who that person was?"

"Fair enough. Gerard owed me big time – and your dad apparently owes him. I thought I might be able to work something out."

"What did you expect him to do, just pop up and give you a suitcase full of cash?"

"I didn't really think things through," I mumble.

"Gerard is a threat to my father and he took that threat very seriously. How could he not when you ring him out of the blue, intimidating him with blackmail?"

"Gerard is *dead*. The only threat he can impose now is to the sanitation industry."

I wonder if they found him yet. He must be liquefied by now. Perhaps Armando rang the cops. They're probably trying to pin the whole thing on him.

"Even if he was alive, I'd hardly consider him a threat. The guy was a decrepit old cripple...he only had one leg, for Christ's sake."

"I don't think you get how powerful Gerard was. He controlled a huge amount of the drug trade in Nepal. He was very close to some members of the royal family here, so close that he was set free after wiping out an entire Indian cartel who thought he was getting in the way of their operations."

"What does that have to do with your father?"

"My father...my father used to have ties to Gerard."

"So he used to run drugs with him? Is that what you're saying?"

"What I'm saying is that Gerard might have been able to make some very damaging allegations against him, just by association. Considering that my father is in line to become the next British ambassador of Nepal, he does not want Gerard resurfacing in any way, shape or form. You realize what a blow having Gerard connected to him could be to his political career?"

"Well, Gerard's dead. I can assure you of that."

"That may be, but it doesn't resolve the issue, not completely. Gerard had several operatives working for him in Nepal. Some might still be here, waiting for instructions."

"I think you're the one being paranoid now. Listen, Maya, I'm not *with* Gerard. I'm not one of his operatives, waiting for instructions from central command. OK, I was looking for a handout from your dad, but I'll drop it. You guys got me out of prison, so let's just call it even."

"Don't get cheeky with me!" she says. "And even if you're what you say you are what about this friend of Gerard's – this John?"

"John?"

"The person whose address you showed me yesterday. John, wasn't it?"

"Oh yeah, John…what about him? Like I said, I don't know anything about him."

"Yes, but you meant to contact him. You're going to drop the *dzi* with him, aren't you?"

"Maya, you're giving me too much credit. I just wanted to talk with him, see what he's about. I might give him the *dzi;* I might not. I don't expect anything in return, even if he is one of Gerard's operatives. What do you think he's going to give me for those stones – a Russian suitcase bomb? He could be just as dead as Gerard, for all I know."

"Well, I know less about him than you do. Father only mentioned Gerard. I don't know what I'm supposed to make of all this now. It seems as if he could be another loose end. My father should be informed."

"Listen, I don't know shit about him. I lived with that old fart for a couple of months. I sold drugs for him so that I could get myself back on my feet…that was it. I don't know anything about any operatives or anything about your old man other than his name. His phone number was on the back of a photo and I called it after Gerard died. I thought he was a friend's of Gerard, thought I might be able to get some money out of the deal. I was high as a balloon when I called your dad; I can't remember half of what I said to him."

"Right. It would be better if you told him all this yourself. I'll arrange a meeting so the two of you can meet. I'll ring him now…"

She reaches for the phone. I slam it down against the receiver.

"What a bunch of bullshit! All his time, you've been lying to me, schmoozing me, and now that I catch you red-handed, you want me to cough up everything I know about Gerard? I showed you my entire hand, and I'm not even holding a pair. Shouldn't you be the one explaining?"

"Listen, Jupiter, I only did it to protect myself…and my father. I believe you, but you've got to speak with him. He got you out of jail. You'd still be there if it wasn't for him. I can't promise anything, but if you talk to him and tell him what you know, he might be able to keep you out. Do not cross him and do not underestimate him: he is a very influential man here. Don't you think you owe him that much?"

"Before I say yes to anything, I've got a few more questions."

"…Go on, then."

"So your father, he's been here in Nepal for a while now."

"Yes."

"And your mother?"

"She moved away years ago. I haven't seen her in over twenty years. She left when I was a child."

The case of the incredible vanishing mother. Mine is still physically present, but emotionally void.

"I know the feeling," I say.

"My father met her in London. He charmed her into marrying him and brought her with him to Asia when he started his overseas service. I think he painted an overly bright picture of what life would be like here. The way he talked it up, she no doubt thought it'd be filled with white-gloved banquets in palatial homes, foreign dignitaries, and romantic Kipling-style adventures. It wasn't quite like she'd imagined, I guess.

"Father's first assignment was in Burma. They arrived in the middle of the monsoon, during the worst of the heavy rains, and were sent straight away to a village far outside of Martaban. Their first year was spent in a stilt house overlooking one of the largest, most remote backwaters on the planet. The only foreign dignitaries she received out there were the fishermen who stole her fruits from the fish basket she used to hang off the side of the house into the water to keep them fresh.

"…Father said she never quite got to grips with the humidity. She had curly strawberry-blonde hair and the weather here made it quite unmanageable."

"Like yours," I say, "only you didn't get the curls."

"Yes, I suppose like mine. Anyhow, a year later, she got pregnant. I don't think she ever factored a family into the equation…nor did my father. He was just a junior clerk then, with hardly enough salary to scratch by on. The pregnancy was very…difficult. In the end, I think it all just became too much for her. And one day she just vanished.

"I hardly remember her. All the photos of her had been lost…in the move. I only know her from father's accounts.

"Since then it's been just my father and I. He had no idea what to do with me, so I was sent to a boarding school near London. After that I only saw him occasionally, over the holidays. Once I passed my A-levels, I took a semester at Cambridge but it was all just drivel. I couldn't stand being in England any longer; I had to get out – I was a time bomb ready to explode. After I got into a huge row with one of my professors, I persuaded father to let me come and stay with him a while. That was more than four years ago."

Cambridge? That's top-notch billing. Makes most of our universities look like low-end, mail-in correspondence crap. Did her wits or daddy's connections and deep wallet get her in? I'm guessing a bit of both.

"He thought it would be a temporary stay – 'til I sorted my head out – but once I arrived, I couldn't get myself to leave. He opposed the idea from the start but I told him I wanted to follow in his footsteps, doing embassy work. I convinced him I could learn much more studying here at his side. And that shipping me back to Cambridge would result only in my expulsion. He wouldn't hear of it at first, so I ran off into the hills until the semester was under way. Eventually, he relented, and I started taking courses here at Tribuvan University. I came out with a degree in International Relations."

"And now you *are* working for the embassy?"

"No, you were right about that. I'm not doing much of anything at the moment. I've gone off on the whole idea of government work."

I check her eyes. Beautiful, cat-green eyes. Watch out; you might get lost in there.

"...So, do you believe me?"

"...Yeah, I do."

"Trust me?"

"OK, but on one condition. I've been playing a straight deck with you; now you've got to start playing straight with me. No more stories, no more spies, no more joker's wild."

"Jupiter, no-one was following you, I swear!"

"Oh, am I just being paranoid again?"

She sighs. That's right – you know you played it wrong.

"...No more lies, OK?"

"Cool. Can I ring him now?"

"...Go ahead."

She picks up the phone, punches in numbers.

"Hello, father? Listen, there's been a change." She shoots me a conspiratorial look. "Well, I had him stay at our flat last night and..."

A barrage of electrically-modulated verbiage erupts from the receiver. *Chill it down a notch, pops* – I slept on the couch. She didn't even get to the punchline yet.

"...Yes, father...yes, he *was* set to sleep at Dharma's. Well, it was late and...father, *he knows*."

I can't hear his voice anymore. That took the wind out of your sails, didn't it, Gunn?

"Yes...everything," she continues. "Look, I don't think he's what you've made him out to be, or rather, what he's made himself out to be. He says he's not involved with Gerard, never really was to begin with. I'm fairly certain you don't have to worry about Gerard any longer, either. He's dead, apparently." She pauses, frowns. "I think you need to meet him face to face. Yes, he's here now. No, he's in the other room."

She offers a rueful half-smile.

She just lied again. And to her own father! How am I supposed to believe this girl? OK, maybe that lie was for my benefit – still, this could be a trap.

"Yes, father...yes...yes...alright then, speak to you soon."

"...What did he say?"

"Not very pleased you're in the know but relieved to hear of Gerard's demise. He'll ring me back later to set a time and place."

"Alright, I guess that's fine, but I've got to get out of here. I'm still a little spun out by all of this. I need a little space right now."

"Yes, that might be best," she replies, stroking her wrists.

"Is this really your parents' place, then?"

"I used to live here with my father but recently he's taken a room down at the embassy."

"The *British* embassy?"

"Yes. At least stay until you meet him."

Never meet a prospective enemy on his own terms or in his own house. Preferably make it somewhere public and busy where you're less likely to vanish into a trapdoor or be hauled into a blacked-out van.

"I'll ring Dharma and tell him you're on your way."

"Who?"

"The bloke who posted your bail."

"No, I need to get my own place. Like a hotel or something."

"That won't do. You'll have to stay with Dharma or here, I'm afraid."

"You said you trust me, right? You also said that there's no way for me to get out of this valley without a passport. The Immigration Office has my passport and you have my word. You name the place and I'll stay there, but I won't stay here. Put Shresta or some embassy cronies outside to keep an eye out. I couldn't care less who keeps tabs on me but I need to get out of here. I'm not going anywhere, Maya. Promise."

She scrutinizes me before jotting something on a message pad in Nepali. Damn, she can write the local lingo as well! Maybe she did make the Cambridge cut without daddy's contribution.

"Right, let's get you a taxi then. Ready?"

"…Sure," I say, slinging my pack over my shoulder.

Stepping into a dusty intersection, she flags down a black-and-yellow, canvas-topped three-wheeler. Gold tinsel dangles from the window in celebration of…the god of transportation?

"They really like to pimp their rides out, don't they?"

Rolling her eyes, she hands the driver the message and exchanges a few words.

"He'll take you to Freak Street just down from Durbar Square. Give him four hundred rupees. Check in at the Tibet Peace Guest House. It's not flash but there are always plenty of rooms. I'll pop by the hotel later this evening, around five-ish, to see how you're getting on. Don't forget your appointment at Immigration…and don't do anything stupid."

"Coolio."

•

I crawl into the back. The driver pops his seat forward and yanks a starter cord…our family lawn mower had a bigger engine! After a few stubborn grunts, the engine sputters into life.

"Oh, Jupiter!" she calls after me. "What about the business at the post office…John's whatshisname's contact address? Did you want to drop a message in his box?"

A cloud of white smoke envelopes us as the driver maxes out the revs.

"I don't know," I cough. "What do you think?"

"I think we should see what he has to say. I'll let father know about him so we have a better idea of who we're dealing with."

"Yeah, do that. Hold on a second." I fumble for a pen.

"Ek chin parkinos!" she tells the driver.

I tear a piece off the brown envelope and write:

John,

> *You don't know me but I know Gerard. I need your help. I'm staying at the Tibet Peace Guest House.*

Jupiter

"Here, it's box 108."

"I know, Jupiter. Please don't do anything foolish. My father might not be so forgiving if you did. And don't forget your appointment."

"Maya," I say, "One more thing. Call me Jay, not Jupiter, hey?"

Maya thumps her palm twice against the roof. The driver pops the clutch. We pinball down a dirt path, swerve left and shoot out onto pavement. Seriously pot-holed pavement. Cars, trucks and motorcycles honk like geese flying out of formation. Veering sharply, we dodge a bicycle loaded down with chickens.

Well, well, we've got ourselves a bit of international intrigue after all! Maya, you've got one hell of a poker face but you played it a little too close to the home front. I botched your operation in the end but overall, not a bad piece of espionage for a twenty-something-year-old. Man, I really slammed her against that wall, didn't I? That's good: shake her up a bit, let her know I mean business! But still, a girl. Anyway, I think she's on the level now.

What about daddy dearest? Well, he is a diplomat and he is British, after all. He must be a fairly reasonable man. I'll just tell him everything I know, be honest about it. Apologize about the extortion attempt but play the sympathy card; tell him my own tale of exploitation *à la* Gerard. He shut right up when she told him the dirty old Frenchman had bought the farm. I'm sure he'll have a hundred questions to ask me. I hope he can get me out of this legal jam, but he might chuck me curbside now Gerard's out of the picture.

A feather twirls through the open-sided door of the three-wheeler... did we just run over a pigeon? Petrol fumes seep into my nostrils. I hate the smell of petrol in the morning. Smells like...misery.

I close my eyes, trying to envision the white-sand beaches in Maya's photos. *Skidding stop.* I twist the handle and push open a warped door composed primarily of duct tape...gotta take care of that, buddy.

"Hashish, opium?"

I've been racially profiled. Sounds like the best damn question I've heard all morning. A little of either wouldn't hurt.

Behind me, four o'clock, bearing down hard. I've got him in my sights. A fine mist of dandruff coats his oily bed-head. That style seems to be all the rage over here. An 'I Am Not Perfect But I Am Limited Edition' T-shirt clings to his wiry frame. I might want to pick up one of those.

"Hashish, opium? Good price."

Fuck it. A lot of shit went down this morning. Need to settle the nerves. I drop back a step; he trundles up to my side.

Scanning my periphery, I whisper, "How much for hash?"

"Good price – Nepali price."

Yeah, right. You're going to give me the deal of the century, right?

"How much?" My eyes flit over his shoulder.

"I show you. *Come!*"

Fish on! I hate this part. I hate stepping round corners into darkened alleys and shady drug deals. When I was sixteen, I tried to buy a bag of weed from a brother at the Greyhound depot downtown Chicago. What an easy mark I must have been, with my Guatemalan pants and Birkenstocks. A wannabe hippie bankrolled on daddy's dividends.

We ducked into a basement well and he rolled up a huge ratty joint of what tasted like a cross between sawdust and Chinese allspice. I knew it was bunk but we kept smoking it...then he jacked me. I could never figure out why he went through all the trouble of rolling up and burning that nasty concoction, though. I was so scared I would have given him my Birks if he'd asked for them.

But I do like drugs. I guess that's the rub. The dried-out cake you have to eat to get to the frosting.

He waves me into an alley. Every few steps, he twists around, checking my shit. This guy's dandruff is killing me. The back of his head looks like a December morning in the Adirondacks. The alley widens, expands into a small square, flanked by crumbling brick.

"This is as far as I go, cowboy," I say.

"*Come!*" he beckons.

"You know you've got really bad dandruff?" I say. "You should get some Head & Shoulders to take care of that shit!"

Perplexed, he frowns. Don't have a clue, do you? Sorry, but I couldn't resist – nothing like a little comic relief to ease the tension. '*Having trouble breaking the ice with drug dealers from underdeveloped nations? Try humor!*'

Sidestepping a pile of trash, he squats; I hunch next to him. His eyes dart about nervously like minnows. He fishes around in one pocket, then the next.

Come on, let's go! It can't be that fucking small...if it's that small, I'm not buying it.

Finally, he wrenches a shiny ball from his pocket, curling back the foil with his thumb.

"How much?"

"Two-thousand rupees, Nepali price. Good price." He rolls the ball into my palm. I take a whiff...sweet Jane!

What is that, not even forty bucks? It would be at least a hundred euros back in France.

There's motion from above. Two men in blue uniforms rush up from behind with clubs at their sides. *Oh shit.*

My stomach drops out from under me. *Run* – no, freeze and change colors! *Do something! Real ease, release, RELEASE!* The hash ball dribbles between my shoes; I step on it. The dealer wheels around... too late. One cop yanks him to his feet; the other pokes him stiffly in the chest with a club. He squirms like a street dog, yelping for mercy.

Every muscle in my lame-assed body is taut; blood hammers through my temples – *tha-thumptha-thump!* I want to run, but can't. My heart feels like it's tearing through my chest. They drag him off into the alley. *Tha-thumptha-thumptha-thump, tha-thump...tha-thump...*

Tha-thump...tha-thump...tha...thump...

Phew. Subsiding blood-pump, adrenal drain...that's all there is. Wow. They didn't want me, didn't want the paperwork. Poor guy, he might be getting my rat-infested prison cot for the night. Watch out for that crusted vomit.

Dazed, I wrap my fingers around the chunk of kryptonite wedged between my Chuck Taylors and slip it into my pocket. Yes, my kryptonite...my eternal weakness, the principal cause of my bumbling and floundering through life. And it appears I haven't learned my lesson yet. Still busy buying up hash on the street, even as smuggling charges are being brought against me.

Chances are likely I'll spend a good chunk of change and do time in a third-world prison. *Can you hack it, punk?* I should get in touch with DARE, see if they need a new anti-drug poster boy.

Drugs are bullshit. I really don't need this in my life anymore.

At least, this time, I didn't have to pay.

"How long you stay here?" enquires a pock-faced boy from behind the desk.

"I'm not sure – maybe one week."

"Passport..."

"Um, I lost it...Here...here's my driver's license..."

He takes it, asks, "What country?"

"America."

"America…America…America," he mumbles, as if it were some secret mantra. *The land of gold and honey.* He scribbles in his ledger.

My eyes scan a small courtyard: vines score the walls, infiltrate the bamboo birdcages tucked into corners. Some beat-up copies of *National Geographic* splay haphazardly across a central wooden table. An Asian hipster in a floppy hat, probably Japanese, is thumbing through one on the couch. I glance at a makeshift message board to my side.

Native English speaking teachers needed immediately in Solu-Khumbu region.

Contact Naropa Institute at 4700801

A myna bird squawks obnoxiously in the corner.

Karoline and Anne,

Went to Chitwan – will be back on the 27th – Fleming…

A couple, clad similarly in loose, vibrantly-dyed clothing, shuffles past. They're speaking to one another in some heavy eastern-bloc tongue.

Looking for trekking partner, preferably female, to do Annapurna Circuit.

See Aisha in room 215

I finally made it: the backpackers' Shangri-la. Maya was stretching it when she said modest. With a couple grand, you could hole up here for year if you played your rupees right.

Flipping open the lock, I flop my rucksack onto a mangy quilt, folded at the end of a forlorn-looking bed in the corner. The choppy melody of a flute flitters in through a window, and the inimitable scent of hash. Seems like I'm not the only *aficionado*.

Now, about that hash…*Sweet, sweet Jane, take me away.* I twirl up a joint, lie back on the bed and study my creation for a moment.

The smoke wafts upwards, hangs from the ceiling, probes the cracks for a passage. A knock on the door – *shit*! Can't a man smoke a joint in peace? I lie motionless, weighing options. Do I put it out? Yeah, put it out and light a cigarette.

Another knock. "...Who is it?"

"I am from the room next door."

Shit. What the fuck does he want? This is the kind of place where you don't ask questions and people don't ask any of you...like a low-rent apartment building in Bed-Stuy.

"Hold on a second." Stubbing the half-joint against the table, I tuck it under a rupee and spark up a cigarette.

"Coming," I say, puffing madly as I open the door.I face a swarthy, long-faced man with a shock of black hair and a six-o'clock shadow. Greek, perhaps?

"Hey."

"May I come in?" he asks, in deeply accented English.

"Yeah, sure..."

He scans the room. OK, Zorba, enough with the detective routine. "What's up?" I ask.

"You should take care when you smoke here. The owner's brother is a policeman. It is much safer on the roof."

"Thanks for the tip."

The accent isn't right for a Greek; maybe he's Middle Eastern.

He scoops my ball of hash off the table.

"How much you pay for this?"

"Two thousand rupees."

"You paid too much – and the quality is not so good."

"Come to think of it, I got it for less...much less."

What the fuck do you care about my expenditures, Ishmael? Get your goddamn hands off my hash.

I remove it from his hands...*leggo my Eggo*, bitch!

"What is your name?"

"What's yours?" I retort.

"…I asked you first," he counters.

I've just about had it with this boisterous whatever-he-is. "Jupiter," I say.

"Like the planet?"

"Exactly. But call me Jay."

"American?"

"Very…you?"

"Israeli…and my name is Baraq…like your President."

I had a feeling he was from that neck of the woods. Couldn't have narrowed it down much more…it's hard to tell a Hittite from a Semite unless they're eating or praying. I think I'm actually getting better at this nationality game.

"…Your money, it's on fire."

"*Shit*." I flip the burning rupee onto the floor, stamp it out. The joint burned right through it. Still, it was only a rupee – I could burn a wheelbarrow full of them and it would only set me back a few hundred dollars. I pinch the joint between my fingers.

"…Want some?"

"Sure," he smiles.

He takes a deep toke. Smoke spills from his nostrils, for an instant transforming him into a boar with tusks.

"When did you arrive?" he asks.

"A few days ago. And you?"

International small talk sucks. *'Where are you from? Israel, oh that's wonderful! I hear the suicide bombers are spectacular in the spring… all those colors, the deep reds splattered in the crisp air… Where are you flying/busing/ferrying from? Oh, how was that, I heard it's fabulous! Service is no longer available to that island? The rates have gone up since the last edition? They've built a hotel right on top of the shrine? What a shame! You should have gone two years ago, before they put in the gondola.'*

I'd rather buy the damn book. And then there are those that turn the whole thing into a competition; racking up countries, cities, airports, visas and permits like notches on their guns.

"…We come from Delhi only one week ago. Such a dirty place, my god."

What did you expect – white-gloved coolies in pith helmets?

"Did you fly into Nepal?"

"No, we come by motorcycle."

I'd heard about these Israelis. Not as widely dispersed as Japanese hipsters, who seem to find their way into every nook and cranny of the globe, but nonetheless a prevalent and hardy species found throughout Central Asia. Fresh out of the army, stoned out of their minds, chugging through Central Asia on salvaged Enfields raised from the dead. Like packs of hyenas. As if there weren't enough hazards on these roads already.

Pinching the roach off his thumb, I say, "Cool – how was that?"

"Beautiful, but dangerous. Sometimes we have trouble with the police, too, always with the *baksheesh*."

He picks up my ball of hash. "Do you mind if I take some of this?"

I knew it. *I knew it.* He didn't give a shit about my wellbeing – he was shaking me down from the start.

"I thought you said this wasn't any good."

"It's not for me."

The nerve of this guy. He tells me my shit is no good, hits me up for some of it anyway, then informs me he's going to pass it off to someone else. Prick. Good thing I didn't have the Planter's out.

"If this is so bad, why don't you go scrounge up some high-grade stuff?" I say. "Should be a cinch with your connections."

"My girlfriend is sick. She needs something for her stomach."

OK, I can understand that. I will retract any previous animosity and refrain from pushing you out the door thanks to your bedridden girlfriend…for the moment. But if I find out you don't have a girlfriend, or she's up and about, I'm keying your Enfield, maybe more.

"I can give you some money if you want."

"No, that's cool. Just take what you need."

He rips off a sizable chunk.

"*Go easy*. I'm giving you some, not selling it, alright?"

A gift of a bud or joint usually serves as a deterrent to future unsolicited purchases, but it doesn't seem to have worked in this case.

"I have to go, my girlfriend is…"

"Sick. Yeah, you already told me that. I hope she gets better real quick. See ya later."

"See you."

Don't let the door hit ya in the ass! I should have taken the money.

Blurry-headed, I lie back and pull the quilt up over my head.

I wake to a loud rapping on the door. Shadows cloak the room.

What time is it? Holy shit, I must have slept all afternoon.

"Door's open," I mumble groggily.

The handle twists back and forth.

"No, it's not."

I lever myself upright, lope to the door, and click the key over. It's Maya.

I flip on the light.

"What, have you been sleeping?"

"Yeah," I croak, clearing my throat.

"…So, did they tell you anything new at the Immigration Office today?"

Damn! I knew there was something I had to do today.

"I uh, forgot to…"

"For *fuck's* sake! Do you actually give a shit about what I've done, about what my *father*'s done for you? You know you'd still be in prison if it wasn't for him."

"Yes, Maya, I am well aware of that. I'm sorry – I was just so beat… my sleep patterns are still screwed up with the jet lag."

Maya's eyes fix on the rolling papers lying on the chair.

"What, too busy getting stoned? I suppose it won't be long before you're off gallivanting with heroin addicts down on New Road."

"Hey now, let's not blow this out of proportion. A joint here and there isn't going to hurt anybody."

"Is that what you thought when you got on that plane? Did you even bother to *think* about the ramifications? After all I've done, and you can't be bothered to turn up…one simple fucking thing! I didn't have to be so nice to you, Jupiter…or Jay, or whoever the fuck you are."

She rounds off a backhand across my face.

"*Jesus Christ*. Back off, Agent Smith! The only reason you yanked me out of jail was to pump me for info on Gerard for your father."

"Don't forget your little extortion scheme," she counters. "Anyway, we're past that now, aren't we?"

"I thought we were past the physical assault, too, but apparently not."

"You said you needed space, needed time to think, so I gave it to you. All you had to do was show up, pop your head in and say 'present.' Would that have been so *incredibly* difficult? If you'd stayed with me, this would not have happened. I'm not even sure if my father will act on your behalf anymore."

"So now he's gotten what he wanted, you're going to toss me in the river?"

"If you can't help yourself, we're not doing a bloody thing for you. Immigration may have even sent some decree off to the courts already stating that you didn't turn up. They might be looking for you at this very moment. You're lucky there was another *bandh* today. Most government officials probably didn't bother to turn up."

"Can't you just call and tell them I'm sick?" I'm in no shape for this.

"You can do that yourself: here."

She throws a cheap, boxy cell phone onto the bed.

"So we can be certain this doesn't happen again, I've programmed my cell phone number and Mr Thapa's in, which is all you need. If either of us rings, pick up. If *anyone* rings, pick up. If you don't turn up again, they're going to come looking for you and when they find you, they're going to throw you straight back where I found you."

"I'll go handle it –"

The door slams shut.

"…tomorrow."

I pull the covers back over my head. Should've stayed in bed.

Shit, they put out an APB for me already? They've got their hands full already with renegade Maoists. What do they care about me?

Should I call Thapa? I have a feeling Maya already did. Damn, she really whaled on me that time – *stop with the hitting, already*. Still, she is putting a lot on the line for me. I shouldn't have let her down like that.

I'm good at that: letting people down. That's the only thing I do with consistency. Launched all my family relations right down the shitter in just one flush. *Get your shit together, man!*

First thing tomorrow, I'll march down there and yell 'present' at the top of my lungs…if only for effect.

"Hello, Mr Jupiter!" shouts Mr Thapa. Steaming tiffins are spread across a sheet of newspaper on his desk. "We were very worried about you."

He sticks a clump of rice into his mouth. "Mr Richardson was very upset," he tells me. "Very upset indeed."

"Mr Richardson?"

"From the embassy…"

"Oh yes, Dick. How could I forget good old Dick?"

"He was thinking maybe you were leaving and..."

"Leaving?" I chuckle. "How can I leave if you've got my passport?"

A *'Tiffin Time: 2:00-3:00 pm'* laminated sign hangs crookedly on the wall behind him.

"Yes, well." He pauses to suck in a limp floret of broccoli. "Please do not scare us like this again or we will have to be putting you back into jail."

"I'll be there soon enough," I mutter.

"What is this you are saying to me?"

Easy on that broccoli, buddy. Need a feedbag?

"Nothing," I mutter. "I'm sorry I didn't show up yesterday. I was sick. From that prison food, I think."

"Is everything alright at Mr Shresta's house? You stay with Mr Shresta, isn't it?"

"Fine, just fine. Peachy keen. What about my case? You didn't send anything off to the courts yesterday, did you?"

"I still have everything right here..." He pats the side of his desk. "Nothing new on your case. Please come back tomorrow. Maybe we will be knowing something tomorrow."

Preoccupied with his curry, he dips his head back into his lunch, gurgling out a *'namaste'* through a mouthful of rice. Damn, that little runt can put it away.

I take one last look at his desk. His feeding frenzy has to be the most action it sees all day. I doubt it's locked. My passport is in there: I know it. They probably haven't even marked it yet. Unspoiled. No cancellations, no deportation stamps...like I never even came to Nepal. If I could just get in there and grab it, make it over the border somehow.

I make my way out into the garbage, horns and dust, envisaging cunning ways to retrieve that passport. I suspect I'll be checking in with Mr Thapa for at least a week before they give me a new song and dance. Security's non-existent in there, save for the old stooge at the door. Maybe play it straight a few more days: show up at different times of the day, try to figure out their schedule... *No, I've got to act fast!* They might shuffle my file off to court and then I'm fucked.

Thapa has to leave that desk sooner or later, and he's the only one in that room. I need to stage a diversion. Maya's not going to help me; I'm on my own. He likes his food, doesn't he? Maybe slip a Quaalude into his lentils. *Shit* – they took all my pharmaceuticals. A laxative could do the trick. Hmm…might take too long. If I could get him to turn his back somehow, leave the room. Ask him for a lawyer's number…

All I need is two minutes; two minutes and that passport will be mine.

Carbon monoxide belches from a cross between a lawn mower and a Rototiller, gears grinding through my head. Cigarettes, rickshaws, rupees. I hack up a ball of phlegm, search for the path of least resistance.

Along the wide, crumbling sidewalk, I spot a bearded man squatting next to a caged parrot. Papers are fanned out in front of the filthy cage. A woman stops, hands the man a coin. Lazily, he slides the cage door open and out pops the parrot, cocking its neck from side to side like an Okie deliberating over a hand of three-card Monte. Suddenly, the bird plucks up a piece of paper and flings it aside. The man hands the paper to the woman; the parrot waddles sadly back to its cage. I know the feeling, buddy.

Beats the 'guess-how-old-I-am?' hoof-stomping pony, but runs a close second to the monkey-organ grinder combo.

I hand the guy a rupee. The bird hops out, picks out another paper. The man passes it to me. Lines and squiggles, lines and squiggles… must be Nepali. What do I win? Maybe I've won the local lottery – who knows? Looks like all I get is this paper. I jam it in my pocket and move on, sidling through smoke, sweat and spit, plowing further into the searing afternoon.

I feel like I'm in the massive, never-ending parking lot of a Grateful Dead show. *The Twilight Zone* meets the Grateful Dead, part one. Hare Krishnas are out in force, threatening to morph into a giant steel-your-face starship and take over the band unless only vegetarian burritos are made. If I can only find the burrito guy and tell him in time, maybe trade a few Gooney Birds for some beans…*I need a miracle, man!*

"Hello, what country?" blurts a guy from a step.

Horns bicker at the intersection. Incense bites at my nose. Exhaust fumes sputter, coating my legs in a sickly film. My white T-shirt is acquiring a brownish tinge. Where can I find one of those 'Limited

Edition' numbers? I can't take it, can't take it anymore. *Retreat, find the burrito guy fast!* Temples poke out from a massive courtyard…Durbar Square. Yes, almost home! I hustle past bells, smells and hellos, into the square and down Freak Street.

"Hashish? Hello, friend!"

I want to stop and shake this person, every person who says this. *I am not your friend! Friendships take years to develop and are based on understanding and trust, not carpets, money changing and THC. Do you understand that?* No-one in Nepal is remotely close to being my friend yet. The only one who might count is Maya and the verdict's still out on her.

Shit, that wasn't the dude who the cops nabbed yesterday, was it? His dandruff doesn't seem as severe today.

I slam the door behind me…*damn*! Sensory overload. I wonder if Maya has been by. She could burst in again in one of her surprise afternoon visits. I've got to get in touch with her, get in contact with her father. I hope he's still willing to listen to my story. I hope she's still willing to give me a shot.

I chug the last warm drops from a water bottle and plop down on the bed. I pick up the phone lying next to me. No incoming calls. Should I contact Maya? Don't bug her – it might send her into another slapping frenzy. She'll call when the time is right. I wonder if there's enough credit on my phone to call Stateside.

I dial in the numbers, the ones forever stuck in my head…nothing happens. Only silence. Exactly what I sound like whenever I call.

The faint sounds of flutes whistle through my ears, and the heady scent of jasmine, sweet jasmine. If only I could find the burrito guy.

I need a miracle.

It's hot, scorching. I try to swallow but my throat is parched.

"Does anyone have water?" I ask.

"*Mellow out,*" hisses a shadow.

"I *need* water."

"There ain't no goddamn water, dig? There ain't nothing 'til we clear this goddamn border."

Where am I? I'm moving, bouncing…in a car – no, a bus. A VW bus…*the* bus. Everything is yellow, glazed with dust. Shadowy shapes bustle around me. In the seat across from mine, a person hunches, piercing his arm with a needle. Gross. I hate needles. I look away for an instant, then back at the man…it's Gerard. A smirk plays around the corners of his mouth.

"Do *you* have any water?"

"Y'all shut the fuck up back there or I'll leave ya here and let the vultures rip your eyes out. Goddamnit, here they come – get out the firepower!"

The bus swerves, pinning me against the window. You're either in the bus or out, and I am most definitely in. *Rat-tat-tat-tat!* A salvo of shots rings past. I should be afraid but I'm not, as if this was all just one big video game and I could reset at any moment.

"C'mon, ya goddamn sand niggers! Give 'em some lovin', boys!"

Someone jumps over me, smashes out the rear window. *Rat-tat-tat-tat!* A shell whizzes past my face.

"*Yeeehaaw!* Come and get it, cocksuckers!"

Why doesn't someone give me a gun? I want to play, too. Someone give me a gun!

The bus veers sharply, catapulting me out of my seat.

Rat-tat-tat-tat…rat-tat-tat-tat!

…knocking. Knocking at the door.

I swallow hard, peel the film off the roof of my mouth with my tongue.

"Hold on a second," I croak.

I'm on the floor, sweating against cement. Water. I'm parched. I reach for the bottle of *aqua* on the table. Come on, c'mon…almost – it bounces off my head. Empty.

"Shit."

Tat-tat-tat-tat!

"Alright, *alright* already."

I waver to my feet, unwind the sheet from my waist and open the door. A small boy looks up at me with fragile, eager eyes.

He holds out his hand, beckoning.

"Aaunos."

"Sorry, kid, no rupees today."

"Aaunos."

Taking my hand in his, he tugs gently.

"What do you need, little man?"

I pull away but he refuses to let go.

"No, no. Hey, I don't..."

"E-John...*aaunos.*"

"E-John? Elton John? John who?"

"Aaunos ta," He jerks my hand again.

"Hey, my name's not..."

John. John Bigby! He must have gotten my note!

"Hold on, hold on a second." I jam on one shoe, then the other.

Wallet, sunglasses, key, passp...I wish. Locking the door behind me, I grab my messenger's hand and we trample down the stairs.

Searing sunlight, bells, petals, dust. The boy trots ahead, his head turning continually to ensure I don't stray. He leads me into a copse of street vendors.

"Hello! Hello – what country?"

Atlantis, ever heard of it?

I inadvertently trounce a stack of tube socks.

"Sorry about that."

I make a half-assed attempt to freshen up the disheveled merchandise. Agitated, the vendor flicks his wrist in dismay.

"Ma chigne," he scoffs.

"Take it easy, buddy, it's only acrylic."

Dodging stacks of polyester and rayon, I cross a congested intersection, squeezing around a stalled taxi. Damn, where did my little messenger go? There he is! I chase the runaway down, spin him around.

"Hey!"

Schoolbooks scatter across the ground. Fuck, wrong kid.

"Sorry."

I scan the fruit stalls off to the side. I might as well be chasing a marble down a drainpipe. *Where* did he *go?*

"Aaunos!"

His hand seizes mine again and he leads me round the corner as if I'm a lifesized toy. A big, blow-up American doll. *'Be the first on your block to own one! What every child wants...act now and receive a complimentary American flag with your purchase!'*

We twist into a tight alleyway and my foot splashes in a puddle of mud.

Shit. That was more than just mud: yesterday's lunch, garnished with excrement...I'm hoping from a dog. Where did...oh, *there* you are, you little bugger!

"Aaunos ta!"

We arrive at a cramped doorway, a wooden semi-circle protruding above it. I run my fingers over the weathered carvings.

"Aaunos!"

He tugs on my arm again, shepherding me into a dark tunnel.

Wait a minute: this could be a trap. Look what happened the last time I tried to contact one of Gerard's old buddies. John might want to do more than just 'have a chat' with me. Maya should be here, too, keeping a lookout from the door. Should I call her? Too late for that. Maybe I should talk to the good counselor first, get the scoop on this character. Maybe I *am* paranoid like Maya said.

Crouching through, I emerge into a courtyard enclosed by brick walls. A pair of doves flickers into the air like startled thoughts. I follow them with my eyes until they disappear into the sunlight. Above, the windows are screened in thick wooden lattices. The boy has vanished.

"Hello...hello, John?" I call tentatively. "Anyone home?"

Shutters creak open on the third floor. A woman's face pops out, hastily retreats. I feel like a gladiator cast into an arena, waiting for my opponent to come charging from behind. At least throw me down a sword so I can stave off the initial attack. I swing around and look expectantly along the corridor. It's clear: I can still make a run for it if I have to.

"Hello...can anyone tell me if a John Bigby lives here?"

Evening rays gleam off the rooftop. A gruff cough resonates through the courtyard. I sense eyes on me: someone is watching through the lattice, calculating, judging. I feel like I'm in a huge confessional. *'Forgive me father, for I have sinned!'* Can a few Our Fathers and some Hail Marys set everything straight? I promise not to think impure thoughts.

"Hello...hello? I'm looking for..."

Another violent spasm erupts from above.

"Hello...John? John Bigby?"

A deep, hollow voice fills the air.

"Who sent you?"

"Nobody sent me – I...I'm a friend of Gerard's...Gerard Fey? I've got something to return."

"Move out into the open where I can see you."

I step towards the center, not knowing which direction to face. Does he want to take a shot at me? I scan the latticed windows for any protrusion that might indicate a gun barrel.

"...You're American?"

"Yeah...it's been a while since I've been back."

From the sounds of it, he's from the States, too. Another flurry of coughs ensues, then a long silence.

"...I think I've got something to return to you...or to somebody you might know. Are you John Bigby?"

"That bastard wouldn't give away anything he couldn't take with him," he rasps. "He's dead, isn't he?"

"Yeah, he's toast. He pissed off a couple of whores and they stuck him like a pig. But it was kind of his dying wish and I figured..."

"Keep it," says John.

"What?"

"Whatever it is he gave you, keep it."

"But can't I..."

"Listen, kid, quit now while you're ahead. You don't want to open this door."

I stand there, scanning for signs of movement. He's definitely to the left, probably second level. Playing his cards close, very close, it seems. I got shaken out of one of the most action-packed dreams of my life for this? Don't I get something for coming all the way out here? No gold stars? Not even a comped shrimp platter? I flew halfway around the world for this?

A pigeon lands on the tiled roof above, sprinkling dirt from the gutter. Slowly, I turn towards the corridor.

"Hey, kid..." says the disembodied voice.

"Yeah?"

"Did he still watch those old spaghetti westerns?"

"Yeah."

"Always thought he was Chuck Conner – strutting through Afghan villages with a holster on his side like some goddamn Karakorum cowboy. He never loaded his shooter, though – not unless he thought he was gonna use it. Never came to that, anyhow. Always finagled his way out with that smooth tongue and that ginger beard... Scarlet bastard!"

Gruff laughter.

OK, here we go: this is what I came for...the wild-west, drug-addled days of glory. Lather him up with a story or two that Gerard told you; let him know you're for real. That should turn this exchange around.

"I always thought he was more of a Gary Cooper, myself," I say. "Like that time you had to dress up as Bedouins with rifles under your robes to slip through Karachi."

A flurry of spastic coughs.

"Remember that?"

Nothing.

He's not taking the bait. 'What am I talking about?' Yeah, right. Of course he remembers that incident; how could one forget?

"Karakorum cowboy – that's good," I persist. "What's that you said about his beard?" Silence.

OK…it appears this conversation is finished. He's not giving me anything to play with.

"Well…see you later," I mutter.

Another wave of coughing; it peters out. You should take care of that cough, my man. Doesn't sound like you'll be around much longer if you don't. I scuff my foot into the dirt, move towards the corridor.

I make one final try. "He still had the beard, you know, when he died…"

More silence.

Alright, I can take a hint.

My stomach growls, urging immediate intake. I check my watch: a hair past eight. Feels like I'm finally getting over this jet lag. Pizza wouldn't hurt, but I'm going to need more than a few slices of pepperoni to solve my problems.

I stub my cigarette against the table, grab my pack, and head out. No calls, no note on the door…I guess Maya's had enough of me for a while. Flushed that one down, too. Maybe she's busy working on an exit strategy with her father. I imagine he isn't going to help me anyway. He'll listen to what I have to say, then leave me to my own devices.

I pick out a battered Suzuki in front of the guesthouse.

"Thamel," I mutter.

I feel like a rudderless boat washing backwards with the tide.

Let's do a quick re-cap of yesterday, shall we? I make it over to the Immigration Office and commence 'Operation Re-Identity' in an attempt to self-repatriate myself. I'm optimistic about this, although I'm still hammering out the details. Security is minimal but still, I need to distract Thapa from his desk long enough to pull my file.

I finally got to meet John, if you could call it a meeting; it feels more like I'm seeking an audience and permission has been categorically denied. Another hung jury in my mind.

And I piss Maya off, possibly enough for her to terminate aid...bad, very bad. I've got to get in touch with her and her father and repent – otherwise they might withdraw bail and unleash the hounds on me.

Bottom line: stop focusing on Maya and John and start worrying about that passport. If I don't get that passport back, things could get real ugly, real quick.

As I slam the taxi door, a woman shoves a deformed child and a bowl into my face. Sorry, no world bank loans today. Is that even your child or did you pick it up out of a gutter in the hope of earning a little extra? Alright, maybe it is yours, but all the rupees in the world aren't going to fix that.

OK, my life could be a lot fucking worse.

Two soldiers in blue fatigues cradling M16s chat to one another at the intersection. I wonder if they carry live rounds in tourist hubs... could make for one disastrous headline. Any Maoists lurking? You never know. What does a Maoist look like, anyway?

A cluster-fuck of signs and wires sags overhead like half-finished thoughts.

Spams (a hand pointing left)

Holy Temple Tree Lodge

Satellite TV, 24-hour hot showers and fax.

Reggae Bar

Live Music Every Night!

Lakshmi Communication Center

Email, ITDs, STDs.

STDs? No thanks, trying to cut back.

Car horns bicker…a police officer breaks it up with his whistle.

Wait…STD, that's some stupid abbreviation for long-distance calls, right? I should try and call again. How long has it been now? Almost a year…

Not to confuse matters, I do call. I did call. I call all the time. The problem isn't calling, it's speaking. There's so much I want to say to her, so much I *need* to say, but when I hear that familiar voice down the line, my tongue does a backflip and…This time, though…this time, I'll do it.

I write down the number and, in the lobby, hand it to the lanky man behind the desk.

"What country?"

"America."

"America!" he beams. "Very good, very good."

The promised land. Fireworks go off in their heads every time I say it. *Ahh-mer-iii-caa!* The very letters expand across the heavens in an effervescent glow. If they only knew how much bullshit they'd find at the other end of that rainbow.

The man summons me to a miniscule stall with a phone on a tiny table. I feel like I'm part of some black-and-white movie, squeezed into this paneled booth in the lobby of a posh hotel. *'Hello? How soon can you press a suit?'* I always wanted to say that, but I don't even own a suit. I had to rent one for the funeral. Mom wouldn't spring for it, considering I caused the whole damn mess.

Now just talk to her: talk about the weather, talk about the Cubs. *'They're in the playoffs? Are you kidding? And how is Jenny doing? The kids? First grade already? That's amazing.'*

The man at the desk signals for me to pick up. I've got a dial tone… *all systems go.* My heart starts to race.

*Bbbrringh…bbrringh…*Oh come on, come on…*click!*

"Hello? Hello?"

It's her.

"Hello?"

She sounds so close. I could be across the street at Rob's house after school. I remember how I used to call her all the time, just to check in. Just being a good son. *'Can I sleep over tonight, mom? I know it's a school night but we'll go to bed soon, and I promise to be back early in the morning.'*

"Hello?"

I take a breath. Maybe she's doing better. God, why can't I say anything? There's so much to be said. Why does nothing come out of my mouth?

"*Hello?* Jennifer, is that you?"

I hang up, throw a hundred rupees on the desk.

"Bad connection."

Damn. I was close. I think I might have even sighed. But what was I supposed to say? Who am I kidding? The Cubs won't make the play-offs again. I'm sure they're chalking up another sub-par year, just like me. What *was* I supposed to say? I can't think of anything *to* say. Fact is it's not the same anymore. Regardless of what I said, the answer would be the same. *'Well, that's good.'*

Here's an example.

'Hi mom. I'm in Malaysia now...no, Malaysia...yes, the country. Gerard? No, he's dead now, mom...yep, dead as a stone. I had to get out of there quick. Didn't want to get implicated for homicide, you know. Anyway, I met up with a bunch of down-on-their-luck surfers cum drug dealers and we got so tripped up on betel nut and meth that one day we decided to rob a gem shop. It didn't go smoothly, mom. We didn't realize there were two armed guards instead of one and, well, not everyone made it. I took some pellets in the side. The shit got infected since we couldn't go to the hospital, you know, being on the run and all. So here I am, half delirious, holed up in a deserted beach shack, waiting for the boys to bring me back some meds. My kidneys are really starting to hurt. I hope they're coming back.'

'Well, that's good.'

Always the same crumbling, despondent tone; the hard-plastic emotion. '*Did you hear me, mom, did you really listen to what I said? Shouldn't you be a bit more concerned?*'

I wonder if she knows all those empty calls in the dead of night are me. She has to, right? Mother's intuition and all. A mom knows when her son's calling, when he's crying, when he's in trouble. I want her to know. But does *she* want to know?

She's got to forgive me, right? I'm her son, for Christ's sake. I don't know. I hear that dry, bitter voice on the end of the line and I know the wound's still festering, that she has not forgiven me – that she can't. Will she ever?

I'm sorry, OK? He's dead now – why shouldn't I be?

But a mother has to forgive her son, right?

I love you; I LOVE YOU, you unforgiving bitch!

Did you hear that, mom?

"*Hello, my friend!* Change money?" barks a man from a roadside stool. "Good rate. Eighty five to one."

Thick carpets, intricately woven waterfalls, cascade over the awnings behind him. An orange boar's head lies atop a butcher's table. Casually, he crisps raw chickens with what appears to be a blowtorch.

"Hello – friend. *Come!*"

So many friends; so little time.

As I round the corner, a Nepali man in one of those funny checkered hats and a slim-fitting vest presses his index finger against one nostril and rips the biggest farmer's blow I've ever seen. A huge ball of mucus splatters onto the street. Damn, he got some distance on that one. Ever thought of competing professionally?

North Face and Mammut jackets are crammed into shopkeepers' windows. They must be knock-offs. Outdoor gear company CEOs across the globe must be fuming. *'If only we'd come up with a more complicated insignia!'* I wonder if they've launched a worldwide anti-piracy campaign. Hologrammed logos might be a good place to start.

The words *'La Dolce Vita'* flow invitingly above a door like twisted ribbon. I climb two flights, exiting onto a rooftop scattered with tables. Two waiters in bow ties are whispering to one another in the corner. One approaches, hands me an oversized, laminated menu that rivals the breadth of *War and Peace.*

"Over by the ledge, thanks."

"Yessir."

"Do you have pizza?"

"Yessir! Which do you like?"

Outside of Naples, they've got more varied Italian fare on this menu than on those you'd find in major cities. A residual effect of Marco Polo's travels? In addition, they offer dishes from every continent bar Antarctica. Chili *con carne*, chicken *chow mien*, *coq au vin* – all on the same menu?

"The *al fungi*…and a Coke. Give me the biggest one you've got."

"Yessir."

Sliding the ashtray towards me, I dislodge a green flyer that had been propped against the ketchup.

Ten Days Down the Karnali – trips leaving every Monday.

Equator Expeditions (next to Kathmandu Guest House)

If only they had rafting trips over the border. Maybe I could arrange that. It couldn't cost too much: a couple grand tops. Maybe the Maoists would take me. Didn't Maya say something about them stealing a raft? And if they weren't up for it, I could buy my own damn raft. Buy a raft and paddle down to India, that wouldn't cost me much…though that could go terribly wrong.

Deliverance with a Hindu twist. *'Excuse me, dear sir, but your mouth is quite appealing. In the name of Shiva, I command you to make noises like that of a pig!'* Being gang-raped by a band of sexually repressed

Indian fishermen on the bank of a river strewn with partially burnt body parts sends a shiver up my spine. So much for escape by water.

Scooting my chair over to the rooftop's ledge, I study the commotion in the street below. Fistfuls of water radiate from a shopkeeper's door. A bearded man beats a tired rug, sending dust billowing into the street. The ubiquitous Suzukis veer at one another like geriatric bulls. There's that distinctive smell of sewage again.

My eyes lock on a young boy dressed in rags that look as if they've been left under a leaky oil pan for six months. A beggar. He raises a small plastic bag to his mouth, then exhales and inhales deeply, huffing noisily. A close second to mainlining in terms of nastiness. As if these kids don't have it bad enough.

Ducking past a rickshaw, he zips up behind a woman as she exits a bakery, muffin in hand. He tugs at her pants, lifts a tiny hand to his mouth, rubs his belly with the other. She tears off a bit and hands it to him. Another boy springs up, gesturing to his stomach. They're like flocks of gulls – one nabs a handout and they all come swooping in for a piece of the action.

Ah, pizza. Not exactly deep-dish but close enough. A taste of home that stops the bleeding for a while – that makes you forget. No more money changers, carpet sellers or pending prison terms…just pizza.

At least I've got food to eat. I better figure out a way to extricate my passport from Thapa's desk soon, though, or it might be years before I see another *al fungi*. I fold a piece and a chunk slides off, oozing molten sauce into my lap.

"Christ!"

Deranged laughter swirls in my ear. Wild cocaine eyes smile behind Lennon glasses. Deep-red dreads shoot out in all directions like loaded springs; a long Rasta braid spirals down one shoulder. The face they encase is gaunt, pale as milk, hemmed by a natty beard. Baggy pants patched with swatches of color hang from a bony frame.

Modern-day troubadour, itinerant troublemaker – the kid who ate his paints in art class so he could go home sick; who tortured cats on the clothesline while you were learning to ride a big wheel;, who was dropping acid when you were sneaking beers from the basement fridge. Always ahead of the curve.

I look down at my deformed slice of pizza. Why do I always end up with this punk?

"They're not as bad as they look, but you've got to watch that the slices don't slip down your leg and bite. Let it cool a spell or you'll be swimming in tomato sauce, mate."

"Is that the trick?"

"That and heaps of alcohol. Keeps down those buggers crawling through your insides – kills them off before they can get a grip. Didn't I see you down by the Immigration Office today?"

"Yeah, that could have been me."

"I just got back from the post office myself. Sent off a load of hash to all my mates back home – must have been well over a hundred grams."

They always pick me. I don't have dreadlocks, never wear patchouli, burned myself the one time I tried to juggle fire sticks. Shit, I'm pretty close to clean-cut from a distance. It's like I've got a hippie-reprobate magnet surgically implanted in my head. It's a sixth sense that they pick up on, an as-yet-unexplained physiological phenomenon.

"One hundred grams? You're kidding, right?"

"Nah, mate! I just come back from the hills only three days ago, aayh. I was staying out in this village, just me and the Abos, and I meet this bloke who wants to shake a lot of gear – an English teacher, for fuck's sake! It's a shame seeing teachers selling gear when they should be setting examples, but he had some top gear, mate. Top gear."

This guy doesn't give a shit about the morality of today's youth. His highest good is to get high, nothing more. A possible fit into Charlie Sheen's entourage... probably a bit too feral.

"So we start to talking and it turns out he wants to sell me a fucking kilo. I only had ten thousand rupees on me, but the bloke says he'll dump the whole lot for eight thousand. Can you fucking believe that? A whole fucking kilo for eight thousand rupees? That's less than one hundred US, mate! That will buy me a proper beachfront spot in Bali if I play it right back home. I've got a front set up in Melbourne who'll buy the lot off of me for eight thousand Aussie dollars...a small fortune, mate! I'm still working on the logistics. It's going to be a bit tricky, aayh."

"I don't recommend taping it to your body," I interject.

"Yeah, that would be a lot of tape, wouldn't it?"

He chuckles.

You could wind up with a hefty spell in prison, too.

"I've been slipping a little through the post to my mates, just for a laugh. The first day, I sent a package with a few grams in it, but I doubt it'll make it past the airport. I just got off the bus back from Pokhara, still a bit delicate from all those amoebas swimmin' through my belly, so I just popped a *tola* in a big padded envelope and chucked it in the mail. But now I've got a system, aayh. I reckon they're keen to any deformities and big parcels and such, so now I've started sending it off in small envelopes."

How did I get sucked into this conversation? I have the urge to pin him down and tell him my ill-fated story – tell him it's not worth it; tell him he'll end up rotting in a damp dark cell if he keeps walking that line. But somehow I don't think that'd stop him. With some dumb luck, he'll probably get away with it, too. At least he's thinking big.

"...First, I find some cardboard and cut it out to the dimensions of the envelope so it fits just right. Then I heat up my block of gear and slice it off to make a patty that's as thick as the cardboard, gut it, and slap it *inside* the cardboard so you can't feel any difference, aayh. Even if only half of what I send makes it, my mates will be psyched!"

Drugs through the post, what an exciting new concept! They'll never suspect the old 'hidden cardboard' trick, will they? For his sake, I hope he didn't put any return address on the envelopes. If he did, he deserves to get caught. For his friends' sake, I hope he didn't use their real names, either. I'm just glad I'm not one of the friends stupid enough to give this joker his address.

"...I just hope they save a little stash for when I get back."

"And where's that?"

"Austraayliya, mate."

I love how they draw out the word, embracing each syllable like a dear old friend.

If he doesn't make it, at least chances are good he'll be in a prison where they feed you pizza and Coke. At least they'll speak English, and toss you a pillow and a blanket when it's cold.

"You're a Yank?"

"You got it."

"What were you doing milling about the Immigration Office yesterday?"

"I, uh...I was just taking care of some business."

"What kind of business is that? You look fantastically suspicious in those sunnies."

Who is this joker?

"I'm a CIA operative."

"Oi, ya bastard! I knew it!"

"Actually, I was trying to get in touch with a friend."

"At Immigration?"

"I wanted to see if they could match a post box to his residence. He's a foreigner so I thought they might have some sort of link."

That makes sense, doesn't it? What do I care if it doesn't?

"Slim chance of that, aayh," he says. "That's about as easy as threading a camel through a needle in this jamboree. I would be surprised if they even know if your mate is in the country."

"Oh, I already met him...kind of."

"Well, did you meet up with the guy or not?"

"Yeah, but he's not taking visitors at the moment. My sleep patterns are all fucked up and I'd rather not get into it right now. I feel like I've been up for days."

"Your goose is cooked, aayh? It's like this time I was down in Benares, jackin' up on some go-ey I picked up in Goa. Really good shit, it was. I got it off this chemistry student studying at uni in Calcutta. Top notch, aayh! I was up for four days straight!"

Smells like you haven't taken a shower in five. I don't understand half of what you're saying to me, but this pizza is good. Something to occupy me while I eat. More entertaining than reading the paper or flipping channels.

"So I'm sittin' down on the *ghats* sweating my tits off, watching bodies cook, and up walks this really fine Sheila I met down in Agra a few weeks back. We start talking, telling each other where we've been. By this time the sun's throbbing. I'm crispin' up like a slab of bacon in a skillet and out of nowhere she leans into my ear and whispers, 'D'ya want to come back to my place for a smoke?'

"Believe me, the smell of that burning flesh was turning me into a predator and I wanted to shag her more than anything, but I could barely breathe, let alone shag. That speed had me by the short and curlies, mate! I was coming up so hard I couldn't talk. Me jaw was wired shut, aayh. A second later, she flitted off into the smoke like some sorta cherub!"

I wish I was in India, wasting away the afternoon with this clown, roaming around priceless monuments on cheap drugs. The Taj Mahal versus house arrest...no contest.

Although I'm not actually under house arrest, am I? More like 'valley arrest.' Whatever you call it, it sucks. I'm in limbo: a man without a country, without a passport, watching helplessly as his fate is determined by a roulettish judicial system that borrows most of its edicts from Hammurabi's Law.

"...So, did you hook up with her?" I ask.

"Never saw her again...hey mate, are you up for a smoke? My flat's just round the corner."

"Let me finish this pizza and I'll think about it."

"No worries."

Reptilian in nature, this creature could no doubt defy all basic laws of human endurance: crawl through the desert for forty days, feeding on grubs, and emerge with nothing more than a mild case of sunburn; dive off a glacier into a crevasse and walk away with a few scratches. Somehow, this dude would survive.

I grab another slice and fold it. A mushroom spills onto my forearm.

"Those things are a bit daggy, aren't they? And they usually end up giving me the shits."

I look to him, then back to the pizza.

"Fuck it, let's get out of here." He smiles, all skewed yellow teeth. Who needs to worry about braces when you've got gum disease? Always ahead of the curve.

We navigate past a herd of taxis, a flock of rickshaw drivers. A blue pickup rushes past, horn honking wildly. The back is full of camouflage-clad, gun-toting soldiers, hands on triggers.

Maoist-hunters. They're a bit close for comfort, aren't they? Closer than these soldiers would like to admit. Instability clings to everything, everyone, like a sweaty shirt. Everyone seems to be holding their collective breath, waiting for something to happen. Carbine-laden Marxists shouting slogans for the masses might be storming the capital any day now. Or is it the Leninist faction they're after? Technically, aren't the army soldiers Maoists, too?

Electric Pagoda is scrolled in cursive script on an electric sign perched on a wall. We clatter up the staircase. A blues riff pours from the second floor like molasses. A swarthy, black-haired girl shoots round the corner.

"*Ciao,* Giovanna! How ya going?"

"*Ciao,* Pineapple. *Come stai?*"

"Not bad, not bad. Do you want to have a smoke with us?"

"Oh, no! I smoke too much today – my head is like a big…how do you say, *forno?*"

"Fair enough."

Pineapple? Did she just call him *Pineapple?* What's his last name, *Express?*

"*Piacere!*" she sings, waving to me.

Yeah, she's hot. What did she say? Fuck, I'm not even stoned yet.

"Now I go take my meal," she says. "Maybe I will see you at the pub later on."

"Yeah, we might join you for a schooner or two. Come by for a smoke, yeah?"

"Maybe later…*ciao!*"

She shoots down the stairs. Pineapple winks at me. A smoke…oldest ruse in the backpackers' little black book. I suppose he'll want to bust out his etchings after a few tokes. I could etch all over her.

It's ridiculous how much time smoking joints, bowls, bongs and pipes plays in the life of the footloose stoner. And there's always a cigarette or two to top it off, depending on the caliber of smoker. You invariably find yourself a smoking with fellow stoners at all hours of the day in countries where you're lucky to speak five general phrases, rendering communication with the locals virtually impossible. These engagements eventually take up more and more of your day, and if you're not careful, you wind up conglomerating them into one massive, infinite session.

"...She's a looker, aayh?" He nudges me. "I'd love to growl her out, let me tell ya! And I reckon she's well up for it."

Growl her out? I shudder at the thought of the naive *Italiana* falling prey to his reptilian charms. It will begin under the innocent guise of sharing a smoke. He'll get her stoned off her rocker, maybe feed her a beer or two for good measure – then he'll close like a komodo dragon zeroing in on a baby goat.

Yeah, I've been watching way too much *Animal Planet.*

"I've got other things on my mind right now."

"Are you kidding, mate? She's fucking gorgeous. You a bum plumber or something?"

"Just got a bad taste in my mouth from the last one."

The *Québécoise* who loved me – and everyone else – with reckless abandon...

"Enough said, enough said. I know the end to that story, let me tell ya. Chuck a left at the top of the stairs."

He swings the door open.

"A bit rough around the edges, just how I like it. The owner of the pub gives me a discount on account of the faulty plumbing."

He points to a sagging hole in a ceiling crisscrossed with rusty pipes. I have no doubt this dude would outlast any cockroach that dared venture into this decaying pit.

"My mates call me Pineapple."

"Pineapple? How do you get a name like that?"

He bunches the dreads on top of his head and snaps a band around them.

"What d'ya think?"

He *does* look like a pineapple…at the very least, like rhubarb.

"A striking resemblance!"

I've never known a man named after a fruit 'til now. *Pineapple.* Has a welcoming feel to it.

A bare bulb dangling from the hazardous light fitting spotlights a mound of clothes on a small bed. In its own feral way, homely, exuding the sort of rustic, lived-in atmosphere that eludes so many aspiring homemakers.

Pineapple pulls out a long green bamboo bong from behind the bed and thrusts it into my hand: the weapon of choice.

"A *Gilligan's Island* deluxe. Where the hell did you pick this up?"

"I made it myself, mate! Bamboo has built-in septums, so all you need is a really sharp blade and you're pretty much set. It's easy as cake with the right stock. Down in the valley, it's hard to find bamboo this big, but up in the bush it grows like weeds…along with other weeds."

Rolling out his palm, he reveals a scraggly marijuana bud that looks as if it has been stuck to his shoe for the past week.

"It's shite, aayh. You'd be picking seeds out of this until the next monsoon, but I've got some hash that'll twist you up like a tornado."

I light a cigarette and drag a tired wicker stool from the corner. Pineapple extracts a chunk of black hash from a multicolored purse.

"Take a whiff of that, then!"

Sweet Jane. My crutch, as Maya so delicately put it.

I've got to start finding new friends.

"You've got an entire kilo of this?"

"Did – it's getting smaller every day. Law of diminishing returns, aayh."

He heats up the chunk with his lighter, kneading flakes onto a tray.

"You should be careful with this stuff. They don't mess around with smuggling here, you know. They'll lock you up in a second."

"Aw, child's play, my boy! I've been running shit for years now, hopping back and forth between here, India and Oz. You've gotta watch yourself down south in India. Pigs fleecing ya for *baksheesh* every chance they get. Fucking unreal. But things are different up here. You've really gotta go looking for trouble up here to find it."

"Lucky me," I mutter.

Shake him by the shoulders, try and talk some sense into him before it's too late. Jump up on his tired wicker chair and scream, 'Youth of the world, abandon your wayward dreams! Smuggling will only end in sorrow!'

What's the use? He's been in the game much longer than I have. Long enough to know, or long enough to think he knows, anyway. You don't really know until they turn that key.

"What about Australia? How do you move it in there?"

"If I told you, I'd have to kill you, mate!"

He spills a cigarette across the tray and packs a hefty pinch of the mix into the bowl at the bong base.

"You're mixing?"

"Gotta give it some fuel, aayh."

Lifting the bong, he tips it toward me. I hesitate for a moment. A joint, maybe, but not a bongload of tobacco/hash. My lungs can't handle this.

"What's the problem mate?"

"My lungs are pretty cashed on tobacco."

"That's right; I forgot you were a Yank. You'd rather be *smokin' the herb*! Except you don't say 'herb', you say 'erb.' Pretty fucking bizarre if you ask me."

Don't start in with the Queen's English, Sir Pineapple: my diction's far closer to base than yours.

"No, this will do the trick."

"There's a shoddy at the back."

"A what?"

He guides my thumb onto the carburetor at the back. And you're giving *me* shit about pronunciation?

Exhaling, I cough violently.

"Easy there, aayh. Don't take it all in one go!"

"Sorry…I'm not…used to…*cough, cough*… bongs." I hack up a ball of phlegm.

"I thought that bongs were the primary means of transport in the States. I never met an American who could skin up."

"I never met an Aussie who could make a decent bong."

"Aw, get your hand off it – that's quality workmanship right there, hand-carved to perfection. I even sealed the two pieces together with a bit of candle wax…have a look!"

If the drug smuggling doesn't work out, you might have a future here – something to fall back on. A little head shop on the corner of Freak Street specializing in handcrafted Himalayan smoking accessories, perhaps…

"Pretty nifty," I say.

"Oi, what are you up to this arvo? I hate mulling about like a corpse when I'm stoned."

Arvo, arvo…I dig deep into my Outback Steakhouse subconscious. He means afternoon, right?

"…I've gotta be here by two o'clock. Can we make it back by then?"

"No worries; I just bought myself a motorbike the other day. It's only a little thing, but it can get you to where you're gawin'."

"Let's go."

"That's the spirit. You can't sit about wasting the high. You gotta use it, mate!"

"Oi, ya cunt!"

A decrepit taxi clatters past, honking hysterically. Pineapple veers the motorbike sharply to the right. Clearing the obstacle, he kicks the sputtering bike up a gear. I tighten my grip round his waist. He screams back at me through his helmet.

"You've really gotta watch these bastards – they think there are three lanes in these little fuckin' roads and they never use their mirrors!"

I'm not sure if careening down a one-and-a-half-lane road with three lanes of traffic in it qualifies as constructive use of a high, but it's exhilarating.

Honk! Beep beep! Honk honk! Agitated jousters, drivers approach head on, sounding their weapons. Immense poplars line the road. I look up: branches blur in the midday light. We speed past fields of crops, some neatly stacked and bundled, others being harvested by clusters of men and women.

Huuhaah-huuuhaaah! A bright-red truck bellows past, forcing us to the side. Pineapple races up to its quarter like a half-crazed dog. We bounce along the gravelly shoulder, squeezed between ditch and spinning tire. Suddenly, I've become sucked into a lost segment of *Road Warrior*, with the action moving twice as fast as it should be. Not too close, Pineapple, or we'll be forced to answer to the laws of physics! Wheels shudder over the gravel, threatening to churn us into a lump of meat and metal. We drop behind.

Dusty men in turbans stare down from a mound of rubble in the back. Pineapple flicks up two fingers.

"Fuck off!" he screams.

He's going to take the truck driver on. Quintessential stupidity, challenging a raging truck full of gravel, but I'm in. This is it; this is where life and living separate. If he fails to make that next bend, a few body parts might separate as well.

Winding out the gears, Pineapple tailgates, eyeing his mark. The men in the back wave us on. We veer into the verge, recoiling in unison as an oncoming truck whooshes past…*that was close.*

OK, wait for it, wait for it…*GO!* Pineapple gooses the throttle. Cheers erupt from the top of the truck. Almost…almost…*yes!* I thrust my arm up in defiance, drop my head back, laugh at the sky. *This is living*. The euphoria that bursts forth like a desert flower after spring rains. That feeling you can't quite put into words, yet that could fill a thousand books. *That is living!*

The bike lurches forward.

"Whoaah! This thing's running like a hairy goat!*"*

Pineapple downshifts. Bridge ahead, jammed with water buffalo in tight formation. Coming in fast. Find the gap, find the gap…collision imminent!

One beast jerks back – the other jolts forward. We skid forward, grazing the glistening coat of the closest.

"Duck!" yells Pineapple.

A bundle of bamboo whooshes past my head. The engine conks, the clutch pops, and we catapult forward. Gliding off the bridge, Pineapple pulls off his helmet; his dreads damp with sweat.

"Faaack! That was a close shave – you nearly got skewered. Like a shish kebab, mate!"

The headline flashes through my mind: 'Shish kebab, American style.' Do you think it would make the front page? Might push the Maoists back a page – for a day.

"Hop off and I'll crank her over," says Pineapple. I slide off the seat. He heaves down on the shifter. I look back to the bridge; a fishmonger sags over his catch, scattering water over shiny carp. An elderly woman brandishes a palm frond, whipping a wayward buffalo's hindquarters. Glancing over her shoulder, she yells something and raises her palm to us…did we just get cursed? Hey lady, we might have been coming in a little too fast but that was a good spot of driving by my man Pineapple. It was either a graze or a skewering.

The engine sputters reluctantly each time Pineapple hits the kick start.

"Doused it. Let's go find some bevvies while she clears her belly."

"Sounds like a plan," I concur.

He rolls off the seat and hangs his helmet off the bars. A mob of children engulfs us.

"Here we are," he says, nodding towards a storefront. "What're ya having? I could go for a Fanta myself."

'Enjoy Fanta'… Remember the seventies? I think it was more imperative: *Enjoy Fanta!* Not much of a choice there. About as much as I have with this joker. The last time I had a Fanta, I must've been in moon boots.

Hindi music meanders from the back room like a lazy, endless river. A bearded man pokes his head out from between a cluster of bright-hued buckets and a wire basket of chips.

"*Dui* Fanta," says Pineapple. The man nods toward a grimy crate at our feet.

"*Neigh – chiso, chiso!*" retorts Pineapple.

The man disappears momentarily, returns with two bottles.

"Trying to pull a swifty on us with the warm shite," complains Pineapple, wagging an accusatory finger. "You've got an esky back there; I know it!"

Bottled Fanta: extinct in most developed nations, a thriving bell-wether in the third world. I swallow until the bubbles burn my throat. I don't think I could've muscled through a warm one.

"*Phew,* how good is *that*? Want another?"

"Nah, can't drink too much carbonated stuff. I'll get this one."

As I dig through my pockets for rupees, I unearth the piece of rice paper I won at the parrot game.

"Do you know what this is?" I ask Pineapple.

"Fucked if I know, mate. It's all cryptic to me."

"It sounds like you have some sort of grasp on the language."

"I know how to order a good whiskey, a girl and a kebab, and that's about it."

Such a pragmatist.

"You know those big sidewalks down by New Road, by that huge deserted field?"

"Yeah. They race horses there in the springtime."

"Well, this guy had all these papers spread out in front of him. I threw him a rupee, he opened a birdcage, out pops a parrot and *voila* – it snatches this one up in his beak."

"Sounds like a fortune teller." He crumples up the rice paper prophesy and throws it into the street.

"*Hey!* What did you do that for?"

"You don't want anything to do with that psychic hotline shit."

"Yeah, but this is a psychic parrot we're talking about. Animals can't bullshit you. What if this parrot it some kind of medium?"

Did I really just say that? Desperation does strange things to men.

"You're not telling me you believe in that kind of stuff?"

"No, not really – but what if it says something cool? Like 'your misfortunes will soon end' or 'wealth and fame are just around the corner'?"

"What difference does it make? Do you really think we've got a say in any of this drama unfolding before us?"

"You're starting to sound like a *National Geographic* special," I caution.

"Fuck off – I'm serious. I mean, look at that bloke over there." He points to the fishmonger.

"That's gotta be the last place in the world he wants to be, but his family's probably been scraping about these rivers for generations. Nothing save winning a lottery is going to change that."

"And what if he wins the lottery?"

"Fuck-all chance of that, mate. There's not much upward mobility around here, especially when you start off down the bottom of the keg. All he can hope for is to keep up the fight and scrape about a little longer, so that his son can scrape around a little longer than him, and so on and so forth. "

I can't shake the image of that poor fellow winning the lottery – festooned in garlands with a big sloppy rice *tika* globbed across his forehead, on national TV. *'And with my first million, I will transform this pristine lake into a sterile fish farm and donate it to all the fishmongers across this nation as a gesture of goodwill, so that the fisherman of Nepal may never again know hunger!'* He'll forget all about goodwill, of course, the second they install the sixty-inch plasma screen and satellite dish...long live *Baywatch!*

Do they even have a lottery in Nepal? Could that trashed piece of rice paper be a winning ticket?

"OK, point taken. I feel for the regular guy out there trying to make a buck. I guess caste systems don't help, either. But I really can't handle any more existentialism in my life right now. I've had enough 'drama of life unfolding' in the past few days to last me a lifetime!"

The gaggle of children surrounding us grows steadily. Giggling and jostling, they whisper excitedly to one another, eyes locked on the best show in town.

An abandoned field slopes toward a creek choked with garbage. In it, a pig churns through plastic bottles and wrappers like a waste-disposal juggernaut.

"Well, he looks happier than a pig in shit," I say.

"Vile creatures, pigs," he says.

"Don't tell me you didn't well up when they tried to send Wilbur to the slaughterhouse…"

"Fuck *Babe* and the rest of them. Pigs don't talk, they eat shit. Look at that monster mucking about in our crap. That's the reality of it – and you are what you eat, as far as I'm concerned."

He's right: the pig that's tunneling through that field of scum is definitely *not* cute. Maybe if you took a hose to it, slathered it in cocoa butter for a few days and slapped a pretty white fence around it…I don't know. Piglets are cute, but everything is cute when it's a baby. Even I was cute as a baby.

"OK, I see your point, but I wouldn't go so far as to call them vile."

"Down in Laos, I got a nasty case of the shits in this jungle village. Giardia, I reckon. I always try to keep a bottle of whiskey on me for sterilization purposes. You know, drown the little amoebic bastards in alcohol before they get a grip. But up in those hills I couldn't even scrounge up a pint of piss."

Shunning modern-day legal pharmaceuticals, Pineapple takes a holistic approach to healing. His insides are probably less hospitable than a dust storm on Mars.

"I was dropping my guts for days, doubled over this hole in the ground, half gone with fever, and those little buggers ripping up my insides like razor blades. I'd spend most of my time perched between two flat rocks on the side of a hill, shitting my brains out, not a scrap of bog paper left. And just as soon as the least bit of liquid came trickling out of my bum, one of those filthy beasts would slip up from behind and snort it up."

"No shit?"

"Once, one was gonna snatch it right out from between my cheeks but I smacked him before he could get his snout in. Disgusting. Then I found myself a decent stick; they kept their distance after that. I beat the whole lot of them just on principle. I haven't eaten pork since. Some days I can barely look at them. Believe me, it would be a far better world without those eaters of shit."

I'm drifting off when a skinny boy on the opposite side of the creek begins yelling and flailing his arms in disgust. Picking a stone off the ground, he aims it at the pig, smacking it squarely in the rump. Oblivious, it prods a cardboard box with its snout. Domesticated animals in these parts seem to have a huge appetite for cardboard.

"What do you say – should we get a move on?" asks Pineapple. "Her pipes should be cleaned out by now, I reckon."

"Sure."

Clinking his bottle into the crate, he flips up the kickstand and guides the bike into the street. Jumping on, he brings his foot down hard on the kick-starter. The engine turns over briefly, reluctantly. Pineapple thrusts downward again…and again…

Nothing.

The crowd of children tighten their ranks around us like famished pigeons. Impending Hitchcockian terror: *The Birds* revisited?

One intrepid youngster sticks out his hand.

"Dat pen. Dat pen?"

What do they want? I have no *dat pens*, nor do I know what they are.

"Dat pen. Dat pen diu!" the kid shouts; another whispers, giggles behind him.

"What's this little guy's deal?"

"He wants a pen."

"A pen?"

"I don't know why, but every one of these runts fancies a pen. They must reckon we've got pens coming out of our asses."

"Hello, one rupee!" blurts another child.

"Hello! Hello, rupee! Give me rupee!" cajoles another.

They're getting bolder, closing ranks.

"Hellowww! Rupee!"

Pineapple stamps his foot, then, pirate-like, he growls, *"Arrgh! Skeedaddle, ya runts!"*

He comes down hard again on the kick-starter. The engine wheezes, dies.

"About as useful as tits on a bull. I don't know what else…aw, for fuck's sake!"

"What's that?"

"We're out of petrol – gas. I was so munted this morning, I forgot to fill it down at *Ghantaa Ghar*. Fuckin' hell."

There's an ear-piercing squeal from under the bridge; the boy is whaling on the pig with a big-ass stick. Bolting along the bank, the pig finds itself out on a muddy peninsula, to the dismay of his attacker. That's not where you wanted him to go, was it? The boy pelts a volley of stones at the runaway; it digs in as if that strip of mud was the Temple Mount. You can beat him all day, kid: he's not moving. That cardboard must taste delectable.

They say pigs are smart but I've never seen it. They know how to rummage around and find food, but so does every animal. This one's a case in point. If the stupid porker would just move its ass, the boy would stop hurling rocks. It's not as if there's a pile of sautéed truffles out there. Parked in the mud, the creature squeals wheezily each time a rock hits it, yet fails to budge. Stupid pig.

An officer in a brimmed hat and a blue uniform advances on us.

"Don't look now but here come the karma police," I mutter.

"No dramas," assures Pineapple. "I'll sort it out."

Sauntering over, the officer puts his hands on his hips and inspects the bike, clicking his tongue like a mother might over a mischievous child.

"Petrol chhaina," says Pineapple feebly.

The officer holds out a white-gloved hand.

"License?"

Pineapple digs through his pockets.

"Aw, fuck. Got a license on you, mate?"

"Sorry."

He turns back to the officer.

"License chhaina," he says, in his best 'dumb foreigner.'

"Chhaina?" repeats the officer.

"Chhaina."

The officer gestures for Pineapple to dismount; he complies, and the cop wraps his gloves around the handlebars.

"Sorry to – *hey*! What are you doing, mate?" What he's doing is steering Pineapple's bike across the street.

"That's *my bike*, mate! Where are you going with my bike?"

"License chainchha," asserts the officer.

"Bollocks," mutters Pineapple, stomping along behind him.

The hapless pig wails as the boy smacks it in the head with a stick. *Weeehh, weeeehh, weeeeeehh.* Meanwhile, it hasn't moved an inch. The boy keeps whacking it in the head. *Weeeehh, weeeeehh, weeeeeeeeeehhh.* Just leave the dumb thing alone.

"...Aw, mate. Can you fucking believe it? They just took my bike! I just bought the bloody thing and now they're going to take it away from me? That's not legal!"

"I'm no expert in international law, but don't you need to have a license on you if you're driving?"

"Yeah, but how was I supposed to know? He's got no right."

"Pineapple, dude, he's a cop in a third-world country – he's got every fucking right."

The officer rolls the beat up bike into a courtyard, propping it against a cement building. He returns with another officer; he points and they both stare in our direction.

"Running out of petrol in front of a police station. What are the fucking chances of that? For *fuck's* sake."

"Chill, Pineapple. All he wants is to see your license. Why don't you just go get it and come back?"

"Fuck-all chance of that, mate. Suspended ages ago."

"So how do we get back?"

"Right. I've gotta get my bike back straight away. Do you have any cash on ya? Looks like I'll need plenty of spendoolash to sort him."

"Spendoowhat?"

"Rupees. How much you got?"

"Maybe a hundred. Here – one hundred and…eight rupees."

I've got at least another two hundred in my back pocket but I'm not giving it up. Sorry, Pineapple, you were a bit shaky out of the gate last time. I'm not putting all my money on you to win in this race.

"I've barely got any left, either. It's Buckley's or fuck-all, then, isn't it?" he says.

"Who's Buckley?"

"Just wait here," he grunts.

"Maybe your passport would be enough. You could use the money I gave you for cab fare to go back and grab it."

"Just chill out, have a Fanta and let me deal with this, alright?"

Pineapple marches across the street and into the station. I plop back down on the bench. Let's hope they don't smell that big slab of hash in his pants.

"Go get 'em, tiger."

A child approaches, two others tucked behind her back. A monstrous orange truck rumbles past, honking just as it passes. *Yes, I see you.* I'm ten feet off the road, by the way. *"Mithai?"* The kid sticks out a grimy hand.

Unless a *mithai* is an empty Fanta bottle, I can't help you, kid.

Across the street, Pineapple exits the station, officer in tow. This ought to be good. 'Pineapple, international man of mystery, takes on Kathmandu's finest in an attempt to recoup a motorcycle that he claims was wrongfully taken from him. He'll stop at nothing to get it back!'

He moves towards the bike as unobtrusively as it's possible to be with a bird's-nest of red dreads. He circles the bike like a dog edging closer to an unmanned plate of food. The officer waves him back. Come on Pineapple, just give him the money.

He leaps onto the bike but the cop rips the keys out of the ignition. Another officer springs from the doorway, grabbing Pineapple by the arm.

"Get stuffed!" he screams.

Wrestling free, he spins off into an alley. The policemen give chase.

"Mithai?" wheedles the waiting child.

*"Grreat...*fucking perfecto."

"Hallow, pen?" she asks, changing tack.I hand her the last of my Fanta; maybe she can get a return deposit or transform it into some rudimentary toy.

And the law won.

I don't get it. You don't hare off into the Nepali countryside on a motorcycle without fuel or a license. All they really wanted was some cash, right? A few hundred rupees to cover their morning tea would probably have sufficed. Now he'll be lucky to get the bike back at all. They might even lock him up.

What was he thinking, trying to muscle his bike away from the cops? He's got some stuff on him, too. You should have left that with me before you attempted 'operation cyclopath.' Not smart, Pineapple. I might not have my shit together, but this guy is making me look good. Quite a character, though he could use some lessons on tact. And personal hygiene.

Godspeed, Pineapple.

I stick out my thumb. A bus blasts its horn as it whooshes pass, coating me in dust...thanks. Thanks for blowing out my eardrums, buddy. Did you really think I didn't see you barreling at me like a herd of elephants for the past two minutes? I'd have to have been in a coma not to notice.

The sun is starting to dip. I should have brought my watch. If I don't get a move on I'm going to miss my appointment at Immigration. Shit. I should phone Maya…except I forgot the phone. *Shit!* That's two strikes: one more and they'll definitely toss you back in the slammer. If Thapa sends my dossier off to the courts, I'm screwed. There'll be no chance of self-repatriation without that passport in my hands.

"O Kuiree!"

A bead of sweat rolls off my chin. How long have I been walking down this road? Am I even going in the right direction?

The sun is sinking fast. It's got to be five by now…*fuck.*

"O kuiree! Haallow!"

A cluster of children is swarming towards me like locusts descending on a field of ripe grain, ready to pick it clean.

"Haallo! Haallow!" they shout, springing over furrows.

Just what I need right now: another cacophany of children. More new best friends to throw into the mix of money changers, *saddhus* and carpet-sellers. If I'm lucky, they'll take me back to their Maoist village for some thought reform.

Toppling over one another to reach me, they then stop and huddle, uncertain of their next move.

"No pens, see?" I hold out my palms. "No pens, no *mithai*, no rupees, alright?"

"…How are you?" stammers one boy.

"I'm fine. How are you?"

Sniggers erupt. English 101: 'Let us now turn to page three of *The Lost White Traveler*. Jay, the large, hairy white man, has become lost in the valley while shopping for carpets and needs your help. Can you help him? Try your English to help the man find his way back to his luxurious hotel room!'

"What…is your name?"

Help. I've been sucked into a third-world third-grade lesson plan and I can't find my way out."Where from?" shouts another.

'What…is you favorite color?'

Am I going to get catapulted into the sky if I don't answer correctly?

They tighten their circle. Not too big on personal space here, are they? Alright, you want a show? I'll give you a show.

"My name is...Action Jackson!" I lunge at them.

"Action Jackson!" one yells as the others jump back.

"Action Jackson, Action Jackson!" they chime.

Very receptive.

I'll bet they'd be even more awestruck and impressionable up in the mountains. That's it: I'll trek up into a remote village loaded down with shiny objects – pens and *mithais*, whatever the hell those are – and transform myself into the white incarnation of a deity. Not a big player like Shiva, but a lesser yet relevant god that's revered in small rural communities. *The God of Dat Pens, benevolent avatar of the God of Learning.* Once I had secured my place in the annals of Hindu mythology, I could proceed to establish a small kingdom and there wouldn't be any need to leave the country.

Low rumbling, fast approaching. I hold out my thumb half-heartedly. A truck roars past, followed by two motorcycles, churning up thick wakes of dirt. Red taillights flare through the dust...astounding: the bikes stopped! I run up. Big, ancient Enfields growl out exhaust; dinosaurs that refuse to die. The driver of the lead bike pulls off his helmet.

"Baraq!" I yell.

"What are you doing out here? Are you lost?"

"I lost my friend, and he lost his bike, so I don't know – does that make me lost? Only metaphorically, I guess."

Baraq furrows his brow.

"Do you want a ride back or not?"

Just what I need: another foreign motorcycle chauffer whose hashish consumption rivals that of the most austere *saddhus*. What am I saying? It's almost dark, I hardly have a rupee to my name and I'm ten miles from Coke and pizza. Of course I need a ride. He owes me one, too.

"Sure. That would be great," I say, masking my enthusiasm.

"This is my girlfriend, Tikvah." Behind him sits a tanned, lanky brunette with a curly mane and pink aviators, in tight rainbow pants. Israelis definitely like their colors. Between them and Japanese hipsters, they've got all the primaries covered.

"Hello," she says, in a dense accent, and smiles.

"...Oh, yeah, the upset stomach..." I snap my fingers. "I hope you're feeling better."

She looks puzzled...wait a minute. She doesn't look too sickly to me, Baraq. Are you sure that the hash I gave you the other day was strictly for medicinal use? More like self-medication.

Oh well, she's hot. I have no problem doling out drugs to hot women.

"She can ride with the others. I'll take you," says Baraq.

"You sure that's cool?"

I'll tell you what, Baraq, don't sweat the hash. Take more if you need it. Go off with your tribal crew and smoke your brains out. What I really need right now is your girlfriend. And your bike, of course. What if I just took off with Tikvah? You see, I'm feeling a little under the weather myself. The hash just isn't cutting it but I think *she* could nurse me back to health. No medication required: just Tikvah in a skimpy nurse's outfit would suffice. You cool with that, Baraq?

"No problem," he says, "but I don't have a helmet for you."

"Do I need one?"

"Just hold on."

I wrap my leg over the seat. Thank god they pulled over; I'd have been lucky to make it back by midnight at the rate I was going. That's if I didn't get run over or rolled.

Children scatter as Baraq wrenches the throttle. The bike reels forward, engulfing them in dust. I look up at the fading skyline, at the jagged white slabs of granite glowing like gods over haze-smudged hills.

The motorcycle's flickering headlight carves our path. Cool air rushes against my face. Red and white lights tango through the dust, veering back and forth across the road. I let my eyes drop out of focus; the lights whirl and blend into one another in the darkness...*love those tracers, man.* How much time left before Jerry and the band hit their next set? I'll drop the other half during 'space.'

My appointment today with Thapa is shot. Maya is going to be thoroughly pissed. Please don't give up on me: I'll even help clean up all those decades of paperwork in Thapa's office if you cut me a break. Hold on: that might be a very good excuse for slipping my passport out of his desk.

Gradually, the buildings rise; streetlights appear. Cigarette and whiskey advertisements perch atop buildings, promoting an easier life through consumption.

Royal Stag...Discover the Hero!

Khukurri Cigarettes. The Hero's Choice!

They really like their heroes around here, don't they? Maybe I could lock into a lucrative advertising deal to fund my up-and-coming mountain kingdom. Maybe I could be the hero.

AK-47s...The Militant Hero's Dream!

This would dovetail nicely with my transformation into a minor deity. Easier said than done, however.

The bike surges suddenly; there's a spasmodic clicking noise. Something's not right. We swerve down a cobbled road; Baraq pops off his helmet.

"What's up?"

"I think it's the chain...*harah!*"

He kicks the bike with the side of his foot.

"Harah!" he yells.

"Can it make it back to the hotel?"

"Maybe, but it will do more damage if I keep riding. There is a mechanic's shop not far from here; maybe he's still open."

"That's cool – I can walk back from here."

"Do you know the way?"

"I think so. I need to get something to eat anyway; I'll see you back at the fort."

"Ciao."

Disconcerting, listening to an Israeli speaking Italian in Central

Asia. What I really need is a drink. Those were two of the most harrowing motorcycle rides of my life and they weren't even off-road.

I saunter into the neon commotion of Thamel.

Half a dozen nappy-headed street kids are gathered to one side, huffing and toking on cigarettes. A man with a shaved head tromps by, jabbering his frenetic philosophy to everyone within earshot. A delicate-boned boy darts up and jabs a flyer into my hand.

Come to New Orleans Café

Authentic Thanksgiving Dinner!

Thursday, November 27th

Thanksgiving already. I could go for a few slices with the requisite trimmings right now. Where the fuck are they gonna scrape up a turkey around here? Do they even have turkeys in Asia?

Thanksgiving...it's been a year. Jenny is going to cry when I call, I know it. Histrionic, perhaps, but at least she shows something. With mom it's just the thousand-mile stare.

She always loses it during the holidays when something's not quite right with the family unit. She sat and bawled for over an hour the first Christmas after our dog Toby bought it, and he died of natural causes. This year, she's got a jarring human death and an MIA to deal with.

I'm going on nearly a year now without a word to her. Only a few brief niceties since the funeral; then I pulled the plug. She's probably got a new house by now (there was talk of that, with the expanded family unit) and a new phone number to go with it. Shit, she might even have another kid. She's really going to lose it this year. Just as mom brings out the turkey. If mom can stay off the meds long enough to *cook* a turkey.

Fuck it, I'm not hungry anymore.

A bowed tin sign inscribed with the words '*TIBETAN ANTIQUE SHOP*' dangles from an awning. This looks as good a place as any. The sign squeaks as it brushes against my head. A dark-skinned, stocky man wearing bifocals glances up from behind a huge, dusty drum. I step up to a glass-fronted showcase crammed with bracelets, pipes and amulets.

"Can I help you?" he enquires.

Swinging my rucksack off my shoulder, I fish out the *dzi* and toss it onto the showcase.

"Can you tell me how much this is worth?"

Those of a hungry tiger, his eyes lock onto the stones. Standing, he draws the stones into his palm, rolling them over with his fingers. He swivels a lamp over and sets a jeweler's glass to his eye.

"Where did you find this?"

"A friend gave it to me."

"You have Tibetan friend?"

"No. I, uh, got it from an old friend who used to live here."

His eyes dart to me, then return to the stones, scrutinizing each of them in turn.

"This is a very nice *dzi*. The coral is excellent also. You must have a good friend to give you such a fine piece. How much would you like for it?"

He pushes the coral to the sides and brings the *dzi* closer to the lamp: an auctioneer sifting through dusty violins in search of a Stradivarius. It seems he likes what he sees. Maybe I should just dump the *dzi* and get on with my life. No, this talisman isn't fated to end its days buried in the detritus of a curio shop.

"Well, I'm not sure I want to sell it just yet. Can you tell me something about it?"

He removes the jeweler's glass from his eye and readjusts the bifocals.

"This one is very, very old – from Tibet. It is for good luck...very high quality. There are many eyes, you see?"

He holds it up to the light, counting off the milky white ovals.

"One, two, three...ten...eleven...twelve. Twelve eyes. I will give you fifty thousand rupees for it."

Tilting his bifocals, he looks me dead in the eye. This guy means business. He was pretty quick to throw that money down. It's got to be worth at least twice that.

"…I really don't want to sell it right now. If I do, I will come back and see you, OK?"

As I grab the beads, his hand clenches ever so slightly. He doesn't want to give them back.

"Really," I say, "I can't sell them right now but if I do, I promise to come back and see you, OK?" I coax them from his hand. *Please release the beads, sir.* Damn. For a second there, I didn't think he was going to give them up.

As I tuck them back into my backpack, he stammers, "Eighty thousand rupees. I will give you eighty thousand rupees right now! This is a good price, my friend."

He leans forward, extracting a pouch from around his neck. From it, he pulls a large wad of silver notes. That's a fair chunk of change. That could help with the lawyer costs, but I need more info.

"One hundred thousand! You will not find a better price, my friend!"

"No. No thanks, really." I back towards the entrance, grazing my head against the sign as I exit.

I take a quick right, jog twenty yards or so. Man, that guy was all over my shit. From fifty to one hundred thousand rupees in thirty seconds? He was all over the place!

Spider webs of electrical wiring sag overhead. A distorted bass line from a Bob Marley tune pumps out from a bar above. One hundred thousand rupees? That's a pretty good chunk of change…over a grand, right?

I take the *dzi* out of my pocket, turn it in my palm. I'll bet I could get more. Maybe I should look around, see what it's really worth. Maya did say I'm going to need a lot of cash for litigation. And if I decide to take matters into my own hands I'll need more for an escape. This, plus what I have left from Gerard, could be my ticket out of this mess.

No, I can't sell it yet: it wouldn't be right to come all the way here and dump it just like that. If I only knew more about it – why Gerard wanted me to bring it all the way here…for Betty. It's not my stone; it's Betty's…but who the hell is Betty?

I run my thumb over a white oval of the *dzi*. You're quite the center of attraction these days, aren't you? There's definitely more to you than meets the eye.

I look up; the stocky Tibetan jeweler is staring intently in my direction from his shop entrance. He is talking with another man, gesturing towards me. I take a few steps and turn – he's still checking me. I duck into an alley and run.

People rush past, horns beep, a bell chimes. I stop in my tracks... which way? The gathering darkness has drowned out my bearings...I'm lost. Are they after me?

Get me out of here.

Somehow I get separated from Thamel. I try to double back in search of La Dolce Vita and next thing I know, I'm walking past the Royal Palace (I check the fifty-rupee note in my back pocket for accuracy). I find myself walking down darker and darker streets. 'Minutes later' are turning into 'hours later', as my growling stomach reminds me with increasing urgency. A child's bike horn squeaks obnoxiously to my left. "*Hello! Helicopter ride?* Hallow, you come for helicopter ride?"

In desperation, I exchange the fifty-rupee note for a rickshaw ride back to Freak Street.

A potpourri of carbon dioxide, ash, dust, incense and mystery filth covers my body with a grimy film. My sweat has dried like lacquer, sealing in the toxins. I feel like a dirty piston in need of a valve job, grime and grease seeping into my skin with every step.

"*Whhuph.*" I sigh, opening the door. I bend over, catch my breath. Now where did I hide my cash? I need a pizza, quick.

"Took you long enough," a voice mumbles.

I jolt upright, curl against the wall.

"*Ahhh!* Who's there?" *GET OUT!*"

I wing a book at the shadow across the room.

"Chill out, man," barks the voice.

"Get the fuck out of here!" I counter.

"Hey, you were the one that wanted to see me. That's the last time I go paying house calls, man."

A harsh cough resonates through the chilled air...I know that cough.

"John? John Bigby? *Dude*, you scared the living *shit* out of me. But how did you –"

"Get in? These Chinese locks are easier to pick than your nose. And enough of this John bullshit: the name is Jack."

His voice sounds like a cement mixer in need of immediate repair. He sparks a match, lighting a candle on the windowsill. I can't see him clearly. His shadow slouches in the chair against the wall. Then he leans forward; candlelight catches his jaw. A heavy jaw: the kind of jaw that bites back even after you've creamed it with a pipe wrench. Eyes scan me from under a mop of stringy hair.

"Is that your real name, Jupiter? Or is that some kind of secret code bullshit?"

"No, it's the real deal. Hippie parents, what can I say?"

"Far out."

"You can call me Jay."

"No man, I like Jupiter...that's far out, man."

Gravelly laughter; then he stoops to light a cigarette off the candle flame.

"Could you not do that, please?" I say testily.

"What?"

"Light it off the candle. Here, use my lighter."

"Superstitious, huh? I can respect that. Lots of superstitions floating round these parts...like ghosts." He takes a long drag. "The note – I got your note. It said you needed help."

"You'd have to use a lot of smoke and mirrors to solve my problems."

"Well, I've been known to solve people's problems from time to time. Try me."

There's a soft rap at the door. It cracks open and Maya sticks her head inside. She looks extremely pissed off. I hope she doesn't have a paddy wagon waiting out front.

"Oh, sorry, kid. I hope I'm not interrupting anything."

"No, this is good. *Maya!* Come in. I wanted you two to meet."

I reach for the light switch adjacent the door.

"Don't! Let's keep things in the dark for now," Jack hastens. "These old eyes aren't too good in the light."

"Why didn't you answer any of my calls, Jupiter?" blazes Maya. "I must have rung you more than thirty times."

"I got stranded outside of town and forgot to take my phone."

"You're absolutely hopeless! I really don't know if my father can –"

Worlds collide – stop!

"Can we talk about that later?"

Don't spill those beans just yet, Maya. We're dealing with a rogue element at the moment.

Maya looks to Jack, then back at me.

"Oh, sorry: Maya, Jack; Jack, Maya."

"Nice to meet you." She smiles.

"Pleasure's all mine, babe."

Oh god, *this* is an introduction I want no part of.

Turning back to me, she continues.

"Right, I spoke with Mr Thapa down at Immigration today. They've finally set a date for your trial. You didn't bother to turn up again, did you?"

Oh shit. Don't start reprimanding me in front of Jack for missing my appointment…again.

"Trial? This sounds juicy." Jack rubs his hands together. "What did you do: get nabbed for burning a joint at some rooftop bar?"

"More like an ounce," I mutter.

"Hell, that's not much! At least half the backpacking community has that much in their pockets on any given day. It shouldn't cost much to pay off the right cop."

"Yeah, but it was on a plane."

"Ouch. That complicates things, doesn't it? Yeah, they don't care too much for smugglers around here. I'd love to help you out but they'd probably lock me up and throw away the key if I showed my face in a courtroom. There's more than one way to skin a cat, though."

"Why? Have you overstayed your visa?" asks Maya. "From the looks of things, you've been here for quite some time."

He leisurely cracks his knuckles.

"Yeah, I've been around here for a while. You could say I've over-stayed my welcome but there's a little more to it than that. Hell, no-one's asked me to leave yet! I figure I'll stick around until they put in the first Mickey D's. Once they do that, it's all over. Say, why don't we get out of this dive and get a few drinks in us? It sounds like you could use one, kid."

"I need food more than anything," I say. "Can I get some *momos* where we're going?"

"*Momos, daahl bhaat, thukpa* – whatever your little heart desires," he says.

"Maya, are you up for it?" I ask.

"Alright, then. But we *really* need to talk, Jupiter."

"I promise, but later, OK?"

We shoot through reception and out onto Freak Street, the birthplace of it all. I try to imagine the hippies stoned out of their minds, squatting in the doorways of decrepit hash bars. The hash bar Gerard used to visit was probably right around the corner from here.

Light pours out of shops, casting bright columns into the street. A string of motorcycles buzzes past like a swarm of irate wasps. Jack leads us into a tight, unlit alley.

"Right around this corner…nice little spot."

Maya drops back to my side, whispers. "He's a bit dodgy, isn't he? Is he one of your mates from the holding cell?"

"No." I grin. "The postbox, remember?"

"Oh, so *he's* the one."

"I just met him myself."

"Whatever you do, don't say anything about my father to this bloke," she urges. "Remember, he's connected to Gerard. It might be dangerous if he finds out about my father's involvement."

"Why do you think I cut you off?" I murmur.

"Are you guys coming or what?"

"Just now," says Maya.

I'm glad she's here: despite the hard time she's giving me, I can tell she's a good person. She's not going to fuck me over, even if her dad did sic her on me and she's batting for his team. You can't blame her for that; it's her father, for christ's sake. And he threw down my bail money.

Hey, I'd do the same for my dad if I still could.

I trust Maya a hell of a lot more than I trust Jack. He's the kind of guy who swears allegiance to no-one, plays by his own rules. How many lies he's told, I'll never know. I doubt he does himself. He has a face that's a little too hardened, too beat-up for his age, like he's been sleeping in garbage-filled alleys for too long. He's into something dark and dirty, I know that much.

Rounding a corner, Jack ushers us into a tweaked Lilliputian doorway with ancient ornate woodcarvings above the lintel. A man works vigorously over a fire at the front. The ceiling is cramped. Jack barks gruffly to the cook; he nods. Men huddle at a table in the corner.

Jack leads us to a dimly lit booth. A boy places three brass cups on the table and pours milky liquid into each. He begins to fill Maya's cup; she slides her palm over the top. "*Pugchaa malaai.*"

Jack casts an inquisitive glance, raises his cup.

"Nothing like a little *rakshi* to calm the nerves." He downs the contents. "*Ahhh...*"

Maya drinks, then, wincing slightly. I do the same. The liquid coats my throat, leaving an aftertaste that's something between cough syrup and curdled milk.

"Man, that's *nasty*."

"Not as smooth as a Manhattan, but it gets you drunk twice as quick. Bottoms up!"

Jack fills our cups again. I throw another down.

"Did you order those *momos* yet?" I ask.

"They're on their way."

A dish clangs on the ground. Laughter.

Jack looks different in the light. Late sixties? No, seventies...maybe older. His face is a parched ravine that's weathered several droughts – the kind of face you wouldn't be surprised to see posted against a post office wall. Greasy, dishwater hair streaked heavily with gray hangs haphazardly across his forehead. Crow's feet radiate above gaunt cheekbones grizzled with stubble. It doesn't look like he's seen a mirror in more than a week.

A scar runs along one cheek from the temple to the crook of his mouth. An earring like Gerard's, made of red and blue stones, dangles from his left earlobe. His eyes, steel blue– as vast and vacuous as the sky. A one-way vault that locks things in, doesn't let them out. The kind of gaze that sucks you in if you get too close.

I don't trust him for a second.

"So, what brings you to this magical land, Maya?"

"I've got a little project going at the moment."

"A GAP program? You look a little too old for that."

"I beg your pardon?"

"Sorry, I didn't mean nothing by it. So what, then, the UN? An NGO?"

"No, it's a little more complicated than that. I've spent a fair amount of time here."

"I guess that explains the language skills."

"Maya works for the embassy," I blurt.

That was stupid. Why did I say that? That puts her in the same ball-park as her father. That could totally blow her cover. Sometimes I say the dumbest things. 'Ruling down to the first-base umpire...he went around! Strike one.'

Maya didn't like that pitch, either. Her smile fails to mask angry eyes.

"Oh, really?" Jack's interest is piqued. "Interesting: which one? Wait, let me guess. You're definitely a Pom."

"That's right," she says, glaring at me. "How did you *ever* guess?"

"Hmmm, that's a pretty posh accent you've got there. I'd have to say somewhere around Surrey. British Embassy, eh? I've got a few friends down there. You wouldn't happen to know a guy named Tony Gunn, would you?"

Oh shit. Worlds collide, worlds collide!

"No, I can't say I do."

"You must have heard of him. What kind of bureaucracy do they wrap you up in there? Don't tell me you live down in that brand-spanking-new apartment complex in Bhatbhatini? You could be in Manhattan and not know the difference."

Uh-oh. Jack's not buying it. He's going to start plying her with questions. He's got friends working there; he knows her dad. All he has to do is pick up the phone. *Why did I say anything?*

"We do some work through the embassy, but I don't actually work *for* them."

"So you'll be around for a while, then. While you're here, I could show you some places that would really blow your mind."

She pulls a strand of hair behind her ear.

"I think I've seen all there is to see, really."

Just like Gerard: hitting on every girl that comes by just to piss me off. Are you serious, Jack? You think she's going to leave me choking here in your grandpa dust?

"You should come check out my pad when you've got time. I've got a cozy little place not far from here. Maybe swing by for a drink some time."

As smooth as a shot of Jägermeister. Asshole.

Maya's eyes, by now bordering on lividly, dart again in my direction. She's not falling for this smooth-talking geriatric. This isn't shaping up to be a good combination. She's not going to buy his shit, and he's going to dole it out every chance he gets. I don't blame her – he's being a dick. I already want to smack him upside the head. He's got a lot of nerve talking to her like that.

He leans towards me.

"So, my intergalactic friend, what's this thing Gerard gave you to pass on to me? Money? He still owes me a bundle. Last time I checked, he bilked me out of twenty grand. Those were nineteen seventy-seven dollars, too. Prick! No, he never gave me shit. The only things I can remember him giving me were some really bad habits."

I don't like Jack. I don't like the way he broke into my room or the way he's hitting on Maya or the way he just called me 'intergalactic friend.' He's as shady as they come. The old friend you haven't seen in years who wasn't much of a friend to begin with. You add him as a friend on Facebook and next thing you know, he's sleeping on your couch, hitting on your girlfriend and making long-distance calls for 'business ventures' somewhere down in Central America. Right now, a good percentage of me is wishing Maya had never slipped that note in his post box.

"Go on, then. Show him," urges Maya.

I extract the beads from my pack, slide them across the table. Jack stares at them for a long time without speaking. That was a breaking ball he didn't see coming!

His eyes glaze over, recalling something. He picks the beads up gently, as if they were dove eggs; caresses them.

"Elizabeth. Well, here you are again… He did love her, I can tell you that."

"Betty," I whisper.

This is it. *This* is what I came here for. Betty Boop: the woman of Gerard's dreams, the only woman who was more than just a piece of ass.

"What *are* you two going on about?" Maya interjects.

Jack shakes his head as if awakening from a confusing dream.

"Gerard's lady. A real firecracker."

She's real, then. Or at least, she was. And Gerard turned her into a cartoon, into fiction. Maybe that was how he dealt with her absence.

Preservation through animation.

Who was she, anyway? What was she like? Was she beautiful? What did she see in Gerard? A thousand questions spin through my head but I don't ask, for fear of cutting the slender thread and slamming shut this portal to the past.

"…She was a junkie through and through, but he loved her like nobody's business. Everybody loved that woman."

"Nothing like drug-induced romance," says Maya.

"You got a fucking nerve talking about dead people that way," says Jack. "You don't know a thing about her, or Gerard. You don't know shit about me, either. Do you even know who Gerard was?"

Thanks for slamming the portal shut, Maya.

"I know some things, yes. Jupiter told me a few stories. He didn't strike me as anyone I'd care to remember."

"He wouldn't give you a second thought, either. Trust me."

"Don't tell me you're going to defend Gerard? He was a prick, Jack, and you know it. Even you said he was a bastard."

"I'll say whatever I *goddamn please!*"

He slams his fist down on the table. The men chatting at the corner table fall silent, as if a gunfight might ensue. I'm just hoping this guy doesn't flip the table on me.

A tic has developed in Jack's left cheek. Man, that's a nasty scar! He doesn't look particularly friendly right now. Acting a bit psychotic as well. One more smart-assed remark and he might staple my hand to the table with his fork.

"…You're right, Jack," I say, conciliatory. "I don't know; I don't know shit. That's why I came to Nepal…to find shit out. That's what I need *you* to tell me. What the fuck really went down with Gerard and this girl?"

'*What really went down?*' I've got to lay off the hippie jargon or he might staple my hand to the table with a fork on principle.

"Things change, people change…hey, Gerard wasn't always that bad of a cat. He was different before she died. What a mess that was… we had to bury Elizabeth ourselves."

A wine buzz begins to lubricate my imagination. Sounds like a mafia hit. Next thing I know, he'll start bitching about how the blood had ruined his bootleg Armani suit. Jack sloshes more *rakshi* into our cups.

"…How did she die?" Maya persists.

"Like I said, she was a junkie – you do the math. She died here, in Nepal…way out west."

"Is her body still out there?"

"Why, you wanna go dig her up?"

"Seriously, Jack? He's just trying to put it right in his head. It's just sad, really. Dying like that, in a strange land, so far away from home."

I glare at Maya. Why does she continue to egg him on? Let the portal speak!

"…Nepal wasn't strange to Beth," continues Jack. "She loved this place – loved everything about it. That was a different time, a better time to live here. Things were so much cooler, so much less fucked-up back then."

"I see so many kids fly in here full of lofty ideology who end up getting completely caned, on permanent vacation," says Maya. "This lifestyle, the drugs become a trap. And now that India boots most everyone out for two months between visas, you've got all of these Goa-trance casualties roaming about as well."

"Shit, there are traps everywhere you go. The drugs aren't the problem, man. It's the ideology that's the trap. Look at all these idiots who fly over here with copies of *The Art of Happiness* under their arms, shave their heads, dress up like its Halloween and go 'trick or treating' with alms bowls. The ones who stay true to themselves are the ones who don't get trapped. You could give them all the drugs in the world and they wouldn't get trapped."

"Is that why you're still here, Jack? Being true to yourself, are you?" Maya says, sarcastic.

"Listen, girl, I'm here because I want to be. This is a hell lot better than most people can even dream of. I'll tell you what the trap is: the trap is being glued to a computer screen in a six-by-six-foot cubicle, with stale coffee and a fake plant for company. Not here, man! Here, life isn't about stock options, plasma screen TVs and partial dental insurance."

"It's not about crack pipes and needles either." I say. "Let them get high, I say! Let the kids have their drugs and figure things out for themselves. What doesn't kill you only makes you stronger. That's what life is all about."

"Well, I guess that's one way of looking at it."

Maya rolls her eyes.

"You should be a spokesperson for drug traffickers. Fucking splendid! *'Let them get high'* – is that your motto? Is that the best you can come up with? Come off it."

I'm not sure I agree with Jack's Darwinian view of drug use, either. What doesn't kill you might make you stronger but usually, it comes at considerable cost – hell, look at Keith Richards. Could certain traits, such as increased lung capacity and greater nostril diameter, be part of the evolutionary process? The scientific community is no doubt waiting with bated breath.

"...Oh, that's right: you work for the embassy. They must have done some heavy screening before they signed you on. Shit, Jupiter, where did you find this one? What a chestnut!"

I brace myself for an explosion. Putting these two in the same room? It's like mixing magnesium and water. Where are the aromatherapy candles when you need them? Quick, light some incense! Should I join us together in a moment of prayer? I feel more like referee than minister right now. Maybe I should find two pairs of gloves and let them duke it out. Maya would probably end up kicking his droopy ass.

"OK, everybody just take a deep breath and relax," I say. "We barely know each other and we're not off to a good start."

"...I know enough already," Maya retorts.

"There's the door," says Jack. "Why don't you use it?"

I'm already starting to feel the fallout.

"Cool it, both of you, just cool it. Maya, I need you to be quiet and listen. Jack, let's start again with the beads...they're Betty's, I mean, Elizabeth's?"

"You can call her Betty, everyone called her Betty...most everyone, that is. Gerard gave them to her when they got hitched."

"Gerard was *married?*"

"Well, not in the conventional sense. They trucked all the way from Marseilles in a VW bus: two kids cruising the world on peace and rainbows, man. When they got to Nepal, they decided to tie the knot – so they walked down to Boudanath one day, went into a monastery, lit a couple of butter lamps and said a prayer: then he gave her this. It was the closest thing she ever had to a ring."

Jack holds the beads out over the table, clicking them against his brass glass.

"...So, what are you gonna do with these babies?"

"I don't know. What do you think Gerard wanted me to do with them? He wanted me to bring them back to Betty."

"It's not about what he wanted you to do with them; it's about what *you* want to do with them. You could sell them – they'd fetch a pretty penny on the market. I've got a couple of friends down on Durbar Marg who'd seriously shell out for these puppies. I could set something up."

Sure. Here it comes...the con. This is what he came for; this is what he's been waiting for all night. I got your number. I see you coming, scammer!

"...I don't know. How much do you think I could get for them?"

"Oh, those look pretty old. I don't know how much Gerard paid, but I'd say at least seven to eight hundred dollars."

You've probably got some beachfront property you'd like to sell me in Florida, too.

"Now Jack," I smile, "I don't know anything about beads, but I do know that I can get a lot more than eight hundred for them."

"I'm no expert, either," chimes in Maya, "but you could probably get at least ten times that if they're real."

"OK, OK. They might worth more than that," Jack admits. "I've got a guy, an antiques dealer close by, who can check them out. He can even give you a letter of authenticity."

Hey, thanks, Jack. Does that come with a lifetime guarantee or a 'your money back, limited-time' offer? I reach over to take the stones and for a second, Jack tugs back before releasing his grip.

What is it with this *dzi*? I feel like I'm holding Bilbo Baggins' magic ring. And somehow, I've been duped into shouldering the burden of deliverance.

"I've got my own guy, Jack, and he offered me a lot more than seven hundred dollars."

"You should be careful who you show those stones to. You never know who you can trust."

"Yeah, I can see that."

"Hey, I'm not trying to rip you off, man," he growls. "I don't know what the damn things are worth; I'm just covering my bases. Another round, anyone?"

You know damn well what they're worth, Jack. Quit while you're ahead.

He chugs another glass of *rakshi*. Maya pushes her stool back, announces: "Well, I'm off."

"Finally," sighs Jack.

"You know what the problem is, Jack?" huffs Maya. "The problem is that you've been boxed up in your own little world for so long that you don't know how to leave it. Like a crusty old crab that's not bothered to come out of his shell, you've stopped opening your eyes at the world. It's changing right around you, mate. It's changing faster than you think. It's not all about peace, drugs, rainbows and rock'n'roll any more. And that scares you, doesn't it?"

Jack smiles into his cup.

"Stay in your shell, Jack – it's too late to come out now. Stay inside and have a wonderfully splendid, drug-addled existence!"

She jumps up and charges out of the restaurant.

"Maya!" I call. "Wait. Let me walk you back."

Jack swills another drink, strums his fingers idly on the table. A real winner: a stand-up guy. Shit, he could be worse than Gerard.

"Maya!"

I'm about to run after her but Jack grabs me by the arm.

"Hey kid, could you spot me some cash? I'm kind of low and can't cover all this."

"You've got a lot of nerve, Jack. I thought you were taking us for drinks."

"Yeah, but you ordered food."

I throw a thousand on the table and head for the exit. "Enjoy your meal, motherfucker."

"...Hey, kid," says Jack, conciliatory.

I turn around.

"Stay between the raindrops." He grins sardonically.

"Not so fucking easy when you've got a cloud of rain following you."

I catch Maya at the end of the alley.

"Maya. *Maya* – wait up!"

I grab her wrist.

"Hey. Sorry about that."

"How fucking rude was that? Never in my life have I met such a sod!"

"I didn't know he'd be that much of a dickhead."

"It's not your fault. You can't be held accountable for all the wankers who pour out of your country."

"That would be disastrous," I say. "I'd have to spend the rest of my days being flogged with a red herring in Piccadilly Square."

"Yeah," she laughs, "I suppose it would be. Listen, you didn't mention my father to him, did you?"

"No. I got there only a few minutes before you showed up. He broke into my fucking room."

"I don't like him one bit," she adds. "If it's genuine, that *dzi* is worth at least a few thousand dollars. I've heard that some fetch prices of up to $100,000 these days."

"Whoa! That's a lot cake! That would definitely help out with my legal fees."

"Did you hear him going on about his friend in antiques? Wanker!"

The streets are empty now, save a few cows lolling near a pile of garbage.

"I saw you pay the bill. You shouldn't let him sponge off of you like that. He invited *us* out for drinks."

"Yeah, I know, but it was just a couple drinks."

"Well, you can't be too careful of twats like him trying to fleece you."

Rounding the corner, we reach my guesthouse.

"I'm sorry about the other day, Maya. I just want you to know that..."

She stares at the ground, describing a small arch with one foot. Then she looks up, and our eyes are snared. She's so pretty, standing there in the shadows: such a little girl. Don't look at me like that or there will be...god, I want to kiss her right now. *So do it. Just do it!*

"...That I..."

Two black figures rush up from behind her.

"*Maya*, watch out!"

One grabs her, squeezing a hand over her mouth. The other draws a huge blade from his leather jacket.

"The *dzi* – give me the *dzi*," he shouts.

They're young: early twenties, maybe.

Wriggling, Maya emits a muffled scream. Her captor kicks her sharply in the shin.

"Here – take it."

I throw down my pack.

"It's in the bag – now let her go!"

As one of the men reaches for my pack, another bolts from the shadows – silent and deadly, like a panther. A higher force hits the fast-forward button. Wielding a metal bar, the new assailant swings at the boy holding the knife, lands a crushing blow to his head.

"Jack – *don't!*"

The boy's body slumps to the ground. Maya jabs her elbow into the other's ribcage and clamps her teeth into his hand. He shrieks, shakes her off and scampers off into the blackness.

The other lies motionless. I can see his skull. I can see brain and blood stuck to his hair. One hand over her mouth, Maya crouches.

"Oh god…" She's whimpering.

Jack, who's been holding the bar above his head, muscles taught, lowers his weapon slowly. It clanks to the ground.

The skull: I can't stop looking at the skull. The brains look like a jellyfish, bulging to free itself from a clam. Jack squats and presses a finger across the boy's neck.

"…He's dead."

Time slows, shudders to a halt. I keep staring at the kid's shattered skull. Stone cold death. All the king's horses and all the king's men couldn't put this guy together again.

"What the *fuck* was that?" I stammer.

"Would you rather be lying there? Because that would be *you* right now if I didn't take that fucker down."

Jack tilts the boy's neck to one side, revealing a crude scar shaped like a dagger, carved into the nape.

"You see this scar here? This is a gang sign. The one that got away, he's getting reinforcements as we speak. Come on: let's get the fuck out of here."

"You killed him," Maya accuses. "You sick *bastard.*"

"Oh – and what was your plan? Curtsy and invite them over for tea and crisps? Look – that guy would've fucking knifed you, for christ's sake! We've got to move. There'll be an army night patrol coming any minute."

Slashed open across her midriff, Maya's gray top is now dyed in fresh blood. A clamor of voices rises in the night.

"Come on," hisses Jack. "Let's get out of here."

"But you just killed –"

"Goddamnit, Maya, it was either you or him. We've got to move…

now!"

The voices are closing in. I scoop my backpack off the street and grasp Maya's hand.

"Let's go."

Jack darts ahead, vanishes into a pitch-black alley. I pull Maya around the corner into the shadows. The voices are close now. A few seconds more and they'll run across the body, lying like a log in the middle of the street. I can't believe that kid is dead...and over a stupid stone. That could have been Maya, could have been me lying there on the ground, all because of a dumb-assed stone. I should've dumped it when I had the chance.

Without warning, the alley Ts. Ahead of us looms a high brick wall.

"*Pssst!* Kid. Over here," he whispers. I spot his shadow protruding from a window above.

"Through the courtyard; stairs on the right."

Maya yanks her hand from mine.

"This isn't right. I am not going up there."

"Why on Earth did you tell him I worked for the embassy?"

"I don't know. It's the first thing that popped into my head."

The voices are closer now.

"Why don't we get off the street for a second, clean you up...what d'you say?"

"Is this your 'sense of adventure,' Jupiter? Roaming about with the likes of this guy? You said yourself he's not to be trusted. He just *killed that boy*, for fuck's sake."

"Maya, he was protecting us. Listen, I know the dude is sketch but we might be dead now if it wasn't for him. Let's just chill for a bit, do a damage assessment. You look like you could use a breather."

"I've got to see a doctor. I'm bleeding."

She holds up a bloody hand.

"*Jesus.* OK, we'll get you to a doctor, promise. First, let's clean you up, though – wash off the blood so it's less obvious."

"*He* cut *me*. This is not my bloody fault! I should not even be here right now!"

Shouting erupts in the distance.

"Maya, calm down." This does not look good. If you walk out into the street looking like this, people – the police, for instance – are going to ask questions.

Breathing hard, she looks up at the window, then to me. "Right, let's go."

I climb the stairs, Maya close behind me. The room is musty, crammed with boxes and bags. Blackened pots and pans and an old-school burner are piled in one corner like an old science-class project. The walls are moldy, bare. It looks like he never really bothered to move in. Half a dozen butter lamps flicker, throwing shadows across the walls. Jack slides a bar across the door.

"Lie her down on the bed," he says. He grabs a cigarette, peers through the lattice. A black-and-white picture hangs above the bed, framed in grime and cobwebs. In it, a man, surrounded by foreign soldiers, stands at attention beneath a flag stiff with wind.

"Is that you in this picture, Jack?"

"*Shhhhh.*"

Someone yells in the street. A flurry of footsteps fades into the distance.

"…OK, let's have a look at the damage."

Lifting her tattered shirt, Maya reveals a long laceration above her belly button. Her clothing is saturated with coagulating blood. Fresh blood oozes from her belly as she breathes.

I've seen enough blood in these past few days to start my own bank.

"Oh, god," moans Maya.

"Holy fuck – look at the size of this cut. We've got to get her to a fucking doctor, Jack."

"Doctor? Nobody here needs to see a doctor."

"This is bloody ridiculous: I need to see a doctor now!" demands Maya.

"*Shhh* – keep you voice down," he hisses. "Word spreads through this town quicker than a flame up a Christmas tree on the Fourth of July. Right now, at least twenty Managis are scouring the streets for us – they'll slice us up like sashimi if they find us, guaranteed."

"We can go to the police," she says. "We have to, that's our only option. It was self-defense; we'll tell them exactly what happened. It's our only option."

"And have our names smeared all across tomorrow's *Kathmandu Post*? You do that and we're as good as dead. The police aren't going to protect you, not against these guys. The kid I took out back there moves a lot of drugs in Thamel. He's got at least five guys under him, maybe more. He's hooked up with some big, bad eggs.

"...And he's a Managi. Managis are no joke. Shit Maya, I think you've been around here long enough to know *that*. That slice they gave you, consider it a peck on the cheek.

"To stick around here is suicide. You take a Managi down and a hundred will come after you, and those cats won't quit until they've evened the score. I didn't recognize the one that got away, but that's not to say that he didn't recognize me. Even so, there are only so many old codgers like me kicking around here. Kathmandu is too small, man – too small for us to hide out in. It would only be a matter of time before they'd hunt us down. We've gotta get out of town."

"And leave her here?"

"I can stitch her up, no problem: I've got a kit."

"This isn't a fucking experiment, Jack. She could fucking *die*."

"Listen, man, I've sewn up dozens of wounds worse than that. And believe me, it would take a hell of a long time for someone to die of a knife wound that shallow. No arteries or organs were hit, just a little capillary spillage."

"OK, tough guy."

"Believe me, it's a stomach wound, no big deal."

Gerard would beg to differ.

"Maya, I'm going to spray a little disinfectant in first: it may sting a little."

"Alright."

The wound bubbles over like a head of red beer; Jack hands her two large gauze strips.

"Put some pressure on it. We've got to slow the bleeding down. Take this Vicodin, too. It might make you a little giddy but it will help the pain."

"OK, Trapper John, patch her up."

"Not until I get some straight fucking answers. You first, Maya. You work for the embassy – the British Embassy?"

Oh, shit. Here it comes. He's going to pick her apart now, find out who she really works for. That wasn't sodium barbital her gave her, was it?

"…Yes, that's right. I do some consulting work for them."

"What the hell does that mean, consulting work?"

"Hey Jack," I interject. "Take it easy man. She just took a knife to the stomach and you're hassling her with her job-related questions?"

"I need to know who I'm dealing with here. I need to know if she's going to run off and take refuge behind those gilded embassy gates. Cry 'diplomatic immunity,' then turn around and point the finger."

He turns to Maya, haranguing. "You need to understand the implications of your actions. You need to understand that doing so would *royally fuck me*. I can't have that, Maya, and neither can Jupiter. Do you realize how screwed all of us, yourself included, will be if you say anything about any of this to anyone?"

"…I guess…yes."

"To do so would be the equivalent of slitting our throats or putting a gun to my head, which also means putting one to *your* head."

"I'm starting to get the picture."

"Good. So, what do you mean exactly by consulting work?"

"I…I don't work for them directly. I work for a contractor, a financial office in London."

"And what does that mean, exactly?"

"I'm not a government employee, if that's what you're after."

"OK, so if I patch you up, you promise not to breathe a word of this to anyone?" repeats Jack.

"You have my word."

"And what's my name?"

"I don't know. I've never met you before in my life."

"OK. I'll take care of you if you take care of me. You've got a ticket out of here; I suggest you tell your company that some 'personal problems' have just come up and you need to fly back to England immediately. Don't show your face in town; stay at the embassy, if you can, until they ship you off. Give it some time – maybe a year or two – before you even think of coming back.

He turns to me. "Now you, kid. Who else have you been flashing that *dzi* to?

"What?"

"The stones, man: the fucking *dzi*. They didn't go after your goddamn wallet, did they?   They wanted the *dzi*. How the fuck did they know you had it – telepathy?"

"I just showed you and Maya, that's it… Wait, there was that guy."

"What guy?"

"The guy…at the antique shop. He looked Tibetan. I stopped off at his store on the way back.""Where?"

"I don't know. Somewhere in Thamel, I think. There was a sign above his shop entrance. 'Tibetan Antiques' or something like that. I just wanted to find out how much they were worth."

"And I'm guessing those kids in the street gave you a pretty good idea. More than I would have thought, too. Legally I can't help you out, but I think I can still get you out of this mess."

"What do you mean, you can get me out?"

"Over the humps and across the border. If you can make it over the pass onto Indian turf and play it off like you got lost, there's a good chance they'll just send you home."

Jack heaves open a massive chest. A wave of dust pulses through the air.

"I've got everything we need: jackets, crampons, boots. What size are you, kid?"

"Eleven."

"That is one of the *stupidest* plans I've heard of in all my life," interrupts Maya. "You really have no sense of logistics, do you, Jack?"

"Oh, you'd be surprised at what I can pull out of my hat. And frankly, I don't care what you think, little lady."

"I'm so thirsty," says Maya. "Can I have a glass of water?"

"No water; not before I sew you up. I know you probably want to suck the sweat off a bull's ass right about now, but things would get real messy down below if you did. Just be still."

Maya lies back down, moans. Her face is pretty green.

Digging into the chest, Jack scoops out a pair of leather boots attached at the laces and slings them at me.

"OK, Jack. We humored you with your little game of twenty-one questions. How many pints of blood does she have to lose before you get out a fucking needle? Seriously, sew her up now or I'm taking her to a hospital."

"Hold on to your horses, son. Nobody's gonna die on my shift."

He unzips a large bag, tears the wrapping off a syringe and sticks a vial. Drops spurt off the needle.

"This is Lidocaine. It's a local anesthetic to numb the area before I start with the stitches."

Maya winces as he zigzags tiny jabs across her stomach. Her hands clench. That has to hurt.

"…Alright – give that a second to kick in," says Jack. "It's not as deep as I thought. I'll give you some antibiotics to prevent infection. Keep it clean and you'll be home free."

"You'll never make it out of here with the strike still in effect. Almost all traffic, in and out of the valley, has been shut down."

"The *bhandh* is the least of my worries right now. I'm gonna head up into the hills and lie low for a while until things simmer down around here. And I thought I could get the kid out of his jam, too…get him over the border before they lock him up. Kill two birds with one stone."

Stop with stones already. That damn *dzi* will be the end of all of us. "Fuck, look at the time. Curfew's going to start any minute now."

"That's what alleys and back roads are for. Besides, nobody's likely to question a couple of foreigners with backpacks on their way to the bus station. You're grabbing at straws, Maya. I don't get why you're so consumed by this. What do you care? You should be happy for us. You should be happy you're headed back to England."

"You're leaving, just like that?" I'm genuinely puzzled.

"Just like that. I'm bailing. I'm not gonna stick around to find out what happens next. So are you in, kid? Or do you want to hang about until they hand you three to five on a cross? Believe me, they'll do it – and it ain't gonna be pretty, shitting liquid 24-7 in a dirt hole with more parasites than there are in the Ganges crawling round your insides."

"You think it can really work?"

"Hold on!" Maya glares at me. "You can't just *up and leave* – you're under house arrest, mind you!"

"I'll be under life arrest if I stick around much longer."

"That's not true. With the right lawyer, we might..."

"Might isn't gonna cut it," I counter. "You know there's a good chance I'll end up doing time. Even if I beat the trafficking charges, I've got the assault to worry about."

"You didn't tell me about that one, kid. Did you beat up a cop or something?"

"A male flight attendant," Maya smirks. "But the poof wound up routing him."

You little bitch. Traitor. *Spy.* I could spill the beans about your dad right now – blow the cover on your whole operation.

"*Really,*" says Jack. "Did he fake you out with the 'chicken or fish' combo?"

"Not now, Jack," I say. This is no time for fucking banter. "How soon can we leave?"

"Tonight, maybe in an hour. You can't go back to your room. It's too risky."

"No problem: everything I own is in this bag right here."

"...So, now what?" says Maya, pouring cold water on our high-stakes adventure. "You're going to do a runner for the border with this cheap excuse for Indiana Jones? I should never have got involved."

"I never asked you to, Maya," I say. "What am I gonna do – spend the next couple of years rotting away in a five- by seven-foot cell with parasites gnawing away at me? I can't do it. No more fucking rats... no more."

"Why do you care so much about his problems?" asks Jack. "Surely you've got enough on your plate as it is." "But..." she stammers.

"But what?" I ask. "And what do suppose is going to happen if we run into any more of those Tibetan gangsters? You know it's true – you know I've got to go one way or the other."

"You'll need your passport to get past checkpoints," she counters. "How do you plan on getting around that? You'll never make it out of the valley, not with all of the checkpoints. They check visas practically every forty kilometers and Jupiter doesn't even have a passport in his possession – do you, Jupiter?"

"Can you please just *call me Jay*?"

She's throwing out all the stops now. Anything to make me scratch my head for a second, reconsider.

"That, my dear," says Jack, "Just happens to be my specialty. From time to time, I deal – well, let's say, dabble – in human traffic."

"You smuggle people across borders? Like, sardining Chinese into cargo holds?" Jack the slave trader, a patch over one dead eye, sailing a leaky, weather-beaten vessel crammed with desperate human cargo into a storm. Scary.

"If you have so much as a trace of involvement in the trafficking of sex slaves to India, I'm going to personally castrate you," spits Maya.

"Try to relax, Maya." I tuck a pillow in behind her. "You're bleeding pretty badly."

"Come on, what do you take me for? Nothing major: just a couple of domestic runs a week. You see, with the current state of affairs, I've carved out a niche transporting certain individuals who aren't in good standing with the government back and forth from Kathmandu."

"You support the guerillas?"

"Hey, I don't ask any questions and they don't tell any lies. Politics is bad for digestion. All I do is to provide a discreet service to the community for a small fee."

"It keeps the country in a constant state of turmoil as well," Maya counters.

"Keeps my bills paid, and coffee and cigarettes on the table. Now I can guarantee that we can make it out of here tonight on a one-way, hassle-free ride out west. I'll handle the rest once we get out of the Kat. What do you say, kid?"

"Fuck it, I'm in."

"Now, all this extracurricular activity is going to involve some costs, and some risks, especially for me. You still game?"

"How much do you want?" OK, here comes the catch I should've expected.

"I don't want your money," says Jack. "I want the *dzi*."

"You can have it. The only thing those ill-gotten stones have brought me is trouble."

"I'll probably wind up getting sacked for this," gripes Maya.

Worse than that: daddy will probably ship you off to a private labor reform school somewhere on the Siberian peninsula for a few years. If you're lucky. Hey, he might even disown you.

"Maya, come on – please don't be angry with me. I really appreciate everything you and your fath… you've done for me, but I'm running out of options here."

"*I'm* running out of patience," she retorts, giving me the kind of glare your girlfriend gives to let you know she's going to backhand you the second you're out of the public eye.

Fuck, I said it, didn't I? The one thing she asked me to not do, and I couldn't even lay the bunt down…strike two!

Behind her, Jack gives me an entirely different look: a *'What the fuck is she talking about?'* look. Later, Jack, later. One lie at a time.

"Well, I'm not doing any time. No way. And I'm not going to wait around and see what those gangsters have in mind. This is it, Maya: this is my chance out. Every minute we sit here, the tunnel narrows."

"Right, but…well…"

"What?"

"…I want to come with you, then."

Jack raises an eyebrow.

"Now why in the hell would you want to hitch a ride with us? You don't even know where we're going."

"It doesn't matter; I don't care. I want to come."

"All you have to do is hop on the next plane to London. They can't turn down the old 'personal reasons' excuse: it never fails. Shit, you might even be able to write it off as a paid vacation if you play your cards right. Think of all the shopping you could get in."

"I'm not going back to London."

She looks up from the bed, still bleeding. "I'm going with you."

"Will you just stitch her up for christ's sake?"

"In a second, kid. Look, Maya. You're not fit to climb a flight of steps right now. You've got an out; the kid and I don't. Why would you waste your time and risk your life hiking into the mountains with a cut-up belly and a couple of beat-up cards like us?"

"If you don't bring me," she threatens, "I'll go to the police and tell them everything."

Wow, OK – I guess she really wants to tag along. Jack glances at me, clocks her, scratches his head.

"…What do you say, kid?"

"She's got just as much right to come as I do. And I never argue with wounded women."

"Three is more than two. Extra liabilities cost extra," he says.

"You get me to the border, get her back down here in one piece when it's over, and I'll give you one thousand dollars plus the *dzi*."

"Three thousand dollars plus the *dzi*. Three's a crowd."

"One thousand five hundred," I counter.

"Two thousand."

"…Two thousand, expenses included."

"Done. I've got plenty of gear to go around but I'm fresh out of boots. She'll have to find her own," he says.

That's pretty much all the cash I have left. Gerard's entire retirement package, exhausted in less than a week.

"I suppose these will have to do," she says, lifting up a Doc. "Do you have any sunnies?"

"Here you go," says Jack, handing her a pair of weathered mountaineering glasses.

"These are huge!" she says, but puts them on anyhow.

"Remember the seventies? How's your stomach feel?"

Maya pokes it gingerly with a finger.

"Fair to middling. I can't feel a thing." She's off her tree.

"Good, the Vicodin is starting to kick in, then. Just make like you're Jackie O, babycakes."

Maya giggles from under her glacier glasses. Maybe my slip about her father made her hate me so much that Jack's become the lesser of two evils. Maybe it's just the Vicodin. But against all odds, it seems Maya and Jack just connected.

I can't quite put my finger on it but a momentous change just occurred. Almost imperceptible, as slight as a breeze rippling across a pond, but it's happened: the three of us have become something more. We've made a pact, no matter what the odds. Signed on to a mission… *Mission Slim-possible.*

I pick up an ice axe and strap on the wristband.

"What are we going to be using these for?" I ask.

"Hopefully, we won't have to use them at all…but you never know." Jack threads a needle with monofilament. "Alright girl, now just lie back and relax. Dr J will have you patched up in no time."

Midnight. A few quick phone calls and a taxi ride later, Maya and I are sitting back to back, our packs slumped against one another like Siamese twins waiting for the carnival to pack up. We're in a ditch. Insects bounce off weeds like loaded springs. Trucks wheeze past, headlights cutting through the dust. Several of them are parked nose-to-tail along the far side of the road. Somewhere among them is our ride out of the valley.

Jack is supposedly locating it. What he's actually doing is anyone's guess. I wouldn't be surprised if he was trying to sell us off into the white slave trade. I stare down at the heavy, weathered boots on my feet.

"These boots Jack gave me suck," I say.

"I wish I'd had time to fetch a proper pair. At least yours are built for the mountains. Mine aren't up to serious trekking. You know, if this scheme of Jack's doesn't work, you're going to be completely stuffed. I don't know how he proposes to conceal us or what route he has in mind, but there will be at least a dozen checkpoints in any given direction. One of them finds us and you're looking at guaranteed prison time, at least three to five years, probably more."

"I've made my decision, Maya. There's no going back for me now."

"I'll be lucky to get out of this without being deported, and will most likely be disowned. He's right about those Managis, you know," she says. "It's always an eye for an eye with that lot. A while back, one sliced open an Italian bloke's neck in a bar fight at Tom & Jerry's, and killed him. The mother flew in and started handing out anti-Nepali pamphlets in the street. The Italian bloke's friend tied a leash around one of the street kids in Thamel, dragged him around like a dog. It was an absolute nightmare."

In less than a week here, I've had more run-ins with violence than I had in a lifetime on the south side of Chicago. Not that I spent too much time down that way.

"Himalayan gang-bangers…they meant business, huh? I thought this was supposed to be a happy mountain kingdom."

"Things aren't always as they seem. These days, there's loads of trouble brewing in Nepal. Things calmed down a bit for a while but now the three Maoist factions can't reach an agreement, it's back on the brink. This place is like a volcano set to blow."

"I can see that…How's your stomach holding up?"

"Jack pumped so much anesthetic into me I can barely feel myself breathe. I suppose I've got a few more hours 'til the pain hits."

I can't believe she's here, tagging along with two deadbeats en route to a currently undisclosed location. Why in the hell is she here? Is she doing more fieldwork for dear old dad? Keeping an eye on his multi hundred-thousand-rupee investment? What's in it for her?

I'm afraid to ask. Does she even like me? Hard to say: I haven't given her much reason to. If I was her, I'd be on the next plane back to London. And yet here she is, lying in this ditch with me, waiting to be whisked off to the mountains by Abbie Hoffman's wily cousin.

Jack slides down into the ditch. Panting, he says,

"OK, our man is here, just across the road. I've got us dialed in for a straight shot to Nepalganj."

"Nepalganj?" quizzes Maya. "Why on Earth would we go there?"

"*Exactly.* It's the last place the Managis would expect us to go, or anyone else for that matter. It'll buy us some time until we get our shit together. It also happens to be the bread-and-butter route of my shipping operation."

"That's a hotspot for the Maoists. It's a fucking battle zone. Doesn't the army shut down all traffic on that route during the night? And what about the *bandh*? There's another one tomorrow in case you haven't heard. I heard they're only letting ambulances and some media vehicles through. All the drivers are afraid to cross the strike line."

"This is where it gets good," says Jack. "We're riding in a food supply truck for the army. Same truck, same driver, twice a week every week. It's the perfect disguise. The checkpoint jockeys hardly bat an eye, and the Maoists don't touch it, since they know it might be full of their comrades. We'll sneak in right under their noses."

"They'll be searching hard at the checkpoints, Jack. I hope you have this fully sorted."

"Smooth as pie."

Smooth as pie. I assume that means Jack has things under control… or thinks he does.

Maya and I sling our packs over our shoulders.

"Keep low, out of the lights," Jack cautions. "I spotted a police van cruising by a few minutes ago. They might be doing freight inspections down the line."

We shuffle past a line of trucks, parked along the shoulder. Streams of gold and silver tinsel adorn their rearview mirrors. Jack steps up to one driver's door and raps hard. A soiled face appears at the window.

"*Jau!*" he says.

The engine roars; headlights blaze. Somewhere down the line, a door slams. The truck's fan belt squeals like a stuck pig. A waifish boy beckons us to the rear.

"It's going to be a long haul," Jack yells, "but we've got the gods on our sides. You see this here?" Grinning, he points to a red eye painted just below the truck's headlights. "That's the eye of Shiva: he'll steer us clear of danger."

I bend down for a closer look.

"*Stay out of the light, damn it.*"

The skinny boy unlatches the rear gate and forces it open...inside, it's all blackness. Jack clambers in, turns back to us.

"Toss up the packs."

I unfasten mine and thrust it upwards – Maya does likewise. I hoist myself inside.

Maya, meanwhile, is struggling.

"Here." I offer my hand; she ignores it.

Ok, be that way. I don't care if you're a man or a woman; you've got a belly full of Lidocaine and a few dozen fresh stitches and I'm offering you a fucking hand. You don't have to prove anything to me, tough girl.

She puts two hands on the tailgate, tries to lift herself up, slips back.

"Grab my hand, Maya – you just had your stomach cut open, for christ's sake!!"

I reach out again and yank her upwards, into the belly of the beast.

I climb up onto a stack of sacks, suck in the musty air. Burlap. Stale burlap. The engine fires up. The horn sounds, something between a startled donkey and a dying sea lion. The tailgate slams shut, sealing us in. We're in complete, utter darkness.

"Jack?" I whisper. "Where are you?"

"Right here...*whooaaah aah ahhhaaah!*"He does his best ghoulish guffaw.

Flipping on a flashlight, Jack holds it up to his chin; the harsh underlighting distorts his features. Gunnysacks...we sit atop a quaking plateau of gunnysacks.

I tuck myself into a crack. Whorls of dust float over the upturned beam. I knock my fist against one of the sacks.

"What's in these, do you reckon?"

"Let's find out, shall we?" says Jack.

Drawing a knife from his coat, he makes a nick in the side of one, splitting it open. White granules spill out.

"Rice. Standard. From our good friends back at US AID."

Well, there's no chance of us going hungry.

"...Here kid, keep the flashlight on me."

Gears wind out; we bounce over a bump.

"OK, here's the deal," says Jack. "Above us is a false roof, concealing a compartment. Access is through a trapdoor."

Muscling over the rice sacks to the forward end of the van, Jack reaches up and trips the hidden door, revealing a square black space overhead.

"You two go first. There's not much room to move around up there, so watch your heads when you go up. There should be some matting or something to lie on."

I hoist myself up into the darkness, smacking my head against the ceiling. He wasn't kidding about space constraints. Splayed on my stomach, I scooch my legs up out of the hole. A secret compartment? Seriously? This has to be one of the oldest tricks in the smugglers' handbook. It's probably cutting-edge technology here, though.

I grope around with my fingers, calculating the dimensions of the space. I've got maybe three feet of space, just enough to allow me to lie flat on my back. What feels like several straw mats overlap one another, covering the floor of the compartment. So much for riding in style.

The air is stifling, thick with body odor, urine and dust. Reminds me of my prison cell, only smaller… What a trade-up. And I paid money for this?

Maya pulls herself in behind me, then Jack. He slams the hatch behind him and wedges the flashlight between two mats, its beam facing upwards. Quieter up here, anyway.

"OK, we made it all aboard," he says. "Now all we have to do is lay back and enjoy the ride…and in twenty or so hours, we'll be there."

"What do we do if we have to use the loo?"

"Just try and fall asleep and next thing you know, we're there."

"It's going to take more than twenty hours, Jack. Anyone who can last that long is severely dehydrated or a liar."

"Maybe we can try the pee-in-a-cup routine."

The truck lurches forward.

"That might get a bit messy. Jupiter, you and I will have to take our business to the back of the compartment when nature calls. Maya, it's going to be a tad more difficult for you, so we'll let you out the hatch in between checkpoints. Let's not make a habit of dropping down below, though. The driver told me that since they found that decapitated journalist last week, the army has really been snooping through their cargoes."

"What about, you know – the other stuff?" I ask.

"That, my friend, is simply not an option. Just try to relax and you'll be dozing off in no time."

Human cargo. Fuck, I've become a commodity. You don't really know the feeling 'til you've tried it. Like the sacks of rice below us, I've got a price tag stuck to my forehead. Prime western rib: two choice cuts. We could be headed to Bangladesh for all I know.

Shit. I never called home, did I? Maybe it's better that I wait. Wait until…what if I don't make it? She'll never know what happened. Quite possibly no-one from home will. Jenny might track me as far as Kathmandu, if she's lucky. I can see her handing out flyers with my picture on them in Thamel, maybe even spending a chunk of her nest egg putting my sorry face on the side of a milk carton.

The caption will read: *'Have you seen me? Last spotted wrestling a male flight attendant. Stoned and delusional; possibly dangerous. Answers to 'Hey, dude!' and likes warm milk and cookies.'*

Another deadbeat lost to the Orient. Years later, a Chinese archeological expedition will find my frozen remains on the side of a glacier and mistakenly identify me as proof of CIA espionage along their borders. I've got to make that call: at least let them know where I am in the world. Give them a fighting chance of finding me after the fact...as if they even care.

I feel a little relieved knowing that Jack, seasoned smuggler, is riding along with the smugglees on this run. Jack the junkie; Jack the slave runner: so multi-faceted. Who's to say we're not headed for the swampy flats of Dhaka? Maybe he's personally delivering such fine stock. A couple of nice white kids like us. Maya could fetch far more than the norm, I'm sure.

"...Hey kid, you want a little something to take the edge off?"

"What's that?"

"Opium. I picked it up off a Thai associate of mine. Top-notch shit. You can't beat it for shitty road-trips and this is one is abysmal. We've got a good long stint ahead of us."

He hands me a green pipe. A glossy stem protrudes from a bowl fashioned in the shape of a hand.

"What's with you lot?" Maya pipes up. "Do you need to be high every waking second to function?"

"Hey, it's consensual, not a fucking crime," snaps Jack. "You should have a pipe or two yourself: it's the best sleeping aid on the market."

"Just keep it over there; I don't want to get a contact high. And mind the flame, will you? I don't want to end up as the meat on a bed of fried rice."

She rolls over, her feline back a reproach. Why is she so adamantly anti-drugs? I mean, I can see why she's got a hang-up with my habits, given that the majority of my shortcomings and this whole fiasco can be linked to reckless, stupid drug use, but why lecture Jack? So he's doling out opium to me – so what? The problem is a lot bigger than Jack and I.

Her father was part of the problem, too, working with Gerard's out-fit. I wonder if he got tweaked out or shot or got uppity and had to have an arm broken. She's definitely got issues around the subject.

I run my fingers along the jade bowl. "Nice piece. Where'd you pick this up?"

"Western China somewhere, I forget. I traded it for some piece-of-shit Taiwanese wristwatch and had to hightail it out of town before the shopkeeper realized it lost five minutes of time a day. Now just kick back and put her in neutral."

Lying on my side, I place the end of the pipe to my lips, rest my head against a sack. Opium: the final frontier. Shouldn't I be propped up in a mass of pillows with an obsequious Chinaman at my beck and call – or is that just in the movies? I guess Jack and these musty mats will have to do.

Gosh, mom would be so proud of me now. Why waste time on pris-on stories when you've got this kind of material?

I look over at Maya, her back still toward me. Don't be mad, Maya.

Jack flicks a lighter over the bowl. The resin froths like a crab's mouth. I take another hit, drawing in the perfumed smoke. Tastes like I'm smoking air freshener: jasmine mist with a twist.

I roll onto my back, now, shut my eyes. The drug gurgles through me like hot, bubbly foam...

Don't be mad, Maya...don't be mad. Sunny beaches...happy place...happy place.

...I walk along the edge of a stream, gazing at the pebbles that line its bank. I pick one up: it's as smooth and green as jade. I want to put in my mouth, roll it around with my tongue like I a Jolly Rancher. Another stone below the surface catches my eye. I look closer: it's the *dzi*.

There you are, Mr *Dzi*...such a troublesome little bugger you are. I reach for it. The water is as clear as glass. I can see every detail under-water, from big fish to tiny strands of algae, clinging to the rocks. As if there was a camera lens attached to my eyes, I zoom in again...

Ah, the *dzi*! I can see every whorl, every eye looking back at me. I crouch down, now, dip my hand into the water. Just a little deeper. It's deep, deeper than it looks. Why can't I reach it? It's right there.

Someone calls from across the bank. Jack. What the hell are you doing all the way over there? He's leaping up and down like a monkey…laughing like a loon. Funny, you know I've never seen you laugh before?

A syringe hangs from his arm. Oh, *that's* why. Back at it again, huh: riding the horse… So what's it like, Jack? Better than sex? Can I have some? Just a little taste?

"Jack!" I say. "Come over here, give me a taste."

Suddenly, the syringe morphs into a lamprey. I slip, slip, slippery! Reel forward, somersault, fall in. The water laps against my skin, flows over me, around me like a dark secret, so warm, even though I know it should be cold. *Mmmmmm.* Tucking me in like a little child. I raise my hand out of the water.

The *dzi* – I've got the *dzi.* How pretty you are with all of your eyes: ever-seeing, ever-knowing. No-one can take you away from me now. Not Jack, not anyone.

Eddies swirl, currents build, moving quickly now. I'm being sucked downstream. Jack, no wait…*Gerard.* I see Gerard running along the bank now. He's really moving. How can he keep up, with just one leg? My head bobs up and down like a rubber duck; images flash before my eyes, switching between land and water. He wants the *dzi.* Hold onto that *dzi:* don't let go of it. He'll steal it from you if he can.

I'm going faster now. *Do not let go, do not let go!* Two boulders, fast approaching. Suddenly, I roll down a chute into a hole filled with churning water. *The hole's got me!* It slams between the boulders, playing with me like a cat toys with a half-dead bird.

My face presses hard up against a rock. Suffocating, I fight for the surface. You're not taking my *dzi,* not taking me.

"*Aaaaahhhhh!*"

I bite down hard. The current slams me back down…no, it's Jack. He claps a hand across my mouth, puts a finger to his lips…his expression is harsh in the flashlight shadows…

Jack the new fucking Ripper: he could kill me right now. One sharp twist of the neck and that'd be it...

OK, Jack: I get the message.

The truck screeches to a halt. No waterfall, no stones, no river or submerged treasure, just a truck. I'm wedged between our backpacks: my river boulders. I wriggle free. Wheezing reluctantly, the engine fades out altogether. Almost at the same instant, the flashlight cuts out and we're completely in the dark.

"Wow, I just had a whacked-out dream," .

"*Shut up*," Jack hisses, shaking his hand as if he's in some kind of pain.

A male voice breaks the silence. A door slams. I can feel the tailgate opening. Footsteps clatter on the boards below us...

Inspection time; the moment of truth. The only thing separating us from an armed, cranky Nepali officer on the dog-end midnight shift is a flimsy half-inch of aluminum cladding.

All I can hear now is the breathing: quiet, steady, calculated breathing. The three of us huddle close; there's a collective sense of impending doom. It's so stuffy up here I can barely breathe. I feel like we're in a submarine that's lost power and sunk to the ocean floor...or trapped in a vault, the hapless victims of a bank-robbery-gone-bad.

Steady now, not too fast. Make each breath count. Only so much oxygen left, only so much to go around. Each breath a little less than the next.

The tailgate, then the doors slam shut. The truck's engine roars back into life.

I let out a sigh of relief. We've regained power; we've cracked the combination...*we're going to live*!

"What's up, doc?" I whisper.

"That was close!" says Jack, adrenalized by the encounter. "If you'd had your little conniption a minute later, we'd be at gunpoint right now."

"Sorry."

"Motherfucker, you've got some fucking bite on you," he adds. "You almost broke the skin when you clamped down."

I can't believe I bit the guy. I've never bitten anyone before. Jack may be triggering my primal instincts. A subconscious action, made to protect myself, perhaps? I fucking bit him in my sleep. That'll learn you.

"...I had a nightmare."

"You were wriggling around like a goddamn hamster on mescaline! Remind me never to sleep too close to you."

A hamster on mescaline? I don't need to know where that simile came from.

"You were in it," I say. "You were in my dream. So was Gerard."

"A nightmare... with Gerard? That sounds about right. He's been in a couple of my nightmares, I'll tell you what! Plenty more time to dream, man: we've got another five or six hours to go. There'll be at least three or four more checkpoints before we're through the woods, so to speak. Hey Maya, how's your bladder holding out?"

"Terrible," she says. "The road is so bloody rough it wants to shake the piss right out of you."

"Alright, I'm not in good shape, either. I'll let you down through the hatch in the next couple of miles...miles...miles."

His voice blurs in my ears like a worn-out bootleg tape; louder, louder, then softer, slowly dissipating.

I lie back down on the mats, opening and closing my eyes, trying to detect flaws in the darkness...perfect. I could lie like this forever, dream and euphoria whirling past. But I'm kinda sleepy right now. Are my eyes even open?

The drug has me foiled again! *Why fight it?* Let the parade march on, the ribbons whirl, the colors dazzle! Razzle dazzle, dazzle razzle. The *dzi,* the *dzi*...I need to find the *dzi* ...

Don't be mad, Maya, don't be mad.

Light swings back and forth, back and forth across my face.

"Rise and shine, sleeping beauty!"

Jack is shaking me, flickering a flashlight beam across my face. Cocking my head, I rub a grimy palm over my face. Oh, my stomach. It feels like a tub of battery acid, churned into an acid bath with the truck's non-stop rattle and roll.

I hope we're there soon.

The engine hums, gears grind momentarily. Maya is pinned against the front of the trailer, now, head propped against her pack, bobbing dangerously close to the ceiling. She yawns, plucks a strand of dirty straw from her hair. It's been a rough night for the contraband.

"...Shit, man, you've been out stone-cold for nearly five hours," says Jack. "I tried to wake you for a piss stop but you were dead to the world. That opium sure put you out for the count. Pretty smooth shit, eh?"

"Where are we?" I croak, dislodging a gob of phlegm from my throat. My head hurts; my bladder's ready to explode. I feel an urge to vomit – but Maya is a few feet away. I can't do it. Should I ask her to turn away? If we don't stop soon, I'm going to hurl.

"...Hard to say," replies Jack, after a longish pause. "I'm fairly certain we made that last turn seventy-odd kilometers back, which gives us around thirty kilometers to go."

The engine slips into high gear as we build speed.

"How many miles is that?" asks Maya.

"You've been here over a decade and you're still stuck on that ancient system? Get with the times, girl...you do the math."

"If it's such a shite system, why does your almighty nation still use it, then?"

"Give me a break: I haven't touched US soil in over fifty years."

What are they talking about? There are more crucial debates, surely, than standard versus metric measurement. Give those two enough time together and they'll be disputing the color of the sky.

The truck squeals to a stop, then pitches forward. Maya's head slams against the trailer wall.

"Fucking hell."

I hear the back door swing open; the tailgate being lowered. Is our prison term up? Are we getting early release for good behavior? Someone raps against the false roof.

"Well, I spoke too soon," says Jack. "It looks like we're here."

Jack pops open the hatch. Light floods in. I shield my eyes with a hand. Jack and Maya shimmy through the trapdoor, drop down onto the rice sacks. I'm not ready to move. The entire right side of my body is numb. And it's so fucking bright. I feel like Papillon after a month in the hole. That will teach to you try and escape, *Monsieur Papillon*! My body protests via throbbing temples and aching joints. I'm starting to sweat in earnest.

Behind the trailer, the rangy boy scans the way nervously for passing traffic. He motions for us to hurry. I wonder how many people he sees emerging from that trapdoor in the average week. He might get the occasional drug smugglers or fugitives like our sorry selves, but most of his clientele are no doubt Maoists these days.

I wonder if he's part of the insurgency – if he believes in the struggle against 'imperialist running dogs' or if he's just trying to make a few extra rupees like everybody else. He doesn't look like a Maoist but then it's hard to discern a person's ideology by looking at their face.

I look out the back of the truck. Flat...empty...fucking hot. We could be in Bangladesh, for all I know.

Jack lobs our packs, one by one, down to the boy. I climb down off the rice-sacks and out onto the potholed street. Get out of my way, rangy comrade, before I retch on you. May your ideologies or pockets be fulfilled – or filled full – whichever you prefer.

Cicadas drone in the sultry air.

"I don't feel so hot," I say. "I think I'm gonna be sick."

"It's the opium," Maya admonishes.

Invisible gremlins are poking me in the temples. Sweat beads off my face, my head reels...Oh man, I'm going to hurl. Nobody told me about this part.

"First-time offender," says Jack.

"Why did you have to give it to him?"

"Hey, I didn't twist anyone's arm."

OK…better. It's amazing how much better you feel after a 'self-purge.' Now if I can only get these two to stop fighting.

"Did you tell him he was going to be sick as a dog the morning after? How do expect him – or yourself – to complete this mission if you're both chock-full of opium?"

"He's a big boy; he can think for himself. I didn't force the shit down his throat."

"As our trusted guide, I would've thought you'd employ better judgment."

"I'll get you where you need to go, but I really don't give a toss what you think of my ethics, Maya whoever-the-fuck-you-are."

Drug pusher, human trafficker, and all around shady guy: that's our man Jack. Our trusty guide. Wouldn't trade him for the world.

A rickshaw driver pedals by, pulls a U-turn and skulks up from behind.

"*Tum kyam jay che?*"

"Is he speaking Hindi, Jack?" asks Maya. I can't make out the accent." Then, slapping the back of her neck, "My god, this place is swarming with mosquitoes."

"*Hotel ma jay che?*" the driver persists.

"Is that Hindi? I can't make out a word he's saying."

"That's because he's speaking Gujarati," explains Jack.

He's pretty good with the regional dialects. I wonder if he picked them up on his own.

"…Welcome to India," moans Maya.

I swat a mosquito off my shoulder. She's right, they are rampant.

"This is Nepalganj?"

"More like Nagraganj," she mutters.

I don't see any signs – at least, none in English. "How close are we to the border?"

"Six kilometers," says Jack.

"That would explain the Gujarati," says Maya.

Six kilometers: I could do that on foot. I don't need Jack for that. Maya can get to a hospital and have that gash checked out by a real doctor, head back to Kathmandu for some much-needed rest. I could go by night; it looks flat as a pancake out here. I could be there tomorrow morning, and I would have a ton of money to spare...

Shit. OK, I do need Jack to manage this. Stay off the roads, lay low 'til I can find a bus or a taxi to an embassy. Delhi would probably be closest. They'd help me out, right? Or would they toss me back to the lions?

"I know what you're thinking, kid, but you won't have a chance of crossing here. The police will be all over your shit, so close to the border without an Indian visa. And the border is swarming with them. They pull passports at every check post. They'll ship you straight back on the next red-eye to Kathmandu. You've got to play the waylaid mountaineer, stumbling off the Tibetan plateau with frostbitten hands and a shit-luck story about blizzards and bandits. It's not even money – but they'll take the bait."

"So...the only way is up?"

"You've got better odds of making it over the top than you do of crossing here. Tell them you got lost on a mountaineering expedition from China.

"My guess is that the Indian authorities will take the bait. We'll slap some climbing gear on you for effect. Besides, they've got their hands full with a nasty drought. And if they do buy the mountaineer story, it could take weeks before they get any sort of response from the Reds – I don't think they'll wait around for one, either. They don't want the paperwork or the headache."

"What a load of shite," says Maya.

"In case you haven't heard, China and India aren't exactly kissing cousins. They went to war with one another back in the '60s. And the border dispute in Ladakh keeps flaring up like a case of herpes. That's pretty damn close to your entry point into India.

"They won't want to play hot potato with you when they're on the verge of settling, finally. It's bad press. It will only stir up old wounds."

"If we're able to get a domestic flight with these passports, why couldn't we just hop on a flight to Kunming or Delhi?" asks Maya.

"Visas. You've got to have a visa in your passport all sorted at an embassy before you set foot in either country."

"Then why don't we get your hook-up to sort visas to India? Wouldn't that be a lot less painful than humping it over the Himalayas?"

"My man only does Nepali visas."

"…What about Bangkok?" I ask.

"Thailand's too high-tech," Jack asserts. "And Karachi is totally out of the question. The only Americans flying in there these days are carrying press badges or heavy artillery."

"Australia?" I counter.

"Same deal. You need a visa beforehand. And with the heightened security these days? Remember, this area has become a hot outlet for fundamentalists. Any way you slice it, they're gonna grind you through the mill before you set foot in their country.

"My guess is they'll ship you down to Delhi, hold you a day or two, then send you off to the embassy for a new passport. After that, you're free as the wind."

"You paint a pretty picture, Jack, but that sounds like a lot of guessing," I say.

"Guesswork is a high art form in these parts. And I'm pretty damn good at it."

So, he fancies himself an artist…sounds like more of a bullshit artist to me. What's your medium, Jack – oily lies? Jack's proposed venture into the icy unknown sounds like a major undertaking to me. I might not be able to speak a half a dozen Asiatic languages but I've got a pocketful of dollars – as proficient in any language as I need to be – and enough nerve to give the lowland border-sneak a try.

Why is Jack so adamant about taking me into the mountains? I'll give him the *dzi* even if I don't go with him. That's all he wanted in the first place: then he can go his way, and Maya and I can each go ours.

That would be ten times easier than lugging us up a Himalayan pass…no, he's hiding something under his canvas. I can see why he wants to keep us out of sight of the Managis. He's protecting himself from information leaks (i.e. us). The 'human cargo' angle? I'll have to play it as it lies.

If I go his way, if I go up into the mountains, I've more to deal with than prison time. I could wind up shellacked to an ice wall or buried in a crevasse for the rest of eternity…

On the other hand, prison time is a bitch. Maybe he's right. I'm certainly not going back to prison. It sounds funny to say it, but I'd rather die than go back to prison. I look at Maya; she smiles, a faint 'I told you so' playing around her eyes.

Another rickshaw swings by. We cram Maya and our packs inside and climb onto the ripped vinyl seat of the second. Jack turns to the driver.

"Hum samjye. Apne jaie!"

The driver jiggles his head from side to side. His calves bulge and strain against our weight like water buffalo to a plow. The contraption rattles and squeaks, gaining momentum as we edge onto the potholed pavement. I don't know how they do it: half our sizes, with bikes that would be better off sold as scrap…and calves of steel.

Twisted shots of rebar jut from the rooftops of drab, concrete-clad buildings. It looks as if a bombing raid has taken place not long ago. A helmeted soldier peers uneasily from the other side of a blackened barricade. Scorched sandbags suggest a recent battle.

Must be Maoists around. I scan the surrounding rooftops for proletariat snipers.

Suddenly, a distorted voice blares from a loudspeaker, butchering the serene early-morning air. A desperate wailing. It sounds like Arabic.

"That's so obnoxious," I complain.

"Dig those satanic verses, man! Nothing like a few lines of the Koran to start your day. Look at this place: a sweaty armpit, complete with ingrown hairs. Nothing but *mahdeshis* and malaria out here."

He's right. Maybe not about likening *mahdeshis* (whatever they might be) to armpits but about figuring this place as a dump at the ass-end of the world. It has all the signs of a frontier town that sprang to life suddenly and was just as suddenly forgotten. The place reeks of low-end commerce: plastic buckets, PVC tubing, welding torches, dusty bags of cement. It's as bland as a rice cake. I'd guess a few hundred tourists would roll through here a year, maybe fewer. Those Managi gangsters wouldn't dream of looking for us here.

A way off from the road, a shiny white-tiled building arches upward, the crescent and star on top reaching towards the heavens. It's a shiny brand-new mosque, pre-fabricated and ready for instant worship.

"I thought this was a Hindu kingdom."

"Oh, there are a few of those pesky critters about, mostly Indians who've come to stay. This cesspit happens to be one of their strongholds. There were some pretty nasty riots out here a while back. A few mosques got torched after Iraqi militants took out all of those Nepali workers...poor fellas. It looks like they missed this one, though. Maybe they'll get it next time around."

Maya swings round to face us. "...Do you have to be such a condescending asshole so early in the day, Jack? As if the Muslim community doesn't have enough problems."

I knew she wasn't going to let that sentiment fly. At least they're not in the same rickshaw. Is it just me, or does Jack have penchant for traveling to politically unstable hot spots? If we make it over the pass in time, maybe we can catch some end-of-season effigy- and flag-burning rallies in Islamabad.

"*Alhamd' Lilah!*" yells Jack.

Somehow, I've become mother to these two squabblers. Alright, you two, don't make me pull over these rickshaws. If I have to pull over, I'm going to start cracking!

Mom would say that every time Jenny and I would get into it the back seat. Start cracking...that always used to make us laugh. She made it sound as if she was a circus trainer breaking in a pair of lion cubs...I suppose she was doing just that, more or less, with two hyperactive hell-raisers on her hands. Half the time, one of us would pick a fight with the other just to hear her say it: "I'm cracking!"

I've got to make that call.

A welder's torch glows in the morning haze. In the distance, the steady pulse of a mill.

"I remember when this was a tiny village and you could still hear tigers roaring in the night," says Jack. "The only roaring you hear now is from those damn loudspeakers."

I'm not certain but I think that was Jack waxing nostalgic. Jack… the (T)ripper: environmentalist? I'm sorry but I just can't see it. If there were still tigers around, he would be the first to exploit them. Probably snatch up the first safari jacket he could find and become a hunting guide. It's a good thing he's dealing in humans these days; I don't see any shortage of them around here.

Alongside the road lies the rusted-out carcass of a school bus and a mélange of discarded objects: Asian Appalachia. A refrigerator, stacks of worn tires, a ladder-everything a toddler would need to construct a post-modern playground. A child, barely school-aged, perches atop a decrepit tractor, smothered in vines, jerking a steering wheel back and forth. A bigger boy rushes past, spinning a rubber tire with a stick. At least he's laughing.

The Star Hotel. The glossy six-by-four-foot poster of a baby-oiled Bollywood star in flyaway shorts and feathery mullet says it all. A gaggle of men in ill-fitting suits sit chain-smoking at reception. A sitar whines from the radio. Everyone's a star at the Star Hotel.

"These shysters have booked the place solid. Something to do with an annual pesticide convention," says Jack.

"Sounds like the place to be," I jest.

"They've only got one room left. You two can take the bed. For an extra hundred rupees they promised to throw a in a cot for me. Go get some sleep. You look like you could use it. I'm gonna go hunt down some old acquaintances and see what I can do about our identity crisis."

The contact. I hope he's not referring to anyone in the slave industry, because I would have a hell of an identity crisis being a slave.

Lugging a backpack over each shoulder, I swing open the door. Maya collapses on the massive bed in the center of the room. Flakes of plaster from the ceiling coat the bed. Tired curtains, their eyelets torn, droop from cheap aluminum rods. Not the honeymoon suite I was hoping for.

"Let's sort this before I forget." Maya coaxes a cell phone from her jeans and dials. *Damn, they look good on her.*

"...Hello father? It's me."

There's a long, long pause, then eventually, she says, "You don't have anything to worry about with Jupiter, he's alright. He's not after the money."

I can't make out what her dad's saying. He's probably not too happy about that last snippet, though. Blackmail's no laughing matter.

"He's just a bit messed up in the head is all," continues Maya. "You might want to blame Gerard for some of that."

Daddy Gunn's ranting now, most likely cursing my name. Settle down, Tony! Maya tries her best to plow a path.

"Dad...*dad. Father!* Listen to me for a second, will you? I'm not in Kathmandu anymore. No, I'm not in danger...just hear me out, *please.* Something happened. He got scared and did a runner." Silence... *Now* he's listening.

That got your attention, didn't it?

"I think I know where he is. I overheard him talking to some back-packers heading to Pokhara and I'm fairly certain he hopped on a bus with them this morning. The hotel receptionist saw them leave together. Look, there's no need to get anyone else involved right now: it will only turn into a – just let me try and sort this on my own. Pokhara is not that big a place, dad. It shouldn't be too hard to find him."

She frowns at me. Is he buying it? He'll be sending a posse to rescue his daughter at some point soon, no doubt. He's probably snapping his fingers at a team of electronics experts who are listening in, triangulating our position right now. It's only a matter of time before a swarm of blacked-out helicopters roars over our heads, then circles back with gunmen hanging out the sides.

The old man's voice is rising in pitch and volume, but Maya cuts him off at the pass.

"I *know* you put yourself out to get him released from prison, but what would you have done if you'd been in his shoes? I think the American consular agent gave him a scare, what with all the charges against him.

"…Just tell them he's fallen ill from the prison food they fed him and had to be hospitalized at CIWEC for dysentery. If they ask to visit him, say he's been released and is under your care now.

"*You* were the one who bailed him out in the first place, so why wouldn't he be under your charge? Surely you know someone there who can make up some charts on him. Have them push the case back a bit."

Tinny chatter emanates from the other end. Maya rolls her eyes, mimics his babbling with her free hand. "Yes, I should have kept a better watch on him, dad, but just give me some time to put it right. They've got his passport, for christ's sake. He can't go very far without that.

"I *told* you I'm OK. Yes, father, I promise to stay safe. No, I won't: if it becomes –"

She stops, listens, rolls her eyes again. A tad more strained than your average parent- child phone chat but still, the classic pattern. How many times have all of us gone through this routine: half-listening to a parent babble down the line, responding on automatic pilot – 'Yes, dad,' – 'No, mom' – to questions we've fielded a thousand times before.

"*Whew,*" she says, finally, stuffing the phone back in her pocket. "I thought that would never end."

"He didn't sound too happy."

"Well, he doesn't have much reason to be, does he? He's going to have to…" She stops, sighs. I put my arm around her. It seems like the right thing to do.

"Thanks. You didn't have to do that, you know."

"I'm aware of that, but you're welcome. He went ballistic when I told him you did a runner. I thought about just coming clean with our little ploy to get you out of the country but I think it would have been too much for him.

After mum left, he was a complete mess – I guess I was all he had to fall back on. If he lost me, I don't think he'd be able to get on."

"I don't want to fuck up anything you have between you and your father." I'm flattered she's confided in me. "Not any more than I already have, anyway."

She pats me on the knee. "That should buy us a few more days, anyway. Once I tell him I've found you he'll calm down a bit. But eventually Immigration is going to want to see you in the flesh. I suppose I'll have to coat this lie with another one. Today's *bandh* should buy you another day at least."

Still lying, but not to me – at least not to the best of my knowledge.

"I'm completely knackered," she exclaims. "I can't wait to take a shower and get some kip."

"Yeah, that was a pretty hellish ride." I brush little plaster snow-flakes off the bed. "A shower doesn't sound like such a bad idea."

"*Mais oui.*"

"*Alors, tu parle bien français! Si j'avais su…*"

"I'm not that good, really," she demurs. "It's been so long."

What a stupid line. Who am I kidding, here? Trying to seduce her with my lame-assed French in some cheap border-town hotel. Doing my best Pepé Le Pew. 'Oh, *ma chérie*, we could make *beautiful* music together!'

Dumb-ass. Don't you know she can see straight through you?

"I took classes through boarding school but that was ages ago. And my dorm mate was French. My French wasn't half bad, back then. Her name was Angeline…such a pretty name, don't you think? We were the best of friends – virtually attached at the hip.

"We'd sneak off to London on weekends and try to get into clubs for a laugh. We used to ride the trains, see how far we could get without paying. Once, we blagged it as far as Glasgow before the conductor sent us back, on the promise we'd go back to school straight away. We must have been fifteen, sixteen then.

"Angeline knew how distant I had become with my father, knew I never really had a mum – that I had nowhere to call home. After we graduated from Seven Oaks, she invited me to stay with her family on the Côtes-d'Armor. It was brilliant. We had just finished our A-levels and didn't have a care in the world. Every day, we'd go down to the beach and collect shells, sit on the cliffs and smoke Dunhills she stole from her father's bureau...it seems like a lifetime ago."

"Where is Angeline now?"

"I don't know. Most likely married, living in some affluent suburb of Paris, I suppose."

"You don't keep in touch with her?"

"No. In fact, I haven't seen her since that summer. She was meant to come for a visit at Cambridge one weekend but it all went pear-shaped: something to do with her aunt falling ill, as I recall. I received an invitation to her wedding in Provence, but by the time it was forwarded from Cambridge, the wedding had already happened. I wanted to call, tell her how happy I was for her, but for some reason I never did."

"It sounds like a friendship that could've lasted the rest of your life."

"Yeah. Funny that. It wasn't even very long ago. And for that slice of time, we were really close. Inseparable. Two lives in complete synchronicity.

"I don't reckon I'll see her again," she says, then, oddly pensive. "All of the obligations she must have these days: visiting the in-laws over the holidays, joining her mum and dad at the beach house, dinner parties for her husband's business associates...and then a baby! With a baby around, she'll barely have time to breathe. No, it doesn't seem likely she'll have much time left for me."

"Did you try emailing her? Or maybe looking her up on Facebook? The internet can hook you up with just about anyone these days."

"Frankly? I can't be bothered. And I don't subscribe to any of those bullshit online networks."

Shunning Facebook! I have to give her props for that.

"I imagine she's most likely changed as much as I have since that summer. We'd be strangers to each other, now – flipping through dusty albums, pointing at yellowed photos of tanned little girls we hardly knew. I can't say for certain, but I just have this feeling I'll never see her again.

...There are times I meet someone in a seemingly trivial fashion, and then run into again, down the track: someone whose name I'd forgotten or never even bothered to ask. Those are the ones you have to watch for: the ones that keep surfacing like tunes you can't get out of your head.

Years later, when you've forgotten all about them, they pop up in the most unexpected places – a train station in Milan, a nightclub in New York, a beach in Thailand. Could be anywhere. Before you know it, they're back in your life again.

Fact is, we're all just random letters in a bowl of alphabet soup: a bunch of charged atoms and fragments floating around, bonding and un-bonding in some twisted chaotic dance. Only it seems that some of us, some of these atoms…It's like chemistry: some bonds stand the test of time; others can't.

Do you know what I mean?"

This is getting a little too *Celestine Prophecy* for my liking. Did she pop another Vicodin?

"…I don't know – call me old-fashioned, but I like to keep in touch with my friends, even if it doesn't amount to more than a postcard a year. People don't change that much in five years, Maya. Let alone over the course of a lifetime."

"Yes they do. Look at you, Jupiter. Look at the people you've met, the things you've done since you've shown up. You may not see it but you've changed a great deal since then. Everyone changes; every*thing* changes…it's like the Buddhists say: the world is in a constant state of flux."

Now she's pulling out the big guns. How am I supposed to pull rank on an Eastern philosophy spanning several thousand years?

"…Do you think *we'll* ever see each other again? After this whole fiasco?"

"Hard to say, really. I don't suppose it will be in Nepal again, unless you're given a pardon by Prachanda or whoever comes out on top at the end of this political nightmare. I will say this: I haven't been able to get you out of my head."

I look up to catch her smiling. And not the cutting smirk I usually get but a real smile, a smile a girl gives to a boy to let her know. I like you too, Maya. I like you a lot. No, I don't want to kiss you now, don't want to risk ruining this moment. I'll go take a shower, clean up, cool my jets.

I dig a bar of soap, a razor and a towel out of my pack. Act casual.

"See you *après mon douche.*"

"Alright then. But it's feminine, you know, not masculine."

"...Oh, OK. Right."

I find a cracked sink within a simple cinder-block enclosure. Mirrors, inexplicably, hang on three of the walls. Mosquitoes coast lazily over a tin of stagnant water. Outside, the sun glares down on bone-dry fields.

She likes me...I *knew* it. Suddenly, this trip has another layer of meaning, a new source of excitement, of inspiration. She'd played her hand pretty close for a while, but she's starting to let her guard down a bit. She's back in the room, waiting for me...should I make a move? Was that my signal? Damn, I wish this water would warm up.

As I scrape the cheap blade along my cheek, a gangly man slinks up behind me, wide-eyed as a lemur. His eyes are locked on the back of my head. I never knew shaving could be so captivating. If I wiped my ass, I might draw a crowd. OK, let's play. You want a show? I'll give you a show.

I look into to the mirror on my left, stare intently into the reflection of his eyes. Following my gaze, his eyes meet mine in the mirror... *gotcha!* He laughs uneasily, vanishes.

I can't blame him; we must be quite the spectacle here, with our light skin and hair and our packs full of strange modern gadgets. It's almost as if we're from another planet. '*Hello, earthlings, we come from a planet of consumerism unrivaled in the universe...bring us to your outlet malls!*' They're curious, brazen yet timid; new kids on the edge of a baseball diamond, waiting for a chance to be called up to play.

By the time I get back, Maya is in bed, curled under the covers. A ray of sun drills through a tear in the ragged curtains. I gently set the soap and razor on the nightstand; she rustles under the covers.

"How was your shower?" she asks.

"I'm starting to feel human again."

"Just wait until we get up to into the hills. This might be the last proper shower you take in some time."

"It might be my last shower ever," I say. "Anyway, I hope we don't spend much more time in this shit-hole."

"...I've got a bad feeling about all this, Jupiter."

"It could be worse."

"Yes, but I'm afraid I've started something I shouldn't have."

"What do you mean?"

"I set the wheels in motion; I put the note in the post box. If it wasn't for me, none of this would've happened."

"The wheels were spinning long before you slipped that note to Jack. I jumped on a flight to Kathmandu with a belly full of hash, all banged up on barbiturates, and got chucked into prison. And if it weren't for you, I'd still be there. If this is what it takes to keep me out, I'm all for it. Even if you didn't put that note in the mail, I would have found Jack eventually. I was *meant* to find him. I think somehow, for some reason, you and I were meant to find each other, too."

"How metaphysically charming of you to say that."

Is she mocking me?

"This whole thing, the reason we're all here, it's bigger than us," I say. "That's what I think, anyway. Do you believe in that kind of stuff?"

"...On occasion."

"Well, it seems to me we're just a couple of pawns, getting moved around on a big chessboard of fate."

"Oh, you do?"

I cozy up against her thigh; she draws back. I guess she's not giving in that easy.

"Thanks for coming, Maya, it means a lot to me." I say, nuzzling her shoulder with my clean-shaven chin. "You mean a lot to me."

I'm schmoozing and both of us know it. Half of me wants to get laid and – well, the other half does, too.

Her warmth; her sweet, wet hair...I nuzzle her neck – or try to.

"What are you like?" she says, kicking me in the shin.

"What do you mean?" I stammer.

"Pawns on the chessboard of fate...get off it! Are you just after a shag, then?"

"That's not true. I…you mean a lot to me, Maya. I'm sorry…I thought…"

"You thought I'd just roll over and spread my legs for you, is that it?"

"Maya, gimme a break – that's not it at all."

"Well, you're going to have to do better than a pawn on the chessboard of fate, mate!"

She rolls and wraps the covers around her, dragging them over to the other side of the bed.

She's right…I've got to get better lines. That was downright cheesy. Who am I kidding? I want to fuck her brains out right now, but there's more to it than that.

I really do like the girl, and all she's done for me, though her initial motives were questionable. I can't believe she's still here, wasting her time on me. Why does she bother? She's not the type to latch onto the first new face of the season …she could have her pick of the litter.

A minute passes…then three. She rolls over to face me. Her eyes are shut; her face is very close.

"Maya," I whisper. "I'm sorry."

Her breath flutters against my neck like a feather.

"Maya…"

She's out.

A lizard scuttles across the ceiling, freezes above the whirling blades. I've got to get better lines. I stare at the fan for what feels like minutes. Strange…when you squint, it goes faster. Blink and it stops.

Either way, it's always moving.

The light flips on.

"Way-key, way-key!" chimes Jack.

I raise my head a tad and look about, groggy. I'm spooned against a dozing Maya. Both of us are covered in sweat. I slither away, hoping I'm quick enough for her not to hold it against me.

I'm trying too hard. Don't try to squeeze the peg into the hole; just let things happen. Yawning, Maya stretches her hands in the air and lazily rolls towards me. Opening her eyes, she rolls away abruptly and sits up. A shag; I probably had it written all over my face.

"Where are your fags, Jupiter?"

"On your side."

Snatching a packet of cigarettes off the nightstand, she lights one up.

"Well, it looks like you two have been enjoying yourselves!" He's so annoying sometimes, such a child. Just like Gerard. He keeps hitting buttons until he gets a reaction.

"...Nothing your twisted mind couldn't fathom, I'm sure," snaps Maya.

"I didn't know you smoked, Maya.""I don't – I quit ages ago. Fucking hell!"

"What is it?"

"My stitches – they're bleeding. Quick, hand me that roll of toilet paper."

She rips off a yard of it, bunches it up, dabs it against her stomach.

"Here, let me see," I say, sitting up.

"It's nothing. Really." She stiffens, turns away.

"That's normal," says Jack in an attempt, I guess, at reassurance. "It'll ooze a while before settling. Here, try using some antiseptic with that mess of germs." He lobs a bottle of hydrogen peroxide onto the bed.

Dried blood is smeared across the palms of my hands, too. Shit, she must have lost a fair bit of it.

"I met up with an old partner in crime this afternoon – he gave me a hand with all the loose ends," says Jack. "We're booked to leave for Simikot tomorrow morning at ten."

"Simikot? Are we on a pilgrimage to Kalaish?" asks Maya.

"Simikot is one of the last big towns this side of India. Flying will save us a week of trekking, give us a jumpstart before the winter storms. We fly in, provision and start heading for the border. It's that simple."

"That's got to be some treacherous terrain," says Maya. "We could easily get lost."

"I know the way," says Jack. "Don't you worry about that."

"Jack, don't you think you should take a look at these stitches?"

"No, they're fine," says Maya.

"And how, may I ask, are you going to get *on* a plane without identification?"

"That's all been arranged: new passports fresh visas."

Jack tosses two red-covered passports into my lap. The gold lettering on their covers is illegible, worn off from years of use. I open one, flipping to the front. A water-stained photo of a forty-something guy with short brown hair stares back at me.

Mr Andrew Minihan...Cork...Republic of Ireland.

"I don't look anything like him. You really think this'll fly?"

"I didn't have much to work with. It was a toss-up between that guy and a Saudi national. You look a hell of a lot more like an Irishman than Osama bin Hiding, or whatever his name was."

Maya reaches into my lap and snatches up the other, opens it, flicks through its dog-eared pages.

"German: you've got to be joking."

"I thought the picture was a pretty good match, myself."

"I don't know if my father would ever forgive me for passing myself off as a kraut. He's still got a bit of post-World War sentiment pulsing through his veins."

"It's only for a day, Maya. Security here's pretty lax; nothing to sweat over. They're looking for rogue Maoists, not *bideshis* like us, in these parts. Relax, you're with Uncle Jack now. You kids hungry, by the way? There's a little dive around the corner that serves up a mean batch of *dhal-bhat tarkari*."

Jack...he actually pulled through for us. At least a little. I'm not overly impressed – in fact, I think we'll be lucky to make it past a half-blind night security watchman with these passports – but he made an effort. We are going to do this!

For the first time, I really feel as if we've got a real shot at making it...a long shot, but a shot nevertheless. I guess I can lay my slavery trepidation to rest, but I don't think I'll ever be quite at ease with Uncle Jack at the helm.

Half an hour later, we're sipping 40s of Tuborg beer in a cramped roadside restaurant. Our table is swamped in empty bottles. Jack tilts one to his lips. He's well on his way to smashed.

"Ahh, Tuborg...wherever you are!" he warbles. A young Nepali girl with shiny black hair lifts a serving tray off the table opposite, smiling in our direction. Jack's eyes follow her back through the curtains, thinking what all men think when they're well on their way to getting smashed.

"So what's in...where is it? Simi what?" I question.

"Simikot."

"Why don't we just truck it up to Jumla instead of Simikot?" suggests Maya. "That would avoid the whole passport dilemma. There's a road up to there now, in case you didn't know."

"It's too far from the pass," vetoes Jack. "We'd never make it there in time before winter set in. One good storm and it will be locked up.... Goddamn, that girl over there's on fire! Would you take a look at the ass on her," he stage-whispers.

"Enough with the girl," I whisper back. "Maya is right fucking next to you...have some respect."- I lean back. "So tell us what Simikot's all about, Jack."

"Yes Jack, tell us about Simikot," says Maya. "Have you even been there before?"

"Yes, I've fucking been there before! I told you I've got everything under control, so just relax."

Maya's feeling the same reservations as me. That's good...it'll keep him on his toes.

Jack cocks his head and points his chin towards the black-haired girl as she collects glasses. Swigging his beer, he bellows."*O bhaini! Aaja raati masanga sutna man laagyo?*"

"You cheeky bastard," says Maya. "You *know* that's well out of line!"

I have no idea what Jack said but it's not hard to figure out the sentiment. I'm sure it had something to do with our waitress's ass... or worse.

"I can't believe you just said that to her," Maya admonishes. "Look at her. She can't be a day over fifteen!"

"Hey, they may be sexually repressed but they want it just as bad as we do."

"You'd be better off visiting a brothel if that's what you're after."

"Not a bad idea. What do you say, kid?" He turns to me.

Oh god, how do I get out of this? Would a sick note from mom do the trick?

"A brothel?" I reply. "What the fuck are you talking about?"

"You know exactly what I'm talking about, kid! A little action before we hit the trail."

Don't drag me into this, Jack.

"I...I don't...no."

"Come on, it'll be a kick in the ass. And an excellent cultural experience as well."

I cast a pleading glance at Maya: her eyes slide away and she springs up from her chair, snatching the keys off the table.

"Whatever you do, keep it out of the room. Prostitution may be prevalent here but I assure you it's not legal. I wouldn't think twice about informing the local police of your whereabouts. I'm sure they'd love to get their hands on you two meaty sources of extortion."

Turning to me, she whispers in French.

"Ne lui fais pas confiance. C'est que de la merde qui sort de sa bouche!"

"Qui raconte de la merde?" says Jack.

Maya looks surprised.

"Ah, tu croyais que je ne parlais pas français, hein? Tu sais que c'est mal poli de parler comme ça derrière le dos de quelqu'un."

I didn't catch much of that. I think Maya said he's full of shit...
nothing new there. OK, kids, don't make me pull over this car or I'm
going to start cracking!

"Fine. I'll just come out and say it, then," she snaps. "I think you're
as dodgy as they come and I have just about had it with your antics."
Spinning round, she marches briskly out of the restaurant.

"Don't let the door hit you in the ass, sister," he mutters after her.

"Hey, that's enough."

Thank god she didn't hear him or I might be out of a trekking partner. I'm going to give Jack a swift upper cut if he doesn't cool it.

"Quit pressing her buttons, will you? If she bails, I bail. We're a
package deal, OK?"

"Wow: I didn't know the two of you were that serious already."

Where is your off switch? A kill switch would be more appropriate.

"I'm not sure why you're so set on taking us into the mountains,
Jack, but if you want us along for the ride, you'd better chill the fuck
out."

"Sorry, man. She's always jumping all over my shit like some goddamn schoolteacher. I know you dig her, but sometimes she just rubs
me the wrong way."

"You're the one who's doing most of the rubbing, man. You're acting like a damn Palestinian in a land grab after concessions have been
made. Grow up! You're at least forty years older than she is."

"Alright, alright...I'll be mellow like yellow. So what do you say –
you ready to take a walk on the wild side?"

"I don't know. I'm not really into..."

"Not into what? Women? Sex? Come on, kid, *carpe diem*! This is
one of the only places around where you can get down and dirty with
the natives. Nothing to write home about, but its only one hundred rupees a pop...strictly Nepali prices."

That's less than one and a half dollars. I've never had a hooker before, but something tells me that if I did, I wouldn't go for one at these
bargain-basement prices. A few fruitless experiences at dollar stores in
my teens have made me wary of such 'irresistible' deals. Maybe a light-

er or some postcards if you're desperate – but a lay? Even the toothless crack whores down on Halstead have to charge at least twenty for a blow job…and most of them don't even have full grills. I shudder at the prospect.

"No thanks. I think I'll see what Maya…"

"Come on, man, you don't want to bring sand to the beach! At least tag along for the ride. All these girls, decked out in red like they're about to get married to you. Every day is Christmas, man!"

Tag along for the ride…in high school, I had this friend: his name was Steve Head. In most local households, saying his name was the equivalent of saying 'fuck you' or 'eat shit.' Many a parent banned him from their homes thanks to his mischievous antics. Steve Head always wanted me to come along for the ride, and if I could figure out a way to dupe my parents, I would, which inevitably resulted in some brush with the law. The last time I went 'along for the ride' with Steve, I got arrested for underage drinking and assault with a stolen snowmobile. I heard he's doing five to ten for breaking and entering down in Joliet.

"You won't see anything else like this north of the border. You've got to come, man, just to see it with your own eyes. You can keep lookout while I…"

"OK. OK already. Let's go, then, before I change my mind."

Why did I just say that? Why am I agreeing to this? I'd rather jab bamboo under my nails. I never had any desire to pay for sex, never understood the Charlie Sheen mentality of it all (although I'll still give him props on being upfront about the drugs). There's no fun in it if you have to pay. There's no challenge. And these days, there are plenty of deadly deterrents. Besides, I've got Maya…well, maybe. She'd never forgive me if I did anything like this. I'm not going to throw that all away for a dollar-fifty fuck. I'm just going along for the ride. I'll be the lookout, like Jack said.

Clearing our tab (there's a first time for everything), Jack leads me into a series of side streets furrowed in tire tracks. Clumps of bananas and plastic buckets line the shop doors. Bright-blue light purrs off a welding torch inside a small building littered with scrap metal. The odor of burning metal hits my nose… Smells like misery. A cramp wrenches through my gut. I bend over, take a deep breath.

"Hey man, you good?" asks Jack.

"I think it was the *momos* from the other day."

"It's probably the heroin we smoked last night. It will do that, first time around. Takes some getting used to."

"Heroin? I thought you said that was opium?"

"Heroin, opium, what's the difference?" Patting me on the back, he says, "Hang in there, kid…just a little further."

I stop, lean against the corner of a building.

"Hey, seriously, you alright?"

He's wondering why I feel sick? Sure there wasn't any strychnine in that batch, buddy? I feel like a cheated consumer. It's pretty damn low, telling someone they're smoking one thing when you know full well it's another. It's people like him that make delusional atrocities like the Jonestown massacre possible.

This time, I'm really going to aim for him if I puke.

"If there's no difference, why the fuck didn't you tell me it was heroin, then? Don't you think I'm at least entitled to know?"

"Hey man, an opiate is an opiate."

I can't believe he wasn't straight with me…actually, I can. I'm giving this two-bit con artist too much credit…and way too much of my time and money.

"Why don't I just wait here?"

"Hey, you've got to check this out, man. It's no Patpong but it's worth a look. They'll be all over us if we stick around too long, so we'll have to be quick, though: know what I'm saying?"

"I'm not fucking anybody, Jack. Prostitution has about as much appeal to me as watching televangelists push Jesus paintings on Home Shopping Network."

He laughs.

"Oh, we're going shopping, but we sure as shit ain't buying any damn paintings. *Hallelujah, praise the Lord!*"

Adrenaline buzzes through my veins. Didn't he hear me? Of course he did. Why the hell do I have to hold his hand all the way to the brothel?

"I've seen this all before, Jack. Gerard showed me all there is to see in that department and it wasn't a pretty picture. *I'm not interested*, get it? Do you want me to watch or something?

"Hey, wait up!"

Rounding a corner, we come out onto a street floodlit by glaring electric bulbs, strung on wires between wobbly cigarette stands. Distorted pop music pumps out of speakers.

"Man, some things never change: look at all these *kumaris* gone bad!" he gloats.

Opposite us, a cluster of women dressed head to toe in red – some in *saris,* some in veils – eyes us apprehensively. A man with a cigarette dangling off his lip slithers over like a carnie hustling a ring toss…I'm guessing he's the pimp. The girls begin to chatter like excitable finches. *Step right up, step right up!*

"This cat wants two hundred a pop. That's less than three dollars. More expensive than last time I was in town, but where else can you get pussy for those kind of rates? He says they're practically virgins – lying bastard. But for three bucks, what can you expect?"

Jack says something to the carnie; he signals to the group of girls. I feel like I'm at a deli counter. *'Next, please take a ticket…now serving number 573. Did you order the ham on rye? How many pounds of roast beef, sir? Wait, hold the roast beef!'* My belly starts to rumble.

Pushing one another forward, the girls shriek and giggle. Jack pulls one to his side, shoves money into the man's hand. Nice pick, Tarzan.

"You like this one? She's been around the block but she's not too long in the tooth."

"She's not a fucking horse, Jack," I'm embarrassed by him, to tell the truth.

"Well, she's not bad, huh? What do you think?"

"Jack, I told you already I'm not doing this. Do what you like but I'm not –"

"Hey kid, don't sweat the Pom. I won't say a thing to her, I promise. This is just between you and me. What happens out here stays out here."

Why did he have to mention her? I could be back at the hotel spooning her right now…possibly.

"Jack, she saw me leave with you. As far as she's concerned, I'm guilty until proven innocent. I shouldn't even be here."

My stomach does a flip with a half-twist. Everything's moving so fast. I've got to sit down for a second.

"Aw, don't be such a pill! You're damned if you do and you're damned if you don't. Listen, I paid for both these sluts." He points to two girls: one tubby, the other as skinny as a pin.

"Here's a couple of Trojans; you take the chubby one first. Meet me back here in ten minutes and then we can switch off if you want another twirl…you can thank me later."

"Look, Jack, why don't you double down and I'll –"

"Have a good time," he answers, winking at me.

"Wait. Jack!"

I reach out to grab his arm, miss. I look around…which way is out? My head is spinning – no, everyone else is spinning and I'm standing still…

I can't do this. Where is the EXIT sign?

The tubby girl wraps her hand around my arm, tugging me away. Why do I get the tubby one? Thanks, Jack. And no thanks, I don't want your sloppy seconds. I look at the girl, her eyes caked with mascara. Twenty years old, at most, but already you can see the miles. She eyes me mischievously. This is crazy; I can't do this…I…*goddamnit.*

Alright: a blow-job and that's it.

"*Chigne?*"

"I – I uh, don't speak…"

"*Chigna man laagyo?*"

"I don't understand what you're saying to me."

Oh, yes I do. I don't need to speak a lick of Nepali to know what she's saying…let's get this over with.

Tightening her grip, she pulls at my arm. I twist my hand out of hers, but she grabs it back and lugs me off to a low-slung, decrepit building constructed of cinder blocks. At the center, a family squats on torn pieces of cardboard huddled around a pot of rice. A weathered man in a checkered hat looks up feebly. What a bonus. I get to meet the family, too!

"Listen," I squeeze her hand. "It's OK – you just keep the money. I'm not supposed to be here. I can't…"

She stares at me, puzzled, then, parting a ragged curtain, pulls me into an adjoining room, where a sagging cot sits in the corner.

I'm actually supposed to fuck her while her family eats dinner in the other room? Do I get a hot meal after we're done? This is too much. My stomach…the heroin. I can't…

"…Just take me back…I…"

I lean against the wall, unable to move. I need to sit down for a second, catch my breath…my stomach twists into a pretzel. Jerking me over to the cot, she lies on her back, slides the red skirt up over her waist and spreads her legs.

"*Chigne ho?*"

Go to a happy place, go to a happy place. Palm trees, sunshine, sandy beaches…

A wave of nausea surges through me. I need air. I need to get…out of here. I rush from the room, kicking over the pot of rice, out the door and down the street. Where the fuck is Jack? The rat-eyed pimp materializes out of the shadows.

"*Raamro sanga haanyo?*" He leers at me, blowing a thick puff of smoke in my face.

Fucking parasite. I step backwards, crouch against a cinder-block wall, and heave into the dirt…. that's twice. I haven't puked this many times in a day since slamming beer bongs that day by the lake. Steve Head was there, too, forcing them down my throat…just along for the ride.

A hand slaps my back. "Easy…easy there, kiddo. Hey, don't freak, man!" Wrapping his arms underneath mine, he yanks me into an alley. "Come on, we've gotta bail. I just spotted some pigs down the other way. They'll be all over us if they find us here." I wipe spittle from my cheek, flick it back at him. Jack swings me around; I slump into his shoulder. Someone shouts; two silhouettes materialize at the end of the alley, moving quickly in our direction.

"Come on, kid, I can't carry you."

Nearby, a dog barks.

"*Move your ass*," Jack hisses. "I think the cops are onto us. You don't want to wind up in the slammer again, do you?"

Jack shoots off down the alley. I trundle after him, holding my belly with one hand. Everything is thick with shadow. I can only see Jack's silhouette a few steps ahead. I trip over a bundle of wire and bounce back to my feet. Suddenly, the alley opens out into a vast field of sparse grass. I stop, gasping for air. Looking up, I see Jack bent over his knees panting.

"Whew – that was close! I thought they were going to nab us for a second there. What a rush, man!"

I fight for breath.

"Damn, I feel twenty years younger. You're only as old as the women you feel! So how was it?"

He's just like Gerard: a letch, using whores to quench his insatiable craving for fresh meat…disgusting.

"…I…don't want to talk about it."

"What? You were driving the lane and you missed the *lay-up*?"

Next time, I swear I'm aiming straight for him.

"I don't…I'm not like *that*," I stammer.

"You a switch hitter or something? You like to putt from the rough? Hey, that's cool with…"

Stop pressing my buttons, man, or there's going to be trouble. I'm a half-step away from detonating.

"Fuck you. Why don't you just leave it alone? First you lie to me about the heroin and then you sucker me into this red-light bullshit. You're probably the kind of filth that slips roofies into girls' drinks when they're not looking."

"What the hell is a roofie?"

I guess he wouldn't know what a roofie is, being the dinosaur he is, but I'm sure he'd use them if he could get his hands on them.

"…Yeah, that's just the kind of trash you are. Shit, you'd probably bang a girl in a coma ward just to get a little side action."

"Don't blow smoke up my ass, kid." He spits on the ground. "What are you trying to hide? Are you batting for the other team or what? You might be better off back in Thailand sipping daiquiris with the lady boys."

"*Dickhead*," I snarl.

That's it, you're going down, you piece of shit.

Barreling into his waist, I tackle him. Together, we tumble backwards into a tangle of weeds.

"Hey man, chill out. Don't lay all this heavy...*Ouch – motherfucker!*"

Jerking his leg upwards, Jack drops to the ground like he's taken a fastball in the shin.

"*Fuck* – I've been bit! Goddamn snakes!" He emits a feeble groan.

Cautiously, I move towards him. Snakes? Is he trying to draw me in for a sucker punch? I half-expect him to leap up and come hurtling at me. I resist the urge to kick him in the ribs.

Clutching his ankle, he rolls on his side. No, he's not bluffing. *Man down.*

"*Jesus*: did you see it? Do you think it was venomous?"

"It was a big black fucker...*son-of-a-bitch!*"

"OK. Just stay calm...you've gotta keep still, man. I'll go find someone to get us to a hospital."

"I'm cool, daddy-O, but I'm sure as shit not going to any hospital."

Gerard had said the same damn thing.

"What the fuck to do you guys have against doctors, anyway?" I ask.

"Just get me to a pharmacy...they should have the goods. Wow, I'm really starting to feel it now...must have been a cobra."

A cobra? That's some serious shit! I guess we are in cobra country. The odds must increase exponentially the closer you get to the Indian border. He had it coming, that's for sure. Only the *fer-de-lance* and some vipers edge out a cobra. How long does Jack have before the venom really kicks in? Between the snake wisdom I've picked up from Riki Tiki Tavi and *Crocodile Hunter*, I'd say he's got five to ten minutes before he loses consciousness. Shit, they dropped old Riki in less than a minute.

Swinging an arm around Jack's neck, I prop him up against my shoulder. We begin to hobble across the field towards lights in the distance. Jack probably thinks he's dying already, moving towards that mythical light at the end of the tunnel. Don't give up yet, my man, we're going to get you out of this!

A bead of sweat dribbles off Jack's brow. He totters like a grazed bowling pin on the verge of toppling.

"Just hang in there, man...nice deep breaths..."

"Deep breaths...deep breaths," he rasps.

We step over a muddy ditch onto a dimly lit road scored with tire tracks. Steering Jack with my shoulder, I make for a cluster of concrete buildings. Make it to those buildings, find a policeman or...shit! Not a soul in sight. I hope there's not another *bandh* in effect. Where's a fucking cop when you need one? Where are the ones who were chasing us a few minutes ago?

Suddenly Jack slumps; I catch his weight.

"Come on, big guy! Just a little farther. Keep those legs moving."

Candles weakly from one of the shops. Go towards the light, go towards the light! Jack trips, drops heavily to the ground. I try to heave him up but he crumples like a sack of dirt."Come on, buddy, we're almost there. I can't carry you, Jack!"

"...Just...let me lie...here...a sec."

"Goddamnit, Jack, get up. Do you wanna die out here?"

"Why not? Don't matter to me none."

Jack is drunk with cobra venom, now, raving to himself, slurring his words .... He just lies there, looking up at me with glazed eyes. Dead weight. I tug at his leg...nothing doing. A grimace contorts his face.

"I'll fucking leave you out here! Don't make me fucking leave you here, Jack!"

From nowhere, a man appears on the road. Thank you, god. He is old and gaunt; gray stubble coats his chin. I don't think he's knows what to make of us: two sweaty tourists, zigzagging towards him out of who knows where in the middle of the night.

"Hey, give me a hand!" I shout. "My buddy is hurt bad!"

Flicking his wrist, he asks, "*Ke bhayo?*"

"I don't under..."

"*Nagale tokyo*," Jack responds wearily.

Scuttling to Jack's side, the man puts a sinewy arm around him and the two of us heave ...dead weight. The old guy is pretty small and doddery: it takes everything I have to keep the three of us moving forward. Together, we stumble down the road like a band of shit-housed sailors out on a bender. *Yo ho ho and a bottle of rum!*

Jack's feet keep sliding out from under him. At this rate, he won't make it to the hospital – or anywhere much. He's only got a few minutes left. I reckon he's going down.

I did this...all of this is my fault. If I hadn't shoved him into that patch of weeds, this wouldn't have happened. *Fuck*. Come on, Jack, you're not going to die on me here! Not now, not like this.

We're approaching a building. My little old helper yells out to someone; a voice shouts back. The man gestures animatedly towards the light. OK, it looks like we've got clearance...we're bringing this bird in!

Stumbling into a narrow doorway, we drag his feet over the steps. Another man materializes from behind a glass counter, sets a stool below Jack. We lower him onto it. Sweat trickles down blanched, waxy cheeks. He's mumbling something between labored breaths. The two men speak rapidly to one another, then dash off into the street, leaving us alone.

"Where did they go?" I shake him. "Jack...*Jack*! Where did they go?"

"To go...hunt down some serum...How much money you got on you, kid?"

"...Two, three...four – four hundred and twenty rupees."

"That might cut it...that's one good thing...yeah, baby...the drugs are cheap."

I might as well be talking to a cartoon character. He's gone, watching this whole thing play out from a monitor in the sky. Jack's in the zone now...the death zone. But he's not going to die, 'cos cartoon characters never get hurt.

"Jack, look at me. Just stay with me, buddy, stay with me. You're almost there."

This can not happen. I can't have people dying like this on me. I can't have this scene playing over and over in my head like a clip from a B-grade horror flick. *This is the end... My only friend, the end...* I'll be in therapy for the next decade.

The men reappear, with a pudgy third in tow. Drawing clear liquid from a dusty vial, he extracts a needle, plunges it into Jack's thigh.

Jack grimaces. I hate needles.

"Doc says he's got a bad vibe about the serum...says it's old...says it's gone off."

"What? Then why in the hell did he just give it to you?"

"We need...we need all the help we can get. He's sent for...a *jhankri.*"

"A what?"

"A *jhankri*...a...a shaman."

"You mean a witch doctor? You think it'll do any good?"

"From the looks of that serum...I'll need all the help I can get."

Jack's face is gray now. A sheen of sweat glistens along his jawline. I probably don't look much better after watching that needle plunge into his leg.

The doctor and the shop owner lift Jack off the stool and shuffle him past the counter into the back. I wait for my bout of lightheadedness to pass, then follow them into the back room.

An oil lamp flickers next to a bed. Barely audible, a transistor radio hums in the background. The men ease Jack's bony body onto a cot. He looks so old. One motions to a stool opposite the foot of the bed; I hunch down on it. Panting, he rolls his head erratically like a busted chronometer.

"Fucking snakes...*ma chigne*! Never leave your man...never...

leave..."

I slouch against the wall, shut my eyes. Don't die on me, Jack.

Voices rouse me. The doctor is gone. A guy slouched in the corner scans radio stations sporadically. Jack is silent. I can't tell if he's breathing or not.

A bearded man enters. The aluminum grate at the front of the shop rattles shut. Jack groans softly...he's alive, at least. Another man appears, tall for a Nepali, his head bare save for a wispy tuft at the crown. A long white linen shirt and trousers hang off his lanky frame. Two long garlands of black beads and bells dip down to a worn waist-amulet. Talismans, made from bone and hair, dangle between the necklaces; bands strung with tiny rattles jingle round his ankles. He's the kind of guy you'd expect to find traipsing around America's Burning Man festival, but his grave demeanor dismisses any such frivolous notion.

This must be our *jhankri*.

The bearded assistant holds out a plate filled with rice and sticks of burning incense, gesturing towards me. A blessed snack, perhaps, to accompany the *jhankri* service? I reach out but he pulls it away. What's this all about?

"Paisaa dinos...paisaa dinos ta," he whispers.

"I don't..."

"Paisaa..."

The *jhankri* plucks a coin from the tray. Oh, looks like they're passing the plate around for donations. Sure, I'll pay to see this; I'll even throw in a little something extra if Jack makes it through the night.

I hand him a bunch of crumpled rupees. Raising them to his forehead, the *jhankri* places them on the tray and sets it at the foot of the bed frame. I guess that was enough to cover the bill. I stare at the shaman's eyes but he doesn't seem to notice. Serious dude: he's all business. His lips move incessantly. Gliding past me, he unearths a small, two-headed drum from his robe. Nothing like a little percussion to get your trance on. Flinging a handful of grain over the bed, he begins beating the drum with a long, snake-shaped stick.

"Omm um um um…Omm um um um

Ohh herrrr, ohh herrrr, ohh bhai!

Ahmmmm! Ohh herrrr, ohh bhai, ahmm mum mum mum…

Brrrrrrgh! Ohh bhai…dindindindin…"

Several candles are spaced at regular intervals around the bed… are those aromatherapy numbers? Candles go well with any exorcism, I guess; they help set the mood. I feel like I'm in a lost clip from *Altered States.*

Jack starts to mumble; he's twitching, like a dog running in his sleep.

"Wangdu," he mutters. "Wangdu…never leave…your man…*Wangdu!*"

Wangdu? Person…place…thing? Whatever or whoever Wangdu is, it seems to be troubling him deeply. Has he been possessed?

The shaman hovers over Jack's sweaty pale form, contorting his body rhythmically. Stretching out a hand, he runs it down the length of Jack's body. As it reaches Jack's feet, the hand recoils: looks like he's located the demons. Putting down the drum, he kneels, bows his head close to Jack's ankle, and abruptly spits out a thick, dark liquid. Slick with cold sweat, Jack's head rolls back and forth. His lips mouth inaudible words.

Then the shaman roars out, laughing uncontrollably. Froth bubbles from his mouth like he's some rabid animal. Vibrating violently, he howls, breaking into a frenzied two-step dance accompanied by the clinking of bells and rattles.

I'm getting nervous…this is some way-out shit. I've never seen a grown man foam at the mouth.

"Ahhh ha ha ha! Ohh herrrr, ohh bhai, brrrrrrgh!

Ohh herrrr, ohh bhai, wha, wha, wha…

Hummmhummmhummumum…"

Gradually slowing, the shaman's chant softens into a whisper. Then, lowering his head, he begins blowing over the length of Jack's body. Slumping back against the wall, I close my eyes, letting my mind drift...

What if Jack does die? That would be a blow. As much as I can't stand the guy, with his sleazy chicanery and seat-of-the-pants logistics, he planted the seed. He's given me a roadmap out of here. Even if it's not the smoothest path and the plan sounds a bit hair-brained, it's the one I'm going to follow. If he dies, I'm not going back. I'll walk, swim, raft, crawl –whatever it takes. But I'm not going back...

I'll do it for Jack – no, for myself – but I'll slip him somewhere into the credits, near 'key grip'...

What the hell is a key grip, anyway?

"Ohh herrr, ohh herrrr, ohh bhai

Ha ha ha ha...ohh herrrr, ohh her, ohh herrr..."

Now Gerard appears behind my eyelids. The years have vanished from his face; his beard is neatly trimmed. A long blond ponytail ripples down his back. Wow, he looks pretty damn good. I never thought of him like that – but then Keith Richards didn't look too bad at one point, either.

Gerard looks almost like a *saddhu, s*quatting on his haunches. He extracts a clay pipe from a leather pouch. Inhaling steadily, he hot-boxes the *chillum,* releasing a cloud of smoke. I'm dreaming again, aren't I? I've never seen this man in my life but a little voice is telling me that this is Gerard, that this was Gerard, that this will be...Why are you showing me this? It's the ghost of Christmas past, present and future, all wrapped into one.

This is not the way I will end up. This is not my path. I adhere to a different creed, march to different drum...

This is *not* my path.

Whoosh! The aluminum door slides back; a burst of bright-white sunlight blows out my pupils. Jesus. I can't see a damn thing in here. I cringe against the wall like a vampire exposed. The stool wobbles, slips out from under me.

"Shit."

My neck aches...must have tweaked it sleeping against the wall. I feel like shit, but somewhere between the chanting and the drumming, I must have dozed off. The shaman is gone. Intermittent globs of melted wax, spaced out around the bed, are all that remain of the exorcism.

An exorcism...never thought I'd be involved in an exorcism. Up to now, the closest I've come to an exorcism was asking a *Ouija* board questions on Halloween as a kid. That always used to scare the shit out of me, but it scared Jenny more. Dad grounded me for a month, once, when I chased her around the house after one of our séances, acting possessed.

The pudgy doctor is standing over me. What's the prognosis, doc? If he's dead, I'm gonna have to light out of here real quick. This is like Gerard all over again. Jack's dead = police + questions = prison. They'll slap me silly with charges when they find the dodgy passports on top of everything else. Jack's no doubt a wanted criminal as well...they'll probably tack on another year just for knowing him!

I scan the room for any belongings I might have to pick up in a hurry.

"*Raamro sanga sutnu bhayo?*" he asks. I smile faintly. Is he buttering me up for the 'it was his time to go' speech? *'We did everything we could, but...'*

"...Is he OK?" I ask.

Kneeling, he drops his bag to the floor and checks Jack's pulse. Should I shake Jack down before I hightail it out of here? Interpol will probably be onto this one too... They won't be able to connect these two untimely deaths, will they? They won't be able to connect Jack and Gerard and me... Do they even have Interpol in Nepal?

"*Bachai raheko chha! Biswas garna nasakine!*"

Is that good or bad? Don't toy with me: give it to me straight, doc!

"He's OK?" I give him a tentative thumbs-up. "OK?"

"OK, OK!" he smiles. "Better...but very...tired."

Better but tired: a thumbs-up prognosis by all standards. Rising, the doc scoops up his bag, shoulders it and shakes my hand, proud as a sheriff who's just single-handedly cleaned up a lawless town. Well done, my man! They should name the new hospital wing after you! I suppose he'll hit me up for a life-saving bonus, but I gave the last of what I had to the shaman. He seems more relieved than me. He must have been sweating about that serum he shot Jack up with last night.

The shaman is nowhere to be found. I wonder how much of a hand he had in keeping Jack from kicking the bucket. Probably more than I could imagine. Coming from a land of CAT scans and stethoscopes, I admit I'd been more than a little skeptical but somehow, he *did something*, and whatever it was, it's the reason this reprobate's still breathing.

Maybe I'm giving the doc too little credit. Even though it was expired, the serum probably was the lifesaver. Either way, I'm not giving him any more rupees. I dust off my jeans. Come on cowboy; let's bust outta this town before the cavalry shows up.

"Jack? Jack, can you hear me?"

He shifts, rolls onto his side. His face is flushed again.

"Jack. Wake up, buddy. Time to go."

"I'm not going anywhere," he grumbles.

Oh yes you are. I poke him sharply in the ribs with a finger. He groans.

"Jack...Jack – *wake the fuck up*. We've got a plane to catch, remember?"

"Not today, kid...doctor's orders."

"The doctor said you're better."

"He also said I'm tired. I feel like ass and my immune system got totally tapped out last night with the venom. I need sleep, kid, and lots of it. Old body can't bounce back like it used to."

"Jack, you know if we don't get out of here, you're going to turn into a morning sideshow. We hang around much longer and people will start asking questions. The cops might even show up."

"Let them show up: what the fuck do we have to hide? We're just two tourists who ran into some bad luck," he says.

"We also ran into a couple of whores down in the red-light district last night," I remind him. "What if one of them saw us as we ran off? I'm sure the whole town's abuzz about the two white boys who got their rocks off."

"You gotta chill, man. Nobody's looking for us out here. You're fucking paranoid."

"Maybe I am, Jack, maybe I am, but there was a shaman here last night, for christ's sake. You don't think people are going to *hear* about that? I don't need this kind of press. I'm giving you five minutes to get out of that bed before I roll you out of it myself. What happened to *carpe diem*?"

"Goddamn, kid." Jack growls but in the end, swings his legs onto the floor and levers himself upright.

"Owwwch!" he howls emphatically. "Throttle back on the leg, man!"

"Show some effort, Jack; I can't fucking carry you."

I steer him into a sidestreet, one arm wrapped tight around his torso. We must look quite the pair, staggering down the main drag like a couple of horny street dogs who've been up all night, chasing bitches in heat. I always feel guilty, walking around like the living dead in last night's clothing after a rough night out. Most of this guilt can be attributed to my Catholic upbringing. This time, though, it isn't by choice.

I hope Maya didn't book out of town already. I wouldn't blame her if she had. As far as she knows we've been out whoring all night. I've got some explaining to do when I get back…if she's still there.

"Oh man. I feel like I was shit out sideways through an elephant's ass! Nothing like a dose of neurotoxins to stiffen up the arteries."

Shut up, Jack…and stop leaning on me like a damn bag of bricks. I can't fucking carry you…I know you can walk better than that, you lazy bastard.

A broken-down horse hauling a wooden cart plods past. For a second, I think about tossing Jack onto the cart and paying the owner to carry him out past the city limits. If I only had some rupees left.

"Fuck, I could use some of that opium now. Maybe there's a couple resin hits left."

Fumbling through his pants, he pulls out a pipe; I snatch it from him.

"Jesus Christ, stash that. Are you fucking crazy?"

"As much as possible," he rasps, then coughs, retches, spits. What a fucking train wreck.

"Jack, look around you for a second...*look*. Everyone is checking us out. We're already the main attraction; we look like we've been up all night...and you want to blaze up a ball of opium, front row center? Keep it up and I'll lay you down right in the middle of this road. I swear I'll do it!"

"OK, OK. I give up. You got me, officer." He hacks up a ball of phlegm and holds his hands up to the sky.

"Damn it, Jack!"

I catch him as he sways, loses his balance...I should have tossed him on that cart when I had the chance.

"That's a nasty cough you've got there," I say. "You should lay off the cigarettes and other stuff for a while."

"No worse than yesterday...*yesterdaayyy...all my troubles seemed so far awaayyyy...*"

Yeah, I hear you on that one. If we don't make that plane it looks like they'll be here to stay...*oh, I believe in yesterdaayyy*. Actually, I stopped believing quite a while ago.

We totter into the courtyard of our hotel. A man drinking tea stares over his paper. Guilt wells up inside me ...he *knows* where we've been – at least, he *thinks* he knows. Almost there, on the home stretch now. Our door is open a crack. Did Maya leave already? Shit.

I kick the door open; it swings forward, reverberates against the wall. Maya pokes her head out of the bathroom, a towel wrapped around her hair. Still here...but she's not happy.

"Boys out on the piss, eh? Lovely!"

Oh shit, here it comes: she's going to rip our heads off and eat them for appetizers. I half expect lasers to come shooting out of her eyes and bore smoking holes through my heart.

I hump Jack over to the bed and flop him down. I'm not sure if the snake bite will be a sufficient alibi.

"Goddamn, I said to go easy on the leg." He groans.

"Sorry we're so late. Don't worry, we're still on line…we ran into some unexpected difficulties last night and…"

"Unexpected difficulties? Is that so?"

'Hurricane Maya, gaining in strength and bearing down on us with alarming accuracy, has just been upgraded to a Class 4. She is considered highly dangerous. Evacuation orders have been issued. Attempts are being made, even as we speak, to divert her path of destruction. Meanwhile, weary, weather-beaten residents wait in fear.'

"…We got tied up last night," I explain lamely.

"Tied up? What, like they tied you up and had their way with you? Don't look so surprised. Did you think I couldn't tell? Or maybe you were hoping I wouldn't broach the subject…you fucking sod. I know you two went out looking for a shag."

Here comes the eruption I've been waiting for. Jack rolls his eyes. Luckily, he's out of her view. Should I duct-tape his mouth shut before proceeding?

"Hey, it's not like that, Maya. OK, we went to a brothel but I didn't… Seriously, nothing hap…"

"I really can't be bothered."

"But Maya, I swear I didn't…"

"I don't want to hear it – I just hope you used a condom, for your sake. There's enough AIDS floating around this country as it is."

I look at her. Head down, she's shoving clothing furiously into her pack. I'm such a bad liar. Classic 'tells' are written all over my face. Even when I'm just feeling guilty, it looks as if I'm lying. I'd be the world's worst con man.

"Hey kid, you want to finish off this bowl? There are still a few resin hits left," says Jack.

Love you too, Jack. How about I chuck you in an incinerator and get a contact high off your burning flesh? You just had to put another log on the fire, didn't you? Superglue would be better than duct tape...that might do the trick. Feed him through an I.V. drip or a hole in his neck.

"What did I come here for, Jupiter?" whines Maya. "I mean, really, why am I here? To get stoned with you and Jack and revisit the ghost of hippie past? To add a woman's touch on an arduous trek? This was a mistake from the start. Do what you have to do but for me, this is not worth the aggro...I'm out."

"Wait a minute, Maya," I say. "You can't go back now."

She stuffs a stray shoe into her pack.

"Oh, I can't, can I?"

"But look at how far we've come."

"And how far is that, Jupiter? A few hundred kilometers away to some tip in the Terai? We're nowhere, Jupiter, *nowhere*. You think you're going to make it over that pass? You have absolutely no idea of where you're going and what you're up against. Count me out."

"You can't go back now, Maya – it's too dangerous, I assert. "What about the Manangi gangsters?"

"The kid's right – go back to the Kat now and they'll find you," Jack adds. We're committed now. We've got to see this thing through."

"What *about* gangsters? I really can't be bothered," she says. "I don't have to stay here. I can take a holiday in India, go visit my mates in England, whatever. My father can have me on a plane quicker than the king of Nepal... if there still *was* a king. .

"And just what the fuck is this *thing* we've got going here? We're going to Simikot and then what? Pray tell, Jack, or I'm on the next bus back to the valley."

"Hold on there one second. How is it that your daddy can have you on a plane so quick?" Jack may be stoned a lot, but he doesn't miss much.

"That doesn't concern you," she replies, cool as water.

Shit, she slipped. If Jack figures out who her father is, I could be out of a mountain guide...or worse. Something tells me things could get ugly quick if Jack gets hot under the collar. Quick, Maya, make something up. Don't throw in the towel yet.

"So what line of business is the old man in, Maya? He sounds pretty well connected."

"If you must know, he's a banker, Jack."

"Right here, in Nepal? Not much volume of cash flowing through here, I'd have thought..."

"Oh, you'd be surprised. And yes, he is well connected."

"Laundering the ex-royals' accounts, is he?"

"I'm not even going to entertain that question."

Nice volley, Maya.

"Banker, huh? Interesting...I mean, you work for the embassy, your daddy works for a bank...sounds like you've got yourselves dug in pretty deep over here. What about mum, does she have a hand in the cookie jar as well? Or does keep herself busy with fundraising dinners for orphans and charity balls? I'll bet she's a real hit with the Ranas."

"My mother's *dead*, Jack. If you mention her again, I'll shop you to the police, I swear. Is that clear enough?"

Her face is flushed. She's livid. *Whoa!* Good show, Maya. That clammed him up, didn't it? He's got nowhere to go with that pitch.

I guess some of that anger was meant for me, but I'll let Jack take the heat. He had it coming.

"How the hell was I s'posed to know that your mom –"

"*Do not mention her*, you sod."

Maya kicks him sharply in the calf.

"*Ouch!*"

Jack buckles slightly, rubbing his ankle. Damn, right on the bite; that's got to hurt.

"Hey. *Eaasy*," I interject.

"*Fuck a duck.*" Jack groans. "Get her out of here, kid, before she kills me!"

Really, Maya: superb acting. You should be up for an Academy Award: Best Supporting Actress in an Asian thriller...Oh god, she's not joking.

Dead? I thought...she'd said she left them...she's going to cry. *Damage control!*

I hustle Maya out of the room, plant her on a stool at the end of the hall and crouch down next to her. "I'm sorry, I couldn't. I couldn't... tell you." She's stammering.

"Hey, hey," I coo. "It's OK....*shhhhhh.*"

Her eyes are red-rimmed from crying. I hug her; keep hugging. Gently, we rock back and forth.

"Shhhhhh......shhhhhh."

"Oh, I'm so embarrassed," she says after a longish while, sitting up and brushing her eyes with a sleeve. "I haven't cried like that in ages."

"Sometimes it's good to cry," I venture. "It's good to let things out."

I wish I could cry like that...it might wash my brain of this guilt that's been brewing inside me like a cheap merlot.

I didn't cry at my old man's funeral. Not one tear. I should have been the one crying the most, the one buffeted with hankies, sobbing in the corner. Everyone said 'It wasn't your fault' but they were only reading from the script. Other, darker thoughts were invading their minds: thoughts of filial treachery, no doubt bolstered by the grieving widow's vacuous stare. And the fact that she kept a minimum of four feet between herself and her not-so-grieving son at all times.

She thought it was my fault and she wanted the world to know. She wanted me to pay.

Still does.

"I'm sorry, Jay," says Maya. "...I wanted to tell you earlier. I never knew my mum, never even saw a picture ...d'you know what that's like? My dad had no photographs of her – not a single one. I thought he was lying at first; I'd scour the flat looking for a snapshot, a lock of hair, an old brooch – never found a thing. I don't think he could stand to keep anything of hers.

"He told me my mother was beautiful – so beautiful it hurt him, sometimes, to look at her. He was floored, devastated by her loss. I could hear the pain in his voice whenever he spoke of her. 'So brilliant; so fragile...like an orchid,' he'd say. But mostly, he said nothing. I guess the way he coped was to act as though she never existed.

"So, in a way, the orchids were all I had. As a kid, I wanted orchids all over the house. My room was a botanist's shrine. I would whisper to them as if I was talking to my mum, like some people sit around a coma patient's hospital bed, telling them bits of news from the world still going on around them in the hope that one day, they'll come back from the dead.

"...It was all a bit daft, I suppose, talking to plants like somehow I'd break through to the spiritual world that way. But in the back of my mind I kept hoping, and that was the only link I had, the only thing I could remember her by.

"I'd tell the orchids if I did well in the piano recital, show them my pictures, confide in them about the new boy in school – or not, the usual lot. Some days, I'd just sit and listen…and wait…of course, they never answered.

"So when Jack made that offhand comment about mother raising funds for orphans, I suppose it struck a chord.

Don't think that I was keeping it from you, Jay," she says. "It's just something I tend to tuck away in the back of my mind. She died while giving birth to me. Father only tells me that there were complications. Being stuck out in the backwaters of a third-world country, I can only imagine. I think he secretly wishes it was me who died and not her."

I catch a tear sliding down her cheek.

"Hey, don't beat yourself up like that," I say.

I hug her again. After a while, she sits up straight like a child and wipes her eyes.

"...Everything else I've told you is true – everything about my schooling, my father, Burma…all of it."

"Hey Maya," I say. "Look at me…that's OK. Don't worry, it's no big deal. I believe you, really. But you've got to believe me, too. I went with Jack to a whorehouse last night but seriously, nothing happened. I care about you too much to do something like that…I swear it."

She puts her arms around my neck. Just like that.

"I knew you didn't want to have anything to do with it," she says. "But I don't understand why you let that charlatan putty you into corners. If you have any intention of pulling off this mission, you've got to be stronger than that.

"I'm worried about you, worried that you're in over your head. If you're not careful, Jack could rob you and push you into a crevasse. Who would ever know?"

She really thinks I'm a country bumpkin, doesn't she? Come on, I got this far. I don't need a lecture from a twenty-something misfit on employing better judgment.

"Maya, I don't trust Jack any more than I'd trust a coked-up arms dealer. And he's the biggest pain in the ass I've ever met. But I doubt he's going to con me."

"Look," she says, "You don't have to carry on with this if you don't want to. You can come back to Kathmandu with me. The Immigration Office might not have even missed you yet, what with all the holidays. And if they did, I'm sure we can sort it out. You don't have to do this, Jupiter."

"...What about your dad? He's got connections?"

"It's...it's not that simple," she says.

"Why not? You said yourself that he could get you on a plane in no time. If he can get me out of the country, I promise I'll pay him back every rupee of the bond. I'll pay him double!"

"He can't do that, Jupiter. He's only a counselor for fuck's sake. Do you know how many favors he used up to get you out of jail in the first place? He must be going spare right now, wondering where we've run off to."

"Then the answer is no. If you want to leave, then, that's your choice: I'll pay for your ticket back and make sure you get home safely. But you need to know that I *want* you to come...I want you to come more than anything. If you don't, I'm going to give it my best shot, but somehow I know that if you do come, everything will work out in the end.

"I know it sounds cheesy, but you inspire me to get through all this mess. It's like you're a constant in this whole slew of variables. You keep it together for me..." I trail off.

"Maya, I'm begging you: come with us."

That did sound cheesy, didn't it? Shit, I actually begged her. I must sound downright desperate. Carry on like this much longer and she'll definitely be on the next bus back to Kathmandu.

"...Besides, if you don't, I might wind up in a crevasse like you said. What do you say?"

I'm digging low now, pulling the guilt card out of my hat. If she bails...I don't want to think about it.

She tucks a strand of hair behind one ear.

"He's part of the deal, then?" she asks.

"I don't like the way he treats you, I don't like the way he treats women. I've got my doubts about this whole hare-brained scheme but it's all I've got right now. Without him, I can't do this."

"...Alright, then," she says, finally. "I'll come. But I'm doing this for you. I want to have as little to do with him as possible. And you need to make sure he stays in line –otherwise I will leave, I promise you that."

Keep Jack in line? Is that even possible? "Well, then, we'll have to pick up a tranquilizer gun and some ketamine on our way out of town."

It's lame, but she laughs. *I can still make her laugh.*

"Why don't we go see how the untamed beast is doing?" I say.

"Yeah, cool."

"You sure you're alright?"

"Yeah," she smiles.

Jack rubs his shin delicately, like it's a newborn pup.

"How's the leg feeling? She got you pretty good, didn't she?"

"I can barely walk, for christ's sake," he winces. "Beat up on an old man, why don't ya?"

"Oh, please," says Maya.

"It's true, Maya, so just chill out. A snake bit Jack last night – right where you kicked him, as a matter of fact."

Jack lifts his shin as I point out the vampiric marks on his ankle.

"You could have kicked my good leg." "Why didn't you say something earlier?" says Maya, unsympathetic. "Are you sure you're up to flying?"

"Yeah," says Jack. "Why not? Nothing a few shots of Demerol and a hash pipe can't handle."

"That's the last thing you need in your state," rebukes Maya. "It would only be another shock to your immune system."

"My system would go into shock *without* it. Hell, I don't think I've gone a day without for over thirty years."

"How impressive," Maya snaps. "Did you want a medal or something?"

"Both of you, stop it." Am I going to have to play mediator all the way to the border?

"Jack, if you get nabbed at the airport carrying shit, you're going to wake up with more than a swollen leg."

"Idle threats," he grumbles.

"We'd better hustle if we're going to catch that plane." I'm impatient now. *Let's go* before anyone changes their mind.

"The kid's right. We've only got two hours before lift-off."

"You know as well as I do that it'll be an hour late."

"If we're lucky, but we can't risk missing the flight. If it rains up there they'll shut down the airport for at least a couple more days. There's a monastery a few days out of Simikot; I've got some old friends up there. We can hole up there and regroup before the pass. Listen, I'll lay all my cards down once we get there. Can we just fucking go now?"

"Hhmph," snorts Maya. "It's like pulling teeth with you."

She winches down the straps on her pack.

"So sassy," sneers Jack.

She stops, twists around. "What are you on about?"

"Your style. I like the 'get fucked' attitude," Jack parries.

"How unfortunate," she retorts, looking daggers at me all the while.

Go ahead: kick him again, Maya, you're a big girl. I've got your back. A little pressure on that snake bite will do the trick.

"Well, bear with me a few more hours, honey. We're married, you know."

"What?"

Gloating, Jack lobs his passport across the room. Maya grabs it, flips hastily to the front.

"Absurd. You're old enough to be my grandfather! The lady in this photo looks twice my age."

"They were the only passports my guy had left."

"So we're going as a couple, are we? I'll give you fair warning then: don't do anything foolish or I'll shop you straight out. Is that clear?"

"Whatever's clever."

"...And I'm not your honey, you old letch."

Voices bounce softly off the inner walls of the terminal like Jell-O. I watch the last of our packs get carted out to the runway...hoping we'll see them again.

"Alright, everyone," says Maya. "Don't forget names and birth dates, names and birth dates."

Andrew Minihan...Cork, Ireland...January 11ᵗʰ...*fuck.*

I crack open my passport; I look nothing like him.

"1970," I chant. "Andrew Minihan...Cork, Ireland...January...11ᵗʰ, 1970."

"Why don't I hold onto the passports, honey," cajoles Jack. "We know how you tend to lose things."

She slaps the passport into his palm.

"Don't push it."

He's back to his old self again, much to our dismay. Maya starts off first – Jack follows, casually draping an arm around her shoulder. So help me god, Jack, if you blow this thing now...

Blue fatigue-clad soldiers in berets. *'Warning, Bill Robinson: metal detectors dead ahead!'*"Here we go again," I mutter.

I fall into line. Adrenaline surges through me. Keep it steady, keep it steady. Don't blow a fuse...

I take a deep breath. Jack hands their passports to a steely-faced soldier with a rifle slung over his shoulder. All of a sudden, his face lights up like a Jack-o-Lantern. Beaming, he turns to Maya.

"Ich habe in Frankfurt fuer ueber fuenf Jahre gelebt, und waehrend dieser Zeit fuer das Britische Militaer gedient.Und sie kommen aus Alzei, das ist ja in der Naehe von Frankfurt, wo ich gelebt habe. In der Fruehlingszeit bin ich oft nach Alzei gefahren, um die schoenen Weinkeller zu besichtigen."

Maya, flustered, casts a distraught glance at the soldier. What the fuck is going on? Was this once a German concession or something? Have the Stasi finally caught up with us? Shit, it's those fake IDs. People are watching, Maya, let's not blow this thing. At least try to speak *wit a Zherman aksent.*

Clearing his throat, Jack chimes in.

"Ja, ja! Der Eein in Alzei ist wunderbar. Als Kind ging ich zu dem Garten mit meinem Vater."

Raising Maya's passport to her face, the soldier asks, *"...Und ist diese ihre Frau?"*

Jack takes Maya's hand in his.*"Ja, Liebchen, wie lange ist es nun her...sechs Jahre?"* he replies.

The soldier scrutinizes Maya, then counters, *"Auf dem Foto sieht sie aelter aus, nicht wahr?"*

Jack squeezes Maya's hand, laughs. *"Danke, es ist night haufig daß wir das ueber unserer frauen sagen konnen!"*

"...Ich – ich nehme nicht an....Ja, sicher, da haben sie recht. Ich wuensche ihnen weiterhin einen schoenen Aufenthalt in Nepal," the soldier replies, cracking an almost-smile.

"Danke, danke!"

Handing the passports back to Jack, the soldier ushers them through. I have no idea what just happened, but it seems whatever rabbit Jack pulled out of his hat has worked.

Andrew Minihan…Cork…January 11ᵗʰ, 1970. Andrew…*luck of the Irish, luck of the Irish.*

Drawing Andrew's, or should I say *my* passport from its sleeve, I hand it to the officer. He flips through its pages skeptically. Is he going to start grilling me about the inner meaning of the Blarney Stone? Will he want me to recite limericks? Hey, I can hold my liquor. That'll be enough, surely.

"Aye, 'tis an old picture to be sure," I say.

I sound more Scottish than Irish. But it's enough. Handing the passport back, he waves me through the detector.

After a feeble body search and a quick visa inspection, I catch up with Jack and Maya.

"What the fuck was that all about?" I say. "I thought our number was almost up. Nice move with the German, Jack."

"Just our luck to run into a goddamn ex-Gurkha who'd been stationed in Germany. What are the fucking odds on that?" He nods to Maya.

"So what's next, Flash?" I say. "Let's keep it exciting, shall we? Why don't we hijack a plane and fly wherever the fuck we like? Maybe a quick stop-off in the Maldives before we hit the hills. What do you say, Jack? Or don't you know how to fly a plane?"

"You know," he says, "I thought you were gonna blow it back there, Maya. But we made it, didn't we, honey?"

"I'm not your honey, you bastard. I can't believe you told him I was your wife!"

At least they're still talking to one another.

"I'm no security expert but were those metal detectors even plugged in? They didn't even check my bag, but it got a little tricky with the pop German quiz."

"That was just bad luck. Anyhow, flying into another country, any country, would be worse than that. But you saw how I got us out of that jam, didn't you? That right there should be enough to let you know I've got things under control."

Bad luck. Let's see, in my past three attempts at flying, I've been borderline detained, arrested, and given a twice-over...and we haven't even left the ground on this one yet. Seems I've got an affinity for stirring up trouble with aviation personnel.

Without trying to sound like a self-help program, I'm going to go out on a limb here and say it's more like 'bad choices.' But with Jack playing the wire, I'm not sure I can turn our 'luck' around. Maybe that damn *dzi* can.

"Listen to me; these passports are stolen," says Jack. "Here, we can get away with that, but everywhere else they've got scanning computers. My guy even added fake visas. But you try and skip to another country on these secondhand jobs and ten to one, they'll nab you. It's all biometrics these days.

"Believe me, where we're going is the one of the best spots in the world to slip between the cracks."

There's that cheap salesman twinkle in his eye. I've slicked back his hair and penciled in a mustache in my mind. *'It's Jack, the wonder guide! Passports, visas? Who needs them? Have I got a deal for you! Why fly elsewhere when you can see the beauty of the Himalayas and escape justice at the same time?'* I feel like farmer Bob from the rolling plains of Iowa, in a bona fide city for the first time ever, about to buy his first car...his first used car. Maya, my wife, looks on nervously as Jack, smooth-talking salesman, feels me out for all I'm worth.

'Jeez, honey, I know it doesn't come with any guarantee but it's such a great deal! That rattle is only when she warms up, and the transmission is as good as new, just like the guy says. Golly, she's a peach, isn't she?'

'...OK, dear, if you say so.'

A little voice tells me there's going to be a catch – something hidden in the small print. Jack hands me a pen and I sign...on the dotted line. *Pre emptor caveat.*

"Do you mind taking that *dzi* off your neck, kid?," suggests Jack. "We don't want to attract attention."

With you around, how could we not?

A wind vane flops around on top of a radio tower. I follow the flow of people to a massive orange helicopter some twenty yards off. A helicopter. I'd expected something more along the lines of a barnstorming biplane. Helicopters are dangerous; every movie ever made about the Vietnam War affirms this. A lone sniper fires a single shot from the jungle into a copter's tail blade and the whole thing goes twirling off into the side of a mountain...*BLAM!*

A white guy in an olive jumpsuit and mirrored shades strikes a heroic pose at the head of the stairs...Hey, *Top Gun* revisited. I hope he knows what he's doing.

"Yo Maya, check out the tough guy," I say.

"At least he looks the part."

Well, confidence is good. But I need more than looks to be certain. Are they actually certified pilots or are they paid to look the part, like captains' doubles on cruise liners, decked out in white jackets with shiny epaulets and always available for dinner?

"Hey Jack – I think you and our pilot must have bought your shades at the same bargain basement sale."

"Give me a break, man, I'm stuck in the seventies," he replies.

Cicadas buzz incessantly like distant lawn mowers. A dozen-odd vultures circle lackadaisically overhead in a hazy sky. Are they waiting for us to crash? Better odds of that, I guess, in this third-world outpost. I ignore the omen and attribute their proximity to an adjacent garbage dump.

"See these puppies?" says Jack, pointing to the helicopter. "They're old Russian jobs: palmed off to King Mahendra in a play against China, back when Mao and Stalin were at each other's throats. Russian pilots, Russian mechanics, Russian everything. They're worn to the bone, but not half as bad as those Aeroflot deathtraps rattling around China."

Thanks for that snippet of trivia, Jack. I feel so much safer.

Inside the 'copter, a circular bench flanks the cabin perimeter. All our baggage is lumped in the center like a poorly laid bonfire. Now all we need is a match to get this party started. Little placards holding words with way too many consonants dot the interior. I scoot down the bench, pressing up to Maya. A stout woman slumps next to me, a stray roll of fat bulging out of her sari. We're packed in tighter than buckshot but I don't care.

"Was Jack's little factoid speech supposed to have a calming effect on us?" I whisper.

"Not to worry." She pats my leg.

At least she's not nervous – or she's trying hard not to show it. A bag bulging with strange fruit, red, yellow and orange, is pressed hard against my back.

A woman in a bright-hued *sari* with shiny hair passes around a dish of candies...and cotton wool? What's that for? Wiping our sweaty brows? It's like the low-budget version of Singapore Airlines.

Grabbing something that resembles a jawbreaker, I pass the dish on to Jack. He takes a chunk of cotton, stuffs a wad of it into each ear. Cotton wool: the third-world's answer to earplugs.

An elderly woman across from me glances about apprehensively as the blades begin to churn. *Fffffth...fffffth...fffffth...fffffth...fffffth, fffffth*, like a giant locust prepping its wings for flight. Seconds later, the roar of the engine drowns out our anxious voices, the 'copter shifts forward, and we levitate into the sky...

Up, up and away.

"Loud sons-of-bitches, aren't they?" Jack screams into my face.

Nodding, I shift around to peer through the thick round window at my back. Fields transform into a vast patchwork quilt, then give way to forest and foothills. I take a last look back; the only way I'll be returning here will be in a pine box.

A weathered man shifts a cage of terrified chickens between his legs. A Nepali 'copter ride just wouldn't be complete without chickensA minute ago, we were down on the plains. Now snow-clad peaks stand stoically like ancient druids' stones. 'Come if you dare,' they say. 'You'll be lucky to pass.' One of the caged chickens flaps wildly. A puff of feathers wafts upward. The nauseating smell of diesel fuel seeps into the compartment and we fall silent, determined not to puke.

Maya, meanwhile, is glaring out at the mountains as if they were the enemy. The mighty Himalayas: some of the biggest, most daunting mountains in the world. How many men have been sucked into their folds and cracks? Damn pretty to look at, but they'll swallow you whole if you're not careful. You mess up: you pay with life and limb.

Doubts and fears well up inside me as we zigzag our way past jagged peaks and dizzyingly deep valleys. This is real. Forget your skepticism. Leave your trepidation back with the snakes and the shamans: this is no place for uncertainty, no place for the faint of heart.

I press my face against the window, scanning ahead as the copter weaves upwards through the canyon. Somewhere up there, we are going to cut a path, cross a pass into freedom. Somewhere up here lies the answer.

"We're really up in it!" I shout.

"In it to win it, baby!" bellows Jack.

That's right, we're going to win this war...or die trying. We're going to beat those stodgy old mountains 'cos we've got game...OK, I'm starting to sound like a NBA commercial.

Prisms of sunlight pierce the window, reflecting off the snow.

Gradually the helicopter drops down...down...down, and the canyon opens into a broad, flat plateau. Houses are scattered throughout a latticework of green and brown fields.. Shangri-La, here we come.

"We're pretty damn low...is this guy gonna crash-land or what?" I yell at Jack.

"Chill out, my man. They land 'em like planes." His hand glides downwards, slides across my knee. So much for my simplistic notions of physics. Surging forward, the helicopter edges closer to the ground. Closer...closer...*BAM*! Billows of dust churn up as we bounce down the runway. The rotors gradually slow, the din diminishes... grinds to a halt.

I step out onto the stairway. A fierce wind sandblasts my cheek. Soldiers are everywhere.

"Over here!"

Squinting, I look up to see Jack waving. The wind is screaming like a witch on fire...blowing forty, maybe fifty miles an hour. *It's fucking cold!* Ducking out of the rotor wash, I turn my back to the onslaught and spit out a few grains of dirt. Tastes more like Kabul than Simikot. We've definitely scaled a few rungs on the climate ladder. The air is dry and thin, the land worn.

Maya runs up, wrapped in a dark blue shawl with only her eyes exposed. Smart thinking, girl; I should get myself one of those.

"Man, I can't believe they actually landed in this crosswind," jibes Jack.

A group of men laboriously coaxes a wagon towards us; others pluck luggage off it, giving new meaning to the term 'baggage claim area.' Sand is everywhere: I can barely keep my eyes open between gusts. It feels as if I'm looking through a thick strip of gauze. We've become trapped in a huge snow globe with some gigantic, demonic child pitching us about for laughs.

Over the screeching of the wind, I pick up the drone of an approaching plane. I turn to see small, single-engine plane wavering towards the runway, a helicopter tailing it in the distance. Without warning, the plane veers to its side; its wings angle dangerously close to the ground. The helicopter lingers for a moment, then arcs sharply upwards. The struggling plane suddenly rights itself and its landing gear slams into the packed-dirt runway.

Whoops and shouts erupt from a crowd that's gathered behind a wire fence atop a ridge to our left. I'm not sure if they were rooting for a safe landing or a crash. *'Thank you for coming out and supporting the Daily Himalayan Air Extravaganza: we hope you enjoyed the show.'*

"Put a tent on that circus!" exclaims Jack.

Slinging our packs over our shoulders, we head towards the throng at the fence. As we approach, a series of eager greetings erupts from the assemblage.

"Hello. Hello, sir! Where you go? Kailash? You need guide? I be your guide – good guide! Hello, *saathi!*"

"You need hotel? Hello!"

As we pass through the fence, a man with a gritty, scaly face shoves a bracelet into my face.

"Hello, you buy! Very old – antique. Hello!"

Here we are: Thamel revisited, minus the smog and autos and with a substantial increase in elevation. Where's a rickshaw to whisk you away when you need one?

Jack plows through the crowd with Maya and I in tow. Before Asia, the only looks I've ever gotten from strangers were from suspicious cops; all this attention makes me feel almost famous. Attaining celebrity status just by being white…imagine. You can live your entire life in obscurity, then gain instant rock-star status simply by entering Central Asia.

Yes, we'll be releasing our upcoming album this spring, and we're going to kick off our international tour in Delhi next week.' 'Hello… friend!' 'Please, no more paparazzi, no more questions!'

We follow a path hemmed by waist-high fences of carefully placed stones. Winding downwards, we descend into the town. Spotting us, a child throws his arms into the air and wails.

"*O Godaa! O Godaa!*"

I'm guessing that means something like, 'The white men are coming; the white men are coming!'

A leathery-skinned woman chortles from the shadow of a porch. Stone fences flow around houses and down streets, constructed with such precision that they look as if they were put together from a huge Lego set.

Stone houses, stone fences, stone paths: everything here, it seems, is built out of stone… *'The 2,567,149-piece, life-sized Himalayan Village set, complete with action figures.'* Atop a handful of roofs, satellite dishes tilt towards the sky, mechanical sunflowers turning towards unseen signals.

I wonder what the shipping would be on a Lazy Boy recliner from the Home Shopping Network. For the sake of posterity, I hope they don't get *Jersey Shore* here.

The path widens into a flagstone-paved street. Weaving through a herd of goats, I follow Jack into a small two-story house with a white flag strung on a pole above it, whipping about madly. Is that the sign of a smugglers' 'safe house,' the symbolic equivalent of the quilt on the front porch of the abolitionist's house? It must be religious.

Behind me, the door squeaks shut and Maya peels the shawl from her head.

"Well, we're not going anywhere today in this shitstorm!" says Jack. "Besides, I'm still feeling a little worn out after last night's escapades."

"Yeah," I agree. "You look like shit."

"Thanks, asshole."A lean brown man with silver hair enters from the back, eyeing our packs with that look. The look that tells you he thinks you're crazy for coming up here and wasting your money, but he'll help you waste it just the same.

In the States, you might find one of his kind sitting on an overturned milk crate chewing tobacco, next to a filling station. *'Out-of-towners, eh? Don't think them fancy packs can save you from those mountains, no sir.'*

"Tintaa dudh chiyaa haamilai dinos!" says Maya.

Beaming, he disappears behind a curtain.

"Maya, no offense – but from here on out, no more Nepali unless absolutely necessary," says Jack. "It could be dangerous."

"Dangerous? I hardly think so."

"Considering our circumstances, yes. Speaking Nepali is going to shine a spotlight on us wherever we go. And we're in Maoist country now. You know how they feel about Uncle Sam. We're the reason the Nepali army has an endless supply of shiny new weapons and has been given the international green light to mow stray Maoists down. We're OK here with the over-abundance of soldiers, but if you start chiming in and showing off your command of the local lingo, they're going to suspect something untoward, like that you're CIA, before you can even show them your passport."

"But we're German and Irish, remember?"

"Forget the passports. We'll be lucky if we just got beaten up and robbed. They might even get creative and try to avenge what happened to their boys back in Iraq. No more Nepali, Maya: that's a fucking order."

It's good to see Jack taking charge, but I'm not so sure he should be issuing orders yet. Not unless he wants another swift kick to the shin.

"How are we supposed to buy a cup of tea and biscuits, then?" she asks.

"Just like every other foreigner that comes up here, Maya."

"Only a handful of foreigners come up here every year. I'll bet even the local English teacher can't speak English."

"You can play the charades just like everyone else. It might take a little longer but it will help us keep a lower profile."

"That's going to put quite a dampener on communication."

"Don't worry; we won't be running into too many people where we're going."

"And where's that, exactly?" asks Maya.

"North by northwest...exactly," he replies.

Their ongoing feud is killing me. They both need a time-out. We all need a time-out. *Each to his or her corner!*

"I'm really starting to feel this altitude." I yawn. "I'm gonna get some shut-eye. Maya, can you call out of the country with your phone?"
"Of course. Why?"

"Do you mind if I make a quick call back home? To my mom?"

"Sure, but don't be too long. Once I run out of credit up here, we can't get any more. This is our last lifeline back to civilization in case things go frightfully wrong."

"No problem," I assure. "I'll only need a few minutes."

"Where are you calling – the States? Tell me the number and I'll dial it for you."

"Ok, it's +1 425 482...no, let me give you another number: +1 206 291 1080."

Let's try and ease back into this family thing, take a more indirect route.

"...OK, it's ringing," she says, handing me the phone. I hustle up the stairs and into an empty room. *Damn*, it's cold up here!

Bbbrringh...bbrringh...bbringh...bbrringh...click!

"Hello?" Her voice sounds a little coarser than it used to. "Hello, this is Jennifer," she says. "Can I help you?"

There's so much I want to say. So much I need to tell her.

"*Helloooooow?*"

"Hey...Jenny," I stammer. "It's me."

"...Jupiter? Is that you?"

I'm the only one she allows to call her 'Jenny' and she's the only one sanctioned to call me 'Jupiter.' It's a longstanding agreement dating back to childhood.

"...Yeah, it's me," I say.

"Where the hell are you? Are you OK? I haven't heard from you in, like, months."

"I'm..."

"Oh my god, I'm sooooo busy with the kids these days, I can barely think!"

That, it seems, is going to be the extent of her questioning, more or less. Her life now revolves around her children. If an event happens outside of a fifty-foot radius of them, it pretty much doesn't exist.

"Jackson is really a handful," she continues. "Throwing tantrums every second, and it seems like Annika has night terrors each..."

"How's mom?" I ask.

"...Mom? She's...still not dealing with things...very well. It's been really hard on her, you know. It's been really hard on all of us, Jupiter," she sighs.

There it is: front row center. The sigh. Her tacit nod to the fact that *I* am the source, the fountainhead, of this tragedy.

"...When are you coming home?" she asks. "The kids would really love to see you."

She always has to speak through the kids, as if they were a goddamn medium. She never says *she* wants to see me – it's always 'the kids want to see you.' Probably because she actually doesn't want to but can't bring herself to say it.

"I'm…on my way," I say. "Might be there by Christmas if all goes as planned."

"Oh, that's great! Do you have a place to stay?"

"I'm…working on it."

"We're completely packed now that we have Annika," she says, feigning regret. "I'm sure mom would love to see you as well, but…I don't think she's ready, you know, to have you back in the house. She's just…having a hard time with it, you know?"

I shift the speaker away from my mouth, stifle an unexpected sob. Mom will never love me again…never. They both blame me. It's always been and will always be my fault. *'If not for Jupiter, none of this would have happened.'*

Yeah, I really shit on the family parade.

High-pitched cries erupt in the background. Jenny to the rescue!

"Jackson, *no!*" she shouts, then, "Jupiter, I've really got to go now. The kids are acting up and I'm late for work. *Annika, stop!* It was really great…"

I drop the phone to my side. I'm not coming home for Christmas – there's no point. Jenny did her best, given the circumstances…she didn't even get emotional like I expected. I'm surprised she didn't hang up the phone on me. I'm so fucking tired…

Footsteps thump up the steps. Peeping out from my cocoon, I spy the silver-haired man as he walks past, an urn swinging from his hand. Give him a funny hat and he'd look like an Irish priest on Ash Wednesday. Shit, I must have slept the whole day away…

Now, I'm wide-awake and appear to be next to a shrine of some kind. A pungent evergreen odor fills my nostrils. Trailing smoke fades into the air.

My eyes follow him to the far end of the room. Against the wall, a multi-limbed golden figure is illuminated by butter lamps. They've probably got a deity for every room of the house.

Is that Buddha? One of his apostles? It's hard to keep track in a place where religion is as ubiquitous as oxygen. Nepali people seem to live and breathe religion. But they don't seem interested in pushing it on passers-by; they're just doing their own thing. Everywhere you turn, there's a sacred stone or flag or statue of some kind, or someone offering up alms or small animals. I kind of like that; a place of worship is always within reach. Easy-access prayer…good old G.W. would love it. Who says you have to separate church and state?

I remain still in my sleeping bag, reluctant to ruin the sanctity of the old man's spiritual ritual. I feel hung over; must be the altitude. Chanting now, he approaches the shrine and bows, trailing sticks of smoking incense around the figure.

"Om mani padme hum, Om mani padme hum, Om mani padme hum…"

I like that chant; it's got a nice ring to it. Who is he praying to? The figure at the end of the room? For our safe passage, perhaps? Keep praying, buddy: we're going to need all the help we can get.

Scooping a plate full of dough tablets from the shrine, he turns towards me. Walking past my supine form, he grins, still chanting, and shuts the door softly behind him.

Slowly, I peel back my cocoon: a pupae emerging into the cold unknown. The wind has died down. A rime of frost is spun across the edges of the windowpanes like spider webs. It glistens in the afternoon light. I slip on my fleece and hobble down the stairs.

Jack sits on a bench to the side of the room, warming his hands over a fire that blazes steadily in the hearth. Behind him, a group of children huddles over a table, watching intently as Maya sketches on a miniature chalkboard.

If only I had a frame for this Norman Rockwell painting! 'Mistress Maya teaching the chillun their Ps and Qs while crotchety Schoolmarm Jack stokes the wood…*Little House on the Prairie: the Mountain Years*.

Taking a seat next to Jack, I rub my hands briskly over the flames. How can they still be up, with their slashes and snake bites?

"Man, it's getting cold out," I say.

"Yep," he replies.

Whenever I get near a fire, I feel an overpowering urge to talk about the weather. Possibly something to do with it triggering a primal survival instinct.

Jack rolls a log in.

"You spend a lot of time up here?" I ask.

"More than my fair share. Yeah, I spent a hell of a lot of time up here, mostly in the '60s. Things have changed a lot since then. Did you see those satellite dishes on the way down here? I remember when there was no electricity here, when there wasn't a single motor or machine up here. It wasn't that long ago."

"You must have had some time together, you and Gerard, making runs across Asia."

"It wasn't all peace and free love, man. There was some serious shit going on out here back then...heavy shit."

Maya exits, a towel over her shoulder.

Is he on the verge of reminiscing? Maya's gone: this could be my chance to get this crusty old turtle to come out of his shell. He said he would spill the beans once we got up here. I turn towards him.

"...Tell me about Gerard."

"What's all this shit about Gerard?" he scoffs. "He's dead – forget about him."

"*You're* going to die some day," I say. "Hey, we're all gonna die. In the end, all we're left with is memories – some good, some bad. And in the end, that's all we have of anyone. Don't forget that."

"...I'm already forgotten – I'm a piece of lint stuck in someone's crotch."

"I definitely won't forget you," I say.

Raising a small leather flask, he chugs a gulp. Chasing it with a few swigs of beer, he hands me the flask.

"Here – try some of this. Kukuri Rum: *Sahaasi ko ek matrai chahaana ho!*"

"...What does that mean?" I ask.

"The choice of heroes, man," he answers, coughing.

The choice of heroes. So which one is it: hero or piece of lint? Tuborg beer, Kukuri Rum...he's a walking advertisement for the alcoholic beverage industry of Nepal. I'm not sure they'd be too thrilled to have his endorsement. Bad press. That would be like sponsoring Idi Amin to promote a set of steak knives.

"Come on, the altitude gives it an extra little kick." He tilts the bottle towards me.

"I'm still zoning from that opium," I say.

Jack coughs. "Nothing wrong with stoking the fire."

"No thanks; I think I'll get some air instead."

Rising, I swing the door open and totter out onto the flagstone street. Push, push, push...isn't happy until we're all high. The Gerard inquiry will have to wait until another day.

Everything is dark save the west, which is muddled in deep shades of pink and green. The air is brisk and still. Quite a change from the sandblasting we got this morning.

Strolling down the street, I spot Maya crouched over a spigot of running water. Sneaking up behind her, I watch as she squeezes the suds from her hair. She *is* a trouper – hasn't complained once about her stomach and that water has to be freezing. Most girls I know would be blubbering about the scar it's going to leave and screaming for a plastic surgeon, yet here she is, taking it in stride at ten thousand feet. All that and she's a looker, too.

I cough. Flipping her wet hair, she jumps back.

"Oh! You gave me a fright," she says. "I didn't know it was you."

She grabs a towel from the stone fence.

"...I can't believe you're still here," I say.

"Yeah, well, neither can I. But here we are."

"How's your stomach?"

"It hurts. It hurts quite a lot, actually, but the stitches are holding. I was well impressed by Jack's needlework. Don't let him know, though – he's got a big enough head as it is."

"This air," I inhale, "It's so pure. I think I'm going to give the hash and cigarettes a miss for a while. Get all that junk out of my system and give my body some down time. I need to recuperate."

She stops drying her hair for a moment.

"Why are you telling me this?"

"I just…I don't know. It's just time. Because if I hadn't been stoned I would have made it to the Immigration Office that day. If I hadn't been toting it around the world, all tweaked out on painkillers and sedatives, I wouldn't have landed in prison.

"Bottom line: the stuff's more trouble than it's worth. Drugs are a crutch, like you said, and I don't want to be a cripple."

"…Like Jack, you mean?" she asks.

"Yeah…I guess. I don't want to end up like that."

"Good for you," she says. "But it might be harder than you think."

I can't believe I just said that. How many pacts to 'smoke bud until death' have I made with myself? How many times have I envisioned myself well into my latter years, rocking on a porch, passing a joint back and forth with my trusted *compadres*? For years, quitting didn't carry the slightest tinge of possibility; now here I am making a statement of abstinence. This mountain air must be getting to me.

Wrapping the towel around her head, Maya pauses for a moment, smiles.

"…So, what *is* our fearless leader up to?"

"About his fifth Tuborg by now, I'd say."

"I've got to ring my father again," she says. "Just give me a moment. Shit, there's barely any reception here."

This should be interesting.

"…Father, It's me," she says. "Look, I found Jupiter in Pokhara and he's willing to come back and speak with you. He's also wants to…"

I can hear loud exclamations on the other end.

"Hold on a second, dad," she says. "I can barely make out what you're saying."

She takes a few steps away from the building and levers herself up onto the stone fence.

"What was that?" she asks.

As Gunn talks, her eyes begin to widen. Are they sending in the Apache helicopters? Hang up before they triangulate!

"...I didn't realize...I see. Right, we'll be on the first bus back to Kathmandu tomorrow morning. I...yes, I understand. I'll ring you as soon as we're back."

She hangs up, sighs deeply. Uh-oh. Did they get a lock on our position?

"Immigration reported you missing to the US Embassy, so they've notified the police and put out an All Points Bulletin. My father tried to intervene but once they issued the bulletin, it was out of his power. I'm afraid you're a wanted man now and there's not much he can do about it."

"Great. I wish it was in more of a loving sense, though."

"Look," she interrupts. "We've already committed ourselves, so let's just focus on what lies ahead. The police in Kathmandu are half-assed and only get off their collective butts if a bribe is involved. They'd never bother out here in the bush."

"Didn't you tell him that we're on the next bus back to Kathmandu?"

"...Yes, I did."

"But..."

"Don't worry about that," she deflects. "Just concentrate on what lies ahead. You can't go back now."

"...Your dad is going to kill you, isn't he?"

"...He'll forgive me," she says. "Eventually."

Grinning, she turns to face the fading horizon. Slowly, pinks and oranges slip from the clouds like autumn leaves.

"Look at that," she says. "It's gorgeous here, isn't it? It's been ages since I've been up in the mountains."

I'm busy looking at an entirely different, more attractive horizon.

"Mmmm."

She turns to me. I want to kiss her so badly, to take her in my arms and squeeze her. I'd probably get excited and end up ripping out her stitches. Should I, should I? Maybe just a little one...

A bell chimes in the distance, as if signaling an end my allotted kissing time: thanks for playing, maybe next time. She slips a hand in mine.

"Let's get inside. It's freezing out here!"

"OK. You're back," says Jack. "Wait here."

He disappears upstairs, returning with a yellowish square of paper, folded several times over.

"Come over here and have a look at this map," he say, unfolding it.

Heavily creased, tattered at the corners, the map is riddled with red marks, yellow marks, dots, symbols and routes, penciled over topographical swirls. Most of the marks are up near the top of the map on what appears to be a border: 'TIBET' and 'INDIA' are marked on either side. There are so many penciled-in symbols and scribbles that they warrant their own legend.

Finally, something tangible – something with which to gauge 'Point A' (you are here) relative to 'Point B' (freedom). Poring over it, I feel as if we're part of some underground resistance movement.

"OK, campers: we are now officially *here*." Jack brings his forefinger down onto the dot denoting Simikot.

"Wow, this map is ancient," I say. "Where'd you pick it up?"

"I can't remember; some old map shop down near Paatan, I think."

"What are all these lines – and these symbols up along the border? Are those supposed to represent garrisons?"

"They're just places we stopped along old trekking routes. Now, if we..."

"What's this?" interjects Maya, pointing to some print in the lower right-hand corner. It reads:

Central Asian Operations

SHADOW CIRCUS

"Geographical notation."

"*Curiouser and curiouser,*" says Maya, then, unable to help herself: "What are you doing with a map like this? This is a military map, isn't it?"

"It's just a goddamn map, OK?"

"Oh come off it, Jack – this is not just a goddamn map, and you're not just a waylaid hippie roaming about the hills, smoking dope and worrying about your *shakras.*

"You know, my father has quite a library back in Kathmandu. Most of the books in it deal with the history of Nepal: some are old, some recent. I managed to read quite a few of them, and I recall coming across 'SHADOW CIRCUS' in more than one. Do you care to elaborate, Jack, or would you like me to speculate?"

SHADOW CIRCUS…is that like an Asiatic version of the Freemasons? Is there a secret handshake? You've got to teach me that handshake, Jack.

"Here we go again with the questions," he snipes. "I feel like I'm in The Hague every time you open your mouth."

Maya's not backing off. "Hey, you wanted us to follow you up here and we did. It's pointless for us to keep secrets from one another like a bunch of petty thieves. If we're going to accomplish anything, we've got to pull together. Do us all a favor – do yourself a favor. Dust off the skeletons and come clean."

He sighs.

"Do you want the page-by-page or the condensed Hollywood version?"

"The Hollywood version will do for now."

No fucking way. This whole time, I've been hunched over the safe with a stethoscope trying to pick tumblers. Then butter-wouldn't-melt Maya sneaks up behind me and cracks the combination in one fell swoop.

"…Alright, then" says Jack. "Where do I start? …I used to teach languages – was a Professor, no less, of Eastern Asiatic Languages, a PhD. I had command of more languages than most UN translators could ever dream of – Mandarin, Cantonese, a little Thai, Nepali, Urdu, Hindi. I had three Hindi dialects down at one point... And Tibetan.

"It was my gift: I'd pick up a book and the words would just flow. I could pick up the basics of any Romantic language in a month; just about anything else in under six. I loved studying languages more than anything in the world."

Jack, a PhD? I had him down as more of a Dr. Feelgood. That would explain his seemingly infinite knowledge of languages. How did he wind up scraping the bottom of the barrel over here? How does an academic become a junkie? I guess you'd have to ask Timothy Leary. I need a jumbo popcorn to go with this story.

"What brought you to Nepal, then?" probes Maya.

"Tibetan...it was the Tibetan. Nobody in the States could touch me when it came to that language. I'd been studying it since I was fourteen. This was at a time when most people only knew the name Lhasa as a breed of dog, and only a few dozen foreigners had actually reached the Tibetan capital. I had already published my own Tibetan dictionary and was working on a grammatical text when they came...I'll never forget that day. That day turned my whole life upside down.

I was teaching a graduate class in Classical Chinese down in the basement of the Oriental Institute at University of Chicago. At that time, I was the youngest professor on the staff. They marched in right in the middle of my class...assholes.

They were dressed head to toe in black like they'd just come from a funeral. Anybody comes looking for you dressed like that, you know it can't be good."

"Who came looking for you?" I ask.

"The Federalis: the CIA. Of course, they didn't just come right out and say it. Parks and Finbaar: those were their names. Straight out of a lost *Dragnet* episode. I 'was needed urgently in Washington,' they said. 'Highly sensitive matters involving US-Chinese relations,' they said. Just the facts. Shit, I thought they might have snuck in a Chinese envoy, hush-hush, and been trying patch things up at the White House.

If only it had been that simple. Before I knew it, I was re-deployed and on a plane to Guam, being briefed on winter survival tactics in the Himalayas."

"What do languages have to do with mountaineering?"

"Not a thing, It all boiled down to politics."

"What kind of..."

"The worst kind. Mix anything with politics and it all goes sour, doesn't it? After Chiang Kai Shek lost mainland China and hightailed it over to Taiwan, Washington freaked. Communism runs rampant across the world! The dreaded domino effect – can't have that.

"They gave it the old college try in Korea, but it was a stalemate. They had to figure out a way to keep Mao in check. We had bases all over the Pacific Rim but they were too far away, so they set their sights on Mustang, a promontory in north central Nepal.

"It's a kingdom, a kind of autonomous region. The king of Nepal never really had control over it. For hundreds of years, the only contact between the two kingdoms came in the form of small, annual tributes. The king had even less control against the CIA setting up ops in this little chunk of rock and ice twelve three thousand meters above the valley."

OK – he just threw out at least one half dozen countries that I know absolutely nothing about, plus a kingdom that I'm not sure even exists. Where can I find a copy of *Asia for Dummies*?

"Wait a minute," I say, "Mustang is separate from Nepal but a part of it?"

"*That's* why the government made that area off-limits for so long!" says Maya.

"Bingo! In order to speed things up, the US government shipped plane-loads of Tibetans over to a base in Colorado, trained them in guerilla warfare and filtered them back into Mustang."

"Like Colorado, USA Colorado?" I interject.

"Camp Hale. Camp Mule Shit. Good old US of fucking A," he replies.

What the hell is he talking about?

"...There was a lot of factionalism between the Tibetans; there always has been. The CIA needed a point man, someone who knew the language, someone who knew the customs inside and out and could keep them together, keep them united as a front...and my number came up."

I knew there was something more to him than trafficking drugs, small arms and Maoists, but I couldn't have concocted this topsy-turvy ride if I tried. When you think about it, the CIA almost makes sense. They're notorious for spitting out used-up operatives that wind up trafficking drugs and small arms, but a professor of languages? I never saw that curve ball coming. Dropped right out from under me.

I'm still having trouble visualizing it. He just doesn't strike me as an intellectual. He seems so…fried. Thrice-baked. And whoever heard of all this far-flung shit going on with the CIA in Tibet? Training Tibetan guerillas in Colorado? Why didn't they teach us any of this stuff at school? I doubt any of my teachers knew about that shit. They had their collective heads so far up America's ass, they couldn't see past WWII. Even if they did, I wouldn't have been listening.

I've got a feeling Maya knows exactly what he's talking about, and she's not calling Jack's bluff. It's got to be real. This is not the kind of stuff you pick up in history books – this is the kind of stuff that gets ratholed in some top-secret file for twenty years and shredded when the last character of the story finally dies off. Looks like Jack is one of those characters; maybe he's the last one. Still, I might as well say it while the cards are out on the table

"Jack, I hope to hell you didn't drag us up here to take part in some bullshit covert government operation. The only operation I want to be involved in up here is Operation Save-My-Ass."

"I'm a freelancer; I don't work for anybody but myself these days. I made a promise to you to get you over the pass and to get Maya back down, and that is what I intend to do. If it makes you feel better to look at this as a business deal, that's fine – but it has nothing to do with the CIA or any of the shit I used to be mixed up in, you dig? Now you have your story for the six o'clock edition, can we continue?"

"…Uh, right – carry on," says Maya.

"Yeah, sure," I add, somewhat superfluously.

CIA? You never would have known it from looking at him. You could say the same about Jack Berry, too. Then again, you're not supposed to tell.

I glance at Maya – she looks a little shocked. She wanted the truth, but I don't think she expected him to dump all that info at her feet like a truckload of wet cement.

"First, we can hoof it up to the monastery," Jack is saying. "That's three, maybe four days from here. Like I said, I know some cats up there, so we can hang out and catch our breaths before heading north. From the monastery to the border, we're looking at a solid two to three days, weather permitting. It's no cake walk, but I was planning on dropping the kid here, up at Tinker Pass."

His finger slides across the map, stopping at a thick dotted line in the upper left-hand corner: Tinker Pass. It's almost at the top of the map, at the edge of the charted territory. It looks like the edge of the world.

"How far is it from the border to where I need to be?" I ask.

"Don't know exactly...never made it that far." he says. "I know that there's an Indian military check post right on the other side, though.

"The pass is over six thousand meters. I've been up to the first saddle. Nothing too technical, give or take a crevasse. I'll take you over the top. Once you clear the pass, you should hit the check post on the other side." He points to a blank space on the other side of the border: a blank white space. "It should be about five, maybe ten clicks below the pass from here. The civilians will most likely be Tibetan, but there may be some patrols from the Indian Army as well."

"How do you know that there's anything there?" I ask. "There's nothing on the map, Jack. Are you sure anybody even lives there?"

"Listen, I know it's over there. I know this. We were set to head over this pass once, but we never made it. I'll give you my compass so you don't stray."

It sounds like a shaky intelligence report at best – right up there with the WMD reports that sent G.W. Bush and the light brigades charging into Iraq. Yellowcake uranium my ass.

"Jack, you can give me a handheld GPS with all the bells and whistles but if there's nothing there, it's not going to help me for shit."

"Just keep going south by southwest after the pass and you can't miss." He's joking, surely.

"Can't miss what – the Indian Ocean? A difference of five kilometers at that altitude is a huge difference. What if it's fifteen kilometers – what then? That could be the difference of days. Don't you think we should have brought a map that actually had the places we're going to on it?"

"It's ten kilometers, max," he assures. "I've never been, but I *know* that. If that's not good enough for you, then figure your own way through the mountains."

If there was something, even a faint speck indicating a military post or even a village, I'd feel more comfortable, but that blank space on the map is unnerving. I'm venturing forth into the blank static of a non-existent television channel. Only the bold block letters of 'INDIA' on one side of the pass and 'TIBET' on the other offer any indication of what lies out there. What if a rockslide has washed away the entire backside of that pass? What if they changed the borders since…when was this thing published?

I might as well be plodding into the depths of an uncharted mine shaft.

"Like I said, I've never been," says Jack, "but I do know that this pass was used for transit back in the '60s and '70s. It's not a major route, but I'll bet it sees at least a dozen salt caravans a year. If the weather holds there should be some semblance of a marked path."

I don't want dated presumptions, variable weather conditions or blank spaces on maps, I want concise facts! But I'm not going to get that with Jack. If you buy a cat one day you can't get mad that it's not a dog the next, can you? I bought myself a cat, one angry son-a-bitch tomcat, so I might as well start getting used to it.

"What about border patrols? What if they spot me first?"

"I don't think this border is patrolled often. Not too much to patrol. They're not going to expect you, that's for sure. They'll probably treat you like a VIP, since you'll probably be the first white boy they've ever seen.

"Don't avoid them – go to them. You *want* them to find you, remember. But don't go running and screaming into their arms, either. Approach them like you would a grizzly bear: walk slowly and make lots of noise. If you sneak up on them, they're likely to blast you to high heaven.

"Keep the ice axe away from your body so they won't mistake it for a gun from a distance. Scrape up your hands a little; maybe scratch your face up with a chunk of ice when you get close so it looks like you *have* been climbing mountains."

I'm already starting to look the part. Shouldn't need any props by the time I stumble off that pass.

"As long as you keep your story straight and your background check clears, the US embassy in Delhi should whisk you back home as fast as lightning."

Easy as that, says Jack.

Back home – it's time for that, too. I knew it was coming. Maybe this whole charade will work itself out and send me back from where I came. It's time to seal the leaks, patch up the holes I've been trying to hold together with Elmer's Glue and Scotch Tape for the past year. Time to get out the hardcore epoxy and clamps – the stuff dad and I used to use on the boat when the cheap shit didn't cut it. Still a long way to go, though, between home and here.

"...Just keep heading south and stay out of the way of the Chinese or they might take you for a stray *chiru*," cautions Jack.

"What's a *chiru*?"

"A Tibetan antelope prized for its soft fur coat. I hear they're a bit trigger-happy up there, with nothing to do all day but shoot at anything that moves."

An image of my stuffed head on a plaque above a group of Chinese police officers playing *mahjong* flashes through my mind. Does a young American male beat out a seven-point buck? They'd stick things like cigarettes and rotten fruit in my mouth every so often for amusement and throw darts at my head when questions regarding their MFN status or human rights were raised.

"And then what?" asks Maya. "What happens after you take him over the pass?"

"And then you and I get the hell out of there before the passes fill up with snow," says Jack. "We'll hoof it back down to here and fly back the way we came. I've already bought two open-end plane tickets for us. When we get back to Nepalganj, I'm not sure what my next move will be, but I can make sure you get on one of my undercover trucks back to the valley. That's as far down the road as I can see before the bend. Does that sound like a plan?"

"Yeah, whatever," replies Maya. "It sounds as if you're sending him straight to his death. I don't want you to even think about leaving him at the top to make his way down on his own. You have to get him over to the other side or he doesn't stand a chance. And if you don't, I will."

"I said I'll get him down. We'll try to get out of here by mid-morning tomorrow. I've already arranged most of our provisions from the proprietor, but I'll head to the bazaar in the morning to score some odds and ends."

"What about a tent, Jack?" persists Maya. "Or didn't that occur to you?"

"It did. I brought an old two-man. It's not much, but the snows are coming and we need to travel light to clear that pass before it dumps. There are plenty of animal shelters below the passes and lots of boulders to protect us from the wind."

"That's great...but there are three of us."

"I've got an extra tarp. You two can have the tent," says Jack.

"Is it going to be enough?" Maya asks, skeptical.

"She was built back in the day when a two-seater was a four – so it's a roomy two, believe me. I'll carry it."

I'm picturing one of those drab canvas numbers that were a staple of the WWII soldier. The Model T of tents, straight-up vintage.

"I'm not talking about space, Jack. We need something that will actually keep out the elements and keep us warm. I've been frozen at thousands of meters less than where we are going, I don't care to repeat the process," says Maya.

I love how the English say 'process.' It makes what you're discussing sound so much more important. As if you're dithering over the advancement of education in the House of Lords or metaphysical theorems at Cambridge. 'All this must involve *due process*.'

I toss a wad of rupees on the map.

"Use everything you need for the provisions...and anything else that I need to make it over that pass and that you two need to make it back. If you think we'll die without a better tent or better sleeping bags, then get them. I want to keep as many of my toes as possible. And I don't want anyone losing any on account of me."

"It's a little late for that now, kid. All of the mountaineering shops are back in Kathmandu, and any gear that does make it up this far isn't easily parted with...but I'll see what I can do."

"What about check posts, Jack? There have to be at least a half dozen on the way, and probably loads of soldiers stationed along the border."

"There aren't any check posts where we're going," he replies.

Maya tugs surreptitiously on my jacket as Jack rolls up his map.

"This is going to be the death of you, Jupiter," she whispers. "I think we should get out now while we still can."

"If you've got a better option, I'd love to hear it."

I pull away from her. Straightening abruptly, she says, "Well, I'm knackered! See you all in the morning."

She stomps up the stairs, laces trailing behind her Doc Martens like pilot fish to a whale shark. Withdrawing a cigarette from my coat pocket, I stare into the fire's dying embers.

"My stomach's not feeling too hot," I say.

"I've got just the thing that can turn that around," says Jack. Rolling his wrist, he reveals a stubby joint tucked inside his palm.

"What is it?"

You've always got to ask with people like Jack. He was the guy at Dead shows who told people to 'have a nice trip' after he'd snuck up and sprayed them with liquid acid from a mister. Consensual crimes should be just that: consensual.

"Just good old-fashioned hooch."

I'm not one to contest the medicinal properties of marijuana, especially when it comes to stomach ailments. It beats all tried and true remedies when it comes to nausea…and leaves with a nice after-buzz, too. Still, I did say I was going to cut back.

"I'll come outside, but I don't want to burn."

"Let's step outside. We don't want to rile the management," says Jack.

The door creaks open. My glasses fog up quicker than a Cape Cod bay on a sticky August afternoon.

"Damn, it's frigid out here!" Unzipping my pocket, I yank out my hat and snug it over my head.

"It does get nipply up here at night. But don't worry, my man, those sleeping bags are heavy duty...US Army Special Ops issue."

"They look more like bar rags than sleeping bags, Jack. They must be at least thirty years old." I reply. "The zipper on mine is practically frozen shut. And they smell like ass."

"A little beeswax should take care of the zipper, anyway. Those sleeping bags will do the trick; they're tried and true...you can have mine if you like. It's got an extra liner in it."

Tried definitely is the operative word on the sleeping bags. And beeswax...where does he get his information, the *Farmer's Almanac*?

"Hey kid," he says, then, pointing to my neck. "I thought I told you to tuck those stones away in a safe place."

Does he honestly think someone is going to run up and rip them off my neck? No, it's more than that: he can't get enough of them. The *dzi* draws him, calls out to him. He needs to see it just one more time.

Gollum just wants 'one more looksy,' doesn't he, Preciousssss?

"They're safe enough."

"Not around your neck, they're not. Those boys in Kathmandu weren't after your wallet; they wanted the stones. People in these parts know the value of stones like that. I can hold onto them for you if you like."

"What a load of crap, Jack: I saw fake *dzis* all over Kathmandu. Tourists were buying them by the dozen. How the hell is anyone going to tell the difference from ten feet off?"

"You won't see fake ones like that – not like that one."

"Honestly, Jack, I really don't think you can tell the difference."

"I can tell, OK? *They* could tell."

I pull the *dzi* off my neck and stuff it into my pants pocket. Does he think I'm that stupid?

"There...happy now? They're tucked away where no-one can see them. Now it's our little secret."

"I wouldn't be too sure of that," he says. "The damage may have already been done. All those people at the airport saw them. And what about the owner of this teahouse? If they have followed our trail, this will be one of the first places those Managis come looking for us. If they put the pressure on him, he'll fold like a cheap suit."

In terms of needing therapy, I'm borderline, but Jack is way over the top. I could be prescribed any number of medications but he's making me look good with his conspiracy theories and KGB paranoia. I guess years of working for the CIA will do that to you.

"You think those kids tailed us all the way from Kathmandu for a *dzi*?" I ask. "No way, no fucking way. They're not going to follow us all the way up here for a few stupid stones!"

"Maybe not for the *dzi,* but definitely for revenge. Don't underestimate them, kid. We got away from the scene of the crime pretty quick, which is good, but you never know who is watching. Even though we snuck out in the middle of the night, we don't exactly blend in around here – white people in Nepal stick out like Masai tribesman at a Ku Klux Klan convention.

"I can't be certain if anyone saw us that night; I can't even be sure that the drivers who carted us to Nepalganj wouldn't sell us out for a few thousand rupees. You don't think they're watching but they are, man."

"We can't be certain how many shots were fired from the grassy knoll either, Jack, but before you get all tweaked out on conspiracy theories, let's take a deep breath and think about this. How many people could possibly have seen us? We left in the middle of the night, for christ's sake."

"Yeah, and we were the only thing moving out of doors besides cows, dogs and rats. We're not that far from Manang, their stronghold. I'm sure they've already made a few calls up there and sounded the alarm. All it takes is a well-placed phone call and they're back on our tail. They ask the right person the right question and they'll be able to follow our tracks as if they were cemented into the pavement."

"But why would the truck drivers sell us out?" I ask. "I thought that was your operation."

"It's kind of like an operation within an operation. Besides, it's not like we're family or anything. A thousand rupees can put food on the table for a couple days. With the Maoists calling *bandhs* every other day, they're already living from hand to mouth. They're looking for us right now, and they're going to turn over every stone before they give up looking – including the ones around your neck.

"These Nepalis notice that kind of thing. You might as well have a big red siren strapped around your neck, and a megaphone, screaming out 'Come and get me!'

"That *dzi* is what anyone who sees it will remember you by. And you know what they'll say? 'A white kid with a twelve-eyed *dzi* around his neck? Yeah, he was here, with two others. They passed by here a few days ago. They went *that* way.'"

Jack points dramatically off into the darkness."

We've got a severe case of what appears to be chronic psychosis here. We're going to have to up Jack's dosage of Haldol to 100 milligrams, *stat*!

"Don't you think you're exaggerating just a bit, Jack? *Shhhh! Can you hear that? Where are those voices coming from? Shhhh!"*

I wheel around to face him. "Is that coming from in there?" I tap my knuckles softly against his head. "See, Jack, now I'm jealous because the voices are only talking to you!"

"I don't think you understand exactly what we're up against," he persists. " I don't think you understand how dangerous this is. Maybe this will help you."

Opening his jacket, he slides out a small pistol. An armed Jack…is this good or bad? Five to one, it's very bad.

"How the fuck did you get *that* through airport security?" I hiss.

"That airport is about as secure as the Sunni triangle. Got the EP gas past them as well. You missed my Bavarian shuffle at the gate, huh? I slipped it right past them when they started going on with that bullshit about springtime in Alzei…Man, I hate Germany!"

"I know that you don't need a fucking gun to climb over a mountain pass, dumb-ass!" I say. "Put that thing away before you shoot yourself."

There goes that tic again, twitching his scar…did I just go over the line?

"Do you?" he replies. "Do you really think you know? Do you really think you know?" Cocking the hammer of the pistol, he pushes its cold barrel to my head.

My body freezes, folds into itself. Christ, he's having some sort of *Full Metal Jacket* flashback. What did I do? Look at his scar the wrong way? Does he flip out when you look at the scar? Was it *zee Germans*? Hey, I hate Germany, too, Jack! *Jack, I'm your friend...FRIEND!*

Is this it? He's going to blow me away. My heart drops to my knees...he's going to off me right here!

"Christ, Jack," I stammer, "Take the stupid *dzi*: it's yours. Take whatever you want, but don't..."

I throw the *dzi* on the ground and instinctively, put my hands in the air. Shit – take the damn stones, take my money. Take whatever you want, just DON'T SHOOT ME.

I'm trying jumpstart poignant, life-changing memories, but all I can think of is that Eddie Adam's photo with the Chief of Police blowing away the Viet Cong prisoner. In the picture, the impact of the bullet has made the prisoner's hair all go to one side, as if the pistol were a blow dryer and the police chief a stylist giving him his final salon primping. One second later, his brains must have been splattered all over the place like spaghetti.

"Do you *really* know?" Jack asks again.

He leans very close to my ear. Please, no spaghetti tonight! Would he understand if I stuck a flower in the barrel? *Give peace a chance, Jack.*

Damn it, if you're going to do it, then, at least be quick about it.The hammer clicks. I'm dead, I'm dead...I'm not dead.

"...Now you know," he whispers.

"Goddamn it, if you're going to do it, *do it!*"

I shut my eyes, wincing with anxiety.

"...What, did you think I was actually going to use this on you?" Jack lobs the pistol back and forth between his palms like a hot potato. "Hey man, seriously, you didn't..."

I inch backwards.

"I don't know what I thought," I say. "Could you just put that down, please? Call me skittish but when someone sticks a gun to my head, I get a little nervous."

"Yeah, sure," he laughs. "Man, I can't believe you actually thought I was going to pull the trigger. I was just fucking with you, man!" He jabs me jovially in the arm.

That was a highly questionable, highly disturbing action. Is this what you get when you don't hire a licensed guide out here? What the fuck was I *supposed* to think, Mr Hyde?

"I don't know if that was some kind of rite-of-passage war game you used to play with your commando buddies, but I don't fucking appreciate it."

"Hey man, it's not even loaded. Here, check for yourself if you don't believe me."

"No, I don't want to know. Where I come from, if you point a gun at any living thing, you want it dead. Just put it away, will you?"

He's got a lot of nerve waving that pistol around like Pancho Villa. I've got a notion to rip it from his hands and jam it down his throat. That would probably be my death knell – he'd pull some Green Beret neck-cracking move on me, and that would be it.

Jack snatches the *dzi* off the ground. Take it. Good riddance…that thing is supposed to bring good luck? Good luck, my ass! I've had nothing but bad things happen since it crossed my path. If I didn't know better, I'd swear it has a special power. And Jack's right: people are attracted to it – like mosquitoes to a bug zapper. Every time it falls in or out of someone's hands, they get fried. Have fun with that. But hold up a sec…I was supposed to deliver it to Betty. Jack knows that. Maybe that's what he intends to do after all. Maybe *that* was the unfinished business he was talking about.

Jack admires the *dzi*, turning it over in the moonlight. *Yesssss, my precioussss!* Now we have the *precioussss!* Maybe that pistol will misfire in his pants and blow his dick off. It'd be the ultimate karmic retribution for a chauvinistic pig. But as much as I hate to admit it, I still need the cunning old bastard. Let's just hope the blast happens *after* we make it to the border.

"…Hey kid, just so we're clear on this, I'm not taking these stones off of you, not until I get you over that pass," he says, and makes to hand them back.

"I hate to correct a man with a gun, Jack, but you just took them. That was the deal, wasn't it? That was my insurance policy. Now that I've paid you in advance, what's going to stop you from bailing on this whole operation?"

"I'm not taking them, just holding onto them. I'm protecting my investment. What if we got all the way up there, only to discover that they fell out of your pocket somewhere along the way? This way, if I lose them, I've only got myself to blame, man.

"Anyway, I got you this far, didn't I? If I wanted to rip you off I would have done it a long time ago. Why the hell would I lug the two of you all the way up here, *then* rip you off? Besides, you haven't paid in full."

"Why the hell would you stick the barrel of a gun to my head? I mean, what on Earth possessed you? I don't know, Jack, but I do know that people have *died* for those stupid stones. And I don't want to be included in those statistics…where's that fucking joint, anyway?"

Sparking a match, he ignites the joint; it sizzles like bacon in the crisp air. I didn't want to smoke, but I'm a bit rattled after being in another life-threatening situation.

A minute ago, Jack had a gun to my head; now I'm smoking a joint with him. A very bizarre twist on the evening's course of events. This is all I need to induce further paranoia. Can I bum some of that Haldol of off you, my man? I'll go with the straight Lithium if it'll help.

"I like you, kid. And the girl – well, she's not my type but I dig her vibe. She's got moxie. She's got a lot of fight in her. She reminds me of Elizabeth. To tell you the truth," he whispers, "It kind of turns me on when chicks get all sassy and throw it back in your face."

I did not need to hear that. You should have held up at moxie. That's just wrong. The thought of Jack harboring lascivious feelings for Maya isn't something I want to entertain. He's possibly old enough to be her great-grandfather, for christ's sake! Dirty old letch.

I hope to heaven I don't turn out anything like him.

Jack, oblivious, takes another hit and passes me the joint. I have a sudden desire to stab the ruby end into his eye. Why do I keep smoking this shit?

"Just like Gerard," I say aloud. "Just like she's another piece of ass. If anything happens to her after I leave, I will find a way to sneak back into this country and maim you, man."

"I'm not like Gerard," he says sullenly. "Gerard left his men behind. I did a lot of fucked-up shit in my life, but I never…I'm not going to leave you behind, alright, kid? You gotta trust me on that."

"At this point, I don't really have a choice, do I? Seriously, what about Maya? Do you think she'll be alright? Do you think dragging her into this was wrong? Her stomach is all Frankenstein-ed together and she seems pretty damned wound up about going up into the mountains without the proper equipment. What if she has poor circulation and gets frostbite or something? What if she gets altitude sickness and dies?"

"Well," reminds Jack, "It wasn't my idea to bring her. But I don't think you've got anything to worry about; she's a trouper. The altitude – well, we'll just have to wait and see. There's no telling how it's going to affect you until you get up there. I've seen beat-up old chain smokers blow by young bucks half their age."

As hard as it is for me to imagine, something tells me that he is using himself as a point of reference.

"There's no rhyme or reason to altitude sickness," he explains. "Besides, I don't think her main concern over the tent was fending off the weather."

He just couldn't resist, could he?

"What's that supposed to mean?" I ask.

"You know what I mean. You're sweet on the girl. You've been following her around like a lost lamb since we left. 'How's your tummy, Maya? Do you want me to rub some cream on it? Do you want some more biscuits, Maya? I saved the last one for *you*.'

"I see what's going on between you two. The connection seems to run both ways. By the end of this trip, I wouldn't be surprised if you started calling each other sweetie pie and sugar plum." He snickers.

I was really hoping he wouldn't bring that up. I didn't think it was that obvious. Taking a drag, Jack coughs, passes me the joint.

"At least I'm trying to be nice to her. Besides, what do you care?" I contend. "A few days ago, you didn't want anything to do with us."

"A few days back, you were some punk in my courtyard, stirring up bad memories."

"Don't call me punk unless you want to start something."

"I'll start whatever the hell I damn please," he sneers. "Hey, where's that joint?"

"Here – I don't want any more, I'm cooked," I say.

"How about a little nightcap?"

He slides a small bottle of rum from his jacket. The triple Xs on the label look like something you'd find on a box of rat poison.

"No, I can't do it," I say.

"Not even through the first quarter and already, you're dropping the ball! This is some prime-time bud, not to be missed. I've only got a little left and then we're back on the harsh hash. I can't believe you're going to pass on this."

Exhaling, he blurts, "*I and I rastafari, bom shankir-jah!*"

He takes a swig of rum. "You know what you're like?" he continues. "A dredger. You know: those huge, hunky machines that come and scrape all of the mud out of silted harbors. The only problem is that the harbor is polluted. There are all kinds of nasty poison and toxins buried below the mud. The people keep protesting, saying that the dredger is going to release all of that shit into the environment the second it starts digging – but the damn dredger goes ahead and does it anyway. Before you know it, half the fish are floating belly up and they've shut down the harbor. Why you got to come in and stir all that poison up, kid?"

Why don't *you* go fuck a whore? Downpressor man has spoken... how flattering. If I'm the dredger, then he's the poison.

"Why don't you just tell me what really went down?"

"Shit, it went out," he says. "You got any matches? I'm out."

"Here." I hold out the Zippo...Gerard's Zippo. That should rile him up.

Jack flips open the top, freezes. He dusts off the buried treasure in his attic, studying it like a script from a language he once spoke but had, until now, forgotten.

"See, now that's what I'm talking about. I've told you a hundred times I don't want to talk about it, but every time you open your mouth, there it is again!"

"You needed a light."

"And just when I think you're finally going to show a little respect and keep it under the mat, you go and pull some shit like this."

He's talking about respect and he has a gun. I've just gone against the cumulative conventional wisdom of every mob movie I've ever seen. Oh shit, I really ruffled his feathers. Please don't pull that gun out again. *'Please, Godfather, I'll never disrespect you again. Let me kiss the ring! Let me kiss the dzi!'*

…No, he's not going to pull the gun on me again. Don't back down; don't show fear…*they can smell fear*. As much as it bugs him; as much as he acts like he doesn't want to talk about this, he really does. And he wants to talk to me about this because I'm the only one who will listen.

Don't let him smell the fear.

"…Hey Jack," I say, "Don't get me wrong – I don't mean any disrespect, really. I know you don't like talking about it but I've got to know.

"I never saw a nice side to Gerard, but you said before Betty died he was different. When I came here looking for her, I guess I was looking for him, too…for another side of him. I can't help thinking that there was some good in Gerard, old bastard that he was. Shit, even Darth Vader had some good in him."

"Who?"

"Forget it.

From what Gerard had told me, it didn't sound so bad. Like a nonstop *kung-fu* movie: you and those good ol' boys from Texas. Drugs, women, guns, rock and roll," I say.

"Yeah, that's Gerard for you. I'll wager at least half of what he told you was a load of horseshit. But you couldn't get enough of it, could you? He was one hell of a salesman…what a salesman! He could sell porn to a preacher.

Hell, when you've got a product with a one hundred percent addiction rate, it ain't too hard, but he sold more than that. That cat sold Gerard…sold himself, the 'Gerard Experience,' and for a while, nobody could get enough. Shit, I even bought into it for a while."

The Gerard Experience: sounds like a psychedelic '60s band, downed in a plane crash off the Jersey coast during the Summer of Love. I think my uncle still has one of their eight-tracks up in his attic.

"I've already got Gerard's angle, but I know that there's more to it than that," I continue. "I want to hear what *really* happened, what really went down. Just tell it like it is and I'll listen."

And then, finally, he does.

"Before Beth died, he *was* different," Jack begins. "When he laughed, his eyes were softer, even. Don't get me wrong: he was still a bastard, but he was a bastard with a heart. Beth was all over the place. One day she wanted to save the rainforests, the next she was trying to adopt every damn orphan in the third world, but she sort of leveled him out. She was the yin to his yang, so to speak. Whenever he'd get a mean streak in him, she could always splash ice water on whatever it was that was burning him up inside and talk him down. But he didn't have much of a mean streak back then, as I recall. He was real happy back then. He laughed a lot. Not that wicked ne'er-do-well laugh you know; a *real*, like you mean it laugh.

"I'll never forget that wedding day of theirs. They had a big hoe-down at a hash den afterwards. What an episode! I got so shit-housed I stole the owner's motorcycle and woke up in a ditch that night to a mailman jabbing me in the ribs with a twig. Gerard had to fork over a fistful of rupees to get me out of that one. On his wedding day…can you dig it? Not many men I know would come bail you out on their own wedding day. I could count on him back then.

"Then she died. One day she was chock full of life, the next she was dead, just like that." He snaps his fingers. "Just like that, she was gone.

"At first he got real quiet. It got so bad that you'd catch yourself tip-toeing up to him for fear of breaking the silence. He stopped sleeping. He started speeding out on the bennies…and the cigarettes. He must have been up to six packs a day.

A month or so passed like that, with us walking around on eggshells hoping he wouldn't explode…and then one day, he just lost it. He blew like a goddamn volcano. Got real nasty. There was no-one to check him anymore; his rage hit no ceiling.

"I guess he wanted somebody, anybody to pay for his loss. He need-ed something tangible to destroy. So he came after me."

"Why you?" He pauses, sighs."…We had just scored some really good junk in Uttar Pradesh and were getting ready to run it back to France. Usually, we would get opium and let the Corsicans mess with processing it. But this stuff was straight-up H and pure as snow. Gerard knew the boys back in Marseilles didn't want to deal with labs if they didn't have to. He knew they'd pay a lot more, so he bought up every kilo that Pakistani had.

"We had all of the tires and rocker panels loaded and were ready to go, but Gerard wanted to swing back into Nepal and pick up a tub of honey. He wouldn't go back without it. Middle Eastern food didn't agree with him. Let's just say it would have been awful for all parties involved, so we didn't think twice about it.

"When we crossed the border at Tanakpur, something didn't seem right. The way they looked at us, held us up for too long, checked and re-checked everything before letting us through…it was like they were onto us, waiting for us. After we cleared through, I told Gerard something wasn't smelling right but he didn't give a shit; the only thing he was worried about was his damn honey.

"The entire time, Beth was dying for a fix, but Gerard had it all locked up. Whenever we crossed a border, he'd keep all the dope under wraps – and everyone straight for at least a few hours ahead of time. Smugglers' protocol.

"That only made Beth worse. She kept begging me like a punk-ass kid…as if I would bust out right there in front of the customs and immigration and cook down for her! Gerard was nuts but she was just as crazy, let me tell you.

"A couple miles later, we pulled over and squeezed some out of the rocker panel because she was kicking up such a fuss. She was sweating hard, yelling at me for not cooking it fast enough. When she got distraught, a tiny bead would form at the top of her lip like a drop of dew.

"Well, we were all getting wound up about the prospects. It had been over a month since we'd scored anything but *charas*, and we were all jonesing hard. Kind of like kids who can't wait to run down and rip the wrapping off their presents come Christmas morning. Gerard even wanted a fix.

Nobody wanted to settle for a snort or a pop. They all wanted the mainline; all wanted to go straight to the moon. And Betty was first in line…ladies first. 'Give me a good one, Jackie,' she said. I cooked the stuff up as fast as I could. Fixed it up real nice for her; gave her a good one.

"Turned out it was her last one. It was too much, too strong: it had been too long and her body couldn't handle it. Beth ODed that day... she was so damn tiny.

My heart misses a beat, almost. OD: those are two letters I don't ever want come face to face with. The guest nobody invited, who sneaks in through the back door when no-one's looking. The fantastic beast that comes dripping out of your scariest nightmares and sends shivers up your spine. Death itself.

There's always room for one more.

"...She died in my arms, right there," recalls Jack. "Tex and Dusty went silent, wide-eyed like a couple of kids outside the principal's office who know there's going to be hell to pay. Gerard had no idea. The whole thing happened while he was up in the driver's seat, singing to himself and rambling on about his honey: how he was gong cook up *chappatis* for everyone and slather them in honey. Might have been the happiest I'd ever seen him.

He pulled over as soon as he saw. Cried like a baby for hours, holding her tiny body in his arms. Hell, we all cried a little. We decided to make camp close by and gave him and his old lady some space to, you know, say goodbye.

"They pretty fucking heavy," I say.

"Yeah, it was heavy shit...

"Turns out I was more than just paranoid back at the border. The guys we had bought the H off of in India turned out to be crooked cops, in cahoots with the Nepali border police. They let us pass through into Nepal, then came after us, disguised as Indian businessmen to avoid detection. They were after the whole kit and caboodle.

"There must have been nearly a dozen of them with just as many guns. They snuck up on us in the middle of the night and all hell broke loose. Blood everywhere. We were holed up in that bus like it was the goddamn Alamo, going through rounds of ammo like candy.

"Towards dawn they gave up and left; they must have run out of ammo. By the time the smoke had cleared, every one of us had been shot at least once.

"...Right off the bat, Gerard recognized one of the cops we'd killed; one of the guys he thought he had in his pocket. Turns out he got greedy and double-crossed us. It was so foggy that morning, you could barely see in front of your face: it was as if we were wedged in the middle of a cloud.

"We buried her right there, right in the middle of that battleground... under a *bodhi* tree, if you can believe it – the kind of tree the Buddha was parked under when he attained enlightenment. I hope it helped Beth get where she needed to be...bless her soul.

"The whole time, not one of us said a word...and from that day on, things were never the same. I don't blame him for taking it out on me; I was the easiest target. If it was my girl, I probably would have done the same.

"I guess you could say it was my fault. It was so damn pure that it just stopped her heart. Everyone was so pumped up to get a fix that no-one tested it out. I should have known."

That's a tough racket, watching someone die in your arms and taking the heat for it. I suddenly have an urge to give the guy a hug, but fear that it might trigger another *Full Metal Jacket* episode stops me.

"Lighten up, Jack," I say instead. "You were all playing with fire; any one of you could have gotten burned."

"Hey man, easy for you to say, but you try fucking living with that kind of guilt. It gets under your skin and leaches into your bones like toxic waste. And it doesn't go away. You can try and bury it in a deep, dark hole; fill it with dirt; plant a garden full of flowers and put on a happy face – but it's still there, man; it's still there. You can wait a hundred years and that shit won't go away."

What do I say to that? He's already convicted and sentenced himself to a life of guilt. Even if I opened his cell door with the key, he wouldn't leave – he'd get back into bed, stare at the ceiling...and wait to die.

"Hey man, accidents happen," I say. "It could have been any one of you who stuck that needle in her arm. Shit, it could have been Gerard!"

"But it wasn't anyone else," he says. "It was *me*."

"Jupiter," whispers Maya, "Wake up, we're set to leave." She shakes me again.

I poke my head out of my sleeping bag. "What time is it?" I ask, rubbing sleep from my eyes.

"Maybe four o'clock," she says.

"What happened to mid-morning?"

"There's been a change of plan: Jack wants to leave under nightfall."

As the client, don't I reserve the right to depart at a decent hour? I am not at all in favor of this boot camp regimen. I reserve the right to a sunrise! First being held at gunpoint and now this? I've got to nip this in the bud right now before it becomes standard.

"Where is he?" I demand. "I'm sick of leading a nocturnal existence!"

A hand cups over my mouth, forces me against the bed.

"You listen up, kid," Jack whispers. "There were two riders, maybe more, that came past here a few hours ago. They stopped in front of this teahouse and started talking to one another. I couldn't make out much of what they said, but I think they were looking for us. If we're going to have any chance at all to slip past them, we've got to move immediately. Now when I take my hand away, you're going to get up real quiet and get your pack together as quick as you can. Use the headlamp I gave you as little as possible, and don't shine it in the window, dig? Then meet us downstairs."

I nod, still half asleep. Whatever you say, Jack: just don't point that gun at me. Peeling back my cocoon, I tug pants over my boxers.

"*Brrrgh.* It's freezing in here!"

Jack slams his hands back against my mouth.

"Shut the fuck up," he hisses. "You've got ten minutes."

I didn't hear any horses in the night. This altitude makes me sleep like a bear, though. Even if he did, how on Earth was he able to hear what the horsemen were saying...about us? I don't know how much of this pre-dawn excursion is being fueled by little voices in Jack's head, but I do know that when he slammed my head against the headboard, he was *scared*. Right now, he's jumping around like a cat on speed. Something in my gut tells me we've got to go, too. Real horsemen or figment of Jack's fevered imagination, we'd better err on the side of caution and get the hell out of here.

Having said that, this sucks. I hate the cold but I hate dark cold even more. Dark/cold is a bad combination – it makes everything feel at least ten degrees colder. I've got every article of clothing I own on my person and I'm still shivering, which is hardly consoling when you consider the higher elevations we're heading for. My hands have retracted back into my jacket sleeves like alarmed turtles.

I thought Jack was supposed to find us some gloves, goddamn it. I'll be lucky to have hands left at seventeen thousand feet. I hope Maya is planning on making body warmth donations.

My boots are still permafrost temperature; my feet feel like iced salmon fillets. Reminds me of Chicago winters, when those Arctic blasts would come swooping down out of the north like vengeful ice-dragons. When you had to drag a hair dryer into the attic and hit the water pipes for twenty minutes just to be able to get enough water for a shower. When car keys would crack off in the door before you could even get in and turn the engine over to discover the battery was dead. Oh, those were the days.

Cold, mixed with darkness and the possibility of being followed, has its own strange energy. It shocks your body into an extreme sense of alertness, no matter how tired you are. Even the slightest sounds seem magnified. It's like some primal survival instinct has been triggered, like you could be prey. Something bigger, meaner and much more powerful than you might be out there in the shadows, waiting to snatch you up in its claws.

Like a mouse, you prick your ears at the slightest movement. The crackle of a bush in the breeze sounds like bones breaking. *Be nimble, be swift, little Indian brave.*

I shift my pack from shoulder to shoulder, checking for load discrepancies. It's an old external frame job in drab olive canvas that straps to my back...thirty-five, maybe forty pounds when filled. It clings to my back like a prehistoric sloth, makes me feel like I'm going off to war. Here I am, ready to gun down any commie bastards that get in my way. Back the fuck up, Maoists.

The whole town is dark. Maya and Jack are bulky, indistinct shapes a few feet to either side of me. OK, the only way we're going to warm up is to start moving. Let's get this show on the road.

Jack is perched at the corner of the building as if waiting for something or someone. Suddenly, he slinks back to us, whispers.

"OK, I don't see any sign of them. Maybe they passed by, maybe they didn't. Either way, I don't want to take any more chances."

I can see his breath in the moonlight. He slings his pack over one shoulder.

"There's a ridge, maybe thirty yards from here," he instructs. "We're going to hike up along it for a few clicks to where it joins up with a livestock trail. It's only used during the monsoon to bring the animals to pasture. No-one will expect us to use it. The owner of this place already thinks we're heading the other way, to Dolpa."

Did we just sleep-and-dash on this teahouse? I hope Jack cleared the check. All we need is another agitated local on our heels. They'll probably form their own search party if there's not one already after us.

"Stay close together and don't make any noise," says Jack, *sotto voce*.

Maya's behind me, now, with Jack out in front. Something keeps twitching at the top of his pack, like he jammed a feather duster into the top flap. Almost looks like it's alive. My eyes must be playing tricks on me.

Damn, he's going fast. This isn't easy when it's so dark. There's not even a moon out. I can just make out the dark bulges of rocks and bushes at my feet. OK, I think I'm starting to…*shit*, I hit a bush. Maya stumbles into me from behind. Dry, dead branches crackle in the midnight air.

Jack flies back in one swooping motion.

"…I thought I told you to keep quiet," he says.

"I'm *trying*," I whisper. "I can't fucking *see*."

"Just stay close to me. Once we get over that ridge, we can pop on our lights."

I strain my mouse ears for the *clickety clack* of horseshoes…nothing. We've eluded the Dark Riders for now. A light gust of wind nibbles at my nose and together, the three of us slink into the night.

I've never been happier to see the sun in all my life. The flashlight Jack had spoken of was an empty promise; in the end, being able to see the path took a back seat to his probably-paranoid misgivings.

The last few hours before dawn were spent stumbling through terraced fields and groping around rock outcrops and brush. The ordeal has left considerable bruising from my knees down. That was the longest, coldest two hours of my life…but hey, *I felt alive*. More alive than I've felt in a long time.

This must have been how the Dalai Lama did it on his way to India, traveling through frosty nights to avoid detection.

I will survive.

The first rays poke over the ridge, flooding the pine forest on the hill opposite with orange hues. The sun has given the land form, definition. I can make out the surrounding countryside for miles and miles. We're in hill country, now, in terrain not unlike that of the Smokey Mountains, but drier.

We took a family trip there when I was seven, maybe eight years old. Dad and I woke at dawn to go fishing. He hated to fish, slamming it as 'a complete waste of time,' but he took me just the same. Because he was a father and I was his son, just like it should be.

It was magical that morning. As soon as my bobber hit the water, I had a bite…a speckled brown trout with a swathe of gold across its middle. It must have been over two feet long, a trophy by any standards. Within forty minutes, we had maxed out our limit for the day, but none were half as big as that first one.

Things were simple then – before all the trouble started, before the fighting began. I've heard there's nothing left to fish in that lake anymore. Acid rain killed all of them off.

Some things are better kept in your head; better flash-frozen and put on ice.

The mountains are flanked with brown and yellow; thick pockets of fog blanket the valleys. We plod across seemingly endless fields, weaving between rocks and clusters of brittle grass. In the distance to our west loom a bunch of snow-capped peaks. That must be where we're headed. Somewhere up in those fog-wreathed folds lies freedom.

Maoist country...looks a hell of a lot like Marlboro country. I have a sudden urge to smoke but my lungs have other ideas.

Cold + altitude + smoker's lungs = hell. We've only been at this for two hours, but my lungs are begging me to stop this madness. Every time I breathe in, it's like opening the door to a blast freezer. My lungs aren't happy: they want out.

The shoulder straps of my old-tech pack are starting to pinch my clavicles. My entire body protests this rash plan of action with every step. Nobody told me this was going to be so physically fucking strenuous.

I'm completely out of shape. The last time I elevated my heart rate through physical exertion was sprinting to catch the midnight train out of Cannes – that was at least a month ago. I'm already winded and we've only been at it for fifteen minutes. Another hour of this and I'm going to need bypass surgery. I'm not going to war; I'm at boot camp!

I look up at the pack rising and falling methodically on Jack's back. Its edges are frayed. These must have been the same packs, the same tent that Jack had used with the CIA, the same gear he'd used with the Tibetan guerillas. It certainly looks old enough to fit the part. In fact, all the gear he's given us looks ready to blow out a seam or strap at any time. Let's hope it can hold up for this one last trek. Just one more trek and we can put all of it out to pasture.

The sun reveals a newcomer to the group, a trussed-up golden-blue rooster. I knew I'd seen something moving around in the dark. His head pokes out the flap on the top of Jack's pack like a puppet...*finger lickin' good*. Our only fresh meat for the journey; a farewell feast Jack has planned for me at the pass, perhaps? And after the dinner, he'll pull out a pint of rum he'd stashed away for that very occasion. Each of us will take a shot and pass it round, share a laugh. But I don't think Jack's 'tendencies' would even allow him to hold onto a bottle of rubbing alcohol for that long.

Jack had bought the bird yesterday when we weren't looking. I hadn't been seeing things after all. The rooster clucks quietly to himself every so often, mulling over his predicament. Confined from the neck down, he twitches anxiously like he's spun out on diet pills. As dumb as it is, he must know something's up. I hope he doesn't register his protest via dawn wake-up calls.

Jack stops and turns.

"Let's take a break. Get some water and biscuits in our bellies."

Maya and I lump our packs together.

"Here you go," he says, tossing me a red-and-white packet with crooked knives on it. "I picked us up some smokes for the trail." Kukkuri: wasn't that the same brand as the rum? They seem to have the sin market cornered.

Just what I need. How the hell am I supposed to quit with him stuffing cancer sticks down my throat? I'll hold on to them, anyway. A few packs might come in handy to butter up the border patrol.

"And for our British contingency…"

Extracting a small jar from his coat, he lobs it to Maya.

"Marmite! My mate!"

Marmite …nasty stuff. I'd rather eat a two-week-old chicken casserole. Eating Marmite is the equivalent to eating salty black sludge. How can something be so repulsive to some and so delightful to others? The answer may lie in the last presidential election. What would possess someone to create an edible product out of the waste products of beer? As strong of the alliance between the States and Britain has been, I am doubtful that the trans-Atlantic Marmite gap will ever be bridged.

"Where on Earth did you find this?" she asks. "Do you think it's still edible?"

"That stuff must have a half-life of at least a couple hundred years."

"Thanks for that," she smiles.

Marmite: a sure-fire way to any Brit's heart. A lovely spread for all things well-boiled and overcooked.

"Oh, I almost forgot." He throws two pairs of nappy gloves in our direction. "I bought them off the teahouse owner last night."

Now he tells us, after my fingers feel like leftovers from Shackleton's voyage and have turned the color of an ice-hockey rink. I rub my numb hands between my legs and hastily don them.

Jack extends a tarnished brass telescope and scans the ridge behind us. He's not taking any chances, is he?

"Don't be so paranoid, Jack," says Maya. "Neither Jupiter nor I heard horsemen last night. You need to stop smoking so much gear and let your head clear."

"Just because I'm paranoid doesn't mean they're not following us."

"You really think those gangsters tailed us all the way up here from Kathmandu and rented out horses to hunt us down?" I ask.

"No, no I don't."

"There's hardly a horse up in these mountains, Jack," says Maya.

"That's what bothers me. These men I heard last night, I doubt they were Managis. They were speaking a different dialect."

"Then who were they?"

He snaps the telescope shut.

"It was hard to hear but I could have sworn...I could have sworn they were looking for us. I don't know."

He's getting that distant look again. He's looks almost scared, like a kid emerging, white-faced, from his first scary movie. I'm not sure whether to believe him or blame it on a particularly vivid and disturbing REM cycle.

"What language were they speaking, then?" I ask.

"Tibetan...a dialect of it, anyway."

"So, they weren't Managis?"

"The dialects are pretty similar, but I'm pretty sure it was Tibetan. It was so damn hard to hear anything through that wall. It almost sounded like...no, I don't know."

Something tells me he does know. A long dog-end of ash hangs off his cigarette. He flicks it to the ground. There is a lot of blame festering between Jack and I, more than you'd find in rival Catholic archdioceses. It coats our friendship, if you could call it that, like a clear lacquer finish. It may be nearly invisible, but everything we do, everything we think is tainted by that coating.

I grew up Catholic...made it to confirmation, anyway. My parents gave up after that. I used to start fights with them on the way to church and would go off about how the church was filled with hypocrisy and there wasn't any god, hoping they'd dump me off on the side of the road before we'd get there. The earlier I started the fight, the better...it made for a shorter walk home.

Jack really thinks he killed Betty. Nothing short of a presidential pardon would relieve his burden of guilt, and I don't see that forthcoming. I know the feeling; I'm still hung up on dad. I wish it had been someone else out there with him that day, but it was me, wasn't it? If only I hadn't gotten into that massive fight with him on the way to church. If only...

"I'm gonna go scout that next ridge; see what's on the other side. I'll meet you there."

Jack shoulders his pack and hobbles off. The rooster stands sentry at his post atop the pack, checking for attacks from the rear.

I slam back some water and hand the bottle to Maya.

"How're you doing? Damn, I wish he would've had given us those gloves sooner."

Then, out of the blue: "...I thought you weren't smoking gear anymore, Jupiter," she says, fishing out her water bottle. "I thought you were going to try and clean out your system."

"...What do you mean?" I ask dumbly.

"Jack told me. Frightfully poor form for someone wanting to abstain, don't you think?"

Shit. Fucking informant. I'd specifically told Jack to keep all drug-related activities under wraps when it came to Maya. That's probably why he did it.

What a stand-up guy! Maybe I'll ask him to be the best man at my wedding. He's volatile; he could do a lot more damage if unchecked.

Which reminds me: I've got to tell Maya about Jack's recently revealed weapon. How do I break the news without adding to her growing doubts about him, about this whole escapade? How do I sugarcoat the fact that Jack put a gun to my head? I don't think there is a good way to sugarcoat *assault with a deadly weapon*. Fuck it, I'll just tell her, maybe garnish the story slightly in my favor.

"You don't understand, Maya. I was under duress. He might have blown me away, literally, if I hadn't smoked that joint with him."

"Right," she says, skeptically. "Look, Jupiter…"

"It's Jay, remember?"

"Look Jay, do whatever you want but remember: you were the one that came to me with tales of your brave new plan to give up drugs. I can't be bothered to be your moral keeper. Go join a church or rehab if that's what you're after."

OK, I'm bullshitting a tad but she's not one to talk. She'd probably still be filling my head with daring tales of embassionage if I didn't check her with daddy's photo. But she's right on this: we have to depend on one another if we're going to survive this journey. We can't afford to keep things from one another. Which is why I've got to tell her about that gun. The fact that Jack's carrying a deadly weapon has tons more bearing on our survival – and ongoing safety – than whether or not I partake in the occasional joint.

"And don't lie to me, alright?" she continues. "I've had enough lies; I simply won't have it."

I rub my eyes. It's hardly daybreak and already, I'm earning demerits. No gold stars for you today, Mr Flip Flop.

I don't feel so hot, either. If Jack laced that joint with anything but hashish, he's got another kick to the shin coming.

Maybe it's just the altitude.

"Forget about the joint, Maya," I say. "I am not lying to you; I'm being dead serious. Jack has a gun; he put the thing to my *fucking head* last night."

She looks me over, scanning my face for signs of deception.

"*For real*, Maya. Why would I make up something like that? I started teasing him about being paranoid and he went all Special Forces on my ass."

She sits down next to me.

"Why didn't you tell me this earlier?"

"I didn't have a chance to. This is the first time that we've been alone. ...It was the weirdest thing. One minute he was normal; the next, he had a dirty nine-millimeter pressed against my temple."

"He's dangerous, Jay. What should we do? Try and take it from him?"

"No...not yet, anyway. He's already on edge. It kind of freaked me out when he did it, but I think it was just a show of testosterone. I know he's a little sketchy but he saved us from those gangsters..."This loose cannon we hardly know sticks a gun to your head and now you're defending him? You must be barking mad! They didn't even want us, Jupiter: they wanted that bloody *dzi*. All we had to do was give them the bloody stone and that would have been that. But Jack had to get in the middle and muck everything up. Now, quite possibly, we're caught in a tribal vendetta with a deluded ex-spy for a guide. *Excellent*."

"Well, that's where we are, Maya, in the middle...right in the thick of things. As sketchy as he is, I think Jack's the sort who likes to make good on his promises.

You can bet there's a reason Jack needs to get me over that pass. I'm not sure what it is, but he needs to get over that pass as much as I do."

"I hope you're right," she says. "My father would strangle me if he knew I was with Jack." Then she falls silent, delicately probing her stomach.

"What are you two talking about?" interrupts the reprobate in question.

Shit, he must have snuck up from behind us. Quiet as a mime but way more freaky. Was he just out of sight the entire time?

"Nothing," I say, guilty. "We were just talking about the pass."

"Yeah, right. What was that you said about your father, Maya?"

"Why on Earth would I be talking about my father?" she lies. "I really don't see what..."

"I've aired my dirty laundry," he replies. "Now let's talk about yours. Why *does* your father have a library full of books on the history of Nepal? Who is he really, and what the fuck are you doing in Nepal?"

"Why do you care about my father?" she snaps. "And you already know more about me than I care to reveal about myself."

"We can do this the easy way, Maya, or the hard way," he says, menacing now. "Your choice."

Grotesque images of gangland-style murders flash through my head. *Armed and dangerous, Maya.* "Just tell him, Maya," I interject. "It's OK."

She looks pissed at me, then uneasy. She seems to be looking for assurance. I give her the nod.

"...He works for the British Embassy," she confesses. "You might know of him."

"I'm pretty fucking sure that I do," says Jack. "What's his name? I want to know his name right now."

"Tony Gunn," she mutters.

"*Goddamnit*, I fucking knew it! I *knew* he had something to do with all this shit. Where the fuck is he? Does he know where we are? I fucking *knew* it!"

"We're not after you, Jack. And Dad isn't after you. He just..."

Jack yanks his nine-millimeter out from under his shirt and points it at Maya's head. Is this guy for real? It's one thing to threaten me but Maya? Jack could probably wrestle her one-handed and win, decrepit as he is.

"You listen, missy, and you listen well," he rants. "I want to know where that fucker is *right now* or you're never going to see him again."

What is this, a C grade crime movie? *"Jack, put it away,"* I say, the voice of reason. "She's not..."

"So you're in on this, too, eh?" he says. The dude's paranoid and he has a gun. Not good.

He brandishes the weapon, swinging it recklessly in my direction. His eyes are wide as saucers.

"Jack, just calm down!" I say. " Just put the gun down and we can talk about this, OK? Maya's dad doesn't want to hurt you. Nobody wants to fucking hurt you! Just put the damn gun down."

"Please, Jack," Maya whimpers. "I didn't…"

"Everybody just shut the fuck up for a second!" he yells.

Oh, shit, we're back to another *Full Metal Jacket* episode. Did you take your Haldol this morning, Jack, like the doctor said? No unexpected movements! There goes the telltale facial tic!

"Jack," I edge slowly towards him. "The only reason Tony's involved in this at all is because of me. I got his phone number from Gerard's little black book and tried to blackmail him, so he sent Maya to snoop on me. She bailed me out of jail and then we met you. Maya being Tony Gunn's daughter has nothing to do with you and him. I swear!"

Jack's not convinced. swings the gun back towards Maya.

"Is that true, missy?" he asks.

"Yes, Jack, it's true. Everything we've told you is true. Please don't point that thing at me anymore!"

She's crying now. I take another step towards him.

"Jack, just put it down," I say, in what I hope is a soothing way. "We're not trying to fuck with you, I promise."

His aim wavers. Slowly, he brings the pistol down to his side. Maya's still whimpering with her head between her legs. This is going to doom their already troubled relationship. Friend, Jack. *FRIEND!*.

"…Tony Gunn," Jack muses, calmer now. "So he's still kicking around here, huh?"

"…Yes." Maya rubs the tear streaks from her face.

"Is this your idea of *freelancing for the embassy*, Maya? Doing a little detective work on the side? Trailing me up into the hills?"

"No, I don't …my father thinks that we're on the next bus back to Pokhara. I've been lying through my teeth to him since we left Kathmandu. Why the *fuck* am I even talking to you when a second ago you had a gun to my head? I didn't fucking sign up for this!"

"I asked you straight up if you knew him and you fucking lied!"

"OK, everybody just chill the fuck out," I say. "Jack, put the gun away, *please*"

He tucks it back under his shirt.

"Now promise Maya and I you're not going to point that fucking thing at us again. I'm paying you, remember? I don't think it's very cool to be pointing a gun at your clients' heads!"

Jack stares at the ground.

"All this time you've been telling me how paranoid I am and now this? If you had been up-front about it and just told me…"

"If we *had* been up-front and told you, you would have wigged out and we wouldn't all be here right now," I note.

"Probably not," admits Jack. "But I've got a right to know these kinds of things. Tony was on the sidelines most of the time but he was still part of the crew. He got in the action from time to time. Shit, I remember one time when…"

"Jack, please – I'm his daughter. I don't want to hear it."

"But I wasn't going to…"

"The past is the past. Everyone has a past, but they shouldn't have to pay for it the rest of their lives. *Please*."

Listen up, Jack. That goes for you, too.

"OK, man, whatever. But I'll tell you, that cat…"

"*Please*, Jack. I don't want to hear it."

"OK, I dig."

"Now," I add, "Promise you'll keep that nine-millimeter in your pants and only use it to protect us, not to threaten us with grievous bodily harm."

"Get your shit together," he says in response. "We're burning daylight."

The sun dazzles overhead. The trail winds into a sparse forest, a scattering of slender pines trailing along a hillside. Brown pine needles crunch below my feet; dark branches undulate overhead.

I don't like forests. Bad things happen in forests. I can recite a whole litany of children's book characters that met untimely ends in forests.

"Jack, can we stop for a spot of lunch?" asks Maya.

He looks around us distractedly.

"Yeah, sure," he says. His pack thuds to the ground. "This place is as good as any."

Maya and I unload. The twenty-five pounds I've estimated I'm hauling on my back is starting to feel like fifty. And this is the easy part. I've seen zero sign of mountaineering aside from a few melting clumps of leftovers. I have no clue as to how I'm going to lug this load over all that ice and snow.

"Shit!" says Maya.

"What is it?"

"My phone – I don't have reception anymore. I still need to get in touch with…my father."

"If you even think about breathing my name I'll…"

"I won't say a word, Jack. I promise."

"Coverage past Simikot is spotty at best," says Jack.

She slowly arcs her cell above her head in search of elusive bars.

"So…that's it?" I ask.

"You might get a signal off a repeater once we get higher."

My last transmission to my family will be a minute and a half discombobulated conversation to my sister over the screams of her kids. Great.

"I promised my father I'd ring him back. He's really going to go through the roof now."

I can feel blisters in the blackened, sweaty caverns of my boots. With each step comes a slight, faint rub between sock and skin. With each stride, the blisters fester and grow until eventually, they explode, then implode. *And therein lies the rub.*

I take off my jacket. Sweat radiates from each armpit of my shirt; my back is drenched. It's getting hot, now, really hot. Whichever god governs climate control in these parts has a penchant for extremes.

Fishing a canteen from my pack, I guzzle a few mouthfuls of water and wipe the perspiration from my brow. A breeze wafts by. Leaning back against my pack, I watch flecks of sunlight dance across the fallen needles while Jack pumps life into the stove.

"What's for lunch?"

"*Chow chow.*"

"What's that?"

"Noodles."

"Just noodles?"

"Get used to it – you're going to eat plenty from here on out."

How many ways are there to cook noodles? Noodles *à la main*, noodles Sassafras, noodles *au pot*. And we're not talking Spaghetti-Os or anything fancy like that. We're just talking straight-up, flat-out, freeze-dried noodles. There's not too much you can do with them when your only variables are boiling water and flavor packets. It's all in the flavor packets. Jack probably got all the same kind: a shitty shrimp flavor, I'll bet. Can man survive on shrimp-flavored noodles alone? I wonder how many days you could go before scurvy sets in.

The water boils; Jack plops the squared white clumps into the pot and crackles up the wrapper.

"When are you thinking of working that chicken into the menu plan?" I ask.

"We've got a week of hard trekking," he says. "Let's not get ahead of ourselves."

"Maybe we should give him a name," I say.

"I wouldn't get too attached," replies Jack. "It might be harder to digest."

I don't care if he juggles and talks, but my hunger is going to beat out any feelings of intimacy I might develop for that rooster. A dog, yes…a pig, maybe – but a rooster, I don't think so. You've just got to look at the brain-to-body ratio: a rooster, familiar or otherwise, is flat out *food*. Let's call him Foghorn Leghorn from here on out.

The noodles bob on the surface of the roiling water like chunks of Styrofoam. Jack vigilantly stirs them with his knife as if he were mixing up a batch of crystal meth.

He's rubbing something in his other hand…it's the *dzi*. *His preciousss*. He'd probably try to claw out my eyes if I tried to take it from him, now, even just for a looksy. Why does he want it so badly? OK, it might be worth a small fortune, maybe more, but it's not just monetary value. It's a lifeline to his past, a lost, grainy snapshot that's suddenly resurfaced, stirring up all sorts of memories.

"…I remember the day Gerard bought this." He rolls the *dzi* in his palm. "I must have drunk fifty cups of butter tea while he haggled with that chieftain. I swear they wear you down with that tea; they just keep pumping it in you until you set a price.

"It was up in Dolpa, a hair east of here. Rugged turf; tough people. He spotted a chieftain wearing it around his neck and he had to have it.

"They had just come over the pass from Tibet. We sat in his tent all day, arguing back and forth, with that rancid, bitter tea flowing all the while. He didn't want to sell it but they were broke. Gerard tried swapping with him – a bundle of raw opium and a couple thousand rupees for the *dzi* – but the man wanted something with more of a return investment. He wanted a gun…so Gerard threw him a couple dozen rounds and a rusty M1 instead."

"A rifle?" I ask. "Then why don't you give me that pistol and we'll call it even?"

Jack ignores me, continuing with his journey down Tibetan memory lane. "This was before the tourists started throwing down serious coin for them…and when times were tough for these folk. People were starving up here, man. Thousands of them would stagger over the passes every year, half dead. Shit, back in the '70s, you could pick up a decent *dzi* for a couple bales of barley if the crops didn't come in."

"But this one is special. Gerard was lucky to get this one, even back then. See the eyes on it?" His finger rubs against a whorl. "There are twelve eyes. You can't find one with more than twelve eyes on it. It's top-of-the-line. They don't make them like that anymore."

"How *do* they make them?" asks Maya.

"That's the problem: they don't really know how anymore. They've dated some of them to as far back as 3,000 BC. They've traced some of them back to the Middle East, near Sumeria.One legend has it that the 'stones' in *dzi* were a type of burrowing beetle. If you were quick enough, you could freeze them with dust before they disappeared beneath the earth. Another has it that they were worn by the gods and were dropped from the heavens if the deities noticed any flaws...but I see no flaws at all on this one."

That would make a good ad campaign. *'The dzi...you too can own jewelry worn by the gods!'*

"The stones are usually chipped or cracked. Even a half of this one would be considered a prize. And these tiny red cinnabar flecks make it even more valuable. This *dzi* is one in a million."

"Why all the fuss about beetles?" I ask.

"Around these parts, they're considered good luck charms. Families will hold on to them for hundreds of years, passing them from one generation to the next. There are stories about farmers stumbling upon unclaimed herds of sheep after finding *dzi* in their fields, and of others meeting untimely deaths after selling or losing them."

"Gerard bought it off a starving man...that doesn't sound like it was sold in good faith. Maybe that's why it's been causing *me* so much misfortune."

My buddy worked a Deadhead over at a show once. He hitchhiked all the way across the country just to see Jerry and Co. The guy had been dropping acid for a week and was on vapors. We took him for everything he had. We wound up with eighteen dollars, a handful of tie-dyes, an eighth of magic mushrooms and a veggie burrito. I never felt good about it. At the time I was too young and high to care but if I could do it over, I would have given him the ticket. We all need miracles once in a while.

"Everyone was cool with the deal; there was no bad blood...you said Gerard gave this to you, right?"

"He gave it to me as he bled to death on the floor but yeah, he gave it to me."

"Good…that's good."

"What about my luck?" I ask. "You said that some people met untimely deaths after selling off *dzis.*"

"You're giving it to me, not selling it," he says.

That, of course, is open to interpretation. I would say some degree of duress was involved, but I'm not going to be forthcoming with my opinion because Jack has a gun in his possession and is likely to lose his cool again. If I considered it a 'sale' for services rendered, would Jack be in the firing line for an untimely death? Interesting.

"…Listen, kid, I won't take it if you're going to put a hex on it. *Dzis* are good luck charms but they have to be given in good faith. If you steal them or cheat people out of them, they'll only bring you trouble. If I stole this *dzi* from you, it would haunt me for the rest of my days. It would turn on me like a rabid dog. Can you imagine my karmic curve if I pulled some shit like that?"

He's superstitious, too. I can respect that. I'm as superstitious as a shaman when it comes to sailing. We had a little forty-two footer on Lake Michigan that we were lucky to use four months out of the year. A five- or six-foot chop in a summer breeze along the skyline was usually as rough as it got, but I fancied myself more a rag-tag whaler aboard the *Pequod.* The other eight months, we were slaves to the cold winters, thawing water pipes with blow dryers. I used to have a book that described all things nautical and inauspicious. 'Never turn over the hatches, all cups facing in, no whistling in the wheelhouse…never light a cigarette from a candle.' I pored over that book all winter long, studying maritime *faux pas* in the hope of tilting fate in our favor for the upcoming season. I abided all the rules religiously. I never flipped hatches, never whistled, never lit a cigarette off a candle. But it happened anyway. Luck wasn't listening the day fate came and swept my dad away. A stick in my superstitious spokes.

"But you have to give the *dzi* back to Betty, right?" I say.

"Betty's dead. Luck is for the living, not for the dead."

"But Gerard didn't say that – he told me to bring it back to Betty, dead or alive. You said yourself it was hers."

"You just let me take care of that," says Jack. "I'll make sure it gets to the right person. I promise you it will get to the right person."

He'd better keep that promise, or he'll be going against the fundamental laws of superstition. Doing so would be the equivalent of not returning the *tiki* doll that Bobby Brady stole on the Hawaiian vacation. As long as I'm in the clear. Maybe I should keep my distance from Jack, like the family in the *Guinness Book of World Records* who ate in a separate room from their daddy because he'd been struck by lightning a dozen times.

"...Alright, *chow chow* is on," he says.

Jack pushes a steaming cup of noodles into my hands. How can he eat at a time like this? Moments ago, he was evoking the wrath of the gods of destiny and doom.

I scoop a loaded fork into my mouth. Damn, they are shrimp-flavored? Guess we'll have to wait until he throws the rooster in the pot for chicken-flavored.

"...Is this really all we have to eat? Noodles?"

"That, some tins of tuna and whatever *tsampa* we can pick up along the way.

"*Tsampa?*"

"Tibetan food. It's their main staple. It's kind of like a paste made out of barley."

"Paste? Sounds delicious," I say sarcastically.

"It's not very high up in the palette department, but it's high in protein and energy," he expounds. "Suck a couple lumps down with some butter tea and you can go all day. Tibetans live on the shit. They can survive on a few handfuls a day. Hey, you should be glad we even have food. Before the days of *chow chow* and chocolate bars, it was slim pickings in these parts."

Here it comes: the old 'back in our day' speech. *Hiking forty miles to school...in a hailstorm...through the forest...each way.*

"Sure, we had supplies some of the time – powdered milk, powdered eggs, powdered everything – but it was pretty bad. And that was on *this* side of the border...that is, if the depots weren't cut off. It was a logistical nightmare, man.

"...People didn't die from bullets; they died from the walk in to the fight and the long haul back. We only had a handful of horses and couldn't use them over the passes. Once they knew a raid was on, the Chinese army would send out patrols to flank us and cut off the retreat. Their men were fresh and they had a constant base to rotate from; ours were half-dead.

"Some of the old-timers, they'd take a whole tin of coffee, mix it up in a bowl of water and slam it. It would keep them going for a while, but after two or three times of doing this, their hearts would just pop."

"That's rough." I take another forkful of noodles.

"...Towards the end, when they really started clamping down, we couldn't get a tin of spam into camp for months. All the horses were long gone, skinned and cooked. Some of the guys just got in from a recon mission, hadn't eaten in days. Half of them couldn't move, could barely speak. A few of the troops who could still walk chipped off some ice from the ravine...Horse saddles – they started boiling down saddles to make them more palatable...they might as well have been eating gravel."

Jack twirls his fork, drops it into his bowl.

"I seem to have lost my appetite," says Maya.

The trail ascends, zigzagging up the mountain. Right, left, right, left, right, left. How many turns before we reach the top? How many steps? How many licks to the center of a Tootsie Roll? Sweat trickles off my chin; blood pulses through my ears. I close my eyes – Gerard's lifeless body flashes by – and open them. I close them again and he is gone.

Up ahead, I see Maya struggling with her pack. Jack is studying a far-off mountain with his telescope. He squints into the lens, adjusts the focus.

"...He's following us," he whispers.

He hands me the telescope. Off on a distant ridge, I barely make out the silhouette of a man atop a horse against the sun and snow. I can't see his face clearly but he seems to be looking straight at me. A shiver runs up my spine...the horsemen: the Dark Riders. *They've found us.*

He's out in the open as if he knows I'm looking, as if he wants me to acknowledge him. I try to focus the telescope, but it catches glare off a rock.

"I spotted him a few days back, just out of Simikot," says Jack. "I thought he might be a herdsman or the scout of a salt caravan...not anymore. I didn't want to say anything 'til I was sure. He's definitely following us."

A bamboo suspension bridge sags across the river like a broken horse's back. Large sections of it are damaged or missing. A dozen-odd haphazardly placed white flags flutter from the tattered rails. Let's hope they're enough to keep the *dharma* alive. This is a bridge long overdue for a service inspection.

"Don't tell me we're going over that," I say.

"It looks like this puppy got munched in the last monsoon. There's no way we'll make it. We'll have to wade across."

"Surely you're joking," says Maya.

"It's either that or turn back to see what our mysterious friend wants. If we cover our tracks, he might think we followed the river upstream or doubled back behind him...if we're lucky."

"Are you sure it's not too deep? Those are some decent size waves," I ask.

"It's still a little high from the last monsoon, but I think we can punch through.

Take off your boots and roll up your pants – we're going for a dip. I'll go first to scout it, then I'll help you two across."

A rancid odor sears my nostrils as I unhinge my boots from my feet.

"Goddamn, that's rank."

"My feet are putrid too," says Maya. "It would've been nice to have brought a change of socks."

"Or underwear, for that matter."

"Let's not think about that, shall we?"

"Come on you two, let's go!" shouts Jack from the middle of the stream. Damn – he's crossed and is back to the middle already! How did he do that so fast?

I turn to Maya. "Do you think we'll make it?"

"Consider this a prelim," she saysMaya goes first, Doc Martens in one hand and a stick from the riverbank in the other. As she wades towards the center, her calves, then her knees disappear below the water. How deep is it? Jack is a few yards off, arm extended towards her. Suddenly she slips and is caught by the current. Her stick floats downstream.

"Maya!" I yell.

With predatory speed, Jack lunges for her and manages to grab a strap on the top of her pack. He's got her! Using all his strength, he turns Maya 'til she's facing him. She still has the Docs in her hand.

Fighting the current, Maya pulls her legs beneath her and gains a footing. Nice save, Jack. Hands interlocked tightly, they wade carefully towards the far shore. Jack pulls Maya ashore, unfastens her pack and sits her down. She's visibly shaken. Without a word, he turns and heads back towards mid-river.

"Hey, kid!"

Jack beckons with a wide sweep of his arm...*next*!

Maybe I should have toughed it out with the lawyers back in Kathmandu. Maybe they would have let me off easy. Shit, I could have bought the judge a shiny new Toyota with Gerard's stash. If I sold the *dzi* I could buy a penthouse in the hills.

What am I thinking? There is no turning back. *No turning back... you are in the maelstrom...*

I edge away from the riverbank, boots in one hand, eyes glued to the water. The din of the rapids drowns all sound. Holy shit, it's cold! My feet hug the contours of the slippery bottom as I navigate further out. *Baby steps, baby steps.* The current begins to tug at my calves, my thighs…

I feel like I'm a contestant on *Fear Factor*. Where's my fifty large? Show me the fifty! Where the hell are the safety lines, though? Why didn't I get kicked off this fucked-up show last week?

I'm not in the water anymore, I'm on it…sailing. Wind rushes past my face…sailing! *Whoah*, here comes a gust through the buildings… almost got knocked down. You've got to watch those gusts – they'll sneak right through those gaps. *'Just ease that jib, son, keep easing that jib.' 'Are you sure we don't have too much sail up, dad?'* He turns to me and smiles   …

"Don't look down or you'll fall!" shouts Jack. *"Look up!"*

I focus on Jack's outstretched hand as I approach, feet inching over the smooth stones, body leaning hard against the current. The water is almost up to my crotch now – please don't go any higher! Just look at Jack's hand…look at the hand. Look…at…the hand. *Baby steps…baby steps…he's got me.*

"I can't feel my feet anymore," I say.

"Come on, kid – we're almost there!"

Oh my god, it's fucking freezing. He tows me towards the far shore. The water begins to recede. I release his hand and make the last few steps on my own.

"Holy fuck," I say. "I can't feel my legs!"

"At least you didn't go for a swim," he jokes. "How you doing, little darling?"

"I'm fine," says Maya, "but my boots and everything in my pack are totally soaked. I'll have to dry out my sleeping bag if I don't want to freeze tonight. And I suppose my phone is dashed as well."

Maya's phone. Our last lifeline to the world. There had been the remote chance she'd get reception if we climbed to the top of the right mountain, but now that's completely shot. Her father is going to be thrilled. I wonder if Jenny is even going to tell mom I called. Maybe her pack didn't soak completely through.

"*Whew*," I pant. "That was little hairy."

"Wait 'til you see what we have to cross this afternoon."

My heart is thrumming. *Holy shit!* If I don't get amnesty based on that last feat alone, I'll be disappointed.

I drop my pack from my shoulders, fish out my water bottle and fill it from the river. Infinite larvae twitch about inside like spastic, microscopic spaghetti noodles.

The perfect recipe for dysentery. How long would I have, I wonder, if I drank it straight up? You're never the same once a gnarly parasite gets a hold of you. Never the same.

"Hey Maya, maybe you should wash out your cut. It looks like there's a lot of stuff crawling around in these waters."

"I can't be assed," she says. " I'm shattered."

I pop open my tincture of iodine and squeeze a few drops into the water. They whirl through the teeming liquid, dying it a syrupy brown. Survival Kool-Aid. Iodized water tastes awful, like a flat Coke that's been simmering in the sun. *Just keep telling yourself it's Kool-Aid.*

Maya sits shivering on a rock.

"Let's get you in some warm clothes, Maya," says Jack. "Here, get out of that cotton and put on this fleece."

"Good thinking. And thanks for your help out there, too," she answers, pointing to the river.

"You'd be a few clicks downstream by now if I'd missed. Not bad for an old-timer, huh?"

I feel like we all won something, like we should all have a group hug and listen to the appropriate Queen track. But before we have a second to savor the moment, Jack marches off up a muddy switchback and into the jungle.

"Well, that was remarkably nice of him," comments Maya.

Several large characters are etched into a massive granite face above the bank. A red hammer and sickle are spray painted over it.

"What does that mean?" I ask Maya.

"*Om mani padme hum* – It's a mantra of Chenresik, god of compassion and protector of Tibet. It translates to something like 'hail the jewel in the heart of the lotus.'"

"Hail the jewel in the heart of the...lotus?"

"Ever seen a lotus flower in bloom?" she asks.

"Can't say I have."

"Lotus flowers like to grow in stagnant ponds. They like water full of muck and mozzies and god-awful smells. What makes them so special is that they can grow in such inhospitable environs and still produce such lovely flowers. The lotus, you could say, is a metaphor to mankind: an example of how we have the ability to escape all the horrors and suffering of this world by transcending to a higher plane – to nirvana."

"How do you know all this shit?" I ask.

"I had a good teacher. It seems we have a clash of ideologies going on here."

Buddhism and Maoism don't seem a hugely compatible mix. Like an oil spill in a maritime reserve. Mao and the Dalai Lama never really hit if off, did they? Didn't Mao tell His Holiness 'religion was poison?' How can you say that to a living god? That must have been an awkward conversation.

"Humla is one of the poorest districts in Nepal. The Maoists have targeted it because of the people's limited options. It's much easier to sway people when they run out of choices."

We pass through several dense stands of spruce. The sun is sinking fast as we reach a small village – a cluster of rectangular stone houses jutting out of the slope bordered by fences of branches and twigs. Tattered strips of white cloth flap from long wooden poles.

A woman with a loom stretched out across her lap stares me down from a flat, sun-baked rooftop. A child shimmies up a notched log. Jack is puffing, standing on a large boulder like Lewis Carroll's caterpillar atop his mushroom.

"How much longer, Jack?"

"A more few clicks…do you want a toke off this?"

"My lungs can't afford it."

"Maya?" he asks.

"You know the answer, Jack."

"Suit yourself. I'm just trying to broaden your horizons. You really need to lighten up, sister."

"I've spent enough time living in a Technicolor pipe-dream, alright? What the hell are you so scared of? Don't look at me like that; I see it in your eyes. There's something up here you just can't face, something you're running from. What *are* you running from, Jack?"

There's that nervous tic again, just like clockwork.

"I'll do whatever the hell I please," he mutters. "And if that involves smoking a joint, so be it. There's got to be something wrong with you if you can't handle a few tokes off a joint every now and again."

Smoke your joint, Jack, just don't freak out again. "You know, Jack, you were right: we *are* alike in one respect. I've been through it all… caned out on lines of charlie as long as the table in decrepit hotel rooms in Bogota. Up three days on your two hundredth fag. Flakes spilling out your blood-caked nose like it's fucking Christmas as you cram another line up your nostril. That's great fun, isn't it?

"Or sweating it out at Bangkok International, wanting to go back in time because you just taped three keys of China white to your best mate's waist…and then they yank him from the line. But you can't go back; you can't make it stop. And then it's not just a game anymore – it's not an all-expenses paid holiday to Bali, is it? It's dysentery and rats and malaria and death."

A tear spills down her cheek. She spins around, walks away. That explains it. She got wrapped up in the drug web, too. She's seen the dark side. She's been as low as Jack, maybe lower. How did she get so messed up in all that shit?

I shake my head.

"*Whoah.* Wow, man, that's heavy ..."

Jack is staring hard at the ground. Maybe she's finally touching something in him. He takes me off to the side.""Why don't we call it a day?" he says. "I'll try and see if we can crash in one of these huts...She gonna be all right?" He looks at Maya with that expression of solidarity one recovered addict has for another. Not the innocent girl you thought she was, is she? She definitely blew my perception right out the water.

Suddenly there's a bond between them. They share the pain, the vacuous sense of loss that only wasted years of addiction can cause.

It's sad that it's taken this for Jack to see her as more than a sheltered princess and occasional object of desire. Is that what it takes, Jack? At least one hard year of injecting narcotics into your system? At least one irreversibly damaged organ?

I slope over to Maya, put my arm around her.

"Hey," I whisper, "How are you doing?"

"...I knew it," she continues, back in her story. "I told him it wasn't right – that he should take a miss – but he didn't listen. And all I could do was watch."-She tucks her head against my chest.

This 'him' she's referring to was more than her best mate. Sounds like she loved the guy. Stupid as he was.

"...It's not your fault," I say, attempting reassurance. How the hell do I know? I don't have a clue – but what else can I say?

"If he only listened..." She's fully sobbing now, burying her face against my shoulder.

Maybe *this* is why she's here. Why she didn't bail on me when she had the chance? This guy running the China white and coke: he was *her* guy, right? She might have been young and deluded but my guess is that she thought she loved him. He got pinched and she didn't want to see the same thing happen to me. Empathy, probably – some weird parallel between us.

She doesn't really like me: she wants to *save* me, to have the chance to rescue some other deluded romantic from a drug cul de sac...Hey, why not spend your energy saving yourself?

She doesn't like me. I can't blame her. Still, I'm happy she came along for the ride.

Clearing his throat, Jack mumbles, "Um, there's an old woman in that house down there. Why don't we warm up around her fire and regroup?"

He gazes stoically at the ground like a child who just threw a rock through a window.

"We'll be down in a sec," I say. "You OK, Maya?"

She nods, wipes her eyes.

"Come on – let's get something in our stomachs. If we're lucky she'll have some of that local brew," I say.

"You mean *rakshi?* Yeah," sighs Maya. "I could use a drink."

Jack is sitting on the porch next to a leathery-skinned woman. Staring off into the distance, she feeds a strand of s wool onto a spindle. A bulky necklace of turquoise and coral hangs over her bosom.

"Uniharu aaye," Jack says.

"Aaunos, aaunos," she replies.

The woman rises, reaches for Jack's hand and leads him inside.

"Follow me," he says.Inside, the smoke is dense, as thick as chocolate mousse. I rub my eyes, sneeze. Then I set my pack against a smooth clay wall and crouch until my face is below the smoke-line...kind of. Stray flecks of evening light poke through the matrix of sticks overhead. Parched corn husks hang from the rafters. A fire smolders in a clay oven.

The woman gropes about for a straw mat and flings it in front of the fire. Sitting cross-legged on one end, Maya pats the floor beside her.

"Down here."

I collapse onto the mat. My whole body feels as if it's been squeezed through a meat grinder and re-arranged. I remove my crusty boots: steam seeps off my socks. Delicately, I peel each one back, exposing red, chafed skin and blisters...not a good omen. Damn, they reek! Steam seeps out from their insides.

Hands spread before her, the woman seats herself opposite us and blows into the fire through a hollowed stick. Faggots scatter across the dirt floor. She breaks a chunk from a brick of leaves, plops it in a pot.

"Is she blind, Jack?" I ask.

"...As a bat. Probably glaucoma. All the years of smoke will do that. Look, I know I'm breaking the radio silence by speaking to her, but she's an old blind lady. She's one of the last one's left in this village."

"What happened to the rest of the villagers?" asks Maya.

"She says most of them cleared out once the fighting broke out. I guess there are a lot of Maoist troops in the area. Not exactly sure which faction – it's hard to keep up these days. They've been amassing near here, getting ready for an attack on the army. I guess they broke into a nearby cantonment and stole a shitload of weapons. The villagers were scared they'd get caught up in it so they bailed. The Maoists will leave her alone, though. This whole area is supposedly under a rebel faction's control now.""What does that mean for us?" I ask.

"It means we get out of here as quickly as possible. The rebels might shake us down for some cash but if we come across any government soldiers, we might get escorted back to Simikot. If they started asking for paperwork, we'd be fucked. We don't even have trekking permits and this is a restricted area."

"I thought you had everything covered, Jack."

"Like I said, my guy only deals in passports."

Turning to the crone, he says,

"Dui jaanaa masanga aaeko chha. Aaja raati haamilai baas paaunchha ki?"

"Paaunchha, paaunchha ni," she cackles.

Leaning towards Maya, I whisper, "What are they talking about?"

"Sounds like we're staying for the night."

Lifting the pot, the old woman pours hot liquid into three tin bowls.

"Chiyaa piuna!"

"Here, our Nepali *aamaa* wants us to drink up," says Jack.

He passes the bowls round.

"Is this that *rakshi* crap again?" I ask.

"No, butter tea. This is the stuff they wore Gerard down with when he bought the *dzi*."

I take a sip; a bitter taste coats my mouth.

"Nasty!"

"Get used to it," says Jack. "It's the *boisson de choix* up here."

"It does take some getting used to, doesn't it?" Maya grimaces.

I dip my head between my legs, trying to escape the smoke.

"Hey Maya," says Jack. "I didn't mean churn up bad memories back there."

"It's alright," she says. "You love to push the line, though, don't you?"I'm sorry. Again. I know, I sound like a broken record. Let's get all of your wet gear out of your pack and dry it around this fire."

He unfurls Maya's sleeping bag from her pack. It's sopping wet. Soaked straight through. So much for a final phone call home. "If you weren't so keen to prod, you wouldn't *have* to apologize so often."

"Listen, there's no way your sleeping bag is going to dry before we crash," says Jack. "Why don't you take mine for the night."

"...Yeah?"

"Positive. I'll be fine. I'm sure this old *aamaa* has a few extra blankets kicking around."

"Thanks for that." Then, turning the tables, she adds, "What about you, Jack? How did *you* get from there to here?"

"There have been lots of turns in my life, some sharper than others. When I left the whole CIA thing behind, I kind of lost it. I *wanted* to forget. I turned into a kind of *yeti* for a while – living off the land, eating berries and shrubs and whatever came my way, which isn't the easiest thing to do at twelve thousand feet. I'm not sure how long I was roaming around like that; it must have been weeks. My hair started falling out in clumps...the shit falls out if you don't wash it, you dig? And my clothes, they were falling apart, too.

"I was a little southeast of here, up on Kangmara Pass. I was wandering around in the fog up there, fog as thick as honey, and out of nowhere spring a half a dozen cats on horses. Funny seeing a bunch of horsemen up here, I thought. Funny seeing Tibetans, too. They rode up on me quick and drew their weapons. At first I thought they just wanted my pack; to them it was space age technology – must've thought I had a genie stashed away in there. But it turned out they didn't want the pack.

They wanted me.

"I tried to make a break for it, but they corralled me like a sheep. I was knocked to my knees, then I remember a knife slicing through my chest. That's a feeling you don't forget, having a rusty knife stuck in your chest. I dropped back. They gave me a few more jabs in the face and left.

"Don't know how long I lay there...I must've passed out for a good while. When I came to it was dawn. The fog was so thick I thought I was dead, floating around in some after-life holding chamber. Somehow I managed to crawl into an animal shelter nearby. And I just rested there waiting to die. I don't know how many days passed. And then in came Gerard and Elizabeth.

Jack looks right past her, deep into the murk of time. He's forty-odd years away, back at that animal shelter, wondering how in the hell he wound up there.

I glance at Maya. We've pounded the tap into the tree; now all we have to do is wait for his maple story to come trickling out. She really got a hold of that one, folks. A deep fly ball against Jack's warning track...let's hope that doesn't go over the fence.

Minutes pass.

"Chiyaa piuna," repeats the woman, gropping for the pot.

"Oh no," I groan. "I can't take anymore of that."

"Puchha-haamilai pugchha," says Jack. His hand hovers over the cup like a goalie guarding the net.

"Ali ali piuna!" she retorts.

Feeling the lip of his cup, she pours a hot stream of liquid over the back of his hand.

"Yeeow!" he yelps. Maya giggles.

"It's hard to deny Nepali hospitality," she says.

Apparently so. This old lady's employing pretty aggressive tactics. 'Drink up or burn' seems to be her motto.

"...Yeah, I should've known better."

He grins...the first time I've seen Jack really crack a smile. These people: he loves them. They make him remember. They help him forget.

Grabbing a stick, then, he pokes playfully at the fire, continues conversing in whatever dialect it is they're using, from whispers to laughter and back again. I lean back on my pack and watch. There must be one hundred and fifty years between them, but Jack and the woman play as if they are ten-year-old siblings. Something inside Jack has opened. Maybe whatever ails him is beginning to heal.

I poke at the fire with my boot. Hissing, it spits out a faggot.

The fire continues to spit and hiss. I peel back the flap of my sleeping bag. Slivers of light drill through cracks in the hut's mud walls. The old woman is gone. So is Jack.

Sliding out of my bag, I pull a sweater, one of Jack's old army-issue specials, over my head and slide out the door. A light frost blankets the ground. I spark a match, raise it to the cigarette dangling off my lip. My eyes fix on a man on a rooftop to my left. Staring, he puffs steadily on a *chillum,* smoke wafting into the breeze. I wave; he nods back.

"Got a spare one of those?" asks Jack.

Crouched against the corner of the house, he's scanning the hills with his telescope. He spits off to his side.

"I'll never forget that morning. As soon as we landed, the Marines marched me out into the field. Light was hitting the mountains just like it is now. They were doing demolition training. They were a pretty ratty bunch in the beginning, before we had any uniforms ready for them.

"They loved to blow shit up...for them, the bigger the bang, the better. The Marines gave them a barrel of M80s to practice booby-trapping techniques and they literally booby-trapped the whole goddamn base. Everywhere you went those damn firecrackers were blowing up.

"They were given American names to make things easier communicating. I always called them by their Tibetan names anyway. That was the first time we met.

"He introduced himself as Walt, but his real name was Wangdu. Until I got there, they played charades trying to translate. After the introductions, Wangdu marched right up to me and requested that they all be given special training for portable nuclear devices. He was pretty ticked off when I told him that nuclear bombs weren't in the itinerary.

"...If he only learned how to work that damn radio, that lazy son of a bitch. When we trained Wangdu, he figured that his servant would learn how to do communications, but the poor guy got so worked up on the airdrop that he started hyperventilating and couldn't jump. We thought we'd never hear from Wangdu again. Eventually he did get it up and running, but he never gave positions for drops. We couldn't make the drops without positions. If he'd only known how to give positions readings, it might have been different."

He gazes off into the mountains.

"Well, get the girl and your shit together and keep on this trail," he says, hoisting his pack onto his back. "I'll catch you later."

He charges past me down the trail. Guess that this healing process isn't going to happen overnight.

Wangdu. So he wasn't speaking in tongues with the shaman. *La Resistance*: a fellow soldier in the fight against Mao's massacre.

"Morning," chimes Maya.

"Morning."

"Where's Mr Joviality?"

"Already gone."

I take a last drag off my cigarette and chuck it into the dirt. A fierce sun slips over the ridge, bathing us in instant warmth. What happened with Jack and Wangdu? What would have been different?

Swathes of pine line a small ridge. Smoky clouds stream down. The wind picks up, whips steadily against my face. I move slowly, sliding occasionally on the large, mossy flagstones forged into the trail. Patches of snow dot the ground.

Winding upward, I see a stone cairn protruding from the crest. Jack is leaning against it, smoking something. Smells like weed – probably mixed in with some Vicodin

he's still holding to give it that extra zing. Behind him, in the distance, lies a chain of snow-capped peaks.

"Man, my leg is killing me! Must be residual venom from that snake bite. I guess I'll just keep smoking *ganja* until I can't feel anything."

Or until you fall off the trail, stoner. Why didn't I hire one of those clean-cut guides back in Simikot instead of Jack? We'd be there by now. We're not exactly playing by the rules, though, are we? Jack is probably the only one around stupid enough to take us.

"...Hey, man, I didn't mean to get into Maya's head back there. If I had known she was in recovery..."

"Hey, I didn't either," I shrug. "That must be why she's so against the shit. Reformed addicts. All the same. Now we know, though. Now *you* know. Listen, Jack, if you want to do your drugs, go right ahead, but I'd be a lot fucking happier if you don't do them around her. Leave me out of the mix, too; I'm done for now."

"Yeah...sure," he says. "You got it."

Sucking in air, he exclaims,

"Smell that fucking mountain air! Makes you feel alive, doesn't it?"

"I think the altitude is starting to get to me," I cough.

"You want any of this action?" Jack waves the joint in my direction.

"Did you hear any of what I just said?"

"Medicinal purposes, man."

"I'm not sick. Why don't you use some of those antibiotics instead? Weed won't help if your leg gets infected."

Maya shows up, drops to the ground, her face as red as a beet.

"I feel like I'm going to vomit," she says.

"Anyone want a cigarette?" asks Jack.

"Honestly, how can you still smoke at this altitude? Do you know how much stress that's putting on your lungs? And what do you need nicotine for when you've got enough weed to smoke out an entire village?" "Don't start with me, missy," he warns. She's right: cigarettes are definitely not intended for consumption at high altitudes.

Bells clang in the distance. Ahead, I spot a train of dark flecks moving across the plain.

"Those are some big-assed donkeys."

"They're not donkeys...they're yaks," replies Jack. He is peering at them through his telescope.

"It looks like they've got a full load. They must be on their way back from the border."

"With what?" I ask.

"Salt. They exchange it for grain down in the valleys to the east."

"Can I have a look?" I grab the telescope from his hand.

I zero in on a dozen black-coated animals laden with what look like burlap sacks. A flash of red yarn sprouts from the lead yak's head. Two men on foot trail them.

"We'll wait here for them to pass," says Jack. "It shouldn't be long."

The clanking of the bells grows louder. The men hiss and whoop at the yaks, meandering towards us like a pagan funeral procession. They're close now, the yaks: something between bulls and bison, with bulging, rectangular sacks slung over their broad backs. Thick mats of black and white hair hang from their massive frames like dreadlocks; smooth, marbled horns jut from their shaggy heads. A huge copper bell hangs from each yak's neck.

One of the men issues a shrill command and the caravan seizes up. Off to the left, one of the beasts grunts, sending a puff of steam into the air, then dips its head to feed. Eyeing us curiously, the men approach, chanting in hushed tones. Each wears a heavy sheepskin coat and colorful felt boots. A thick band of red yarn is tied about one's matted hair; the other wears a woolen cap.

"Om mani padmi hum, om mani padmi hum, om mani padme hum..."

They approach a rock cairn adorned with prayer flags. Extracting a pouch from his breast pocket, one of the men produces what looks like a clump of dried leaves. Bringing the leaves to his forehead, he drops to his knees and lights them. They crackle and pop like gunpowder. A stream of smoke flows upwards, sweetening the air.

"What's he burning?"

"Smells like juniper," replies Maya.

"Om mani padme hum, om mani padme hum, om mani padme hum..."

"That's the chant that innkeeper was repeating when he lit the candles for his shrine, wasn't it?" I ask. "That's what was written on the granite face, right? Hail to the jewel in the...heart of the..."

"...lotus. You remember!" *"Lha sollo! Lha gyello! Kei-kei! Ho hoo!"* cries the herdsman.

Clutching the burning leaves, he bows to the north, south, east, and west, then, rising to his feet, lets out a long sharp whistle. The caravan slowly churns back into motion, passing to the right of the cairn. Slowly, it draws away, eventually disappearing over the ridge, leaving us once more in silence.

Clambering to his feet, Jack places a stone on the cairn and walks off.

"Come on, we've got to pick up the pace." I watch his figure diminish in size until it's no bigger than a mouse. I place him between my thumb and forefinger and gently squeeze.

"...So, who was your teacher? Your father?"

"The only thing my father taught me – or should I say, tried to teach me – was how to pour tea for affluent young Englishmen. They'd smoke their pipes by the mantelpiece. I guess he hoped that they might one day take a liking to his darling little object and strike up a contract with him to purchase her."

"...The dude in the pictures."

"What pictures?"

"The ones that I was...The ones at your parent's house – with the beaches and palm trees."

"...That would be Simon," she sighs.

"He was the one, wasn't he? The one they locked up."

"...We really should crack on."

She jumps to her feet and offers me a stone.

"What's this for?" I say.

"Our luck," she says, smiling.

Rounding the cairn, she places hers on top. I walk up to it and slide my stone in among the others. Guess a little luck can't hurt.

Breaking out of a forest, Maya and I find ourselves in a high meadow. Thick bushes and spruce line the trail. I let my pack slide to the ground, wipe the sweat from my brow.

"Where's Jack?" I ask. "I haven't seen him all morning."

"He's probably doubled back to Kathmandu to shop your *dzi*."

"Do you really think he'd ditch us out here in the middle of nowhere?"

"I don't trust him. He's a heroin addict, mind," says Maya.

"He hasn't shot up in years."

"Is that what he told you? He was smoking opium with you only a few days back. You don't have to stick needles in your veins be a junkie. You've been letting him take advantage of you from the start, tossing rupees at him as if he were a snake charmer down on Durbar Marg. Have you been paying his way all along? I haven't seen him use a single rupee of his own."

"Hey, take it easy girl," I say. "His expenses were part of the deal, remember? Truth be told, I don't trust Jack either, but if he can get me over that border and out of this mess, I really don't give a shit about the money. He got us this far, didn't he?"

"And where's that? You don't have a clue where we're going, do you?"

"And you do? I saw the map, just like you did."

"The map is not the territory."

"Don't get semantic with me. Do you have any biscuits on you?"

"A few."

"Bust them out – it looks like that's our lunch."

"Oh. I've got that jar of Marmite Jack gave me as well."

"No, thanks."

Unscrewing the lid of the jar, Maya dips a biscuit into the tarry goo and takes a bite.

"Mmmm…"

"I don't know how you do it. That stuff tastes like treated waste.

What is that stuff made out of, anyway?"

"An acquired taste, darling," she replies, popping another in her mouth. "Can't be worse than a Twinkie."

At dusk, we come to a clearing with a stream running along beside it.

"Thanks for waiting up, Jack."

"You guys were lagging," he replies. "We've still got a lot of ground to cover before the pass, and I'm not waiting around for the spring thaw. Did you want me to leave a trail of gingerbread snaps for you?"

Not much chance of an apology, I'm guessing.

The last remnants of light fade out over the mountains. Wrestling the tent bag from my pack, Maya spills its contents onto the ground.

"Damn, it got dark quick. Lend me your flashlight for a sec, Jack," I say.

I point the beam down onto the deconstructed tent. Blotches of mildew dapple the clump of canvas at my feet. Bending down, I run my fingers over the thin material. Several small tears dot the seams. The aluminum poles are warped from years of use. A pole slips from my hand as I try to fit it into another.

"How old is this tent, Jack? It looks like a Snickers bar that's been lodged under a sofa for a decade."

"I know it's not the Ritz-Carlton but..."

"It's complete *shite*! Look at this – the zipper's frozen solid," says Maya as she tugs at it.

"A little wax will take care of that," instructs Jack.

"When was the last time you used this? There's not even a tarpaulin for ground cover."

"I've got a tarp, but..."

"But what?"

"If you're going to keep bitching we might as well call the whole show off."

"Listen Jack, I'm not whinging – I'm talking about our survival. It's suicidal to go up into those passes without proper equipment."

"You'll survive," he says. "I've spent years in places that make this look like a Tahitian beach. Do you know how long you can stay alive by eating boiled horse?"

"I'd rather not. I didn't know I was signing up for an iron-man marathon when I decided to come," Maya retorts.

"You have to admit, Jack, it is a pretty sad excuse for a tent," I chime in. "This thing is hurting. This is just canvas, right? Are you sure it's insulated enough?"

"We'd be better off burning it to keep warm," adds Maya.

"What the fuck is that supposed to mean?" Jack's riled now. "You wanted a tent so I got a goddamn tent! These are the same tents we used up in Mustang – I don't see why they won't work now. Sorry I couldn't pop down to the goddamn Camp-O-Rama outlet to get you a fucking triple-ply GORE-TEX dome, but I was in a bit of a rush."

"I'm out. Seriously. This trip is definitely not worth the aggro!" shouts Maya.

Maya and Jack glare like panthers, taunting each other with steamy breaths.

"Alright, everyone, just cool down," says Jack after a tense couple of seconds. "Maya…I'm sorry about the tent. You're right; I would have come up with something better if we had time. Kid, I think I owe you an apology as well. I didn't mean to railroad you into coming up here on an Amnesty trek to freedom. Fact is I'm not even sure it will work."

"That's great, Jack, just great," I say. "Is there anything else you need to let us in on – besides the lack of cigarettes and the high possibility that I'll end up a frozen fixture on a mountain pass? What the fuck did you think I came up here for, anyway?

"I'm sorry, kid. It seemed like a good idea when things got hairy with those punks in Kathmandu. You wanted out of the country and we needed to disappear…kill two birds with one stone, right? And I've got my own reasons for being up here as well.

"Don't get me wrong; I'm going to try and make this happen. I owe you huge, kid, for helping me back there with that snake bite. I would have died if it wasn't for you. And Maya, I've got to hand it to you for sticking with us – you've got a real fire in your belly.

"...I know I'm just a boil on your chests, I know I'm like that, but I *need* you guys up here. Yeah, I know this country; maybe I can get by eating boiled horse and sleeping in caves, but you're right, Maya, there are a lot of skeletons up here. Skeletons I thought I'd never see again... and they scare the *shit* out of me. But here we are...time to face the fucking music.

"...So listen, if you've gotta go, I'm not going to stop either of you. I couldn't have gotten this far without you, and if you leave, I leave. But if you stay, I will get you over that pass and Maya back down or die trying."

I take the tent in my hands and stick a pole into a grommet.

"Jack, give me a hand, will you?" Traipsing over, Jack grabs the flimsy canvas, almost jerking it out of my hand. The poles arch upward. Reluctantly, the tent rises off the ground.

"There ya go – slick as shit," he grouses.

Yanking her sleeping bag, Jack's sleeping bag, from her pack, Maya joggles the zipper of the tent door; a seam tears.

She tugs it again; the zipper flies open. Maya slips inside.

"*Phew.* Funky in here, isn't it?" she says. "Smells like the inside of a bus driver's glove. When was the last time you cleaned this: summer of '65?"

"I think it was '69."

Smart-ass.

Jack is rummaging through his gear. He pulls out a few packets of dried noodles and some tins of tuna. Strapping on the headlight, I stab through the dark in search of firewood. Ten minutes later, I drop a bundle of mangled twigs in front of Jack as he pumps the stove to life: my tribute to the god of *chow chow*.

"Forget the fire, kid."

"Low profile?"

"You're learning. That was the same problem with the Tibetan guerillas. We just couldn't bang it into their heads to work in small units. Traditionally, they always brought wives and children with them when they went into battle. Strength in numbers, you know?

They were damn good fighters, but that was their downfall. In the end, the Chinese would hone in on them with their planes and mow them down. If only we'd gotten that into their heads."

The tent rustles.

"Jupiter, should I clear a space in here for you?"

Jack nudges me.

"Go on, kid," he whispers. "She wants it."

"Shut the fuck up, Jack," I hiss. *"You go!"*

"Yeah, right. If I was twenty years younger, I might have a shot at the title. He croons softly. *'Young American, young American, she wants the young American...aaall night...'*

"Fuck off." I'm surly now.

"Take a chill pill, *hombre!*"

Scooping up my gear, I slouch off to the far edge of the meadow, my unfurled sleeping bag trailing over one shoulder. As much as I want to cuddle up next to Maya, I refuse to let Jack win. My sleeping bag catches on a bush. Shit. Bending down, I coax the bag off its thorny snare, drop my pack, then crawl into the bag and zip it tight. My own rapid breaths resonate in my ears; my body shivers against the inner lining. Gradually, my breathing slows and the temperature inside the bag rises.

Just as I begin to slip away, I hear the thud of footsteps, followed by the distinctive click of a flint. "Pretty rough country up here, kid. It's best not to stray too far from camp."

"You know, you're just like Gerard," I say. "Constantly degrading women as if they were some subhuman life form. What did Maya ever do to deserve your derision? What did any woman ever do to you?"

"Alright, but don't say I didn't warn ya."

"Warn me about what?"

Hacking up a glob of phlegm, he says,

"I don't know – I thought I heard something. It's probably just this opium playing with my head. You want a toke off the dream weaver?"

"That's all you, bud."

"There it is again – did you hear it?"

I pop my head out of the bag.

"Quit fucking with me, Jack," I say. "I've had enough of your shit for one day."

"Hey, man, my ears might be fucking with me but I'm not fucking with you."

"What do think it was?"

"Never can tell. Maybe it's our mystery tracker… or snow leopards."

"*Snow leopards?* Give me a break."

"Hey man, this is their territory. There's not too many of them left now. The Chinese mowed most of them down with AK-47s and hand grenades but there are still a few lurking in these canyons. All of these guys racing up here to collect *yarsa gomba* for the Chinese *nouveaux riches* isn't helping, either. If you're lucky, you might hear one. We might even get a surprise visitor tonight with that rooster around."

"Just what we need right now."

Something trickles across my face. Opening my eyes, I look into the illuminated lining of my bag. I'm sweating like a rapist. Ok, maybe these sleeping bags will work. I peel the sack down to my trunk; frost spills off the outside of my bag. Fifty yards away, Jack is perched on a boulder with his telescope. As I wrestle on my boots a blister pops. I stumble off to the edge of the stream to swipe a few handfuls of icy water over my face.

"Morning."

Looking up, I see Maya a few yards upstream in her sports bra, dabbing her stomach with a damp cloth. A bottle of hydrogen peroxide is balanced precariously on a rock at her side. I gaze down at the rough zigzag of stitches encrusted with blood on her abdomen.

"Does that feel as bad as it looks?"

Turning her back to me, she slips on her shirt.

"Only when I breathe. It's a bit revolting but I think I'll manage, as long as it doesn't go septic."

"Est-ce je peux t'aider?"

"No. I'm all right, thanks."

"Well, just let me know if you need a hand with anything. I can help carry some of your stuff if it starts acting up."

"Ta," she says, smiling up at me.

I saunter over to Jack, whistling as I draw near.

"Don't whistle, it's bad luck," he growls.

"Why, are you afraid I'm going to whistle up a storm?"

I would never whistle on a boat, but given that we're landlocked I sputter out a few more notes just to test the waters. Shit, he always pushes the envelope with me. What are *you* gonna do about it, old man? Pull that gun? Why don't you pull it out, wave it around a little and give your courage a boost?

"Hey man, I'm not kidding. It's disrespectful. The gods don't dig it…they get bad vibes."

…He just might. We don't need another show of force. I fade out on a low C. What a grump: the god of bad vibes.

"So, did you spot any snow leopards last night?" I ask.

"Can't say I did…you?"

"Nah."

Loading a cup of hot tea with sugar, he hands it to me.

"Man, that's sweet."

"I like my tea like I like my women: *sweet and hot*," says Jack.

Urrgh ah urrgh ah uuuuuurrgh! crows Foghorn.

"Again with the lines," says Maya.

A string of multicolored prayer flags, bleached and soiled with age, flap drowsily from a shrine at the top of a ridge. I've got to take a shit so bad I can taste it. Where's the toilet paper again? My body has surrendered itself to Nepali microbes, embroiling my stomach and ass in chronic states of emergency.

Jack and Maya are well out of sight, Maya in front and Jack behind me. I'll only have an issue if Jack catches up, but I can't see him. If Maya were at the rear I don't think I'd risk it, but…it would be a bit awkward having him round a boulder to see me squatting, pants around my ankles.

But shit man, I've gotta go! Fuck it, this boulder will do. I start to rip off layers: belt, pants, then thermals. My skin bristles with the first blast of frigid air.

"Shit." I exclaim – aptly, given what's about to transpire. Before I can get my boxers down, a stream of brown liquid begins splattering off my ass cheeks, accompanied by staccato guttural sounds. I groan, half relief, half agony. Clearly, the microbes have gained control of my intestinal conflict.

Oh, god, please stop.

Then suddenly, it's over – at least, I think it is …for now. The waves of intestinal malfunction come and go, with all the uncertainty and intensity of an equatorial microburst in the Pacific Ocean. Maybe I should hit Jack up for some Imodium. Sixteen thousand feet above sea level is not a good place to have diarrhoea. I need to keep the fuel tanks topped up at this height.

Oh fuck, where's the toilet paper? Now I remember I don't have any on me…well, this might be more awkward than I ever imagined. What to use, what to use?

The prayer flags. Fuck it: bet if I asked him, the Dalai Lama wouldn't mind. I'm in a time of need here, a sentient being seeking material yet essential goods to avoid an ephemeral yet uncomfortable situation. My boxers are on their last legs already. I rip down a yellow flag. It tears away easily, battered thin by the wind. Not nearly as soft as the two-ply to which my ass has become accustomed, but it does the trick.

"What the fuck are you doing?" screams Jack.

"Hold on – just give me a second," I stammer, hiking up my pants.

"What does it look like I'm doing?"

"Did you just wipe your ass with that prayer flag? Are you fucking *kidding me*?"

"I...didn't have any toilet paper."

"That is just so goddamn wrong. It's fucking *sacrilege*. How the hell are we supposed to build up any *dharma,* man? You think the gods are actually going to let you get over that pass when you pull this kind of shit?" He shakes his head in disbelief.

Jack, who's no doubt amassed a lifetime of bad karma, is giving me shit about one little prayer flag?

"...What was I supposed to do, rub my ass in the dirt?" I say. "I needed something! And I'd appreciate it if you didn't tell Maya."

"You actually still think you've got a chance? Give it up, kid, it's not happening."

"Promise me anyhow...please."

"...Fine," he says then. "I won't say anything, but clean that shit up. Bury it or something...and apologize. Here." He tosses me a roll of toilet paper and lights up a cigarette.

"To who?" I ask.

"Buddha, Padmasambhava, the Dalai Lama – whoever you can think of. I just hope the gods weren't watching."

"I'm sorry, Dalai Lama, I really am, but I hope you understand that I was in a time of need. I hope that incident won't affect my karmic status. I had limited options. There was no intent to desecrate your shrine."

"If you're not careful," he says, "you're going to come back in your next life as a bug."

If I'm going to be a bug, Jack is most likely going to resurface as one of the microbes that have been wreaking havoc in my ass. I buckle my belt and sensation begins to return to my lower half.

"I'm out of here," Jack moans. "That was just so *goddamn wrong*."

The three of us pass a small compound with a few flat-roofed houses at the top of the slope. A wrinkled man in a woolen coat is smashing rocks with a hammer above the trail. Strands of hair escape the plait that's wrapped around his forehead. He stops, holding the hammer in mid-air as he studies us. I feel like he knows something. His eyes focus on Jack.

"*Shit*," Jack hisses. "Come on, let's get out of here."

Head bowed, Jack is almost running. Maya and I exchange quizzical glances.

"Hey Jack – what's the hurry? Can't we chill here for a sec? Maybe this guy can sell us some biscuits," I yell ahead.

"Not here," he growls.

"*Jack* – Are you fucking deaf or something? Like it or not, we're stopping."

Suddenly, the man pounding rocks shouts in our direction, freezing Jack in his tracks.

"*Thrhtug kherang thusr gyogpa logzhag. Drubdre gang yongi yodpa kherang khennam. Ngyurdu Azhang Choekyi Gyalpoe ngahog du yong!*"

Jack grabs my arm.

"We move…*now!*"

Mr Rock Chopper lets out an eerie, animistic scream. Swinging round, I watch him hold the sledgehammer above his head for a second, then bring it down against the rock. It cracks like a cue ball against a fresh rack, splitting into fragments...*whoah.*

Jack hesitates, then trots off, disappearing into a copse at the far end of the compound. I look up at the man, at his insidious smile. Maoist? Nah, that guy swears no allegiance to anyone. Rip out your eyeballs just for kicks. Like Jack, maybe worse.

He knows Jack, doesn't like Jack. That rock was supposed to be Jack's head...

Here, things could get real freaky real quick. Who's afraid of Maoists when you've got a Central Asian version of Leatherface in hot pursuit?

Breaking into a jog, I run into the forest with Maya at my heels.

"Hey Jack, what was that all about?"

"He didn't seem very keen on us," pants Maya.

"What did he say, Jack?" I grab his shoulder.

"I didn't catch it," he mumbles, staring off into the forest.

"Come on, what did he say? He *was* talking to you, wasn't he?"

He pulls free of my grip.

"Just keep moving," he snaps.

His eyes are wild. He's scared shitless. Yeah, Leatherface has his number.

"Just let's go!"

He hustles off, leaving Maya and I full of questions in afternoon shadows.

The trail continues to descend, dipping down into a canyon with a quick clear stream. Steep clay walls hem us in on both sides. Jack is out of sight, now, booking way ahead of us. We wind in and out of small copses broken intermittently by meadows of juniper and grass. As we pass near the stream, I notice an assemblage of wooden aqueducts fashioned from tree trunks. Water gurgles incessantly through the bored channels. I follow them downstream with my eyes to a small hut, perched precariously over the river.

I lean back into the warm, moist padding of my pack and close my eyes. Maya rumbles up, brushes an arm across her brow.

"Have you seen Jack?

"Not since we passed that dude chopping rocks."

I hand her my canteen.

"That was bizarre, wasn't it? It seemed as if he knew Jack, d'you know what I mean?"

"He knew him all right. And I don't think he was a big fan, either. Why do think Jack skittered off like a skink? Jack sure didn't want anything to do with him, whoever he was. Must be another skeleton in his closet."

"A right fright. You'll think that bloke will come after us?"

"I think he would have made his move when he saw us," I say.

"Jack might be thinking otherwise."

"I think...Jack would stick with us, if that guy was gonna make a move on us."

"Are you sure about that, Jay? Jack looked as if he'd seen a ghost back there. I think he's beginning to wonder if he should have come at all."

"...I'm not sure of much anymore." I look away.

I wish I was. Truth is, some days I trust Jack and most days I don't. He's saved us a few times, but he's also pointed a gun at both of our heads. That's a bit of a mixed bag. I wouldn't put it past him to bolt on us, especially after being spooked like that. But...no, he's not gonna leave his men behind. There's some unfinished business at that pass. He's not going anywhere but there.

Steadily, we cut up a series of sharp switchbacks. A cluster of birds chirrups in the branches above. Perspiration pours off my body; my clothing's soaked. I look up into the dense brush, darkness obstructing my view.

I never made that call, did I? Not even so much as an email. If something happens up here, they'll never know what became of me. I'll be an image frozen in the family album, the one they all pray for during the holidays...or don't. Maybe it's better that way...to just fade away. Be frozen in time like skinny Elvis.

The forest is no longer pine, now, but a mix of hardwoods and brambles.

Ferns poke out of decaying logs fallen across the path. Weren't we in a desert yesterday? We've been dipping in and out of microclimates on a daily basis since the trek started. Pausing at a turn, I drop my pack and fish out a scuffed iPod (why the hell do they scratch so easy?) from the bottom...a remnant of another world. Thank god it was on me when we got jumped. Wrapping the headphones around my ears, I slip into some Hernán Cattáneo. *Baam baam budupdudaam!* The beats blast into my mind like a needle-gun chipping away a sandstone wall. Just the ticket to stop the doubt running through my head.

Where the fuck is Jack? Did he really bail on us, leave us up in this soupy mountain fog? I shiver, stop the music. The sun has disappeared. A chill nibbles at my neck.

We should have stopped hours ago for lunch. That bastard; he has almost all of the food with him. How did he end up with the food in his pack anyhow? I was carrying at least half the tuna yesterday. I don't think Maya's got anything except a few packs of *chow chow*, maybe some biscuits. He's got Foghorn Leghorn, too. *And* the stove; he's got the stove. Even if we had the food, we'd have to eat it chilled.

No-good piece of shit...hoarder.

Maya trundles up behind me.

"Where's Jack?"

I look at the ground. Please don't ask me again.

"...How much food do you have on you?" I ask.

"A few packets of coconut biscuits...I think that's about it."

"Bust them out."

The white plastic wrapper is off before they hit my hands. Fuel...energy...*food*! I devour half in one handful and guzzle down some water. I can feel my strength returning with every swallow.

"Oh my god, those tasted *so good.*"

"*Damn*, I was hungry! I can't believe how good...what's the matter?"

"...How many do you have left, Jupiter?"

I freeze up in mid-chew.

Maybe we shouldn't eat these all at once."Jack's got all the food, hasn't he? You should have at least savored it a bit: that might have been your last supper."

I pop the last biscuit in my mouth dejectedly. We'll be lucky to make it through tomorrow on our own. She sure knows how to ruin a food buzz.

"He's probably set up camp and started boiling up *chow chow* for us by now."

"Are you that bloody blind?" she says. "This is it. Jack's *gone!*"

"You don't know that for sure. Why do you always jump to conclusions?"

"Why do you think he squirreled all the food into his pack this morning? He's been planning this all along, you fool. We're not going to see him again. Maybe if we're lucky, he'll leave a few tins of sardines along the way. Bloody hell, he might even toss in a fucking can opener."

She stares up into the canopy. "Thanks for that, Jack. Thanks for *fucking looking out! Wanker!*"

"Fuck him: we've got the tent ..."

"He doesn't need the tent, Jupiter. When did you ever see Jack set foot in that bloody tent? The only reason we have it is because he doesn't want the weight. And anyhow, why do you even have it? He offered to carry it in the first place. The bloody thing is worthless. We need food! We barely bought enough to make it up to the pass, let alone back to Simikot. And guess what? Jack has the bloody map as well. Oh, what good is it, anyway? Half the trails we took weren't even on that map."

She slouches down to the ground as if a puppeteer had suddenly dropped her strings. Damn, she might be right. I dropped the strings: I didn't see it coming. Leatherface might have spooked Jack back into his hole for good.

A cool breeze slides past; I shiver. A raindrop spatters my head. Rain – great. Just what we need right now.

I lean over Maya, offer her my hand.

"Come on, it's going to rain," I say. "Let's get off this mountain and find a place to set up camp."

A monotonous drizzle whispers through the forest. Steam rises off my shirt like vile thoughts. Mud begins to cake my boots, enlarging them as the trail softens; I feel like a mobster about to be thrown into the river, feet set in two pots of cement. I bang them against a stump, shaking off the excess.

Why like this, Jack? Why let us starve to death in this moist wound of a jungle? Just put a bullet through each of our heads and be done with it. Let it be quick. You're too much of a coward, though, aren't you? You don't have the balls. Probably did the same to Leatherface's boys. That's why he's after you.

The drizzle has shifted now to rain, steady and looking as though it's set in for the duration. Peering up the trail, I see winding rows of switchbacks fading into the forest. How many switches to the top of this lollipop? I slow my pace, wait for Maya to catch up. I lose her and this game is over.

I hear bells, getting closer. Guardian angels? The ice cream van? Either right now would be a heavenly sight.

Rounding a switch, I spy a flock of piebald goats rambling up over the ridge. Twisted pairs of horns protrude from their shaggy gray coats; bells clank from their necks. Nearing me, they hesitate. I reach down to pet one but it veers away, emitting a startled bleat.

They must sense my hunger. How hard would it be to cook one of these guys up? Maybe we could salt the meat: a big one might last us a month.

A boy brandishing a long stick with a tunic wrapped about his head brings up the rear of the flock. Uttering a shrill cry, he slams the stick against a tree. The goats bolt past in a stream of white and black. *Wait, come back.*

"Namaste."

"Maya, ask the kid how much he wants for one of these goats!" I shout as he passes.

They exchange a few words.

"…They're not for sale."

"Tell him we're going to starve if he doesn't sell us one."

"…He can't; they're not his goats."

"Ask him if he's seen Jack."

"…No, he says he hasn't."

Shit. Where the hell did he go? Thick vines and ferns form a maze-like tangle on both sides of the path. Can humans eat ferns? Not much protein in a fern, I'm guessing. Some are probably poisonous, too. We don't want a sequel to *Into the Wild.*

Hell of a place to ditch us, Jack, you ass…couldn't you have left us a tad closer to civilization, near a teahouse or something?

Had he picked up another trail? I hadn't seen any forks in the track. I'm betting he didn't loop back and have a Scotch with Leatherface for old time's sake. No, if he's ditching us, he's using an alternate route. What are you up to, old-timer?

I take a swig of water…nearly on empty now. Peeking through a hole in the canopy, I catch the unmistakable silver flash of a river below…a big river. OK, we've got one of the necessities in range. Don't freak out just yet. Water is more important than food. And where there's water, there's food! Shit, I might be able to spear a fish with some of this bamboo. Then we'll find another goat herder who's willing to part ways with one of his flock.

Fuck you, Jack. We'll do just fine without you.

"There's no water up here so he must be going down," figures Maya. "We haven't seen so much as a puddle all day. Whatever Jack has up his sleeve, he's going to need to replenish his supplies. Five to one, he's going to make camp somewhere near that river tonight. If we're lucky, we can catch him."

The trail begins to twist downwards. My calf muscles bulge as my knees struggle against gravity's pull. Moss curtains the canopy; the trail weaves through dense jungle, dropping off treacherous ledges, over fallen branches and craggy boulders.

I keep scanning side to side, looking for signs of movement, signs of Jack. *Come out, come out, wherever you are...* Reaching a steep ledge, I ease myself down backwards, rappelling with exposed roots. These rocks are getting slippery with the rain.

The music in my ears begins to cut out...damn, I'm almost out of juice. I stare down at the LED as the flashing icon signals the end. That's it. No more Renaissance, no more Radiohead, no more escaping this grim reality. My last link to civilization...gone. Maybe I can trade it for a goat. If only...

Something moves in the canopy above. I half-expect to see Jack curled up in a tree fork, face painted Rambo-esque in streaks of mud. A branch quivers as a shadow lunges off...a monkey! Another tree thrashes nearby. Within seconds, the canopy is filled with black-and-white shadows, darting through the mist.

Instantly, the tumult above ceases; only the patter of raindrops persists. Looking upwards, my eyes meet many more, all locked on me. Never seen monkeys in the wild before. They look threatening. Like some radical Special Ops battalion trained by the Maoists to roll tourists along the trail... If they could only imprint the local monkeys with Marxist-Leninist thought.

"Ooh ooh, ooohooohoooh aahaah!" I howl.

Like frozen ghouls, the creatures stare intently back.

I wonder what monkey tastes like...chicken? There's always the possibility that I could be a conduit for a mutated virus but damn, I'm hungry.

Thick clouds collapse against the mountainside. What I'd give for my childhood slingshot right now. Let's see, they're not that far away. One is practically over my head. There are some decent-sized rocks around; if I threw a fastball right down the pipe and pegged it in the head...

A huge tree trunk blocks the way...just a little closer. Don't scare them off now. Yeah, they look pretty tasty. A little closer now...

I slip, hard.

Falling, FALLING....*whuf*! Suspended over a cliff, I land on my stomach on a thick clump of bamboo. A sharp pain shoots through my thigh as I try to disentangle myself. Oh, man, if I broke my leg...

"Fuck! Mayaaaah!" I scream.

"Mayaaaah!"

My sunglasses dangle from a fern a few feet below. I stretch my arm out through the bamboo; blood trickles off my wrist.

"Mayaah!"

"...Jupe?"

Extending my arm, my fingertips grovel for the glasses. Sliding off the fern, they tumble into the tangled foliage and over the ledge.

That *sucks*. There's no replacing those. Now the sun and snow are going to double-team all of the life out of my retinas until they're like stale, shriveled raisins.

Maya's voice: "...Where *are* you?"

"Down here," I groan.

I roll over and gaze up through a hole in the foliage. Suddenly, Maya's head pops into it. I need to get back to that hole.

"Oh, dear!" She clutches her mouth. "What happened?"

"What does it *look* like happened? I fell off the fucking trail! Give me a hand, will you."

Slowly I writhe myself up towards her with branches and exposed roots. The rain has turned the ground into mud. Clinging to an exposed root with one hand, I stretch out my other. Our fingertips brush...she's laughing.

"I can't reach."

She turns away, trying to keep a straight face.

I lose my grip and slide back down the muddy face.

"Come on," I snap, "It's *not fucking funny!*"

"Yes it is," she giggles.

"I can't…I'm too far down…"

"OK, OK – stay where you are," she instructs. "You might be closer to the switchback below. I'm going to follow the trail down and see if it leads below you."

Nice move, dumb-ass. I'm not even stoned. Minimal water, no food…and now skewered on bamboo like some exotic Asian dish in the midst of a remote mountain jungle. Gliding through the branches above, the monkeys drop out of sight. Laugh it up, you little shits. I'm the one with opposable thumbs and you're already down the mountain.

A rope drops down to my side. I look up into the opening.

"Jack!"

"Stop yelling, damn it. Now listen: the rope is secured to a tree trunk. Tie the rope around the strap on the back of your pack. Just brace your legs against the hill and pull yourself up. I'll pull as you climb, alright?"

Easier said than done. I've got a twenty-five pound pack on my back…this could be a clip for the US Army Reserves. Right now, I feel about as smart as the fresh inner-city recruit. Let's see if I'm as out of shape as one.

"I'll pull up on three. One…two…three!"

I heave myself up the line. Mud and rock slide away as I cram my feet into the slope, exposing gnarled tree roots. *You can do it in the AAaaarrrrrrrmy!*

"Come on, you're almost there, kid," grunts Jack.

I wonder if he's just fucking with me. Maybe he'll cut the line at the last second, just for kicks. Maybe he wants to tap out my cash reserves before finally booting me off a cliff. Maybe he'll just leave me hanging there until I hand over my wallet, then cut me loose.

"Ready? One, two…three!"

Grabbing my hand, Jack hoists me up.

"One…two…three!"

I wriggle over the ledge like a salamander.

"Jack" I gasp. "Nice move…that was clutch."

"Shut up, will you? Where's Maya?"

"She went down…the trail," I huff, "to see if I could get out that way."

"Come on, let's bail."

He yanks me to my feet, takes a quick look over his shoulder.

"We've got to keep moving."

We're almost running down the trail. Rounding a bend, we almost barrel over Maya.

"Jupe, are you alright? Oh my, look at you!"

I check out the long scratches on my forearms.

"It looks worse than it feels – nothing a little peroxide can't fix."

"Oh, you've waxed your head as well!"

I lightly touch the throbbing bump above my ear…blood.

"It doesn't feel too bad. Fuck, I lost my shades…*goddamnit!*"

"…You're going to need them where we're going. You'll go blind without them. Here, let's have a look at you."

She licks her palm, carefully wipes the mud from my brow.

"Thanks."

"No problem, *dude*," she giggles, drawing out an American accent.

I glimpse the violent, muddy river through the leaves. The water level is high. I hope Jack isn't entertaining another crossing.

"*Jaack.*" Maya turns to him. "So nice of you to pop by! What's this all about? To what do we owe the honor?"

"Not now, Maya," he says. "There'll be plenty of time to talk when we get to the bottom. Bust out your ponchos: it's about to come down."

Jack glances behind him, then disappears behind a tree. He's going native – becoming like one of those mysterious, almost-mute game-trackers from the wilds of Africa, ready to pounce out of the bush at any moment…scary.

A heavy mist creeps into the forest, seeping into every nook and cranny. A damsel fly hovers silently, whirring about my head like a lost fairy. We curl down several switchbacks in close succession, segments of a monstrous centipede. The light is fading into shades of gray.

Each step, I strain back, trying to subdue the awkward, pestering weight on my back. My clavicles scream out for reprieve. I must have tweaked my knee again when I fell…an old sailing injury that never healed properly. Banged it against a winch during a fast tack with dad out on the lake. I can feel the cartilage grind with every step. Last time this happened, it swelled up to the size of a small grapefruit. I need to rest; I'm tired as fuck. I just want to crash. Oddly enough, my poncho won't allow that to happen. It's not doing shit to keep out the rain but the god-awful stench keeps me awake. It's like smelling salts.

I've unwittingly entered some lesser stage of hell, condemned to torture but not thrown straight onto the burning coals. Higher forces must have seen some of the good things I did…way back when. Before the accident.

The rocks and logs along this section of the trail glisten with water; the mud is a glossy black. I grab onto slick branches for balance. Pebbles roll under my boots like marbles. Rain ticks harder and harder against my poncho.

Then the trail widens, the turns decrease. Entering a field of boulders, I stare at the white flashes of the frothing river before me.

Massive and muddy, it produces a dull, constant hum, its churn and flow an unwavering mantra. Still swollen from the monsoon, it rushes bullishly past, flaunting its power.

Maya trudges up behind me, slumps against a boulder, and downs the last drops from her canteen. Streaks of mud score her pallid face. A twig dangles from her hair. A week in a spa and an intravenous electrolyte cocktail wouldn't hurt. I'll go with the straight up blood transfusion. It worked for the Stones, right?

"You don't look so hot, girl."

"You're one to talk," she retorts. "Look at your arms."

"No, really. Your face is so pale I can almost see through it. Are you OK?"

"I wish I had time to fetch some gear before we left," she says, stoic as usual. "This poncho is as minging as sewer pipe. And my boots are definitely not going to last the entire trip. Look, the sole is already separating from the toe. I've already had to mend my laces twice, and the eyelets are beginning to pull out." To demonstrate, she stomps one into the mud.

"Mine are fucked, too. And I've lost count of blisters."

The odds don't look good for either pair surviving the journey.

"I think I tweaked my knee."

"Your pants are ripped as well," she notes. "And you're bleeding."

I touch my head.

"Not there, that's stopped. Your leg"

My pants are torn from the fall. A trickle of blood runs down my leg. I notice a slimy, stringy, worm-like creature inching up my calf.

"Hey, what the fuck is *that*?"

"Land leeches," she says, plucking the critter off my leg. It writhes in her hand like a miniature eel out of water.

"They hang about on vegetation waiting for animals to wander by. They hone in on motion and heat. When one does tramp by, they drop or slither their way onto you and fill up. Looks like we're in for a bit of bloodletting."

She's joking, right? Parasites with advanced tracking systems: bad evolutionary joke. They should have never been allowed out of the water. Sounds like a twisted version of *Night of the Living Dead*. The whole sanguine concept is not sitting well with me. Palm-lined beaches, palm-lined beaches, palm-lined beaches...

I curl back my sock; a fat, slimy black blob plops off my shin. An unwelcome security breach. I kick it away. Another stretches off the toe of my boot, groping blindly in the air. Something wriggles up my neck. Reaching round, I pluck off another. It convulses as I pinch it...*gotcha*, you little fuck. I squeeze until blood oozes from its sides.

"Shit, this place is infested."

"My god, you're covered in them," says Maya. "It must have been from when you fell into that bamboo thicket. Let me have a look."

If I'm going down, I'm going down fighting. I zap the leech on my boot with my lighter...this is war. *No free lunches, bitches!*

You've got to wonder why such nasty creatures need to exist.

They're right up there with mosquitoes and ticks. And Jack.

OK, that's not true; I don't hate Jack anymore. I can't hate him. There was good in him, there is good in him. He's sketched out by something bigger than him...events out of his control. He's become something he is not. I can pity him, yes, but not hate him. I hope he can hold onto his noble past long enough to get me over the border.

"OK, I think that's the last of them," she says, pulling another writhing sucker off the back of my neck. "Are you alright? You look a bit peeked."

"Yeah, I'm fine."

She pecks me on the cheek. I could really use a hot, passionate kiss to take my mind off the leech violation, but a peck is better than nothing. Slits of rain are coming down steadily now.

"Can I get another of those kisses?" I venture.

"Given the circumstances, yes."

She kisses my other cheek, this time for a little longer. Do I have to lose a finger to get one on the lips?

"Hey, you two – I don't want to ruin the moment but we are in for one mother of a storm." It's Jack, huddled in the shadow of a boulder. He's been sitting there the whole time, watching us. Pervert. Just like Gerard: scared off every girl that got near him....every girl I tried to get close to.

"Let's make our way up the shore another click or so," says Jack. "If anyone *is* following us, they'll think we went the other way and crossed at the bridge."

"Did you see the horseman?" I ask.

"We'd better keep moving," he says. "It's almost dark."

"Does he really think...Leatherface? I can't imagine him chasing us all the way down here. He looked pretty arthritic. If he really wanted Jack dead, he would have had a better shot wielding the sledgehammer on the spot at Jack's head instead of at that rock. But revenge is a dish best served cold, right? He might call in his posse do the dirty work for him. Hobble Jack, then drag him back for the good stuff.

I totter over slippery, rounded stones, trying not to sprain an ankle. That's all I'd need, an ankle with a twist, to go with my grapefruit knee…that'd be a debilitating cocktail.

Banked black clouds threaten overhead. The wind surges violent-ly."Fuck it, this is good enough," says Jack. "You'd better get that tent set up. Keep it over to this side so it's out of sight. I'll be underneath that outcropping, setting up shop."

"What, you're not going to help us?" asks Maya.

"I'm not sleeping in it – make your own bed. You can come join me under that slab of granite over there, but I'm calling the inside spot."

"These ponchos are the rat's ass, Jack. They leak like sieves and they smell like ass. Do you have any more rain gear?"

"If you don't want it, I sure as hell could use it. It'd make a nice cover for my pack."

"Don't you have *anything* with GORE-TEX in it?" asks Maya.

"Negative."

"Do you even know what GORE-TEX is, Jack?"

A gust of wind sweeps through the canyon. Thunder bellows across the sky.

"Right – let's get the bloody tent up before this storm hits!" yells Maya.

I flip the tent pouch upside down and spill the contents onto a small wash of sand. I toss a few rocks to the side in an attempt to clear a spot, but find only more. It's going to be a rocky one tonight. Heavy fat rain-drops begin to fall. I slide the poles into the sleeves and arc them into place. The tent suddenly pops to life, catching the wind like a sail. A gust flattens its side and it nearly rips from our grasp.

"Jack, give us your tarpaulin!" shouts Maya.

"Damn, sister, you've already got the tent."

"Bollocks! This tent is meant for all of us. Whether or not you share it with us is your decision, but if we don't use that tarpaulin as a rain cover, we'll all be soaked!" Maya isn't happy, and I don't blame her.

"Bleed a man dry, why don't you…here!" Jack throws the tarp to the ground. Another gust kicks up, spinning it over the rocks like tum-bleweed. *Asshole.*

"Hold the tent, Maya!" I yell.

I give chase, cornering the blue bundle between two pieces of driftwood. This is all my knee needs: a high-speed chase through a slippery field littered with rocks. Good thing I got that nifty health insurance policy before hitting the slopes.

Jack's tarp crackles like electricity in the wind; trees moan. Maya looks as if she's about to go into orbit, the tent surging over her head. I jump on the tarp and subdue it under a rock. Grabbing a corner of the tent, I work a stake into the ground. A fresh slew of rain pelts down.

"...I've got three stakes in, Maya – chuck our packs in and get inside! Goddamnit, Jack, get over here and give us a hand!"

Clutch, my ass – inconsistent at best. Never know what you're going to get with this guy. The only team he plays for is his own.

The tarp flaps wildly as I lash it over the tent. That's alright, big guy – we didn't need your help anyway. I crack open the zipper, chuck our packs inside.

"Well, this is cozy, isn't it?" Maya sniffles.

"It feels like we're sitting on a pile of monster-sized marbles."

"Nice work with those knots!"

"Oh...I had a good teacher, too. My dad taught me most of them."

"At least we're out of the rain," she says. "Another minute and we would have been drenched."

"I already am," I gripe, shaking drops off my arm. "Can you believe that shithead not giving us a hand with the tent?"

I fumble with my shoelaces, pull off my boots. The back of one sole is clearly coming undone. A smear of blood has crusted on my ankle. My feet look more like ground chuck than ancillary appendages. I quickly tuck them into my sleeping bag so Maya doesn't see...or smell.

"He's a loner, Jupe. Loners play by their own rules, not ours."

"I hope he's chilled to the bone. Motherfucker."

Somewhere between here and Nepalganj she's started calling me Jupe. I've given up on her calling me Jay, but *Jupe*? Every time she says it, I think of French skirts. I'm not sure if I like it.

"What's with this Jupe?" I say.

"Oh, don't be such an old stodge. It's cute…cuter than Jay." She smiles.

'Cute' isn't exactly what I was going for. Cute's right up there with teddy bears and baby seals – great. I'm drenched to the bone, though, and too tired to protest. I peel off my poncho, polypro and pants. Another black blob, drunk on my blood, flops to the tent floor.

"Fucking leeches."

I point towards the engorged creature now writhing on the tent floor between us. A streak of blood trails from one end of it. I guess that's its mouth. Gross. Did you have a good feast, you slimy beast? Bloodsucker.

"Um," she whispers. "I think you might want to check your knickers."

I look down to see more blood, dribbling down my inner thigh. Oh fuck.

"Can you give me a second?"

"Certainly," she says, suppressing laughter.

She turns away; I peer into my boxers. Front row center, right on my nut sack, is a big fat leech, latched onto me like part of some primeval torture. Laden with my blood, it plops off before I can grab it. *Hope you enjoyed your last meal, you smug little sucker.* I try to ignite it but the flint on my lighter's wet. It clings to my hand. I flick it outside the tent.

"…OK, Maya, you can turn around now."

"Where did it get you?"

"Right where it counts."

Now, a fresh trickle of blood from under my boxers. A shiver shoots up my spine.

"Fuck. It won't stop bleeding."

"Take it easy, Jupe," she says. "Don't have a fit. When they attach themselves they pump an anti-coagulant into your blood to keep it flowing. It'll stop in a half an hour or so. Not to worry – they don't transmit disease. Not as far as I know."

"I'm…not good with blood," I say.

"Oh, now *you're* as white as a ghost. Are you going to faint?"

"Just…let me lie here…for a moment."

There's that smirk of hers again. This is not going to help me shake the 'cute' tag. Not fucking funny, Maya.

Her hair is matted against her cheeks. I close my eyes in an effort to stop the blood rushing out of my head…*no blood thoughts, stop with the blood already!*

Twisting her torso, she slips off her T-shirt… OK, then. Damn, she's got a killer body. Suddenly I feel better. It's amazing what a taut stomach and a wet sports bra can do to distract you from just about anything. Her wound is still looking pretty nasty. Is it infected? Maybe we should take those stitches out. Raindrops explode incessantly against the tarp like supercharged popcorn.

Then, "You're not having a good day, are you? Here, let me hold you," she says, taking my head in her lap.

She starts caressing my ear delicately with her fingers. I look up at her perfectly rounded breasts, at her nipples protruding under the soaked fabric. Blood starts rushing to another part of my body.

"Do you feel better now?" she asks.

"I feel violated," I say.

"Poor thing; stripped of your manhood." She rocks my head in her lap.

Damn, those are really beautiful breasts. An overwhelming urge to throw her down and make passionate love to her takes charge of my lower regions, notwithstanding the recent leech invasion.

"Alright, I feel better now," I say, sitting up, making sure to hide the swelling in my boxers. "We might as well get this over and done with while you've got your shirt off."

"What are you on about?" She looks down at her breasts, back at me. "You've got to be joking."

WhaadIsay? Call me Jupe if it helps.

"About what?" I answer, Mr Innocent. "I meant the stitches – you said they had to come out, didn't you?"

Her face is flushed red. At least my hard-on's disappeared.

"Why, what did you think I meant? *You didn't…?*"

"I meant…I thought you weren't good with blood," she says.

The tarp stops crackling; outside, the wind has dropped as the rain builds in strength.

"Only with my own," I say. "Other peoples' blood doesn't bother me. It's a subjective/objective kind of thing: when it's someone else's blood, it's like I'm detached from the whole scenario. It brings out the doctor in me."

"Interesting. Well, they are starting to itch. Jack said to take them out when they start to itch."

You think she'd be up for a game of doctor? *I'm going to need to run some more tests to determine exactly what's wrong with you, miss. Now, if you would lie down on the operating table… Just relax as I examine you…'*

"My father was a doctor," I say.

"What does that make you: a wet nurse? Right – let's just get this over with," she says, briskly. "They're starting to itch quite a bit. If you don't mind, I could use a hand with the scissors."The rain has turned into a soft but steady downpour. Maya sets out peroxide, gauze and scissors carefully in a small semi-circle in front of her.

"Now, look," she says. "This is a rolling stitch so it's quite simple. Cut the thread at every stitch and you should be able to pull them out without much effort."

Taking scissors in hand, I coax the blade underneath each stitch, clipping them into pieces. Maya whimpers as I slide bloodstained bits of monofilament from her belly. Tragic, for such a tight little midriff.

"Does that hurt?" I ask.

"No…not really."

This scar is not going anywhere soon…looks like it might never go away. She's being a real champ about it, playing it off like it's no big deal. I'd be more worked up about it than she is. I'd probably be a whiny little bitch.

"Jack is no plastic surgeon but he did a bang-up job keeping it together. I don't suppose they would have done any better at the hospital."

I jerk out a piece stuck into a scab. She grimaces. I can't believe she's talking to me as I'm doing this. I would need restraints, a pint of ether and a bear tranquilizer before I'd even think of letting anyone coming near my sewn-up gut with scissors.

"Maybe not in Nepal, but those plastic surgeons can pull some pretty fancy shit out of their asses these days."

...And some pretty hefty paychecks. That's what my dad used to say. *'Nip-tucks and lasers, that's where the money is these days.'*

"I don't reckon cosmetic surgery would have helped...the cut was deep enough that it would have left a scar regardless. I suppose I won't be able to wear bikinis on the beach any longer."

"Why not? It's just a scar."

"I may be tough but underneath it all, I'm still a girl," she says. "You're a boy: you can't possibly understand. Actually, I used to be a real girlie girl, dressing up in my mum's heels and evening gowns. I'd have to dig them out of the boxes my dad had forgotten to throw out in the corner of the attic. I found her jewelry box in there, too. I used to sit at her mirror and try on each piece, running her antique ivory comb through my hair. It's a girl thing."

"I used to try on my mom's dresses and earrings all the time."

"Well, that explains a few things!" she laughs.

"...But for real, Maya: I wouldn't care about the scar. It's just a scar...it'll heal better with time. Everything takes time to heal. Besides, with or without the scar, you're still beautiful...and I'm not just saying that for a shag," I add.

Shit, I backpedaled too fast – kicked the chain right off the sprocket. I shouldn't have said that. Oh Christ, she's going to launch into a feminist tirade.

"That's sweet of you," she replies, patting me on the cheek.

The cheek pat – it reeks of sarcasm. I never was too perceptive when it came to English wit; had a hell of a time following *Fawlty Towers* when my dad tuned in every other Saturday on PBS. I don't think he got most of it either.

She doesn't believe me... half-believes me is probably closer to the truth. Of course I would love to shag her – who wouldn't? But I want more than that. I could spend some serious time with this girl, as much as she'd give me. By now, the bond I feel with her is strong.

She's cautious, though. And I don't blame her. Simon burned her bad, and some scars just don't heal so quickly. I wish I could take that pain away. I wish I had that gash on my gut instead of her, too.

She's here, here with me, here *for* me. We've been locked together for nearly two weeks straight now, but backcountry mountain trekking wasn't exactly what I had in mind. Lack of showers and palm-lined beaches tend to take the romance out of things. And we've had enough drama to fill half a dozen soap operas for the upcoming season. If we can get through this, we can get through anything, right?

What's left, though? We're almost there. After we reach the border, that's it. We'll hug goodbye, then Jack and I will inch higher and higher over the pass. Maya and I might wave to each other at intervals – maybe shed a few tears as we walk. No rendezvous back at the secret hideout in Delhi…I'll be lucky to get deported.

'Don't forget to email…' Yeah, right.

Fact is, once we're over the pass, I'll probably never see her or hear from her again. I tweeze the last piece of monofilament from her belly, dab a peroxide-soaked cloth across the scar. It froths up like the mouth of an angry dog. "There you go," I say.

"Does it look infected?"

"Maybe a little here, but you should be good to go. Just keep it clean and don't forget to put on that antibiotic cream. The scabs should start to disappear soon. Another few weeks and you won't even notice it…I guess some scars heal quicker than others."

There's a pause, then, "What are you on about?"

"That guy Simon…you really loved him, didn't you?"

"Simon," she sighs. "Yes…I loved him, still do love him…the love of my life, I guess you'd say. He was such a magnificent person, incredibly smart.

"I'll never forget when I first saw him, leading a group of English prats around Bhaktapur. You could tell they were all little horrors, the sort who'd whine if they missed elevenses –but he had them all enraptured, going off on tales of kings and jealous gods as if he'd seen them happen himself.

"Such a fabulous storyteller," she says. "He had a way of telling a story that would almost hypnotize you: do you know what I mean? He sparked something inside me I never knew existed – something that made me realize what power knowledge could be.

"Any religion, any incarnation, any deity: he knew it. He was brilliant. He would take me through the city at night after everyone had disappeared and blow my mind with his knowledge. But of course there was a downside."

"What was that?"

"He never had much money. He was obsessed with having it, with being able to pay his way. Straight out of the steel mills of Newcastle, but he was no Geordie – he wasn't going to get stuck in the mills like the rest of his family. He used what little he had to get him out of there.

"Grants and scholarships got him an education. He could have got a top job at an academy, but he never wanted that. 'The world is my classroom,' he'd say. So after university, he came to Asia.

"That's when I met him. Those kids he was showing around Bhaktapur? He wasn't getting paid to do it or anything. They were just some GAP kids out sightseeing before they headed off trekking; he'd just picked them up in the town square for a laugh. That's the kind of person he was – just sharing for the sake of sharing. After the kids left, I watched the sun go down with him. He left on a bus to India the next day. He got as far as Goa.

"A few months later, he wrote me a letter asking me to join him. I didn't know it at the time, but he'd run out of cash and started selling drugs at the clubs to pay his way. I had heard all about those mad ecstasy raves on the beach and couldn't resist the offer. I fell so hard for him it didn't matter to me. And once he found out I had a diplomatic passport on account of my father that was it. It was the perfect front.

"I suppose he loved me as well, in his own self-absorbed way.

"When I told my father about Simon, he wouldn't hear of it. He was always more concerned about a person's bloodline than their happiness – as if we were bloody thoroughbreds. And Simon was much older than me. I'd have had a better chance of winning the lottery than of gaining his approval.

"Money was a problem from the start. I had enough money for both of us, but he'd never let me spend a quid of my own. 'A kept man is a dead man,' he'd say. I think the whole money thing really got to him, what with my posh upbringing and all. Thought he needed to support me; thought I'd leave him if the money ran out. Silly boy.

"After a while, things started getting hot in Goa. Everyone knew Simon was dealing; it was only a matter of time before he got pinched.

"He'd met some people...traffickers. So we left India to move some gear. He was right: my diplomatic passport worked like magic. We were the young backpackers in love, too charming and innocent to be suspect. It was exciting at first, like a big game...and we were winning large.

"Once Simon found a good contact in Bangkok, we were laughing, mate. Money, hand over fist. We'd bring a huge shipment to India three, maybe four times a year and then fuck off to a beach on Bali or the Buenos Aires or wherever we liked for the rest. The world was our oyster. We were Bonnie and Clyde on a shoestring.

"But Simon's ego was getting out of control – he always thought he was smarter, always thought he could walk between the cracks. That was kind of the beginning of the end.

"He started using...a lot. Went flat out against his own rule: never partake of the product. Our travels started to focus on where he could find the best meth, coke or heroin, not where the best surf or beaches were. Drugs started running the show, ripping us apart.

"I tried to get him cleaned up but he would always go back, sneaking off in the middle of the night to get his fix. I couldn't stop him.

"He got a right scare when a Belgian mate of his ODed in a Bolivian backstreet. Swore he'd never touch it again. I spent three weeks nursing him back to health; it was a nightmare cleaning him up but we did it. He did it. My old Simon was back.

"By this time, both of us wanted to come back to Nepal. It held a special place in our hearts; I think we were both getting a bit homesick. Simon started studying again. He had a plan. He wanted to open a small school for Nepalese students. Give something back to the people who had given him so much. But he needed money...and of course, it had to be his *own* money. That meant one last run.

"Simon knew of a massive heroin smuggling channel running between Bangkok and Kathmandu. They would pay him to move a couple of kilos: one shot, fifteen thousand dollars. He'd dump the whole lot to the liaison once we arrived in Nepal. Fifteen thousand dollars: just enough for a fresh start. Enough to get the school up and running.

"We flew into Bangkok and he sorted it straight away. A day later, they delivered the gear, and we had our tickets booked.

"...I knew it was wrong the second they changed our tickets. 'Better to go later in the day,' they said. I knew it was a set-up...but Simon seemed so sure. So confident...and I loved him.

"I'll never forget how he smiled at me as I sat there in the corner watching him pack it on his body like a soldier preparing for battle. He had such a lovely smile. You always see those movies where the guy is sweating bullets as he steps up to the ticket counter. Not Simon; he never showed it. You'd think he won an all-expenses-paid tour around the world, the way he beamed.

"But all the composure in the world wasn't going to save him that day. They came straight for him – shuffled him off with our entire kit. I grabbed his hand for one second and then he was gone. ."

She turns away. I put a hand on her shoulder.

"Listen, we don't have to talk about this..."

"No." She wipes her hand across her eyes. "No...I want to tell you. You wanted to know why I'm here and I'm going to tell you. You need to know.

"...They locked him up in a...an absolute tip. Most Thai prisons aren't that bad, but he happened to be moving heroin for a dealer who had done away with some high-ranking judge who happened to be related to the king...or something like that. Most first-offence traffickers get five, ten, maybe twelve years. He was looking at fifteen to twenty, case closed.

"I tried. I tried every channel I could. I knocked on every door, met with every official, paid off anyone I thought could help. I went back to my father, begged him to help, but he wouldn't hear of it. It probably wouldn't have done any good anyway.

"So I dipped into my trust fund, hoping some amount might at least lessen the sentence. I must've given away nearly 10,000 pounds, hoping it might help, hoping something would happen. In the end, I just paid off a lot of mortgages and sent a lot of Thai sons and daughters off to private schools.

"I would go to visit him, when they let me. It was awful. I would hold his hand through the bars – tell him I was meeting someone or another, a very influential man, and that we would get through it in the end. That it would all be over soon.

"But something broke inside him when they locked him up. I don't know what they did to him in there, but he was all mashed up. You could see it in his eyes; they were dead. He was gone ...and all I could do was stand by helplessly. He was dying in there and there wasn't a bloody thing I could do about it.

"Every time I visited he was thinner. Then they wouldn't let him see me at all. They told me he had become violent. It was 'for his own good' they said. I suspect he had come down with something as well... maybe pneumonia. No more visits...doctor's orders.

"But I kept going, kept paying people off, kept trying to get my foot in the door. And then one day, I went, and they came out and handed me a box...it was his belongings. All that was left of him. They said he had hung himself...I didn't doubt it. He'd lost all hope. There was less and less of Simon – until there was nothing at all.

"...So there it is," she says, sounding sad and weary. "That's why I'm here; that's why I care even though I don't know you from Bob. Because I didn't want to see that happen...not again, not to anybody. Because this time I *could* help, this time I *could* save someone..."

She buries her face in her sleeve.

"Listen, I'm sorry," I say lamely. "I didn't know."

I can feel her sobbing against my shoulder. I knead my fingers into her back.

"It's OK. *Shhhh,*" I whisper.

I guess I've got to tell her now. Tell her my *why.* She told me, now it's my turn.

"...We grew up on the lake...Lake Michigan, near Chicago," I begin. "Not right on the lake but pretty close, only a few miles away. The winters were hell – when it blew, the wind chill off the water made it feel forty degrees colder than it was. And it was *cold*, believe me. So cold you'd have to hit the water pipes with a blow dryer to take a shower in the morning. Shit, if you weren't careful, you'd have frostbite by the time you got to school. But the summers...the summers were spectacular. Couldn't be beat. As soon as it warmed up, we would spend as much time as possible down at the lake: swimming, fishing, sailing.

"My dad was a sailor – at least he thought he was. I sure as hell thought he was. He was really a doctor, but everything he did revolved around sailing. It was like an obsession. He even dressed nautical: everything was either blue or white or had an anchor or a boat on it. We always gave him shit for that. He even signed his name with a hook. His dad, and his granddad were merchant mariners. Even though he was a landlubber, he had a lot of the sea in his bones.

"We had a nice little boat we would sail in the summers. Nothing fancy, but she cut through the waves like a knife...I loved that boat. She was built like a brick shithouse: the hull was over an inch thick at the keel seam. Before they knew how strong fiberglass actually was. We could have circumnavigated the globe with her, easy, but she never saw any action off the lake.

"Every August, we would sail all the way up to Door County for a week or so, sometimes bring the whole family and the dog. But that didn't work too well: my sister got seasick and mom, she said, 'would rather sleep in a bed that didn't feel like the inside of a washing machine.'

"The dog didn't work out too well, either. Old Toby was a water-dog and would jump overboard the second you took your eye off of him. Great for man-overboard drills but a pain in the ass if you wanted to get anywhere. We eventually started clipping him into a harness to avoid delays.

"So most of the time, it was just my dad and I. Sailed that boat up and down every mile of that coastline I don't know how many times...

"One thing we agreed on was the sailing. 'You should work a boat, see what she's got,' he'd say. 'A boat shouldn't sit in a harbor, going green.' But as time passed, she did start to go green. Our relationship started going green as well.

"At first we'd be gone every weekend, just me and him. We'd even do sunset sails mid-week after he got home from work. But once he took an admin position at the hospital, it was usually just Sundays.

"He'd take me every week after church. I couldn't stand church. I swear the only reason half of those housewives showed up each Sunday was to show off their new minks. Constantly kneeling, standing, sitting, kneeling…it never made sense to me. It would take everything I had to sit still for that hour, but I knew that at the end of it we'd be headed for Montrose Harbor. I couldn't care less about the Holy Trinity, but the knowledge that afterwards we'd go sailing kept me from pinching and punching my sister during Mass. For me, if church was the stick, sailing was the carrot.

"I was eighteen when the bad shit went down. Things were getting strained between us by then. Dad was bogged down between his practice and the hospital. Somewhere between seventeen and eighteen, I turned into a complete delinquent, going on a spree of vandalism and theft that would give an adolescent psychologist a hard-on.

"Dad had an idea of what I was up to, but what blew the lid off it all was when me and my buddies got caught stealing beer out of a Budweiser distributorship… a *whole fucking train car* full of beer. That got everyone's attention, including that of the officers down at the local precinct.

Next day, dad decided to raid my room and found close to fifty pairs of Ray-Bans and a dozen iPods. He thought it was his fault; that he'd been too easy on me, hadn't hit me enough when I was a child. He always blamed himself.

"Fact is, I was just bored. Everything had become so fucking *normal*. Something needed to happen…so I made things happen. I became a kleptomaniac overnight, jacking everything from fishing lures to fur coats.…went on a complete rampage.

"We'd still go sailing, dad and me, but it wasn't the same anymore. It was like we were married and he'd finally found out I'd been having a full-on affair. I guess I killed the trust.

"One chilly November afternoon, I decided I wouldn't go to church. We got into one of our usual en-route arguments. It was a particularly nasty one about pedophilic priests. I went too far, asking dad if he'd ever been felt up as an altar boy. He was really ticked off…didn't drop me at the curb until we were almost there – must have been an eight-mile walk. But I didn't care. To me, church was part of the problem, part of the normalcy, the nausea that constituted our bland existence.

"But dad was still trying, I guess, and winter was right around the corner…so when they got back from church, we took a drive to the harbor. I could never say no to that boat. There were maybe five words spoken between us on the drive down but in the end, I couldn't help myself: I made some smart-assed remark about the Pope shuffling Nazis off to Argentina. "He just lost it then. Said I was always pulling shit like that, 'pressing buttons just to press buttons.' If I knew so much about god, he said, I could sit on the goddamn dock and watch. So I did. I didn't even help him drop the lines. I was so angry back then.

"Nobody else was going out that day; it was already blowing a steady twenty knots when we got there. By the time he cleared the harbor, it was gusting to thirty. Fat ugly clouds were ripping across the sky; it was getting cold. So I went back to the car. It was locked so I sat on the trunk...and waited.

"An hour later, I watched the harbor master put up a gale warning flag in pouring rain, but I was so pissed off I didn't even go out to the breakwater to look for our boat.

"Two hours passed, maybe more. I steeled myself against the cold and trudged down to the dock master's office. The breakers on the beach were at least six feet high by then. I knew he was in trouble.

"They radioed him on 16 but he never came back. He probably never thought to turn the damn thing on until it was too late. A search party went out. They found the boat...capsized. They found the body the day after."

"Oh, my god. Jupe..." Maya puts her arm around me.

"When my mom came, I was still sitting on the trunk of the car. It was raining hard...I was sopping wet and silent; she was hysterical, screaming at me like a banshee on crack. *'Why did you let him go alone? What kind of son lets his father go out alone in this weather?'*

"She didn't even hug me. She tried to pull me into the car but I wouldn't go. I felt like I *couldn't* go...I had to stay put and pay.

"I sat there for hours, half-frozen in the rain, 'til finally my sister came. I didn't go home that night. In fact, I never slept in my bed again.

"...Things fell apart fast after that. My mother wouldn't look me in the eye during the entire funeral. My own mother...is that cold or what? Jenny, my sister, tried to keep us together as best she could, but it wasn't happening. I cruised outta there as soon as the dust settled.

"It's just not fair, you know? Things go bad between kids and parents all the time – but then you grow up, and you make up. I never had that chance. He's dead and I can't apologize; we can't put that behind us and laugh about it over Christmas dinner. Because there aren't any fucking Christmas dinners anymore."

"…You're still running," she says, "aren't you?"

"Aren't we all?"

I awake to voices outside the tent…has Leatherface tracked us down? Or Maoists?

Urrgh ah urrgh ah uuuuuuurrgh!

Foghorn Leghorn sounds the alarm, but invaders have already penetrated the periphery. Jack's probably got them in his sights at this very moment. *I'll provide the bumbling distraction so that he can move in for a better shot.*

Sliding out from under Maya, I move to the door and grab the zipper. It catches on the cheap canvas of the tent. I yank at the zipper again. Suddenly it gives, tearing a hole in the canvas.

"Goddamnit."

It looks like we've got the open-air model now. Folding back the door, I pop my head out into the fresh, rain-swept morning. The sky is cloudless. A cluster of men in brown woolen vests with white cloths wrapped about their heads hovers over me.

There are three of them. On his back, one has a large bamboo basket, attached by a thick strap that runs across his forehead. Muslims? Sikhs?

A large hooked knife with a wooden handle protrudes from bamboo-basket guy's waistband. Another stands apart, a long, blackened musket propped over his shoulder. They look more like Bolsheviks than Maoists. Could be Leatherface's posse. Still, no match for Jack's nine-mil.

I look over towards the granite outcropping…no sign of Jack. Where is the old devil? Perhaps he's already positioned on the grassy knoll. He's got them in his sights… Or did he bolt-again? OK, let's play this one off the boards.

"Namaste," I rasp, squinting in the bright morning sun.

"Namaste." One takes a step forward, flicking his wrist upwards. *"Kahaa baata aaeko?"*

I smile, grab the pack of cigarettes lying behind me. Nicotine: the perfect diversion. Each man reaches down to take one, smiling. I grab one too, knowing it might be my last.

"Nepali auunchha?"

"Auunchha," replies Maya from the tent.

"Maya," I whisper, "Jack said not to speak Nepali."

"Oh, I can't be assed," she says, nonchalant. "He's *so* paranoid."

"Well, one of them does have a gun. Could they be Maoists?"

"Not from the looks of it, but I can't say I've ever seen a Maoist in the wild."

"As opposed to in a zoo?" I joke.

She rolls her eyes.

"What about the rock chopper, old Leatherface? Do you think he could've sent them?"

"They look more curious than malicious to me."

Without warning, my stomach twists into a knot. *Shit.* I've only got seconds before my ass explodes. Grabbing the roll of toilet paper tucked in a side pocket of the tent, I shoot outside.

"Where are you going?"

"I'll be back in a sec!"

Oh god, this is going to be messy. I brush past the men and sprint towards a boulder, ass cheeks clenched. Unzipping my pants, I squat – out of sight, I hope – and open the floodgates.

"Bort, bort, bort…pllbbbbbgh…"

Fuck. That was pretty gross. And loud. Maya probably heard that. Maybe the river drowned it out. Couldn't I have had another minute of warning? This is going to blow any chance I might've had to seal the deal with her.

Oh, god.

"Pllllbbbbbbbbggggh!"

One of the men, the one toting the musket, appears around the corner.

"Yahaa esto garnu hundaina," he says, shaking his head. *"Hamro ghat ta ho!"*

Could you give me a minute? I'm a little tied up at the moment.

Then a bare-chested Jack barrels out from behind the outcropping, shouting and flaunting his pistol. Startled, one of the men stumbles backwards, almost falling onto the tent.

"Jupiter, pull up your fucking pants! Maya, get the fuck out of the tent!" yells Jack.

"Who are they?" I ask.

"If I knew, d'you think I'd be waving a gun in their faces?"

Maya scrambles out of the tent. I hastily yank up my pants – just in time. A rushed job but could have been worse. I run over to his side. Jack barking orders while brandishing a gun scares me, but I'm getting used to it. Better to be out of the line of fire.

"Jack, I really don't -" "Shut up, just shut up for a second, OK?" he snaps. A bead of sweat drips off his chin.

"Maya, just get over here *now*," I insist.

"Turuntai jaanos!" One man waves his arm in the air. *"Yo samisthaan ta ho! Haamro purkhaalai apamaan nagarnos! Paap lag- chha ni!"*

"Shit," grumbles Jack.

"What's wrong?"

"He says this is a sacred cremation site. This place is full of spirits, spirits of their ancestors. We've gotta pack it up."

"Bhut pani hunchha!"

"Yeah, OK, already – *haami ta gaihalchaun*," Jack grunts.

"Cremation site? You've really got a knack for logistics, don't you?"

"Hey, that storm was brewing and it was so dark by the time we got here I could barely see," he gripes. "And I told you two to keep the tent out of sight. You parked the damn thing right in the middle of their fucking cemetery. Let's go, let's go."

"Christ on a bike, give us a second."

"Aw, the hell with it!" He flicks his cigarette to the ground and begins to strike the tent.

Maya totters down to the river's edge with peroxide and towel in hand.

"Hey Maya, not here!" yells Jack.

"But I've got to –"

"Later. This is bad karma, man. We've gotta get out of here."

"Don't get your knickers in a twist," mutters Maya.

"He's the one with twisted knickers," Jack says, pointing to me. "Couldn't you have at least run off into the bushes before taking a dump all over their ancestors' turf?"

If he didn't have a gun in his hand right now, I'd punch him in the face. I can't believe he just said that. I run over and hastily kick sand over the evidence. I'm not going to be able to look at Maya for the rest of the day.

Jack yanks the poles out of the tent. "I should've known better," he grumps. "This is bad karma, man, really bad."

"What's so bad about camping here if a funeral's not in service?" I ask.

"This is where they burn their dead. This whole place is swarming with spirits."

The men conduct an animated exchange as they examine our tent. One reaches down timidly, runs his hands over the fabric. Jack raises his gun in the air and lets off a round. I dive to the ground. The men book into the forest; Foghorn Leghorn cackles nervously (the next round might be his). I dive to the ground, then sit up slowly.

"What the fuck!" I stammer.

"Just letting them know who's in charge," says Jack.

"Nice touch, Jack," sighs Maya.

"That wasn't very karmically correct."

"My karma is already fucked. Throw everything in your pack double time, and head along the riverbank. They said there's another beach a couple clicks down that won't

piss the spirits off."

That really tweaked Jack out, camping on a burial site. He probably thinks we're done for now. Maybe he'll counter with an offering to the disgruntled spirits. Don't sacrifice poor Foghorn Leghorn for some deadbeat spirits. He'll probably splay that poor rooster out on the ground, in a crystal-studded circle for cosmic compensation.

Up the riverbank a ways, I spot him hunkered down by a log. I walk up near him and start to spread my wet clothing across the rocks. It steams in the mid-morning sun. Muddied and swollen, the river looks like a massive serpent.

"So much for our low profile," I say.

"What? Oh, *that*. Sorry, kid, sometimes I get a little jittery when it comes to spiritual shit like ghosts. It didn't help matters that you had your pants around your ankles."

"Dude, I didn't really have a choice in the matter. My stomach has been on end since we left Kathmandu. Did you have to say that in front of Maya, though?"

"…No, I guess I didn't."

Squatting near the water's edge, he skips a stone across the surface. One, two, three…four skips.

"Not bad," I remark.

He lobs another stone out. Easing myself down next to him, I pluck a smooth flat one from my side and chuck it into the water. It thumps heavily into the current; Jack chuckles.

"It's all in the wrist, kid."

Not long afterward, Maya hobbles up to the bank.

"There's no sense washing up in this cesspit," she says. "The river must have risen a foot overnight."

"Use your drinking water," says Jack. "In fact, *always* use your drinking water to clean up your wound. This river may as well be an open sewer, especially around here, with all the leftover body parts floating around." *'Always* use your drinking water to clean your wounds.' *Survival rule number one hundred and sixty seven from troop-master Jack.*

"Hey Maya, let me have a look at your stitches," he says.

"Don't worry about it."

"Come on, sister, I'm not trying to sneak a peek. Let's have a look under the hood; make sure there's no infection."

"I can assure you that it is perfectly fine, Jack, but since you're not going to leave it be until I show you…"

She lifts up her shirt. Red blotches cake her stomach like a row of sun-dried tomatoes.

"You took the stitches out already!"

"Jupiter did, actually."

"Good job, kid," he says. "Didn't leave any stragglers. Have you been using that Neosporin I gave you?"

"Yeah."

"Does this hurt?" He presses his fingers into her abdomen; she winces.

"Not terribly."

"There might be a little pus at the ends: just keep hitting it with the peroxide. Not bad work for a strung-out hippie, huh?"

"Do you want a medal for it?" she retorts.

"Here: this is clean water." Jack hands her his canteen. "Find a shady spot down by the river and give it a good soak."

She stalks off.

"One of the men I trained had a scar like that," he tells me, when she's out of earshot. "His name was Tsewang. The first week they arrived, he was awfully quiet, kept to himself. Then he told one of the Marines he had stomach pains.

"At first, we thought it might have been a change in diet or stress, but when the doc examined him, he knew right away it was his appendix.

"...When they opened him up, there were only tiny chunks left of it. The doc figured that it had erupted before Tsewang even arrived at the base. On top of it all, the power cut out in the middle of the operation. They had to finish the job with fucking miner's caps on. After he picked out what he could, the doc dumped every Sulfa packet he had into Tsewang's stomach – literally salted him down. He gave him a fifty-fifty chance of survival, and that was only because he'd never taken antibiotics in his life.

"Never saw anything like it. A week later, that little devil was running with us in the morning as if not a goddamn thing had happened. Got a hell of a lot more talkative after that. He became a prankster, too, loosening the salt-shaker caps in the mess hall so you'd wind up with a mound of salt on your grub."

Jack chuckles, and his coral-and-turquoise earring bobbles. His lobe droops under its weight like a willow in August heat.

"Your earring," I say, then. "It's the same as Gerard's."

"Yeah, so what? I almost forgot about that bastard 'til you brought him up."

"Did all of you guys wear them?"

"What are you talking about?"

"Tex, Dusty, the rest of your crew."

"...Those cats would never wear them. 'Earring's are for faggots,' they'd say. You'd be better off branding a bull in a snake pit. Only Gerard and I wore the earrings."

"Why do you wear yours?"

"Tibetans believe that a man will come back in his next life as a donkey if he doesn't pierce his ear."

That's why Gerard was talking about coming back as a donkey. "Do you really believe that?" I ask.

"Some days I do; some days I don't – but I'm not taking any chances, man."

"So you're a Buddhist?"

"I'll pray to Shiva, Ganesh, Buddha... whoever's listening. When that's all you've got, you take it. And if a couple of turns on a prayer wheel and a mantra are gonna better the odds of me making it through a whiteout at six thousand meters, I'm game.

"Just like those spirits back there by the river: I don't know for sure, but I don't want to push the envelope...when in Rome, you know? I figure the earring can't hurt. I've been enough of an ass in this life; I don't want to be one in the next."

"Do you believe in reincarnation, then?"

"I'm not making any bets on that. I'll take the even money."

"If you came back and had another life to live, what would you be?" I ask.

"...I'd be in love."

"You've never been in love?" I ask.

"Once. Only once – a long time ago. Caterina Geromino was her name. *What a face.* So damn gorgeous...straight out of a Fellini movie. She was the most amazing woman: always laughing. You could count on it, like waves against cliffs after a big Mistral. Silky blonde hair down to her ass that you could spend days wrapped up in. Golden-brown skin as sweet as honey; eyes that sucked you in and made it so you never wanted her to let you go. She was from La Maddalena, an island just off of Sardinia."

"Where?"

"Off the coast of Italy, in the Mediterranean. Sparkling waters, desert cliffs, pink-sand beaches. Seriously, the beaches are pink, dig...like paradise, man.

"I met her during the summer of '59. I was checking out the Trevi Fountain in Rome: taking pictures of it from all kinds of funky angles, playing with the lighting, you know? Well, every time I shot a photo, she would jump into the picture at the last second, laughing.

"At first it kind of pissed me off. I was really big into photography, then: wanted to be the next Brassaï. So I went over and started ranting about all the film I'd wasted on account of her...but she was so damn beautiful.

"The angrier I got, the more she laughed; the more she laughed, the more I melted. Next thing I knew, I was asking her to join me for a coffee. Three weeks later, I kid you not, I asked her to marry me."

"So what happened?"

"After that summer, I went back to teach in Chicago. I promised to be back in Rome for our wedding at Christmas, but then I opened up this can of worms with the CIA. You know the rest of that film."

"You never fell in love again?"

"I spent the next fifteen years of my life fighting the Chinese in godforsaken mountain passes. I got so wrapped up in fighting the Chinese that I forgot all about love.

"In the beginning, she was the only thing I ever thought about — the only thing that got me through the cold, blood and guts. But years passed, and my doubts grew.

"It's not like I could expect her to wait. I started to half-hope she had found someone else. Every day, she became further out of reach; every month, a little less. Until she was nothing more than a grainy snapshot in my mind. Towards the end, even the snapshot disappeared. *Poof!* She was gone.

"I had a new obsession by then, and it was killing. It became a perverted passion, the urge for vengeance. I wanted to fuck the Chinese like no-one's business. I dreamt about murdering the little commie bastards...tell me that's not fucked up.

"The best years of my life were wasted in a frozen hell, fighting against an enemy as infinite as stars. We were stronger and harder, but they had the numbers and the weapons. There was no beating those PLA fucks.

"...Then I got hooked on smack. It was like switching cellblocks, man. But with heroin, the demons are inside you. Not so easy to locate in your sights. More time went by; more junk went up my veins. Eventually I kicked the brown, but there was no going back to Caterina.

"There was no going back to anything. By then, I was comfortably numb. I would take a knife to myself just to feel, to feel *something*. You think I'm a pathetic asshole now: you should have seen me thirty years ago. I was a sorry excuse for life.

"Eventually I did start to forget some of the pain. Eventually, I started to function again…and in a way, I did find love again."

"With who?" I ask.

"This country, man. It's the most beautiful place in the world. It's like a fairytale: I can't get enough of it. I really dig these people. There are sinners and saints everywhere you go but these are the most sincere, most honest bunch I've ever come across. Complete strangers referring to each other as mother, father, sister, brother. It's like one big family, keeping it together, y'know? Shit, I could leave a sack of jewels worth more than they'd earn in a lifetime in one of their huts for six months and wouldn't have to think twice about it. They barely have enough to make it through each winter but they're so proud of who they are – most of them are, anyway. The times they are a'changing, though. Kathmandu is fucked, and these damn Maoists are ripping a hole in all of that."

"Why aren't you proud, Jack?" I interject.

"…I used to be," he muses. "I used to think I was fighting for a noble cause, helping Tibetans fight for a country that was rightfully theirs. But Uncle Sam didn't care if they got it back, didn't give two shits if they lived or died, as long as a Chinese outpost was ransacked or a military convoy was sabotaged every few months…and I was behind it all, pushing the lie."

"Helping oppressed people is a lie?"

"But that's the thing: I wasn't helping. It's like donating blood your whole life, thinking you were helping people, only to find you had AIDS the entire time. I *did* care about them like family; they were some of the most amazing people I ever met. I gave everything to the fight. But it seems I was the only one. The other CIA operatives were just playing the game, moving pieces on the chessboard until the timer buzzed. *Sorry, time's up, on to the next political hotbed!* One day, we're in; next day, we're out.

"Do you think the CIA really gave two shits about Tibetan independence? About as much as they care about Kurds and Kuwaitis, right? It's all vested interests, but 'fighting for freedom from oppression' always looks better on paper. Sounds better, too…more romantic than oil or the 'communist threat.'

"In the end, I was only propagating their schemes, protecting their interests. I was the poison, not the cure."

"Jack," I say. "You've gotta stop beating yourself up, man."

"Thing is, we weren't fighting with the Tibetans for a new Tibet. We were just using them to keep up the arms race."

He's tuned me out. *Free-access Channel Jack, now transmitting.*

"Tibet never had a chance after Chiang made a fast break for Taiwan. Mao stocked up on all the weapons we'd been mainlining the Nationalists through the Burma Road. Those commies snatched them up as quick as Chiang could dump them. All made in America, too – Truman had a hell of a time trying to dodge complicity with *that* one. Put a damper on US-Chinese relations for a few decades.

"Now it's the same story in Iraq and Afghanistan, *sans* communism. It's a great recipe for military superiority. Sell them some tanks and anti-aircraft guns, train a few hundred guerillas, and stir. Wait for the tide to turn, then send in some crack troops to get a few licks in and practice.

"The Tibetans thought America was the shining star – the fucking prophet of democracy. The big brother, who was going to get the bully off their backs and set them free. They fucking *loved* us, man. Why wouldn't they? We were training them, airdropping in tons of guns and ammo to save them from those damn Chinese.

"Any one of them would've died for me, would've died for any American, because they really thought we were helping them. They *believed* in us. But it was all a sham. All we were doing was biding time.

"You know how to fight a military threat? Scatter a bunch of remotely linked aggravators around the globe, then keep pressure on all points. Commies, Mujahadeen, doesn't matter who. Keep constant pressure up but never cut off the flow, like a time-release tourniquet. If you cut off the flow, the enemy dies. No more arms-race, no more military contracts, right?

"But eventually, the tables turn; the pressure points shift. When Nixon finally kissed and made up with Mao in '72, the CIA pulled out of here faster than an altar boy out of a preacher's daughter.

"I couldn't leave. I stuck with the Tibetans, swore to fight it out till the end…what a shitty ending that was. When the smoke cleared, I was so whacked I didn't know what to think, who to trust.

"Gerard and Beth saved me. I trusted them: I didn't have a choice…

somebody saves your life you trust them. Back then, they were all I had. Sometimes I wonder if things would've been better if they hadn't found me, lying there in that animal shelter, that night – cut up and half-frozen in the dirt.

"But what about you kid. *You* ever been in love?"

Shit, it's that obvious. There's no way I'm going to show him my cards; I'd rather talk about masturbation with my mother.

"…I don't know…maybe," I demur.

"Like *now*, maybe?"

"Maya and I are just friends," I say.

"And I'm one of the twelve disciples. I may be old, kid, but I'm not blind. You think she came all the way up here just to be a Good Samaritan? I'll bet you'll find a way to get it on with Maya – if not now, then some day. You two fit pretty well together. That's not something you find often in life."

"We're not together, Jack. Why are you always trying to inject drama into things? This isn't an episode of *Days of Our Lives*, you know."

"*Days of Our Lives* – what the hell is that?"

"It's…it's a TV show. I used to watch it with my mom, sometimes. It's complete bullshit, a 'who's fucking who?' series, but I really got into it one summer. It was more of a bonding thing with my mom than anything else. Anyway, that doesn't matter. The point is that Maya and I are just friends, got it?"

"Whatever you say, kid. I'll bet you find a way to be with to her… *or don't you have the balls to chase her?* Going to run back to mommy? Cozy up on the couch and watch sappy soap operas …You act all street but really, you're a bit of a momma's boy, aren't you?"

I swallow, say nothing. I refuse to answer that last question, on the grounds that I might be infuriated. If I kicked him hard enough in the ass I might be able to rupture a disc or two. Maybe just a well hurled stone. His shirt is off. Chest and belly sag with age and abuse, but even so, I can discern an athletic body of yesteryear.

I close my eyes; imagine the inimitable thud of stone against bone. Small, round, discolored scars bulge across his back. Attack of the giant leeches? Hardcore S&M session at Plato's Playhouse? Looks like some esoteric form of torture. *Damn, somebody beat me to it.*

"What are those scars on your back?" I ask.

"These?" He rubs one with a finger. "They're from a long ways back…when I lived up in the mountains. It's called *mo*. It's a treatment used in Tibetan medicine. They use fire-tips to exorcise demons.

"We got jammed up in the teeth of a storm. Only half made it back, and that was pure luck. We stumbled into a monastery on a re-con mission.

"I was frostbitten, half dead. That's where the tips of these fingers went." He wiggles the nubs on the end of one hand.

"We lost a lot of men on that mission. A fever ripped through me for days without any sign of breaking. I really thought I was done. I was so weak at first that they wrote me off, but I kept ticking. The monks thought there were demons inside of me, so they called in the shamans."

"You're all about the shamans, aren't you?"

He glowers at me…OK, I had that coming, maybe more.

"…They performed an exorcism – the *mo* was part of the package. Half a day later, the fever broke."

Exorcisms seem to be *à la mode* out here.
They should have opted for a lobotomy instead.

"…You really believe in all that crap?" I say.

"*Amchis* and *jhankris* have saved my hide more than once. I don't know if it was the dancing, the fire-tips or the talismans that did it, but when that's all you've got, you take it. You saw it work back in Nepalganj, didn't you?"

"I saw a doctor inject some serum into your arm, that's what I saw."

"I'm telling you it works."

I roll a stone over in my palm.

"…What else do you believe, Jack? Do you think we're gonna make it over that pass? Do you believe you and Maya will make it back down before the winter storms?"

"We'll all get to where we're going in the end," he says. "But you've got to believe too, kid. You let up in your head and the demons will get you."

"Do *you* believe, Jack? For instance, in yourself?"

"Hell, don't make me look in the mirror after all these years, kid," he says. "I wouldn't know who I was looking at."

He skittles a rock across the surface of the stream.

"...If you're lucky, you'll make a few ripples on the surface before you sink. That's all there is to it. I've got my own reasons for being here, kid, and you've got yours."

He skims another stone.

"Seven skips: that was your best one yet!" I exclaim.

"Lucky number. Maybe that'll change our luck."

Maya trundles into view, peroxide and canteen in hand.

"Come on," says Jack. "Let's get the hell out of here before the ghosts catch up with us."

I study the huge boulders that protrude from the roiling rapids. One day they'll be smooth little stones, perfect for skipping...

It's only a matter of time.

Ahead, Jack is talking with a woman who's hauling a basket strapped to her back. She's laden with jewelry: large bangles on each arm, large silver hoops in each ear, a nose ring and a necklace of silver coins, hanging heavy from her neck. That's the first person we've seen in over a day.

They turn as Maya and I approach.

"Wassup?" I ask.

"Her kid's ear is all banged up...she wants to know if I can do anything," says Jack.

"Where is it?" asks Maya.

"In the basket."

"Oh, what a little cutie!" she exclaims.

Nestled in a checkered blanket, a well-swaddled baby looks up with rounded, olive eyes. I stick my finger into the netting; he wriggles about like an oversized grub.

Releasing the strap from around her forehead, the woman lowers the basket. Gently turning the infant's head to the side, she points to his ear. Dried blood is scabbed over it like patches of lichen.

"Fucking hell," says Maya. "That's really gone septic."

"Yeah – he'll be lucky to hear anything after it's cleared up...*if* it clears up," says Jack.

"What are you gonna do? You must have something for him."

"Give me that tincture of iodine, then."

Maya asks the mother to steady the child's head, pours iodine into his ear. The kid lets out a horrendous shriek. Maya whispers reassuringly, caresses his cheek.

"Oh, poor thing," she says. "It's really infected, isn't it?"

The mother yanks her ailing infant from the basket, puts it to her bosom, cooing to it all the while. Liquid dribbles out its ear.

After the kid calms down, the woman sticks out her hand, pointing to her eyes. She needs something...I'm guessing something for eyes.

"Jack, she's got a problem with her sight," says Maya. "Have you got anything for that?"

"Can't help her," he says. "She needs an optometrist, not meds. We're almost tapped out as it is. It's from all of these damn wood burning stoves."

"At least give her something...."

"Listen Maya," he says, a tad impatient. "We've got to take care of ourselves. That stuff we've got strapped to our backs – it's for *us*, nobody else. We can't go doling all our shit out just because someone's got a fucking bellyache. *This hospital is closed.*"

We push steadily upwards into a forest. Broad-leaved jungle eventually gives way to a rhododendron forest of towering proportions. Parasitic veils, green and blue mosses hang from gnarled branches; a flock of birds rustles through the underbrush. Deep blue, with iridescent splashes of red across their necks, they look like...they'd be good to eat. A few of those would make a nice addition to Foghorn Leghorn, I'm thinking. We could have ourselves a little banquet.

Maya marches up to my side. "Pheasants," she whispers.

"Can we eat them?" I ask. "They look pretty tasty."

"They're endangered and the national bird."

I don't need any additional counts – such as butchering national symbols – on my record. I guess we'll have to stick to the *chow chow*. "Do you think it'll rain again?" I ask.

"I hope not; I'm still soaked from last night." She sneezes.

She looks pretty beat up. Her face is flushed. Breathing heavily, she whimpers.

"You alright?" I ask.

"Yeah...I'm fine."

Like hell you are. Just keep her moving until she can't say that any longer.

"Come on, we'd better keep going, then." I take her hand and we trudge on.

Looking out across the canyon, I gaze down at the fog oozing over the treetops. The rhododendrons, in this light, look massive – mystical even. Silvery, gnarled branches twist above like frozen demons. I am walking through a forest of rhododendron: distant cousins of the scraggly plants my dad planted in our backyard and refused to let die. We had a shrub or two around the house, but the soil was never right. He pumped all kinds of nutrients into them but they never took. If he could see this!

Aggressive experiments with Miracle-Gro? They're so gigantic, so surreal, that I half-expect to bump into a band of elves...or a *yeti*.

We're at the edge of a landslide. A hundred feet below, the river roils angrily. Jack slaves over the old stove. Hopefully, it'll work its magic one more time. One more time; one more step – that's all you can ask for up here. Maya leans weakly against her pack.

"This trail used to be different. It must have washed out a few years back," says Jack.

Good to know. Maybe we should have looked into a purchasing a more recent map. Hell, ours is probably the most recent version. Who the fuck would want to take the time to survey this?

I take the cup *of chow chow* he is offering. What I'd give for a sopping double-bacon cheeseburger right now. I look over to Maya. Eyes shut, she's breathing laboriously – lying down now, with her head against her pack.

"Lunch is ready, Maya."

"You go ahead and eat mine," she says. "I'm not that hungry."

"Not hungry?" says Jack. "You're gonna need some fuel later on." He points to a landslide up ahead. "We've gotta clear that before night-fall."

Maya groans. Leaning towards Jack, I whisper, "She's not feeling well. I think it might be a fever." "*Ke bhayo, bhaini?*" he asks her.

"I think it's a fever. Do you have any more antibiotics?" asks Maya.

"No. You went through the last of them a few days ago. Let me feel your pulse."

It looks like he'll be lucky to get a radial pulse, in her state. Stretching out a hand, he wraps it around Maya's wrist.

"It came on rather quick..."

"*Shhh.* Don't talk...just breathe."

Jack feels her forehead, her back and again, her pulse.

"You're definitely not firing on all cylinders," he pronounces. Fishing through his gear, he pulls out a small vial. "Here, take this."

"What *is* it?" she says, dubious.

"Medicine."

"Antibiotics?"

"Not exactly, but it should help."

"What about the Cipro, Jack?" I say. "She's still prone to infection...and so am I."

"Gone."

"What do you mean, gone? You had a huge bottle when we left."

"I took a few for my snake bite," he says. "I haven't been feeling too hot lately, either."

"Well, that's wonderful. You know, antibiotics don't work for shit if you don't take enough of them, Jack."

"Yeah, well, I didn't know that we would all be gobbling them up like candy," he bristles.

Candy. I could really go for a Mars Bar right now...or maybe a Bounty.

"We've just got to make do with what we've got."

He's probably crunching them up and smoking them in a crack pipe in a futile attempt to get buzzed.

Unscrewing the cap of the vial, Maya swallows some of the liquid, coughs violently.

"Here, chase it with some water," I say. Chugging a mouthful, she grimaces.

"*Yeech.* That was horrendous. Truly horrible."

"It's got a bit of a kick to it, huh?" says Jack. "Not the smoothest ride, but it should give your system a boost."

"What on Earth was that?" she asks.

"I'm not sure exactly," says Jack. "From the taste of it, I think it might be snake-oil extract. The shaman who pow-wowed for me down in Nepalganj stuck it in my pocket when I was passed out...it can't hurt."

Always the optimist, Jack. I'm not sure if I agree with his bush-doctor philosophy, but we're going to need all the help we can get.

"You got any more?" I say.

We pass over a patch of scree. The trail is almost undetectable through the loose stones. Maya dislodges a small rock and it tumbles down, spinning and bouncing off of the cliff face into the raging river. She looks decidedly shaky. *Keep it together, girl.* She slips, stumbles onto one knee. I grab her wrist.

"Come on Maya, we can do this," I say, encouragingly.

"My stomach doesn't feel right at all. I think it might have gotten infected when I fell in the river."

"We'll have a look at it as soon as we clear this stretch, OK?"

She winces in the affirmative. Goddamn, I hope to shit that snake oil is working.

"This is going to be a single-file drill, dig?" Jack instructs. "Maya, I want you in front of me, and you bring up the rear, kid."

Our path hangs precariously over the slide; a foot wide at most, the trail winds along an exposed rock face strewn with fallen rocks and loose dirt. There's nothing to lean on, nothing to grab on to bar some small roots, dangling enticingly at eye level. *Jesus, Jack, if you want to kill us, just pull out your damn pistol.*

"Shouldn't we be tied together or something, Jack?" I ask.

"If one of us went, we'd all go. Each of us has to make this on our own, kid."

High-altitude lifeboat ethics. The water rushes noisily below, drowning out my footsteps.

I'm tired of this high-adrenaline *Survivor* crap. Keep your fifty large, keep it! I never wanted to be on this fucking show in the first place.

I reach out for a root – it pulls free, spilling dirt as it does so. I sway back and forth, the now-useless root dangling in my hand.

"Forward – lean forward!" Jack screams. "Goddamnit, don't go grabbing things like that or you'll be all busted up at the bottom of that ravine. Keep all your weight *on* the trail…and use your hands to balance."

I drop the root and look down at the trail, then a lot farther down, at the water. That's a fucking long way down…it wouldn't be pretty. Wouldn't be much left to send home in a body bag.

Maybe I should have left a note with Jack, or Maya, or somewhere along the trail… I should have at least written a letter. Let mom and sis know what happened. How I tried to sneak over the border to beat a drug smuggling rap to make it back to them. Otherwise I'll just be eternally 'missing.'

At least give them closure. They deserve that much.

OK, let's get this over with. *Fucking focus.* I inch along the tightrope trail, eyes pinned on my feet. *Keep moving, no whammies!*

The trail widens a little, dips around a corner. Suddenly, gravel slides out from under my foot. I swing my arms frantically for balance. I drop to my knees, feet hanging precariously over the ledge. My heart spikes another twenty BPM as I hover between path and death. *Lean… forward.* I place my hands lightly against the loose dirt of the slope. I'm shaking.

"*Relax*, kid," shouts Jack. "Take a deep breath and come up nice and slow. You'll be fine."

Slowly I bring one leg, then the other up towards my stomach. Leaning forward, I shift my weight gradually to one side and rise to my feet. *Baby steps…baby steps…weight forward.*

"You're fine, Jupe," says Maya, who's caught up and is right behind me. "Nice and slow."

If I can just make it, I promise to call home. *I promise to be a good son… a good boy…I promise…* And then the path widens; the ledge dwindles, disappears. Baby steps become bigger, bigger, big boy steps.

Jack pats me on the back. The river growls; we stare at each other in silence. My body's still trembling. That…was…*close.* Too close for comfort. It seemed fucking close, anyway. You never really know how close you are until you're dead.

It's dry up here...and fucking hot. Deserted mountains...mountain desert. Strange how quickly the weather can turn on you up here. Talk about microclimatic mood swings. Seems like only a few hours ago, we were in lush jungle...or was that yesterday?

The sun is like a diesel stove. It takes a while to start heating up but once it does, there is no stopping it until the sun drops. Then it's straight back to the freezer. My shirt is sopping with sweat.

The valley opens before us like a mouth, its teeth the distant foot-hills. Melting patches of snow leave damp imprints on dusty soil. Trails of smoke curl up from a cluster of earthen huts in the distance. Maya and I move on, side by side, boots kicking up dust from the parched earth. I squint through the hazy heat at the huts....something is moving out there...moving closer.

Two clouds of dust churn towards us.

"Maya, what do you make of that? It's coming straight for us."

Raising her head, she says, "*Bloody hell!*" Then, "Do you have a knife?"

"No."

"Quick, grab a stone, then."

"*What?*"

"They're bloody mastiffs, for god's sake."

What next, a fucking Hydra?

"*Find a rock!*" she screams.

My eyes scan the ground...it's all dirt. Wait...I scoop up some small rocks, more like gravel, really.

The dogs hurdle towards us, dust billowing in their wakes. Missiles locked on target. T minus, 10, 9, 8... I need another rock, a real rock, but I am loath to take my eyes off of them. Burly, solid high-altitude killing machines, not like their skittish, flea-bitten cousins down in Kathmandu.

I grope at the ground...a real rock. Snarling, one of the mastiffs barks ferociously. The other wheels round to flank me. Teeth glistening, drool dripping from gaping mouths, they make Cujo look like a Pomer-anian. These dogs want blood and they're not leaving until they get it.

I raise my weapon.

"Come on, you fuckers! Fucking mutts – *bring it on!*" I shout.

Flinging my only substantial stone, I hit one squarely in the breast. *Fastball, right down the pipe!* Doubling back, it lunges forward, then stops, readying itself to spring. It snarls. *Shit.* My heavy artillery didn't even faze him.

Dust wafts about, momentarily blurring my vision. I hurl a handful of gravel, miss.

"Come on, you fuck!"

I reach for another rock – see a burst of motion from my periphery.

"Watch out, Jupe!"

Springing from my undefended side, the other dog lunges, taking me down. I fall sideways; my pack thumps to the ground…dead meat. The beast bites down hard into my thigh.

There's a soft, fleshy thud…the sound of tooth hitting bone. My stomach reels with nausea. I try to shake it off.

"Ahhhhh! Help me!"

The dog burrows into my thigh and twists its head in a death shake. Screaming, I bash my fist into its head.

"Cocksucker!!"

A cloud of dust barrels up. In a flash, the other dog springs toward me, lunging for my neck. I raise my hand. Its teeth sink into my arm.

"Get this thing off of me!" I plead.

Suddenly, three metallic blasts ring through the dusty air. The dog at my leg drops like a sack of rice. The other yelps, recoils into a furry ball.

I look up through the dust to see Jack standing in the distance, lowering his pistol. Whimpering, the live dog limps away, my blood oozing from its fangs. Following it in his sights, Jack fires another shot, echoing in the distance.

With a yelp, the cur slumps to the ground. I crouch, clutching my leg. Two hands lift up my head.

"Oh my god, Jupiter, are you alright?" Shifting my hand, Maya bends to examine my leg.

"Bloody hell, Jack, he's bleeding badly. *Come quick.*"

Jack pushes her away to get a better look. "Let me see."

Blood – lots of blood, like molasses, dripping onto the sandy ground.

"Jesus H Christ," he says. "Fucking mongrels took a piece, didn't they? Raise his leg above his head. Here, put this bag on him. You stay here; I'm gonna get help. Keep talking to him...him...him..." Jack's voice drifts away.

"...The thing is...I like dogs...fluffy ones...I really like dogs," I say, deranged.

"Not these ones you don't."

Maya tucks my head against her breast.

"Jupiter," she says. "Jupe, look at me. You're going to be alri..."

"Call me...Jay."

Maya's head spins, swirls...and then everything's glazing over...

Jack's spent cartridges...scattered on the ground.

A fire is burning. My head is in Maya's lap; her hand is wrapped across my chest.

"...You know, sister, you and I are a lot alike," says Jack.

"Is that why we repel each other so much?" contends Maya.

"My mother was English, you know."

"*Really?*"

"How do you think I picked up on your accent? My mother was from Surrey and yours was from Kent, right?"

"That explains it," she retorts. "Though your English wit and manners seems to be lacking."

"Very funny."

I shut my eyes, still tottering on the edge of a dream.

"My father was an archeologist specializing in Early Eastern civilizations. He had a fellowship from Oxford but I never saw him in a classroom. He was gone most of the time. Sometimes he'd bring things back from where he was doing fieldwork: ivory bracelets, human skulls emblazoned with gems, books...the most amazing books. When I was thirteen, he took my mother and me on a liner from London to Calcutta. He was working on a dig just outside of Darjeeling. We took a house up on the hill in the old city, near Chowk Bazaar."

"Curiouser and curiouser," says Maya.

"...We stayed there for four years – probably the best four years of my life. We took in a Tibetan maid to help mum round the house... Karma. She had studied English in Sikkim, but her father had taken ill. She had come to us looking for a way to earn enough to make it back to Lhasa. But before she could get back there, word came that he had died...so she stayed.

"When my mother didn't have time for my lessons, Karma would teach me. She was wonderful, filling my head with stories of yaks and noblemen, of palaces in the clouds. Sometimes she would take me into town to run errands and introduce me to the Tibetan pilgrims in their *chubas* and leather boots, clicking their wooden rosaries, the women with silver braided into their plaits. They seemed to me quite magical – exotic, mystical creatures from another time come to life, as if from a picture book. Lone horsemen cutting across the vast high plains in a flurry of fur and talismans...

"That's when I began to learn. What were their lives like? What did they think? What did they feel? I needed to know.

"Karma started teaching me basic Tibetan after the first monsoon. By the following spring, I was speaking basic conversational Tibetan. An academic himself, my father was delighted. He gave Karma full tutorial reign over me. On his days off, he would take me to the monasteries in the hope of giving me the chance to draw traveling monks into conversation. He always told me that the more languages I knew, the more people I knew.

"But it was more than that. I was an only child. There were other children around but they never interested me. They were content with their toys and sweets and etchings of the Queen; they didn't see the world out there, the energy that would run right through them like a bolt of lightning if they only reached out and grabbed it…but that was all I wanted, and Karma was my conduit.

"Wherever she went, I was there with her; buying spices in the market, washing linens at the tap, sending letters off in the post. She became my sister…and the Tibetans became my people."

I cough.

"Hey, you're up!"

"Jupiter – you poor thing. How does your leg feel?"

"It doesn't. I don't feel anything."

"I jacked you full of Demerol. Let me know when it starts to fade and I'll give you another hit."

"Do you have any aspirin? My head is killing me."

"That's the attitude, kid. Hey, it was a pretty rough day today so I figured we could cash in on our meat rations. Members of the council?"

"I'm well up for it," says Maya.

Might as well have a halfway decent meal before we all bite the dust.

"…Sounds good to me," I say.

"A couple of bowls of Jack's chicken noodle delight will be just the thing to get your strength back before we get up in it." Foghorn cackles nervously as Jack eases him from the top of his pack. He's been eerily silent the last few days. I think he knows what's coming. "You two hang tight – I'm gonna go out and read him his rights. Come on, little buddy, go easy and there won't be any trouble."

He ducks under the cloth curtain at the door and disappears.

"…What the fuck is he talking about, 'before we get up in it?'" I say. "I can't walk. This trip is *done*."

"We've come a long way, Jupe." Maya puts her head in my lap. "You made a decision back in Kathmandu that this is what you wanted to do. Just hear him out before you make any big decisions."

"…Before we get up in it…*huh*. He's joking, right? We're already up to our eyeballs in it and it's all bottled up."

"I know…I know," she whispers, stroking my hair. I could lie here forever, looking up at her as she caresses me... I close my eyes, shudder minutely as her hand brushes past my ear.

"What if I changed my mind? I don't want to go anywhere anymore," I say. "I just want to lie here with you."

She's looking down at me with those green doe eyes...why does she have to do that? They're definitely not helping motivate me to get out of here.

"You miss your father, don't you?" she says.

I look away. What's with the interrogation? "...After you passed out, you were ranting on for some time before Jack gave you that shot of Demerol. You kept saying my name, and going on about some sailing trip. You were talking to him, Jupe ..."

"So, what's wrong with that?" I ask.

"I was the same way with Simon, for a long time. I know where you are right now – I was on the same track...the same circular track, going round and round, going nowhere."

"Why do we have to talk about my father again? I'm tired."

"Listen, Jupiter, I'm only trying to help. You need to talk about this with somebody or the guilt will suck you dry. You've got to move on; you've got to forgive yourself. I was there.

"For the longest time, I tortured myself over Simon's death. *I should have stopped him. I knew it was a set-up; I knew something was off that day in the airport. What kind of a girlfriend was I to even let him get involved in this smuggling racket, anyway?*"

"Yeah, but you really tried. You went to visit him, used up all your money to try and get him out – and now you're helping me...you couldn't have tried anymore."

"But it didn't work, did it? It wasn't enough. I probably couldn't have stopped him even if I'd tried. And the truth of it is that the future isn't clear until it's right on top of us; hindsight is always 20/20.

"You can't rewind life. How were you to know that a storm was bearing down on your father that afternoon? How was I supposed to know that I would never see Simon again? We didn't, we don't know. But to keep skipping back to those fateful moments as if they were broken records is not the solution. You have to let it go and move on."

"It's more than that, Maya," I say. "It's my mom. I told you about the funeral – how she wouldn't speak to me. The thing is, she'll never forgive me; I don't think she's capable of it. Deep down, even though she doesn't say it, my sister feels the same way. I don't know – I'm not too hot at expressing my emotions. I think they thought that I didn't give a shit. But I was every bit as cracked up about the whole thing as they were."

"Have you tried picking up the phone and telling them how you feel?" she suggests.

"I want to…almost every day. *Every damn day.* I wish I could just call up and talk to them – tell them what I'm doing, how I feel – but every time I pick up the phone and dial, my mind starts freewheeling, my circuits short. And it takes everything I have just to sit there and breathe."

"What about a letter?""I've tried that. I can't…not anymore."

"Jupiter, you've got to let go of all that stuff about your father."

"He saw that storm coming…he knew better, I knew better. The only reason he went out that day was to spite me."

"But Jupe, you simply cannot think like that. It was an accident. You didn't mean for it to happen."

"Sometimes I wonder about that."

"Seriously, *stop it*, Jupiter."

By now, though, I'm broken down, blubbering like a kid. Maya is hugging me and stroking my neck.

"It's OK," she soothes. "It's alright…"

I look up, right into her eyes. She brushes my hair from my forehead. I kiss her; *we are kissing.* I cup my hand around the back of her head…hard, unabashed kissing.

Suddenly, the rooster crows.

Urrgh ah urrgh ah uuuuuuurrgh!

Foghorn Leghorn…stick a fork in him.

We separate: *passion interruptus.* Maya wipes her lips.

"…I'd better go see if Jack needs a hand with supper."

"…Sorry," I say. "I'm sorry, Maya – I didn't mean to…"

"It's alright," she says.

She kisses me on the forehead.

Jack stumbles in, then, searching for something in his pack.

"Can you guys help me outta this gas chamber?" I ask. "It feels like I've smoked a carton of cigarettes in the past hour."

"You bet," says Jack.

Grappling my shoulders, he hoists me up. Maya wraps my arm round her neck.

"It's alright, I've got him, sister."

"Can you walk on it?"

"Yeah...I think so. *Ouch!*"

"Steady there, partner." Jack catches me around my torso. "That mongrel took quite a chunk out of you."

My leg throbs. Gingerly, I test my weight.

"It feels like Jell-O," I say.

"I'll give you some Demerol with dinner."

"We're back to Demerol? Did you swing over to the 24-hour pharmacy at the last band of huts...and what about rabies?"

"Well, we'll just have to wait and see," he says. "Like Old Yeller, dig? We'll give you a couple of days and if you start foaming at the mouth, I'll take you out round the back of the shed and shoot you."

"Fuck you."

Together, we stagger out of the house into the graying light. Seems like only yesterday I was lugging Jack through Nepalganj; now I'm on the other end of the bargain.

A warren of clay huts and fences winds down the hillside. A gust of wind whips past, sending a chill up my neck. Without warning, a dog springs out from behind a wall.

"Fucking A!" I scream.

Jack tries to catch me as I trip backwards. A hot flash of pain sears through my leg.

"Oww shiiiittt!"

"Don't worry, kid, it's..."

The hound lunges, is jerked back; a chain rattles on its peg.

"...chained up!" yells Jack.

A wrinkled woman shuffles out of her house and places her hand over the dog's head, scolding it with hisses. Dropping to the ground, it growls feebly. She laughs.

"Yeah, real fucking funny," I grumble. "Why do they have dogs around, anyway?"

"Protection."

"From what? Seems sadistic for Buddhists, if you ask me."

"...Protection from bandits."

"Gimme a break."

"No shit. The nearest police office is days out – it'd take nearly a week for them to get here. A dog is like a built-in security system."

My legs are stretched out before me. I look down at my wound. Caked splotches of blood stain the heavy gauze wrapped around my thigh.

"Well, I guess this trip is over."

"Over? We're just getting started."

"Look at my leg," I say. "It's fucking toast!"

"We've already crossed the Rubicon, kid."

"What the hell are you talking about?

"I am talking about the point of no return. The only way to go is up."

"I'm not buying it, Jack."

"Listen to me. Remember that guy Tsewang I told you about?"

"The one with appendicitis?"

"Yeah. Well, he had something like this happen, too. It was getting pretty close to re-infiltration time, and the trainees were getting all amped up to get back and use all their new gear on the Chinks.

"We had them out on the firing range fine-tuning their target practice. One of the instructors shouted something – Tsewang twisted around and shot himself in the damn foot.

"It was pretty bad; he hit an artery. Everyone was pretty down at first because they knew he wouldn't be cleared to jump on that first sortie. But he hung in there and within a few weeks he was back on the ground in Tibet."

"Then I'll stay behind and chill for a while," I say. "I can wait until my leg heals and then cross."

"It's not that simple," says Jack. "In a few weeks, those passes will be snowed in for the winter. Getting you here is one thing; getting up and over is a whole different ball game. We're already pushing the envelope. If you want to do this, it's now or never."

He grabs a saddle that's sitting next to the hut, flings it over his free shoulder.

"I got all the bases covered, man. While you've been recuperating, I have been modifying our game plan. I spent the entire day haggling for a little pack mare...only one in town. Come on and have a look at her."

A diminutive pony raises its head as we round the corner, its shaggy mane ruffling in the wind. Dappled grey, with a colorful woolen blanket thrown over its back and strands of cloth woven into its tail. Streaks of black shoot up its legs. Doesn't look thrilled to be here.

Jack's knee-jerk optimism isn't rubbing off on either me or the pony.

"...Looks more like a banged-up, broken mule to me," I say.

"Yeah, well, she's not gonna win any derbies but she'll make it – won't you, girl?" He pats its mane. "These Tibetan ponies are tough as nails."

"...But what are you gonna do once I cross over? You just said yourself that those passes are going to snow over. There's not enough time."

"If we're lucky, maybe. I'm not so sure where I'm going after this. Let's just get you over the border first."

"And what about Maya? If I'm crossing over to India and you're up in the air, how the hell is she gonna make it back on her own?"

"I'll make sure she gets home," he says. "Safe and sound."

"That had better be a promise," I say.

"I swear it."

Using my good arm, I pull him by the collar so his face is right up close to mine.

"She has to make it back, Jack, understand?"

"Get your hands off me, kid, for christ's sake." He swats my hand away.

"Understand?" I reiterate.

"That's the deal, I remember, kid. Two grand, plus the stone. Hey, I'm a man of my word."

"Are you?" I say. "Then why the hell is that Tibetan following us? Is he waiting for the right moment to come up and get your fucking autograph? What about Leatherface? Is he a member of your fan club, too?"

"Hey, take it easy…"

"Take *three* grand – I don't care. And I don't give a shit about that fucking stone, either… Just get her back in one piece, if that's not too much trouble."

"You don't have to ask me twice," he says.

"I'm not asking you."

Above the curtain-door, there's a drawing of an animal on a tawny scrap of leather: a four-legged animal, a dog, entangled in a mass of thorns. Looks a bit like the one that took me down.

"Hey Jack," I say, "What's this drawing here?"

"It's a charm against dog bites."

Just my luck.

Jack slings the saddle over the pony's bowed back. Before he can grab the strap from under its belly, the pony jolts forward, shaking the saddle off.. Jack runs after it, cursing. He's tugging on the reins and the pony's leaning backwards, digging its hooves into the ground.

"Come hold her for me…damn animal."

"You shouldn't talk to her like that." Maya grabs the reins, pets the pony's neck. "No lady in her right mind would listen to you if you talked to her like that."

"It's a goddamn horse, not a lady," says Jack, and tries again. Again, the pony shakes the saddle off before he has time to secure it.

"I thought you said it was a pony, Jack?" I say.

"She's a stubborn son of a bitch, whatever she is."

The pony grunts in protest as Jack cinches the strap at last around its belly.

"She's adorable," says Maya, stroking the pony's cheek. "Should we name her?"

"Knock yourself out," grumbles Jack.

"Eeyore," I suggest. "She's stubborn enough."

"Eeyore is a boy's name, silly! She needs a girl's name, like Isabel or Chloe."

"Looks more like an Eeyore to me," I say.

"She's a miserable bastard," agrees Jack. "Eeyore it is."

"Not as miserable as you! Ladies should never be spoken of so disrespectfully – isn't that right, girl?" says Maya.

Eeyore snorts in approval…I think.

"Maya and I will have to split most of the load," says Jack. "She won't be able to handle much more than you in weight. We can put some of the light stuff in your pack. Well, hop aboard, sailor."

I put my good foot into the stirrup and ease the other one over Eeyore's back. She *hhrumphs*, shifting uneasily as she accommodates my weight. Taking the reins, I say, "Now what?"

"When you want her to go on, just give a good nudge into her sides with your heels and say *'Dro!'* When you want her to stop, just pull back on the reins and say, *'Dyed!'* I don't think this old mare will run on you."

"How do I say, 'Turn around and get us the fuck out of here as fast as you can?'" I retort.

"That's pretty funny, kid. Just steer with the reins and the rest will fall into place once she gets to know you."

I dig my heels in, give the command…nothing.

"I don't think she's going anywhere. Did I say it right?"

"Dig in like you mean it! Come on, girl…*Dro!*" He slaps Eeyore's hind quarter. I steady myself as she lurches forward.

"…Don't get too far ahead of us," Jack shouts. "It's gonna get tricky up a ways."

The early morning clouds lift, revealing a bold sun. We traverse broad expanses of sparse shrubs and rock, crossing a high, arid plateau devoid of trees. The ground is cracked into a million hardened plates of clay, a bleak reminder of water long gone. Undaunted, my pony trots out far ahead.

"Where are you going, little buddy?" I say, pulling on the reins. As Eeyore bends her head to graze on what grass she can find, I watch two vultures wheeling in the distance. They fly in silent unison, gliding effortlessly on the wind.

Massive clouds gather on the horizon. Flakes of snow begin to swirl in the wind.

"Winter's coming early this year," remarks Jack. "This doesn't look good. Check out those rollers. " He points to the churning bank of clouds, rapidly approaching. "We could be in for a mother of a storm."

"What are we going to do, then?" asks Maya.

"Hold on a sec. I'm gonna have another look at that map." It crackles in the wind as he flattens it out on the parched ground. Maya places stones over the corners.

"We are…not in a very good spot," says Jack. "This valley is going to become a wind tunnel if it picks up any more."

"Any suggestions?" says Maya.

"There's a monastery up that valley, the one I told you about." He points upwards to a craggy face almost directly in front of us. "But I don't know if they're going to throw out the welcome mat."

"Why wouldn't we be welcome?" asks Maya.

"Well, for starters, you're a woman."

"Oh, come off it, Jack – they're Buddhists," she says. "They're not going to turn us out in a storm."

"Probably not, but you know how touchy they can get about that. Especially up here, You might be the first white woman they've ever laid eyes on."

"Well, I'd rather take my chances breaching monastic etiquette than spending another night in that shite tent of yours. They're not a bunch of drunken sailors, after all."

Running his fingers across the map, he says. "Alright, I'd say that's about six or seven clicks off. If we hustle, we should be able to cover that in under three hours. And if we don't make it that far, that ridge ahead should give us some protection from the wind."

"And what if it's *not* there, Jack?" I ask.

"It's been there for eight hundred years," he says. "They didn't have any plans to relocate it last time I checked."

"Are you *sure* it's there, Jack?"

"*Yes, I'm fucking sure.*"

"All I'm saying is that it's been a while since you've been up here."

"Think I've lost my game, don't you?' he counters testily. "I know where I am and I know it's up there. If you don't believe me, take your chances by yourself…but I know these clouds, too, and they mean trouble."

Something happened this morning. When I was packing up, I finally stopped worrying about the plan, about whether or not I was going to make it. I didn't give up; I just stopped weighing all the variables as if they were horses laid out on a race form. Why worry about it now? I've already placed my bet. All my chips are in. The horses are coming round the final stretch. As if I ever had a choice.

Cigarettes. We're down to half a pack now and they're all Jack's. At this altitude, I've lost the desire to suck in anything except what little air there is. Jack had one yesterday, nearly coughed up a lung.

His weed went bad a few days back, too: froze up before it dried. He baked some on the stove, but Maya wouldn't let him burn any more fuel to feed his bad habits. He was too tired to fight her...or maybe he knew we were damn low on fuel. He looks like shit – his lips are chapped to hell; the skin is half peeled off his face. This is taking every last cent out of him.

I save one for the end of each day, a cigarette, before the cold slithers into the tent and starts to constrict my lungs. That's the only time I can breathe enough to smoke one. Doesn't sound too appealing, does it? The only thing I should be putting into my lungs up this high is oxygen. But right now, I need the reassurance of nicotine. It's easy to forget what you are up here. This scowling landscape offers no escape, no reprieve.

Oh yeah...Jack fucked up. He's been saying that our destination's right over the next ridge for three ridges now. I don't know if it was the mountains or his brain that shifted, but there's no monastery up here. In fact, there's nothing much of anything up here – it's almost too cold for death. If you died up here, you wouldn't decompose. You'd just freeze. I half-expect to run across an ice-coated face staring up at me through the permafrost. A blizzard-besieged pilgrim, a casualty from a long lost expedition marooned in a whiteout...

Dumb motherfuckers. That's what they'll say when they pass by our glazed-over faces, our rigid bodies.

Eeyore is a wash as well. The trail is too slippery for her to maneuver, at least with me on her back. The saddle keeps slipping. I don't think Jack tightened it enough. The strap is chafing her belly in a bad way. When she's had enough, she just sits there and shakes until I slide off one way or another. Three times is enough. Smart fucking animal. She's got enough instinct to know that we're leading her up the proverbial garden path. Maybe we'll use her for backup when rations get low...poor girl.

It's incredibly still; the clouds hang low. Low, woolly suckers. They've been hanging here for days, following us like vultures. Just like the ones that would come out of nowhere on Lake Michigan. Every so often, a snowflake spirals down, a sparrow lost at sea. The mountains are poised, waiting stoically for the next storm front. Throw whatever you want at them; they can take it.

Jack's a half-mile ahead with Eeyore, trying to figure out where we missed the turn. Maya's a couple hundred yards behind me…and here I am, stuck in the middle with a bum leg and a frozen bottle of iodized water. A lot of good that will do me. If I keep it tucked in my jacket for an hour, maybe I can squeeze out a few sips.

We don't talk – it requires too much energy. I wonder if I shouted, would my voice echo or would the clouds swallow up the sound? Jack said not to shout up here: 'It pisses off the gods.' Besides, Maoists might hear, or Managis. Or the tracker.

All I hear is the snow crunching under my feet…and my breath, pouring out of me on every down stroke like a strained engine.*The little engine that said he could, said he could…but maybe can't.*

Every so often, one of my feet plunges into a snowdrift – right up to the knee and sometimes past it. I use my arms as levers, then, pressing against the sides of the bank to winch it out.*Just stay on the tracks.*

I've read it isn't that bad, being frozen to death. Everything just gets all warm and fuzzy, they say. Kind of like drowning. Wonder if that's what it was like for dad.

I picture a scribe, scribbling frantically next to a man encased in a block of ice who's forcing his last words through creaking lips. Is that how the Tin Man felt? We'll have to ask the boys over in cryogenics, if we ever do make it back.

Cryogenics. What a bunch of nonsense. What a waste of money. Why don't they just ship the bodies here, drop them into crevasses below the permafrost and mark the spots for safekeeping? And if a foolproof method of reconstituition does turn up down the track, well…

Would your thoughts be frozen as well? Imagine having an eternity to ponder that last idea, that final figment of thought – the one that passed through your brain at the very moment of death?

I wonder what dad was thinking when he died. Probably 'I'll get that prick – if that little shit was out here with me, we might have had a chance…'*Stop it.* Think good thoughts. Keep…thinking…about a beach. A beach in…Florida…no, Bali. Wait, I've never been to Bali. *Focus.* And there's a girl…Maya. I'm on the beach with Maya, lying in the sun. That's it: that's how I want to die. On a beach, with Maya.

"How long have you been sitting here?" says a voice through the chill.

Maya drops her pack and plops onto a boulder, steam chugging out of her mouth faster than a locomotive.

"How's your leg holding up?" she asks. "Where is Eeyore? Why aren't you riding Eeyore?"

"She wasn't cooperating...I kept falling off. The whole relationship was going nowhere. We gave her the right name, though, didn't we? Stubborn little devil. Doesn't matter; I can't feel my leg anyway."

Maya takes her mitten off, presses her hand against my thigh.

"Can you feel that?" she asks.

"Not a thing," I say. "Let me ask you a question: where would you want to die?"

"What are you on about now?" she laughs. "Have you completely lost the plot? I hope that dog wasn't rabid."

"I'm just thinking...everyone dies. So in an ideal world, where would you want to die?"

"I refuse to answer that question at this altitude," she huffs. "Here, have some biscuits and water. You need something in your system – you're going to dehydrate if you're not careful."

"I think I'd like to die on a beach. One of those long, white-sand crescents you see on postcards, with translucent water and puffy clouds, and a little boat bobbing in the water at the far end. ...And some palms – gotta have palm trees...I'd be drinking a rum and Coke...with a squeeze of lime...I guess that would make it a Cuba Libra. I'd turn to you and say..."

"Right, up you go." Maya offers me a hand.

I tug her onto the ground.

"Kiss me."

She pecks me on the cheek.

"There. Come on, then."

...What if we died here, just like this? Would it be so terrible? It would free us of all obligations. Death in a place neither of us belongs.

Years from now, other explorers will trudge by and find us embraced in our puffy jackets like a couple of freeze-dried grubs. 'How lovely,' they'll say. 'They must have been very much in love.'

"I can't think of anyone I'd want to die with more right now..." I muse.

"You've really gone off your trolley, haven't you?" she says. "The altitude must really be getting to you." Her voice seems far away as if she's at the other end of a long tunnel. I pull her closer.

"...Come on," I urge. "Let's lie here for a while."

"*No* – sort it out, mate! *Neither of us is going to die here, do you hear me?* I'm not going to lie here snogging in the snow while that storm moves in on us. Look – there are your puffy clouds. They don't look so inviting to me!"

She points up to the ridge ahead. Low, milky clouds, lower than the others, seep into the valley like molasses. A faint breeze announces their arrival.

"Jack's already well past that ridge, and we're going to be in a real mess if we don't get over it soon," she tells me. "Once it starts to snow, we'll be lucky to see each other two feet apart. Here, tie this round your waist."

She drops a rope onto my lap. I pick it up, slowly finger the coils. Snowflakes bounce off my jacket. I stick out my tongue, hoping to catch one. A sudden crack rings against my cheek.

"*For fuck's sake, Jupe!*" She slaps me again. "What, do you think it's pretty? Take a closer look. Why don't you give it a taste?" She shoves my face into a snowdrift. "Can you taste it? *That is fucking death, mate.* That trail is going to vanish in an hour, once that lovely snow picks up. Now get up off of your ass and get a move on!"

She smacks me again across the face. Suddenly, I'm back out of the tunnel. I shake my head as if awakening from a drug.

"Alright, already!" I yell. 'You don't have to hit me."
"Are you with me, Jupiter?" Her green cat's eyes are so beautiful... "You've got to be here with me right now or we're both dead."

She's tying the rope around my waist, now, cinching it up to my stomach. "Right – there's no losing you now," she says, matter of factly.

"Inseparable..." I say.

"Shit. Jack is well ahead of us. Can you see him at all?"

I gaze upwards. Over the ridge, near the top of the pass, I think I spot him: a tiny black fly clinging to a vast white curtain.

"Jack!" she shouts. *"Jack – wait up!"*

Her shouts are muffled by the low-hanging clouds. Jack appears to stop for a moment; then a cloud washes over him, erasing him from the mountain.

"Shit – he must be a mile ahead of us!" Maya tightens the rope around her waist. "Well, we'll have to do the best we can. I'm going to lead. All you have to do is hold onto the rope and stay on the trail." She takes my face in her hands, stares earnestly into my eyes.

"Jupe," she says. "Can you do this for me? It's you and me now, alright?"

"You and me," I whisper.

Snow is coming down hard and thick now. My footsteps are muffled in the fresh fall. Sometimes, I slip into snowdrifts that bury me up to my waist. It's strange how snow shrinks the world around you. The peaks surrounding us are lost in the clouds. It's as if they don't exist.

Jack is gone. Even Maya's gone. For all I know, I could be walking through a dust storm on Mars. Or back in the womb, umbilical cord hanging from my hand.

Oh, here comes the wind. Snow swirls violently round my head. Now my world is me, just me, and this umbilical cord that keeps me attached to life like a fetus to its mother.

Mom. I wonder what she's up to at this moment. Probably on her fifth vodka tonic by now. Wait…it's got to be early morning in Chicago. Shit, it's a whole other day over on that side of the world. So if it's… What time is it here, anyway?

I feel a sharp tug on the cord. I tug back.

Maya materializes.

"Jupiter, are you with me?"

"Right behind you, mom" I say.

She punches me in the arm.

"Ouch!"

"That was your *last fucking warning*. If you want to cuddle up in the snow to die, do it, but you're not taking me with you! I know your head is a bit messed up but if you don't focus and get over that pass, you'll be lying *here* for eternity... not on some beach with palm trees and a little boat at the end of it. Dead – frozen solid. *Dead. Do you understand?*"

"Yes," I mutter.

"Any more games and I'm going to cut you loose to die, *got it*?"

"Got it," I say meekly.

She punches me again.

I roll my tongue across my lip...blood.

"What the fuck was that?"

"Just making sure you're paying attention. Steady on!"

Each step I take, the wind bites into my face like coarse-grade sand-paper. Lambasted. Sandblasted. Every step I take, my body tells me to turn back, cut this umbilical cord and retreat from this land where I do not belong, where life is as fragile as lace. But I dig...I dig in. Take another step forward.

Just...keep...moving.

I can feel the warmth seeping from my limbs. The thermal under-wear, the jacket...none of it's enough. Not enough to stop my extremities from shutting down. Slowly, slowly, I feel them separating from my core. Slowly, each will be sealed off from the mother ship by ironclad sea hatches in a last-ditch attempt to save her.

I reckon my feet will go first, definitely the feet. Slowly it will inch up into my legs. Once my legs are gone, it'll domino to my head, then...

"Jupiter!" yells Maya.

The wind shrieks like a mad whore.

"Jupiter – can you hear me?"

I nod.

"We're almost at the top but this storm is really picking up!" she shouts into the gale. "It might be too risky to descend with such shocking visibility. I don't know how much farther we can go."

Gusts pummel us as we near the top. I feel like a napkin in a dust bowl.

"Here, come on!" screams Maya. *"We'll hide behind the chörten."*

She grabs my hand and pulls me to the lee side of a small pile of rocks. Prayer flags whip and crackle above our head; the wind has become a deafening roar.

"We've got to get out of this," Maya says, not quite shouting now. "We've got to get down...for fuck's sake, *where is Jack*?"

A hand jerks my shoulder back.

"Hey, funny running into you guys!" It's Jack the fucking joker. "Get up off of your asses: we are outta here."

"It's suicide to try and descend in this," says Maya.

"We're not going down – we are going *in*, sister!" he crows. "Follow me."

A gust sways me as I strap on my pack again. Grabbing Maya by the waist, Jack yanks us along into a drift. The wind howls.

Dropping over to the other side of the bank, he changes direction and pulls us around a massive boulder...into a cave.

"...Where's Eeyore?" I ask.

"Dead, most likely," replies Jack. Not a fucking shred of compassion.

"Did you just leave him out there to die?" asks Maya.

Jack looks down at the ground.

"Heartless bastard." she stammers. "I can't believe you would do such a thing...wanker."

"Listen, Maya, I didn't just leave her out there," he explains. "I couldn't see. I went to grab the two of you and when I turned back for Eeyore, she was gone...she couldn't have run very far; I'll go out and look for her as soon as this storm settles down."

"...Do you have any clue as to where we are, Jack?" asks Maya.

"Alive...that's good enough for me right now. That last valley we were in must have been almost five thousand, five hundred meters. We're a little higher up on this ridge, maybe six or six-two. I really didn't want to stay up at this elevation, but we don't have much choice in the matter.

"That translates into not too much sleep tonight: we're really not built for anything over six-five. Keep drinking water and listen to each other's breathing. If you hear gurgling noises, that means we've got to get down quick."

"Fuck, it's cold in here," I say, rubbing half-thawed hands together.

"Get out your sleeping bags and get inside," responds Jack. "We're here for the night."

The cave is black save for a small hole that allows a sliver of grayish light to filter through. Small flurries of snow pulse in sporadically.

Jack walks off into the darkness, flips on his flashlight.

"...This is a lama's meditation cave. I've been here before. Doesn't look like anyone's been around for a while, though."

"Look over here," calls Maya. "There are some texts on the floor!"

Jack and I walk over. In the center of a small circular chamber are several long, rectangular books. The color is washed out of them; only a few traces of gold and red tint the edges. Jack takes one in his hand, folds back the cover carefully and directs the beam of a flashlight onto it.

"It's a *sutra*...looks like the diamond *sutra*. You know that was the first text ever printed," he says.

"It's amazing you're able to read that so easily," says Maya. "You've got enormous potential."

"For what – rehab?" I mutter.

Jack shoots me a nasty glance.

"And what have you done lately that's worthy of such praise, Jupiter?"

"Why is it so fucking difficult for you guys to call me Jay?"

"I wouldn't chalk up smuggling hash into Nepal as one of your greatest achievements...though I'm sure it would rank highly in the 'dumb and dumber' category."

"You calling me stupid?" I bristle.

"You did it," he says, "not me."

"Mainlining heroin isn't exactly brilliant, either," I snipe.

Maya clears her throat. "That's enough, boys," she admonishes. "Anyway, as I was saying – there are probably less than a hundred Western scholars in the world who could've identified that *sutra* so quickly. And then there are all the languages you know."

"I can't really say I know any one language completely anymore. It's just bits and pieces floating through my head – an Italian joke to make a pretty girl smile; a phrase in Cantonese to wow a table of whiskey-flushed Hong Kong jewelers; a command in Tibetan to run for cover when we were being outflanked... all just bits and pieces now. Alphabet soup. I can't even conjugate half the verbs anymore."

"Come on," encourages Maya. "You speak perfect Nepali – and I'm certain your Tibetan is even better."

"Where's that going to get me? Maybe I should be a trekking guide, huh? Yeah, that's the ticket: scrape up just enough to live on day to day, leading a pack of fat, whiny Americans up Annapurna base camp."

"You're not doing much better than that now, though, are you?" I venture.

"You don't understand," he says. "I'm *not* here. I don't have a visa, a passport or a nice two-bedroom apartment with cable to go back to...*I don't exist.*"

"Spare us your tales of self-pity, Jack," I say. "Every time you open your mouth, you're telling us about potential lost, about how things might have been different, how you could have been a contender. Otherwise, you're glossing over the choices you've made in life with lame-assed excuses. *Get real.*"

"*Fuck you*, you prick. So tell *me*, Jupiter, why the hell did you turn up here, anyway? We wouldn't be out here in this mess if you didn't spring up out of nowhere: a Manangi wouldn't be dead, I wouldn't have nearly died from a cobra and Maya's stomach wouldn't have a huge gash across it. You're the one who's so quick to dismiss his own short-comings as fate – every time your hose gets a kink in it, you play the hapless victim. "Why *did* you come here? Was Nepal just another push-pin on your map? Just another 'wish you were here' postcard to send to the folks back home? Or was it the crystal-ology crap you were after? Did you come here to refute all that bourgeois Western ideology you were raised on? Hey, maybe you should shave your head, dress up in saffron robes and join a monastery. That might be the ticket!

"I know it wasn't for Gerard – not for him. You liked him less than shit on a shoe. And you haven't done me any favors. Since you showed up, there's been a distinct downward spiral in the quality of my exis-tence. Is that why you came here: to fuck with me?"

"Don't flatter yourself," I say.

"You're a skimmer – one of those birds that flies across the ocean and dips its beak below the surface, not getting wet, just taking what it needs to get by. That's how you go through life: just skimming along, not really getting too involved with anything or anyone, taking a bit here, a bit there but not really getting anything out of it. You know what? My time with the Freedom Fighters might have been all for noth-ing, but I gave it everything I had."

"Why aren't you still fighting, then?" I retort. "Why did you give up and stick a needle in your arm? Couldn't hack it anymore?"

He walks up to where I'm sitting, scuffs a puff of dust into the air. I kick him in the shins – he tackles me to the ground.

"You little shit," growls Jack.

Pinning my arms, he punches me – *bam* – in the face.

"Stop it!" shouts Maya from the sidelines. Suddenly, Jack is off me. Blood rushes through my ears. The ringing fades...

"For fuck's sake," snaps Maya. "Can you two tune down the testos-terone? As if we aren't in enough of a mess already."

I run my hand along my cheek, wipe off a warm streak of blood.

"So...you spent some time in Chi-town, huh?" I say. "That's my home turf. Are you a Cubs or Sox fan?"

"I lived down in Hyde Park," says Jack. "South side all the way."

"South side trash," I mumble.

"At least they can fucking win," he laughs. "What's it been, like a century for you guys?"

"A hundred and four years...and counting. It's not a very profitable relationship."

"I'll never forget when the Sox won the 1959 pennant," he pronounces. "They set off so many fireworks it was like the whole city was on fire, man! Yeah, that was a day. A perfect Indian summer...right before those Federalis came and carted me off to Washington...Gotcha pretty good there, didn't I," he chuckles. "Well, I guess we're even for Nepalganj."

I lick blood off the corner of my mouth.

"...You're right," I say. "I am a skimmer. I didn't come to fulfill Gerard's dying wish; I just knew I had to get the hell out of France before Interpol rapped on the door. And so much blew up in my face when I got here, I didn't stop to think what I was doing...but I know now.

"I couldn't fucking stand Gerard: his wrinkled, sweaty head, that rotten pirate's crutch, his raspy laugh scouring my brain like steel wool. He was a smelly geriatric tick, Oliver Twisting me all the way to the bank.

"But the stories he told – about you and him, hopped up on amphetamines for a week straight, hiding out from Pakistani bandits in mountain caves; about the time they let you through a Kashmiri check post after Tex clipped off a half dozen rounds in their faces, then invited you for tea because they liked Gerard's ginger beard. I mean, that's like *Butch Cassidy and the Sundance Kid*, man. That's *real*.

"...When my dad died, it triggered something inside of me, as if I'd awoken from some deep trance. It wasn't a great feeling but at least I was *feeling*. I could finally taste how bland this spoon-fed, freeze-dried crap was I was weaned on my whole life was. I was never hungry, never cold, never lied to. But how can you really taste if you've never starved a little?

"My senses were dulled, atrophied like some dormant appendage. I felt like the boy in the bubble. Sterilized by tract housing, perfect lawns and soccer moms; choked by pre-shrunk, acid-washed, Dairy Queen, fat-free, mini-van bullshit. That climate-controlled hospital smell you can't get out of the back of your throat.

"No, there weren't any real smells, any real pain, just a big void, filled with Prozac and plastic and pre-packaged emotions.

"I knew I had to get out – live outside the lines, or maybe between the lines. To feel, smell, touch without banal, meaningless, sterile certainty. 'Cos that's what life *should* be...that's what life's about.

"This is exactly where I want to be."

Jack's not buying it, though.

"...Living outside the lines," he mocks. "Venturing out of the brave new world and tasting the pain? So some day you can sit and tell your spoon-fed offspring what it was all about – how you once got frostbite on a mountain pass; how you *really lived*? That's a glorified crock of shit, kid.

"Dip your hand in that fire too many times, you'll get burned. It will scar you until you can't recognize yourself. And don't think you've got any say in where you're going, either. You have about as much control over life and where it leads you as a cloud does in the wind.

"Yeah, you can see where you're headed – make predictions as to how long it will take you to get there – but they're only good for so long. Pretty soon the wind shifts, and you're moving in an entirely new direction."

"Stop making excuses for your own deficiencies, Jack," I say. "We've heard it all before."

"Did it ever occur to you that being a junkie was not my first fucking choice in life? That maybe I had other aspirations, other shit going on? You think you've heard the whole story, do you? Got me all figured out?"

"Yeah, actually, I..."

Maya interjects, then. "Let him speak, Jupiter."

"...I was a teacher, I told you that much," Jack continues. "A damn good one, too. Then forces started to pull me in a different direction. A few years later, I was on the other side of the world, helping to train Khampas."

"What the hell is a Khampa?" I ask. "Anything to do with *tsampa*?"

"Are you going to shut up and listen?" he gripes. "Don't make a fucking joke of it, kid, or I'll stop right here."

Maya glares at me.

"I'm sorry," I say. "I'll shut up."

"*Kham* is a region in Eastern Tibet. *Pa* means 'people of.' They're the horsemen of the plains... crazy motherfuckers. I've never seen a braver, more ferocious breed. These guys make Managis look like schoolboys – they could take you out with a sword before you blinked. Most of the men I fought with were Khampas...good, solid soldiers who would never turn away, who'd fight to the death. Good to have on your side, not theirs.

"...I spent three years helping train those guys. I wasn't the one showing them how to shoot or dig trenches. I was a teacher, what the hell did I know about that? I was the liaison. I had no family left, no friends, a great ear for Tibetan – and a genuine passion for the place. Back at University of Chicago, I wrote a few articles on the need for Tibet to be recognized internationally. I guess somehow the CIA must have gotten hold of them and thought I was right man for the job.

"At first I thought I was only there to translate, but they put me straight through artillery training. Next thing I knew I was digging trenches. I went through basic training with six groups – we covered everything from Morse code to Molotov cocktails.

"A few years later, I was fighting side by side with them, watching them die on a frozen plateau. When I look back, it's hard to remember how it all started – how one thing led to another. Pretty soon, twenty, thirty, forty years pass, and it's all just a big ball of twine with buried ends you can't unravel.

"Things started going south back in '64. We had this guy in charge: Baba Yeshi. He was a real charlatan. He could really spin his words. Rumor had it Baba Yeshi could tear up at will, untrustworthy little liar. He was skimming off the money the CIA was giving him, skimming the goddamn meat ration money while his troops were starving. He even charged them for their damn ammo.

"To top it off, he was stealing from his own people. He would stop refugees coming across the border and shake them down, take anything they had on them. He even let his bodyguards rape the local women. It got really out of control.

"One of the guys couldn't handle the corruption so he took off, with his wife and a few others who'd had enough. Baba had that guy and his wife shot in cold blood.

"Some of the men wanted to do away with Baba, but I explained that it would be the end of US support if they did. When Washington and Dharamsala finally got wind of Baba Yeshi's antics, the Dalai Lama's brother had him replaced by my buddy Wangdu as commander of the entire operation. Yeshi was really pissed, getting caught with his hand in the cookie jar.

"He left Mustang peacefully enough but within a month he was back for a fight, with two hundred of his tribesmen as back-up. He kept attacking the fort, accusing Wangdu of treason and embezzlement... complete bullshit. We fought back.

"When word got back to the capital, the king of Nepal ordered Baba Yeshi back to Kathmandu...and he crumbled like the sniveling bastard he was, giving away detailed accounts of our supplies, weapons and positions in exchange for political asylum.

"Henry Kissinger...what a prick! His secret flight to Beijing in July of '71 was another nail in our coffin. Suddenly all support from Washington started to dry up. I was issued a tourist visa in a fake passport and ordered to report back to Delhi...I never went. I ripped it up and threw it in the fire."I was on my own after that as far as Washington was concerned. They never sent anyone up to come weed me out. I suppose they would have had me killed if they'd known what I was up to. Maybe they thought I was already dead; maybe they thought Wangdu would take care of me...who knows? I suppose they had more important things – like *détente* – on their minds.

"So I stayed. Wangdu was a good general, a good man. He was one of those friends that never die, that stay in your heart. The ones you still laugh with, thirty years after they're gone.

"But '72 was worse: King Mahendra, who was pro-Tibetan, died, leaving his son Birendra in power. Chinese-Nepali relations were at an all-time low and Birendra was scared China might invade. Mao eased his fears, sucking him in with foreign aid and goodwill projects. Kathmandu launched propaganda campaigns accusing the Khampas of banditry, rape and murder. There were a few isolated incidents, but it was a sham! Trying to smear the mud on someone else's hands.

"In '74, they really turned up the heat. Mao personally threatened King Birendra that he would take action on the Mustang camp if Nepal didn't. Ten thousand troops marched up through the Kali Gandaki gorge to Jomsom, demanding our surrender."

"And did you?" asks Maya.

"Surrender? Fuck that noise. After fighting a country as big as China for fifteen years, you think we were going to roll over for Nepal?"

"Ten thousand troops is not something you can shake a stick at," I say.

"We weren't afraid of them and they knew it; we knew that country better than anyone. One of our men was worth at least a hundred of theirs. And they were holding one of our leaders as a hostage. One thing you don't want to do is get between a Khampa and one of his tribesmen. They'll take down everything in their path like a fucking hurricane if you piss them off enough.

"It was tense; something had to give. And we would have kicked the living shit out of them if it wasn't for that goddamn tape."

"What tape?" Maya's hanging on his every word.

"Towards the end, the Dalai Lama and his government in exile wanted nothing to do with us…we were an embarrassment. Think about it – why would they want their peaceful, non-violent image tarnished by bloodthirsty tribesmen, skinning Chinese soldiers and festooning their remains around Tibetan border towns. But we were the only ones doing anything about Tibetan independence. Bullets and knives were the only thing that was gonna work on those damn Chinks.

"They sent one of their own, their Minister of Security in Dharamsala, with a recording of the Dalai Lama telling us to surrender…I'll never forget the Khampas' faces when they heard that tape. Some of those men, as fierce and brave as they were, wept like babies. Confusion and anger swept their faces. Lost children stripped of their sacred cause.

"Then one of the chieftains spoke. 'How can we surrender to Nepal,' he asked, 'if we have never surrendered to the Chinese? We should all return to Tibet and fight rather than live in shame.'

"Everything they were fighting for, gone in ten minutes. The time it takes to eat a meal… Fifteen years of fighting, just like that.

"Fifteen years...that's got to be over five thousand days. It's like ripping your soul out every one of those days and placing it on a chopping block to be cut up into a thousand pieces. It hurt. And I wasn't even fucking Tibetan.

"I had somewhere else to go, something else to do. I could have packed my bags and got on a plane. *'Thank you very much, wish I took more pictures...'* What the fuck did *they* have left? After half of your country has been crucified, dismembered, burned and scalded alive, what do you do then?

"Children had been forced to shoot their parents, monks their teachers. Monks and nuns, the very core of Tibet's existence, forced to fuck one another in the streets...*what the fuck*??

"...You know all those weapons the CIA air dropped up in Mustang that I told you about? They never cleaned them up. Just like all those fucking oxygen cylinders up at Everest base camp. Mopping up that mess would've been an admission of guilt, I guess. *'Neither confirm nor deny'*...that was the line.

"Last year I was down at Boudanath for *Lhosar* – Tibetan New Year. I saw a yak herder circumambulating the temple. His right hand, or what was left of it, was heavily bandaged. I could tell by his dress that he was from near Mustang. Seeing him and his fucked-up hand sent me right back into the shit. I could almost hear bullets whizzing by my head. After a few minutes, I got myself together, asked him what had happened.

"He was crossing a pass up near the border, he said, when he stumbled upon a box full of grenades. He didn't have a clue as to what they were – tried to break one open to see what was inside...poor fucker. Now he can't even spin his damn prayer wheels when he goes around the temple. How do you live with that? All he wants to do is spin his damn prayer wheels."

Jack drops to his knees, then, shaking and sobbing. Tears stream down his cheeks. Maya covers him with a blanket.

"Shhh," she soothes.

"Leave me alone."

"It's going to be alright..."

"No, Maya, it's *not going to be alright.* Nothing you do or say is going to make it all fucking right," he snarls. "So why don't you save it for somebody else – 'cos it ain't fucking working on me."

"Hey," I sling an arm around him. "You remember that night in Nepalganj, Jack?"

"How could I forget?"

"…Thank you." I say."For almost getting you arrested?"

"No, seriously. There was more reality packed into that night than in the past twenty years of my life…as real as this blood on my cheek. I don't care if it leaves a scar and I don't care where it takes me. That's what I want; to be exposed to what's real in this world…"

"Don't wish too hard, kid, 'cos we're in a damn scary situation," Jack reminds me.

"Well, I'd rather die up here tomorrow than have lived my life inside some goddamn cubicle, writing up memos for the company picnic," I say.

"Stop talking like that," Maya yelps. "*Nobody's going to die.* We've just got to wait things out – right, Jack?"

"You're running a fever and on the verge of dehydration. *Jupe* here is about as lame a three-legged dog. That storm out there doesn't show any signs of letting up and we might be three feet under when it does. The only choice we *have* is to wait."

Great, Jack. Thanks for the fucking morale boost.

The three of us are curled up in our sleeping bags, pressed against one another for warmth. I tuck my hands between my shivering thighs. Sleep comes and goes – mostly goes. I might have slept a few hours at most. The trick is to keep everything close to your core, to lie in as close to a fetal position as possible, and hope that you warm up enough to doze off for a while…but it gets trickier by the minute. Sharp pebbles poke into me through the sleeping bag, gnawing at my back like tiny mites. I keep shifting, rotating parts of my body against the frozen ground…*fuck this.*

"I think it's stopped," whispers Maya.

I poke my head out of my bag. Light peeks in through the cave entrance.

"...Shit, it's already morning,"

"Did you sleep well?" she asks.

"Like shit," I reply. "You?"

"Pretty much the same."

I peel the sleeping bag down; frozen air wraps around my body. Stepping over Jack's prone form, I limp across to Maya.

"Wow – he's still asleep for once."

"I don't think he's well," she whispers. "Listen to how erratic his breathing's become. I think he's showing signs of pulmonary edema."

"Fuck. Seriously? Is there anything we can give him?"

"Nothing short of descent to a lower altitude will help, I'm afraid. How's your leg?"

I shift my weight, flinch. "Stiff. It seems worse than yesterday."

"Could be gangrene," she says brightly. "We might have to chop it off before we're through."

Funny girl. With any luck, it won't spread to your stomach...

"Holy shit, there's a skull in here!" I exclaim.

I hold up an opaque, half-broken orb. Maya brings a forefinger to her lips and nods towards Jack.

"*Shhh!*" she whispers. "If Jack wakes up and finds out we've been sleeping in another graveyard, he'll completely lose the plot."

"Here's a femur. How did we miss it?"

"It was a lot darker when we crawled in here, and you two were too tied up in your tiff. Let's try to get all these bones out of sight before Jack wakes up. You saw how he reacted when we camped on that burial site. He'll have a conniption if he sees this!"

I look over – Jack's still snugly tucked in his bag with his back to us. Quickly, Maya and I gather up the bleached bones and fragments.

"There's a small opening behind you. Let's stash everything in there."

I steal another look at Jack and scan his periphery. Shit – there's a rib bone right next to him. I creep over to his side and pluck it up. Jack stirs briefly, mutters, shifts. *Please don't wake up, please don't wake up!* I retreat slowly and tuck the bone carefully with the others. "Do you see any more?" asks Maya.

"There are some fragments over there but other than that, no."

"Most likely belong to the *lama* who was studying that *sutra* over there." She points at the Tibetan text.

"It seemed like there was more than one person, though," I say.

"Yes, you're right. They might have been yak herders, or even Tibetan refugees who got trapped in a snowstorm."

"I hope we don't add to the pile."

"It's a good thing we cleaned up before Mr Superstitious woke up. It's a lot brighter in here now. Let's have a look outside."Ducking under the cave mouth, I step out into blinding snow.

"Damn, it's bright out here."

"A winter wonderland, isn't it?" she says gaily, as if she's completely forgotten last night's misery. "Look, there's Eeyore!"

I squint down into a valley whitewashed with a thick fresh coat of snow...amazing. A solid-white landscape, dazzling under a lapis-lazuli sky. I wish I could show this scene to my sister, mom...to my dad. *I feel so fucking alive.*

Shaggy head bowed, Eeyore shivers off a layer of frost. Poor pony, she must have had a hell of a night. I'm surprised she didn't get buried in a drift.

Maya tramps down the hill to Eeyore's side, rubs a palm against her hairy cheek.

"Silly Eeyore. We thought we'd lost you!" she croons.

The pony snorts, pushes her nose into Maya's chest.

"Her mane is frozen solid. Hey, Jack...*Jack.*"

"What do you want?" he grumbles, emerging from the cave.

"Eeyore is alive. Give us some food for the poor pony!"

"We dish out any more food to that donkey and we might end up eating her," says Jack.

"You jackass," Maya retorts. "No-one is going to eat our poor little Eeyore. You touch her and you'll be putting some stitches across your own belly."

Jack's not listening; he's surveying the terrain. "It must have snowed at least a foot overnight," he pronounces. "Look, you can't see our tracks from yesterday."

"*Fuck.* We'll never make it out of here," I gripe.

Jack coughs.

"That's where you're wrong, my friend."

He unfolds the map, scans the horizon.

"Climb up over the top of the ridge and tell me what you see."

"I got my half my leg ripped apart by a dog yesterday – you climb it!"

"Maya?" he suggests.

"Wanker!" she shouts.

Jack coughs again into the map.

"Ok, I'll do it. Tell me there's a Hyatt with a jacuzzi on the other side," I mutter.

"Luxury is for the weak, kid," he declares. "Twenty more feet and you're there."

I plow forward, getting sucked further into a drift. "This is more than twenty feet, already, Jack." He doesn't answer. A breeze hits my face as I clear the summit.

"Now, what do you see?" he asks.

"A lot of fucking snow. Wait…there's smoke. *There's smoke. Yeah, baby!*"

A string of smoke meanders out of a chimney in the distance.

"There's a building," I shout. "A bunch of buildings!"

Jack trudges up, matching his footsteps to my tracks.

"That's our monastery," he says.

"Hallelujah."

It looked a lot closer from the top of the ridge. Before the wind picked up. Before my leg started to feel like an abused chew toy. Before the fierce sun came out and melted all the snow into our boots...and pants...and socks...this weather is so extreme with it's hot and cold swings.

"This looks kind of like the place where Gerard found me," says Jack.

"But you and Gerard were tight," I reply. "He was one of your boys, right?"

"Not really. Even from the start, we weren't that good of friends. He was jealous as a tomcat, always worried that I was trying to get in with his lady. Betty loved to practice her English on me, and he was always worried she'd run off to America with me some day."

I don't find that hard to believe – Jack's hit on every girl I've seen him come across so far.

"Hell, when I signed up with Gerard's crew, I knew it was going to be a bad gig from the start, but I didn't care. I was tired of calling the shots; I just wanted to forget. No, I wouldn't call him my boy. We worked together and that was about it.

"Gerard was the puppeteer and we were his puppets, too hooked on junk to give a shit. Beth adored him – why, I'll never know exactly. Tex and Dusty were just a couple of angry steers – only needed amphetamines for fuel and the occasional spur in their bellies to drive them to the next watering hole. Load them up on speed and watch them go. They were the perfect watchdogs of the operation: tough as steel and up all hours."

Poor Tex and Dusty...Texas cowboys turned into cattle.

"As for me," he says, "as long as that needle was in my arm three times a day, I didn't give a fuck. We could have been twenty thousand leagues under the sea for all I cared. Heroin's funny like that."

'Funny' – never an adjective that springs to mind when I think of heroin. Tragic, maybe, or 'fatal' but not funny. Never funny.

"...The CIA, Tibet, the Freedom Fighters – the fifteen years of my life I spent fighting for that poor, fucked-up country's independence. I cared so much...I gave them everything. Those Feds walked up to me one day and I gave up my whole fucking life like a goddamn disciple.

"It's hard to turn your back like that, but sometimes if you don't, it will tear you up on the inside until there's nothing left...so I did. If there's one thing heroin can help you do, it's to forget. You stick that needle in your arm and at first it's like going to the moon, man. Far fucking out. The sunshine through the clouds; the rainbow behind the rain. It's a party you never want to end. But no party lasts forever, man.

"Sooner or later, you're upping the ante to keep that buzz and before you know it, you almost OD. Maybe you do OD. Your heart almost stops; you swear you'll never do it again...but by then, you're hooked.

"When your body buys the lie, the party's over. After a while, you don't even get high; you just shoot up not to get sick. And you don't want to know what it's like to get sick: your whole body seizes like there's a hundred-amp current running through it; your organs shrivel up like salted slugs. You can't eat, can't shit. You just want to die. And the only thing that can stop the pain – the only cure – is more junk."

Sounds glamorous. Makes me want to run home and join a goddamn church. You can put all the money in the world into anti-drug campaigns, but a semi-reformed addict like Jack is a far more convincing deterrent.

"...Must have shaved off at least twenty years off my life, easy."

Only the good die young.

"You don't look so bad," I say. "Better than Gerard, anyway."

Most things well past dead looked better than Gerard, even when his heart was still beating. Smelled better, too.

"Don't be fooled, kid: my insides are all beat up. Just like Charlie Parker said, 'A thirty-five-year-old living in the body of a sixty-five-year-old.' And I'll tell you, I'm nowhere near thirty-five anymore. Half the veins on my arms are collapsed: a bunch of dead twigs on a rotting trunk. My bones creak more than bedsprings in a whorehouse. Every time I break a sweat, I feel as if my heart might implode…all systems shot. I'm like one of those Aeroflot planes the Russians panned off to China: should have been grounded years ago."

'An Air Jack flight bound for Shanghai crashed last night when the pilot suddenly started jonesing and diverted the plane into the Golden Triangle, where it ran out of fuel and nosedived into a local opium refinery. There were no survivors.' I feel like I'm in an AA, or NA, or some kind of scrape-myself-together self-help meeting. 'Hi, my name is Jay and I'm…well, I was a fledgling junkie, but after listening to this guy's hard-luck story, I'm never touching that shit again.'

"…Gerard never used like we did," Jack says. "He only shot up now and again, speeded out once in a blue moon with the boys, but that was it. I don't think he was really hooked. I think he was hooked on watching *us* shoot up and use, if anything. He was hooked on being the contact, on being in control, on being the *man*. Just like the man said, the contact high was always the most addictive."

I can attest to that. Selling drugs is a powerful rush rivaling that of the best opiate. Before the hash, it was mushrooms, back home. Before that, it was weed. There's something seductive about walking into a party where everybody knows your name, where everyone wants to know you. You *control* that party: you control the high, the horizontal and the vertical."

"If you're so beat up, why the hell did you decide to truck all the way up here?" I ask. "Couldn't you have found a more hospitable place to hide out?"

"Something told me that this was the place, this was the time. And this is *your* time, kid. *Your* time to shine. *Your* time to do something so fucking crazy that nobody besides us will ever believe you actually did it. We're gonna beat all the odds and get you over that pass, even if I die trying. Another hour and we'll be at the monastery."

"Didn't you say that a few hours ago?" asks Maya.

"Nepali time…you know the score."

The sun is setting now. Three, maybe four hours must have passed. We lost the trail (if you could call it a trail) early and had to beat through drifts all day. The sun kicked our asses. Our ass, meanwhile, is not co-operating; she freezes up every so often, point-blank refuses to budge. Jack wants to leave her behind. Maya wants to leave Jack. My face feels as though it's glued to a heat lamp; my gammy leg's on fire. I tweaked it again on the way down, slipping on a batch of scree concealed beneath a fresh drift. At least the wind has throttled back.

Once we reached the valley, Jack and Maya stick me on Eeyore, much to her dismay. Sometimes when we hit a drift, she falters, feels as if she's going to collapse and burst into a thousand pieces like a *piñata*...poor beast of burden.

A rectangular, near-windowless maroon building looms ahead. Light peeks faintly through the stones like secrets. Around the large building are smaller stone huts. The smell of burning wood catches my nostrils.

Jack brings us to a halt."OK, you two hang back for a couple minutes. I'm gonna see if anyone remembers me around here."

"Is that a good thing?" asks Maya.

"Good as far as I can remember."

She turns to me, then.

"How's your leg holding up?"

I look down at the dried blood on my pants.

"A lot better," I say, "since I've been back aboard Eeyore. She hasn't tried to shake me off lately – too beat up to fight anymore. Poor thing doesn't seem to taking our adventure too well."

"You had a rough night, didn't you, girl?"

Eeyore *hrumpphs* amiably as Maya rubs her neck.

Voices. A gaggle of young boys dressed in saffron monk's robes is scampering towards us across the courtyard.

Jack tracks through the hardening snow, grinning as he gets closer. *Jack – smiling.* He looks so different when he smiles. You hardly notice the scar.

"Alright, kids, they'll let us stay for a couple nights and help us get our act together. I didn't ask about food yet. I'll wait a while and feel out how much they can afford to give us before asking, you dig? I can't believe they still remember me!"

"Coolio," I say. "But how could they forget you?"

"I haven't seen these guys in over thirty years."

"Well, *I'll* never forget you. I can tell you that."

Jack's already back to business. "We can't stay in their quarters but they've got an extra building out back. Most of them are praying in the main courtyard right now, so let's do our best not to disturb them."

A young monk with close-cropped hair and a tanned, angular face approaches.

"Tashi delek," he beams, his smile as wide as the sky.

"This is Dorje," says Jack. "He'll take the two of you to our sleeping quarters. I'm going to go speak with one of the head monks about our predicament. I'll be back in a few."

Dorje leads us behind the main building to a dark stone shed. Whipping back the cloth curtain that serves as a door, he gestures for us to enter.

"Tujeche," says Maya.

"Kherang bodkyed shekyi yodpey?" he asks.

"Tis," she replies.

Candlelight wavers against the walls. It is bare save for a few mats at the center.

"Well, it's no Hyatt, is it?" I pronounce.

"It still runs circles around Jack's excuse for a tent," contends Maya, then, nodding towards the doorway: "It looks as though we've got an audience." I turn to look and two heads duck down out of sight, ruffling the cloth curtain.

"Ya pesh, ya pesh!" says Maya.

"I thought you didn't speak Tibetan."

"Just a little," she replies.

Dorje stands in the doorway with a smile as wide as the sky.

"…What does he want us to do: tip him?" I ask.

"It's probably the first time he's seen a foreigner in ages. It might be his first time ever."

"…Well, how long is he going to stand there?"

"Stop being so cheeky," she reprimands. "Let him have a look."

"*I* know what he'll like."

I fish around in my backpack and pull out my iPod. Dorje, transfixed, draws near, watching me untangle the headphones.

"Here, try these on for size." Dorje flinches a little as I place the headphones over his ears."It's OK, buddy," I say. "I'm not about to hurt you."

Fingers pressed to the sides of his head, he looks at me expectantly.

I try and turn it on – there's still some juice left! I press 'Play.' His eyes bulge; he shakes his head. Pulling out the headphones, he hands them back quickly, sticking his tongue out and waggling his head.

"He didn't like that too much. What were you playing?" asks Maya.

"I think it was the Beastie Boys."

"Well, what did you expect?"

"Didn't like that, huh?" I say, pointing to the iPod.

Opening his mouth as if to speak, Dorje half-smiles in amazement.

"Khande duwa?" asks Maya.

"Ki saabu du!" he exclaims.

"What did he say?"

"Cultural overload, I'm afraid." she says. "Play something chill for him. Do you have any classical music?"

"I'm afraid not."

"That explains a few things," she says.

Maya keeps talking with Dorje in Tibetan, hesitant, like someone tapping at the keys of a piano she hasn't touched in decades. Keep hitting those notes: it will come.

Half an hour or so goes by before Jack opens the door.

"How's everyone?" he says, jovial. "I see you're making friends already."

"Can I go have a look around?" I ask.

"This isn't another temple you can poke around and then buy post-cards," says Jack.

I yank the ice axe off the back of Jack's pack.

"What do you think I'm going to do – hack off ancient relics with this and smuggle them off to Singapore?" I say. "Cut me some slack..."

"Let him go, Jack," says Maya.

"What if he comes with me?" I ask, pointing to Dorje. "He could be my tour guide."

"OK," says Jack. "But don't stick your hand in any honey pots, dig? They're not used to tourists feeling up their monastery. This place is sacred to me as well; I don't want anything getting fucked up."

A row of bronze prayer wheels flanks the inner courtyard. Passing swiftly through it, Dorje leads me into another room, where clusters of butter lamps flicker to each side. In the wavering light, I can scarcely make out a jewel-encrusted Buddha with a round golden face, sitting serenely against the far wall, dozens of white silk scarves adorning his neck. Brightly colored silk banners hang from the ceiling.

Silently, after a while, we slip back out into the courtyard. I smile stupidly at Dorje, who smiles back like a kid showing off a shiny new bicycle.

I spin one of the prayer wheels. Squeaking erratically, it slows and comes to a shaky stop. I look at the writing etched across it, run my fingers over each embossed character, feeling each contour as if it were Braille. The same characters, over and over again, a thousand times.

Hail the jewel...in the heart of the...lotus.

A gray-haired monk shuffles up, flips his wine-dark robe over one shoulder. Deep wrinkles score his face like dried-up riverbeds. He exchanges a few words with Dorje and the young monk vanishes down a dark corridor.

"…You are curious about the meaning?" he asks me. "These words have many, many meanings."

"Uh, yeah," I reply. Then, stupidly, "You speak English?"

"Yes, though not so well, I'm afraid. I can speak French if you like, but I'm told you are an American." He beams.

"No, no," I reassure, "you're doing fine. This place is so remote, I just didn't expect it."

"That is good. Expectations can cause a great deal of misfortune at times. Allow me to introduce myself: my name is Nyima Lama."

"But how did you…"

"How did I learn? Circumstance. Circumstance takes us places we would never dream to go to, teaches us things we would never learn otherwise. Many years ago, I was a young boy studying in a monastery near Lhasa. Then the trouble began with the Chinese. When the soldiers first came, they were curious, too.

"There was a young man, maybe a few years younger than you. He was a soldier. I couldn't speak to him but we could communicate. I could see compassion in his eyes.

"Sometimes when the leaders were busy inspecting our quarters, he would cut up an apple and share it with me. We would share a smile. I had faith in these smiles. I believed smiles would evolve into words, words into trust, trust into friendship.

"But there was no time for words. They did not want to learn our language, our culture…it was easier for them that way. It is easier to beat a strange dog than one you know, to steal from a stranger than a neighbor. Soon, the smiles disappeared. Each time they came back, they were bolder. They began to steal, to beat us.

"Once they told us all to meet in the center of a courtyard. The translator told us we were being liberated and to do so, we must undergo revolution. I didn't understand. My people were not at war. Who were we being liberated from?

"They told us we were to strip off our robes and place them in the center of the yard. When we resisted, they began to beat us. A club struck me to the ground. When I looked up, I looked into the eyes of the young soldier who had shared the apple with me. How could this happen, I thought.

"I was young and naïve. I became angry and bitter. I could not control my anger then as I can now. I wanted to kill this soldier who had betrayed me, killed my brothers. You could not imagine the rage inside of me then.

"But I have forgiven him. You see, he could not control these events. They were prophesized long ago by the oracles. Once set in motion, a wheel is very difficult to stop. Just as your wheel is spinning now."

Where it stops, nobody knows.

"Bad things like this kept happening," the *lama* continues. "A few years after that, there were uprisings, and many Tibetans were killed. That's when we decided to leave, traveling over the mountains to India or Nepal. The elders objected, insisting that the trouble would soon be over, that His Holiness would soon make amends with the Chinese, but I knew it was too late. I saw it in the eyes of the young soldier when he beat me.

"So one night, a group of us wrapped ourselves in wool robes, loaded a donkey with *tsampa* and water, and left the monastery. For many of us, it was the first time we'd left our monastery. None of us knew how to survive in the mountains, read the weather, navigate the passes. So we began our journey south. "We walked through the nights and into the day, sleeping a few hours here and there. When we reached the mountains, our troubles grew. Many suffered frostbite, some died. Still we tried to cross the mountains – there was nothing left to turn back for.

"I thought we were all going to die but one night, a yak caravan came upon us. A caravan heading for Nepal. They gave us proper clothing and food. Without them, we would surely have died.

"When we arrived in Kathmandu, I went to Boudanath to pray for the brothers I had left behind. I told others of what was happening, of the atrocities. A Swiss man and his wife had formed an organization to help Tibetans in exile. They wanted me to tell my story to others, to the world. So I was sent to Switzerland, to study and tell others of Tibet's trouble.

"I spent the next twenty years of my life there, helping them build a new monastery for other exiles, helping those who fled Tibet adapt to their new world. But eventually, I grew tired. I had to be close to this land where I was born.

"I may not return to the monastery I studied at when I was a boy, but I can feel her heart beating over the mountains…maybe I will escape and reach her in the next life."

"But you've already escaped," I say.

"Come. Let me show you," says Nyima.

We enter a building to the right and pass into a hall. The walls are lined with fantastic colorful paintings gilded in gold.

"This," he points to one, "Is *samsara,* the wheel of suffering." Its claws dug into the sides of the wheel, a massive red demon sinks his teeth into the sacred circle. "This is your life – all of our lives. It is the never-ending story of man's struggle to break free from this world. In the wheel, you see the cycle."

The circle is sliced into sections, each showing a different scene with creatures scattered like fated ants in Bosch's *Garden of Earthly Delights*.

"Each of these sections represents a world in which we live, the higher being more virtuous than the lower. It shows us how our actions will affect our place in the future world. Look at these men and women." He points to figures of men and women fornicating and eating lavishly. "Through their sinful acts, they will slip into the lower realm of Hungry Ghosts."

He indicates a cluster of sickly-looking creatures with distended bellies and pencil-thin necks. "Do you see how their stomachs are so big and yet their necks so small? They eat without satisfying their hunger. They drink without satisfying their thirst. Nothing satisfies them. Vices of previous lives have placed them here, and so they will forever remain hungry, unable to fill their stomachs.

"And there is *Yama*, the god of death, who holds this all in his grasp. You see, everything in death is life. Everything in life is death. Nothing is permanent. But most importantly, everything is illusion."

At the center of the painting, a pig, snake and rooster form a mini-circle, biting the leader's tail as if engaged in some twisted circus act.

"...What about the animals in the middle?" I ask.

"These three animals represent the main vehicles that perpetuate man's inability to escape the wheel of suffering. The pig is ignorance, the snake hatred..."

"And the rooster, lust or desire," says Maya, breaking from the shadows.

"Ah, very good," smiles Nyima. "It seems as if we have a scholar in our midst."

"Just a good listener...who had a good teacher," she says softly.

"These three animals," Nyima continues. "They are forever bound to one another, forever binding us to this world."

"So how do you break out of the wheel?" I ask. "Or are we just stuck in the spokes?"

"It is possible to transcend the suffering, but it takes time," the lama explains.

"How long?" I persist.

"That is a hard question to answer. For some, a lifetime; for others, several hundred. Some may never find it. It is dependent on one's karma from previous lifetimes and their ability to accept truth."

"Truth?" I need clarification. *One man's truth...*

"Before young Gautama attained enlightenment," says Nyima, "he was the prince of a wealthy kingdom to the south of Nepal. His father gave him anything he wished for or desired, but he wanted more: he wanted to seek the truth. On several occasions, he snuck out of the palace against his father's wishes. On his first outing, he encountered a leper, illustrating sickness and pain. On the second outing, he encountered an old man. This represented aging and the slow decomposition of all our bodies. And on the third, he witnessed a dead man lying on the street.

"All of these images were different forms of *dukkha,* or suffering. All of these images were events that every man must endure. In Buddhism, suffering is the highest truth, the absolute. Until we accept suffering as an inescapable part of our lives, we will continue to suffer."

"What happens when you find the truth, then?" I ask.

"Nirvana. Nirvana is an eternal state of bliss and happiness, the end

of suffering. You see, life leads us either in the direction of *samsara* or *nirvana*, depending on our karma.

I do a quick calculation of the actions and misdeeds in my lifetime. I don't think I'm in the red…yet. But still, there was that time I terrorized the block party with my BB gun. Dad put an end to my firearms aspirations right then and there.

"…Still others will become *bodhisattvas* – enlightened beings who have transcended this human form, but decide to remain in this world to help others on their journey towards *nirvana*."

"Like teachers…"

"Yes, exactly. The Lord Buddha was a *bodhisattva*. I think your friend may be close to discovering the truth."

"Who – Jack?"

Jack…an enlightened being? I just don't see him in saffron.

"He has been running many years now, but finally he has come back. You remind me of him when he was a young man…when he was lost."

"You knew him before…when he was here?" I ask.

"Oh, yes, he came a long time ago. He was so young, so full of anger, just as I was. He is the only foreigner who knew of this place – you are the first we have seen in many, many years. He was a brave man in his youth, fighting with our men against the Chinese. Sometimes he would bring his troops here when they could not reach their base in Mustang.

"We did not agree with their fighting, but they were our people and they were fighting for Tibet. They would hide their arms outside of the monastery before entering. The last time, he came with a French couple."

"Gerard and Betty," I whisper.

"All of his men had been killed…wiped away in an ambush near the Indian border. He had escaped the attack but later, he was robbed by some bandits. They left him to die in an animal shelter on top of a mountain pass. That is when the French couple found him.

"He was badly wounded and was close to death. Many of his toes were lost from the cold. He couldn't walk alone, but he guided the couple here, and our doctors nursed him back to health with our medicines and powers."

"What happened then?" asks Maya.

"I am not certain. Soon after Jack regained his health, he left with the couple...that was a long time ago. The man, I forget his name... He was French, I remember."

"Gerard?" I say.

"Yes," he says. "You speak of him as if you know him. He had a very strong energy about him, like lightning just before it strikes. You know it is coming but you don't where it will strike. It was unclear which path he would choose in life.

"At that time, even the elders had little contact with the West. Not one of us could speak English or French. We were only able to communicate through Jack, yet he made many of the monks restless. He was troubled as well.

"We were relieved when they left. I do not know down what paths he has wandered since, but I sense that he has endured a great deal of pain over the years. This is why he has come. He has come to end the pain.

"Look into his eyes. Jack is a very clever man, but his spirit is restless. I have let go of my anger, turned it into something else – he has kept it close to his heart for all these years. But I sense a change. Maybe now he is ready to let go.

"...He is not finished searching, but for what he is searching, I do not know. Men such as him need time and space to find their truths, roaming alone as a snow leopard over these mountains. There are many paths a snow leopard may take, but if one is tainted with the scent of man, they will choose another, no matter how difficult.

"The leopard is growing tired. Let us hope he finds his way before it is too late."

His face rugged yet his eyes oddly serene."The day is growing old...come, let us go from here."

He ushers us through a long corridor lined with prayer wheels. I slide my hand against them lazily, as a child might run a stick along a fence, coaxing an occasional creak or turn.

Nyima jogs ahead of us, then suddenly stops and turns. "I'm sorry.

I've neglected some of my duties during our conversation. I must go, but I hope to talk again with you soon." His saffron robes whisper in the muted air and then he's gone.

"Well, that was some pretty heavy stuff," I say.

"As real as it gets."

"You really know your shit, don't you?"

"I know what I know," says Maya.

"That's a fairly moderate statement," I say.

"Moderation is the key – or weren't you listening?"

She smiles, spins a prayer wheel playfully. Damn, she looks good. Don't look at me like...don't do that. I thread my fingers into her hair, wind her in, press her lips to mine. Her tongue darts past my ear. For a long moment, we press hard against one another. Then, off balance, we bang off of a prayer wheel and tumble to the ground.

Ouch, my leg! Fuck it. A cloud of dust wafts up around us. She pushes me back – not now, Maya; don't deny me now. I kiss her hard. My hand is under her shirt, sliding upwards towards her breasts. I...I...

She strikes me sharply across the face; I step back.

"Stop it!" she hisses.

I stare at her dumbly, taste blood on my lip. Opened up the scar from Jack's punch.

"Didn't you hear them?"

"Who?" I'm perplexed.

"The monks, for fuck's sake. Oh god, they must have seen every-thing."

The faint squeaking of prayer wheels rotating can be heard along the corridor.

Maya puts a hand to her head.

"Oh, this is bad. *What were you thinking?"*

"It was just a kiss. You said you liked it last time."

"Sod off! You don't understand. It's bad enough they're letting a woman stay here but once this gets around...bloody hell."

She pats the dust off her pants.

"We've got to find Jack and tell him before they do. Give me your hand."

I groan as she pulls me to my feet.

"You've hurt your leg again, haven't you?"

"Yeah, when we fell," I wince. "Don't worry…come here."I pull her close, kiss her neck. She pecks me back, then flounces away.

"*Enough*, already." Grabbing my hand, she pulls me outside into the night. A fresh wind is brewing.

In the distance, a circle of monks chants on the moon-washed flagstones. By the time we reach Jack, he's already packing.

"Here they are, ladies and gentleman, after a trying day out in the Garden of Eden…"

"Listen, Jack," says Maya, "Jupe didn't know."

Suddenly a gust wafts through the doorway.

"Didn't know what? That rolling around on the ground French-kissing with your hand up some white chick's blouse in a monastery might be frowned upon? Couldn't you have had the decency to wait *one fucking day*? I told you not to mess around. I guess I should have specified 'each other' when I said not to touch anything."

"It's my fault," I say, "not hers."

"Well, it's too late now, isn't it? A midnight trek in the breeze should give you time to think it over."

"…So…they've asked us to leave?" asks Maya.

"Do they really need to? You know the rules, Maya. We come crawling into their monastery with a woman who shouldn't be here in the first place and then have the audacity to eat their food – which, may I remind you, is probably donated and in scarce supply. And then you've got to go rolling about like a couple of dogs in heat at the feet of Buddha, no less! We have just officially bottomed out on the karmic scales. We are *leaving*."

"For the love of god, Jack, they're monks!" I say. "Can't they forgive, just like any other men of the cloth? And while we're being so karmically sensitive, you might want to watch your language."

"First the shit with the prayer flags and now *this*?"

"What prayer flags?" asks Maya. "Did you do something with their prayer flags as well?"

I lock eyes with Jack. *Do not* say another fucking word, or my hands will be at your throat.

"…*No!* Nothing happened with the prayer flags. Right, Jack?"

"Whatever you say, kid," he sighs. "It's not as simple as slipping into the confessional booth and getting a dozen Hail Marys from Father O'Leary. It's a little more serious than that up here. These Tibetan monks are more superstitious than a flock of Salem witch-hunters. They are going to take this as a personal slight against Buddha and any other local deities and demons they can dream up. And you know what? I'm superstitious, too. I can't sleep here…this place means too much to me. The best thing we can do now is bail."

He throws my backpack towards me.

"Fill it up, Romeo," he says. "I'm going to see if they'll spare us a little water and *tsampa* for the road."

"Can't we stay the night?" I ask.

"Not if you want to have any positive karmic flow left in this lifetime," replies Jack.

"But Jack…*fuck*, man – my leg."

"What about your leg?" he counters.

"I…can't really walk on it."

"That's what Eeyore is for. You've got the easy part: all you've gotta do is sit on a goddamn pony! That's not too fucking hard, is it? "

"This is the first rest we've had in over a week. Come on, have a heart," I groan.

"Look, Jack," chimes in Maya, "you're right – it was terribly wrong for us to act in such a disrespectful manner…in a monastery, of all places. But we'd be hard put to venture into the cold tonight. How many more days do we have until we reach the border?"

"Two…if the weather holds," grumbles Jack.

"With Eeyore?" asks Maya.

"Just shut up and let me think!" he yells. "…Three, maybe three days."

"I thought you said before it was going to be only a day or two from the monastery, Jack," rebukes Maya.

"Just shut up and let me think for a goddamn minute… Yeah…two, maybe three days. We're moving slower than I planned."

"Well, don't you think we should have a look at your fucking map and suss it out before we go marching off into a sodding windstorm?" I add. "We're honored to have your superior guiding skills at our service, but don't you think you should have a definite number of days in your head, given the fact that the only edible thing past this monastery is snow?"

"I said two or three days, alright?" shouts Jack.

"Look. Jupiter is simply in no state to travel yet, and you know it." Maya, always the practical one. "That's at least three days hard going, then possibly another two or three days by himself – at altitudes of over sixteen thousand feet. The wind is freshening as we speak. Leaving tonight is tantamount to murder."

"It's not what *I* think, Maya – it's what the *monks* think," says Jack.

"Come off it, Jack. We all need the rest, including you. *They're monks*. You've gotten your knickers in a twist over some trumped-up, melodramatic charges that have only been filed in your head. Have Ny-ima or any of the other *lamas* even said anything to you yet?"

"You could shoot them in the foot and they wouldn't ask you to leave – they're so goddamn polite," he says. "But ten to one they're freaking out right now."

"Look, they might be a little upset but they're not going to turn us out into the cold. Besides, I'm sure this is more excitement than they've had for some time now."

"Not funny," snarls Jack.

"I'm going to speak to Nyima just now and…"

"No, I'll do the damage control," he says. "Just stay the fuck off of one another. I'll be back."

Maya and I crawl into our sleeping bags. The temperature is dropping faster than bricks. We squirm next to each other like a pair of gigantic larvae.

"...Are we really as fucked as Jack says we are?" I ask.

"He's *completely* lost the plot," she asserts. "I've never heard of a monastery kicking anyone out into the cold. Jack's being rather melodramatic about the whole thing. But he does tend to take these matters rather seriously, doesn't he?"

The door swings open; steam rises from Jack's mouth.

"Alright, we can stay – but you two have to keep your hands off each other and sleep in separate rooms."

"Says who?" I ask.

"Says me, goddamnit. Just keep a lid on it or I'll kick your asses back out into the cold. Oh, and one more thing...they want to do an exorcism on Jupiter before we go on," Jack says.

"An exorcism from what? I haven't been foaming at the mouth, have I?"

"They sense demons. Some of the elders think demons entered your body when the dog bit you. They think the demons are stubborn – they don't want to leave your body now that they can't go back into the dogs' bodies. The demons are strong, too...strong enough to kill you. So they want to perform an exorcism."

"Spooky," says Maya.

"They want to do it tonight," adds Jack.

"Tonight?"

I'm seriously unsure about this.

"Yeah, right now. Nyima said he sensed the bad energy radiating out of you the second we entered the monastery. They were already planning on it. I told them that we're out of here first thing in the morning, so it's got to be tonight…sorry, kid."

"Is this optional?" I ask.

"What is your *deal*, man? They're trying to help you – you should consider this a favor."

"Yeah, but tonight? It's fucking freezing out there and blowing stink."

"It's an auspicious day in the Tibetan calendar. Don't worry, it's not going to entail any Latin or head-twisting…this is a good thing. A few chants, a fire… maybe some effigies of the demons, as far as I know."

"What do you mean, as far as you know?" I ask.

"Well, I'm just going off of what I've read and heard. I used to teach some of this stuff way back when but I can't say I've ever seen a *phurba* ritual…They'll come for us when they're ready."

"Hold on a minute – I haven't decided yet," I protest. "Does the fire involve hot pokers or scarification?"

"What, like the scars on my back?" he says. "I doubt it. Listen, if you won't do it, we're not staying the night. What's it going to be?"

"…Alright," I say. "Let's do this."

The wind howls like an predator closing on a kill. Prayer flags slap frenetically in the gale. In the courtyard, a fire whips and twists, embers spraying into the night air like molten mercury. Opposite the fire sits a small group of monks. A hand beckons…Nyima Lama.

With Jack on one arm and Maya on the other, we hobble over to him. I release my arms from their necks and they ease me onto an embroidered mat on the ground.

Jack trots off, returning with a bundle wrapped in a white scarf. Bowing low, he lays it at the monks' feet.

"OK, kid, good luck," he says, and turns to go.

"What? You're not staying?"

"They don't want the two of us around," he explains. "They need to focus on the bad energy. They don't want the deities they invoke to confuse Maya or me with you."

Maya blows me a soft kiss. Jack nods his head slightly.

"You'll be alright, kid. Nyima will be here with you. Just do what they say."

Nyima takes my hand in his. "Do not worry, my boy. These deities are powerful, but they will come to help you. This can only help you."

Drums begin to beat, then, pulsing to the rhythm of the wind. I shiver, wrap my arms around my knees. Out of the shadows darts a figure in a blood-red wooden mask. Fangs protruding, lip curled, eyes bulging from their sockets, he looks like a devil on PCP. Five skulls grin salaciously from atop his crown. His body is wrapped in a heavy brocade, shimmering red and gold. In one hand he holds a metal dagger, with pieces of cloth flowing off its shaft.

The drums grow in strength and urgency; cymbals slice through the constant howl of the wind, followed by low, ominous trumpets. The figure begins to whirl, cutting through the air with his dagger.

Four other figures appear, twirling around the fire in large-brimmed, pointed hats covered in small skulls.

"Drink this," says Nyima, handing me a bowl of darkish liquid.

I take a sip, smack my lips. Foul.

"It is medicine…it will help weaken the evil forces that trouble you."

The masked dancer spins faster, dipping and slicing, slicing and dipping, blurring into a cloud of color and cloth… He lunges in my direction. Instinctively, I recoil.

"Do not be afraid, Jupiter. You should never show fear in the face of demons," says Nyima.

Hovering over me, the demonic figure jabs at the blackness with his dagger; he shouts into the night.

"Lhaaa Gyaloooo! Kiii! Sooo! Tat!"

He thrusts the dagger downwards, freezing inches from my leg.

"Sooo! Sooo! Sooo! Kye ihasooo! Yul ihasooo! Ta ihasooo!"

Cymbals hum. I look down at the dagger hovering above my leg. Copper, maybe brass: three blades chipped with age, meeting at a pointed tip. Three fearsome skulls glare from the top of the handle.

The dancer jumps away towards the fire, spinning furiously. Again, he lunges at me with the dagger, this time at my arm. I take another sip from the bowl. The bitter liquid begins to warm my body, numb my mouth.

One of the dancers begins to draw on a sheet of paper. The masked demon figure jabs harder, moving towards him. He snatches the paper away and tosses it into the fire.

"Lhaaa Gyaloooo! Kiii! Tat!"

The morning is calm, the dancers gone, but my leg still aches. Sunlight frames the edges of the cloth-hung doorway.

Nyima brushes back the curtain, smiling.

"Are you feeling better this morning?" he enquires.

"Yes, thank you."

Nothing like a little exorcism to flush out the system.

He wraps a white cloth around my neck.

"This is a *kaathaa*, blessed with good fortune…for good luck on your journey."

He throws another *kaathaa* around Jack's. Clutching the back of Jack's head, Nyima pulls him near so that their foreheads touch.

"Thar thug zhidey gangsing yongbar zhog."

Jack brings his hand to the back of Nyima's head and replies,

"Zhidye di zhedrag kyi…nedam yod."

Their foreheads touch, and Nyima chants something under his breath. Then they break from one another. Nyima pats Jack on the shoulder. "Now I must go," he says. "Jack knows these mountains well and can lead you to safety. May you pass before the snows come."

He smiles again, and is gone.

Hey, if you can't trust a monk's word, whose can you trust?

Jack kneels down beside me. "How do you feel?"

"Better," I say, rubbing my thigh. "It hurts, but I should be able to walk soon."

"Good. I'm sure your buddy Eeyore will be ecstatic…Listen, about the other night in the cave…I didn't mean all that shit. Some of that stuff you said just got under my skin…that cave had bad memories for me. You're alright, kid – and you've got some balls to come up here and pull a stunt like this. Maya, too…shit, I'd probably fall in love with her myself if you weren't around to stop me…and I weren't so goddamn old."

"I'm sorry…for everything," I say. "I didn't mean to jump to conclusions and I know it doesn't mean shit to say it, but I'm sorry."

"No, kid, it means something…everything means something. You know the one thing I don't understand, though…why do you two even give a shit about me? Why would you care?"

"I guess you're getting under my skin as well," I say.

Eeyore. She mustn't be too happy with the way things are going. Every day a little colder, every meal a little smaller – and this big white ass on top of her to boot. That's what she gets for not wearing an earring in a past life. When I begin to feel her struggling through the drifts, I get off and walk. The leg's not so bad now, but it's still touch and go. If I only had another day or two to rest. I don't feel much pain, though… don't feel much of anything, come to think of it.

Jack is not looking good at all. He hasn't smoked a cigarette in days – too busy coughing. This morning, I swear his face was blue and his eyes were all puffy like he just got off a seventy-two hour bender…

I think he could be next on Eeyore's list of passengers.

…Only fifteen *chow chows* left. Fifteen packets of *chow chow*, five tins of tuna, half a dozen biscuits and some *tsampa…and I ain't got no cigarettes!* Not that I want any. I tried to smoke yesterday, couldn't do it...hacked up phlegm for a half an hour. I don't think we have enough food left. Jack wouldn't let the monks give us more than a few handfuls and there's no 7-11s between here and Tinker.

I haven't taken anything resembling a solid shit in over a week, and we ran out of toilet paper two days ago. The crumpled pages out of Jack's notebook just aren't cutting it. Frostbite, lame leg, nothing to eat but fucking chow chow...I guess I'll have to add this to the 'just deal with it' list.

Two days left to the border...or did he say three? I'm not hungry half the time anyway. Altitude kills your appetite like Claude Von Bulow killed his wife. Precise, calculated injections over time – increase the dosage in miniscule amounts. Above fifteen thousand feet, you feel a little more tired with every step, but strangely you don't feel the need to eat. Maybe that's how these mountains deal with strangers. *Let them come: we will make them forget to eat. Before they know it, they'll be wasting away on our slopes.*

Our stove sputters valiantly in the bitter air, the only sign of warmth in this frozen desert. Sometimes I catch myself holding my hands near the little blue flame as if it might warm me... Jack places chunks of snow into the pot, careful not to spill the precious water inside. I grab a chunk and crunch it up in my mouth.

"Don't do that," he cautions. "You'll get dehydrated."

"A little snow never hurt anybody," I say.

"Suit yourself."

I pick up another chunk and the pile collapses, knocking the pot off the stove.

"Goddamn it!" yells Jack. "We're almost out of gas and you pull a stunt like this. I've had it – *you* melt the fucking snow!" Jumping up, he trudges away, coughing loudly.

Fine. I'll melt the snow, bitch.

Righting the stove, I dig out my lighter. I keep flicking but it's not happening.

"Toss me your lighter," I say.

"He lobs some matches over and directs his telescope in the direction of the monastery, pressing his eye to the lens.

"He's still following us," he whispers. "I thought we lost him after the storm but he's still there. I thought Maya might be right: maybe I *was* getting paranoid. Thought he might be a herdsman or the scout of a salt caravan...but not anymore. He's definitely following us."

It wouldn't be hard, with the never-ending trail of shit and half-buried piles of converted notebook paper I've been posting as trail markers.

"What makes you so sure?" asks Maya. "He might be lost."

"Those kinds of men don't get lost up in this country – they own it." He coughs into his sleeve. "This is their turf."

"Maybe he's come from the monastery," she posits. "Maybe he's come to help us to the pass."

"There are no horses at the monastery. If he'd wanted, he could have caught up to us in a few hours with that horse. No, he's holding back on purpose, keeping his distance. It's almost as if he's waiting."

"Who would have followed us up here, Jack?" I ask. "Could those Managis still be after us?"

"No, not this high up. They're mean, but those Managis are city-bred. They know more about MTV countdowns and Bollywood actresses than tracking people in the mountains.

"They wouldn't have wasted their time – they would have finished the job a long time ago."

"Maybe that guy I showed the *dzi* to in Kathmandu had somebody tail us."

"They're not after the *dzi,* kid," Jack says. "They're after me. They don't forget."

"Maoists?" "This guy is riding alone."

"What about that dude we passed chopping up the rocks?" I ask.

"Let me have another look through that telescope, kid."

I hand it back.

"...He's so far away it's hard to tell...but I'd swear that was a Khampa."

"That's not good, is it?" I say.

"No stronger horsemen, no better trackers than them. The fiercest warriors I've ever seen. There was a battle in the end, wiped out all our men. As far as I know, I was the only survivor."I'll bet the others know I got out of there alive. And I'll bet even more that they think I set them up.

"Hell, I wasn't one of them. By '62, I was the only white boy up there. Half of them didn't trust me after the CIA cut off aid, but I stayed. It's hard to put down a gun after you've been sleeping with one under your pillow for years.

"No they didn't trust me – nobody trusted anybody in the end. And when my body didn't show up with the rest of the dead, They figured I had a hand in the ambush."

"…Do you think they still recognize you?"

"That guy smashing rocks sure as hell remembered me, didn't he?"

"Well, does *he* bring back any memories?" asks Maya.

"These people don't forget faces, especially foreign ones that speak their language. And they don't let scores like that go unsettled."

"Should we travel by night and try to lose him?" Maya suggests.

"Too late for that," declares Jack. "All he has to do is follow our tracks in the snow… No, let him come. Let's see what score he has to settle."

It's still…as still as ice. A heavy fog begins to roll down off the pass. No wind, just the breath of it spilling off the distant peaks like smoke chugging from factory chimneys.

"Tinker pass…we made it." Jack points upwards to a glacier squeezed between two peaks. "The other side of that ridge is India or Tibet, depending on which way you go. You don't see any *bideshis* up here, man, I can tell you that. Probably half a dozen including Tinker, the guy who named it…and us.

"Imagine that guy Tinker, coming all the way up here just to name this goddamn pass. Why the hell would anyone want to do that?"

A weathered raven caws coarsely from a boulder.

"Doesn't look as if anyone's ever set foot here, does it? Funny how the snow covers things up. But we were here, man. You better believe we were here. Look a little harder, look down on these rocks...they've got a story to tell."

He kicks at a loose stone.

"Yeah, you don't have look too hard. Time freezes up here, man, no matter how hard they try to cover shit up."

He bends down, picks up a rusted bayonet.

"Well looky here! Here's a little bit of history they never taught in school. This is it...this is where is all went down. The final stand."

He scrapes the bayonet across a boulder, revving up some sparks.

"You see, after they played that damn tape from Dharamsala, all hell broke loose up here. One of the chieftains felt so betrayed by the Dalai Lama, he cut his own throat then and there...fucking freaked.

"Wangdu tried to keep it together and cut a deal with the Nepali army, but he didn't want to give up his weapons. You can't take a weapon from a Khampa...that's a part of them, that's who they *are,* man! Wangdu knew they were already holding some of the chieftains hostage and he didn't want to go to jail. He tried to stall the army, promised them that they would give up their weapons slowly over a period of time.

"He told them, 'Give us amnesty and we will surrender.' They agreed. That was the deal. But those Nepali soldiers never kept their end of the bargain. They never meant to. As our men started to filter down and give up their weapons, they locked them up.

"After that, there was only one choice, really. Mao had his men up against our backs, and with ten thousand troops in front of us, we decided to make a run for the Indian border. That was our only hope."

Jack stares out across the clouds. He isn't talking to us any longer; we're listening by default.

"Hell of a trek, let me tell ya! Running through the night, starved and half-frozen, getting ambushed by both the Chinese and the Nepalese soldiers every twelve hours or so. Low on food, low on ammo, low on life. We had to leave half of the wounded behind, just fucking leave them there to die. If they had found a stray wounded fighter, they might have given him a cup of tea, plugged him for information, then put a bullet in his head after they'd gotten all they needed.

"You think I didn't see those skeletons back in the cave? That wasn't a monk, they weren't Tibetan refugees – those were my fucking friends, man! Tashi was hit when we crossed over the Chinese border. Tsering got hit when we raided the police station in Simikot. We had to hole up in there for days...*those were my friends!*"

Maya and I look at one another. He *knew*. He knew all along.

"...Truth is, I fucked up. One night, a couple of our yaks wandered off. Wangdu ordered me to send out a reconnaissance team. I picked two men, two of the youngest. They were maybe twenty years old, the last out of a batch of fighters who'd been trained by the Indian army. They'd grown up in Dharamsala, never even saw Tibet. They'd had an idea of what was happening there but they didn't really know. When you see your mother, father and *lama* killed, your monastery destroyed – that's when you *know.* They never saw that, already a generation out.

They'd only been with us for a month or so. The only action they'd seen was Tibetan fighting Tibetan, when that fucker Baba Yeshi stormed our camp.

"I don't know what I was thinking...I should have gone after those yaks myself. You could see it in their eyes: these boys were scared. They were too young – they didn't have any fight in them. I don't blame them. It's hard to imagine a free Tibet when you've never seen one."

"They gave themselves up?" I ask.

"All we knew is that they didn't come back. They might have gotten lost. They might have been captured...we didn't know. But we did know that it wasn't good. There had already been so much double-crossing going on that no-one really knew what it meant. But *I* gave the order...I should have known."

"Maybe they did get lost," says Maya, only half convinced.

"That I could have lived with...but it turned out worse than that. Much worse. For years, I could only imagine what actually happened to those two. Finally, I got some intel through one of my old contacts. They were captured.

"They gave up the entire mission…everything. They offered up everything they knew about us: how many men we had left, how much in the way of weapons and supplies, possible positions…and worst of all, where we were going.

"I'll never forget how it was when we got there…here. So damn still. It was late in the day. We knew we were close and we knew they were close, too. There were maybe twenty of us left by the time we got here. We'd been taking a heavy beating from both sides.

"Wangdu sent a few men up to scout out the pass, maybe find some water for the horses. The rest of us set up in a circle and started gnawing on frozen pieces of yak fat. We were hoping to sneak over the border that night…but they'd gotten here before us.

"The Nepali army had already sent troops up here to intercept us… must have been at least a thousand of 'em. They made damn sure we didn't slip through the cracks and into India.

"So goddamn still. All you could hear was that frozen fat, crunching in our mouths like gravel. I remember a huge raven circling overhead, landing on a rock next to me and cawing like some evil witch…and then all hell broke loose."

"The first wave of men came from that direction over there." He points to a long string of boulders. "The scouts jumped on their horses and went straight for them; they were the first ones down. The next wave came from over there – it must've been at least thirty to one and they were already in position. We didn't have a chance in hell.

"I don't remember much after that. Bullets flying, men screaming, complete fucking chaos. I grabbed my gun and ran at the line, charging like a bull in heat."

He scraps the bayonet angrily against stone.

"Then I see this soldier. He was running right for me. I knew the gig was up. This was it: Custer's last stand, the final cut. Bullets flying everywhere. All of a sudden, he fell into a drift up to his waist, kicking his arms up in the air like a roach stuck in treacle. I ran at him, stuck him like a pig."

He laughs.

"He looked so damned surprised, like he expected me to come up and shake his hand or something. I'm sure he didn't expect to see a white boy teaming up with the Khampas.

"I froze, bayonet stuck through his middle...and watched him die. It was the weirdest fucking thing. I just stared into his eyes and watched him melt away. Soldiers and Khampas were all around, shooting each other to pieces...and me standing there, fucking bayonet stuck in this poor sack of jelly, staring into his eyes.

"You might kill one man, you might kill one hundred, but there's always that *one*. There's always that one makes you wish you could take it all back.

"...I don't know how I made it out of there without being captured – hell, I don't know how I made it out alive. You know, there's something to be said about walking out of a situation like that. Walking between the raindrops, man. It was just too damn easy for me not to get killed that day, to walk off without a scratch.

"Somebody must have been watching. Maybe the Nepali soldiers thought I was an informant on their side. Those two boys I picked for the recon mission could have said something. There might have been orders from the boys back in Washington not to touch me. Maybe they thought I was part of the act, playing both sides, waiting 'til the last second before I switched allegiance. Maybe Shiva was in a good mood that day and let me slide out of there alive...I guess I'll never know. But every day, I wonder if I might have been better off dying up here with some heart than living down there with nothing left in it."

"Not like I gave a shit if I died at that point, but I'll bet if I'd made a run for it, I'd still be frozen in between these rocks. Yeah, that's what happened...I just dropped my gun and walked. Left my men to die. Left my cause to die. Turned my back on the one thing I really cared about, the only thing I ever believed in.

"...You know what, kid? I lied. Remember when I told you that I never left my men behind. Well, I lied...I fucking *lied*!"

He yells this so loud his voice reverberates around the valley.

"So in the end, I gave up. I guess we all give up in the end."

He coughs into his hand. "Everything seems clearer up here in the cold, doesn't it? ...So damn clear."

He drops to his knees, then, and scrapes the bayonet blade against a boulder. He looks up at me with moist, red eyes. A tear dribbles down the scar on his cheek.

"You're right, Maya. I've been trapped my whole life. You lose hope when you're in a trap...until one day, there's nothing left."

He lifts the rusted blade in both hands, then, as if in prayer. Gently rests the rusty tip against his forehead. Raising his head to the sky, he takes a long, deep breath.

Then, "Nothing left to do," he whispers.

"Jack. No!"

Before I can move, Maya lunges at him, kicking the bayonet free. It spins in the air, plunges into the snow.

Jack drops his head into his lap; Maya drapes herself around him like a shawl.

"I fucking lied," he sobs, ducking his head into her bosom.

"You didn't lie," she says. "You didn't have a choice."

"Some days I think I should have never left that classroom in Chicago. Maybe I could have written another book or two, mopped up a couple Quantrell awards, maybe made it to a professor emeritus, sipping tea at the Oriental Institute. Shit, if I'd played my cards right, I might have been able to snag a Nobel Laureate, pushing the Tibetan cause and actually making a difference. Instead, I wind up on a godforsaken frozen plateau, fighting some lost cause – killing people in the name of Buddha. How fucked up is that?"

"Look at your life, kid. You came here on a whim looking to return the *dzi* to Betty...but you're looking for something more now, aren't you? On the way from point A to point B, you hit a little turbulence and wound up steering for point E, which isn't even on the map. Think of where you'll be headed ten years down the line. What the fuck will you be looking for then? It's scary how the cookie crumbles."

"Things didn't work out the way you thought they would, but you haven't changed, Jack," I say. "You're still stuck on pause in this moment. You keep rearranging how things could have worked out. *If only you'd put more pressure on your liaisons in Kathmandu; if only they'd sent better weapons. If only you stayed and fought valiantly instead of running off like a coward.*

"But you can't go back, it's frozen in time like an insect in amber and there's nothing you can do about it. Believe me, I know. Every day, I'm sitting out on a breakwater on Lake Michigan on a breezy November afternoon watching my dad sail out of the harbor. What if I hadn't been such a shit on the ride down to the lake? Why the storm? Why did I let him go out there alone? Why did he have to *die*?

"Regret is a nasty feeling…it will gnaw at your insides until there's nothing left. It takes over every waking thought, negates every action. I can calibrate and question every single event of that afternoon, over and over again in my mind, but nothing is going to change it…there's not a goddamn thing I can do about it."It's done: leave it."

"The fact that those men turned against you was not your fault," reassures Maya. "Look at me, Jack: it was not your fault…it was *not your fault*! You were loyal to your cause to the end. You fought as hard as you could. You couldn't save those men. You had to save yourself… that's all you could do."

Jack looks up, clouds in his eyes.

"Someone saves your life, you trust them." He kisses her on the forehead.

Then, unwrapping himself from Maya's grasp, he stands and turns to me.

"Here," he says, "This is yours."

He digs into his jacket, pulls out the *dzi* and hooks it around my neck.

His eyes are swollen, tired.

"No, the deal was to get me up here, in exchange for the money and the *dzi.*" I say. "You held up your end and I'll hold up mine. There's no bad blood."

"Hell, I barely got you to the pass." He coughs. "We still have to get you over it. But it's not about that anymore. You got me here, too, you know. I needed to get up here just as bad as you did – maybe more."

"This isn't mine," I say. "It belongs with Betty, not with me."

"*Dzis* are for good luck…and luck is for the living, not the dead. If you want to make it to the other side in one piece, you're gonna need more *than chow chow* and *tsampa.* Take it," he says. "It's yours. You earned it, kid."

We eat in silence. Everything that needed to be said has been said. The wind has kicked up, scaring off the fog. Jack stares up at the pass behind us. Eeyore shifts restlessly in the glare.

Jack muffles a cough into the side of his jacket. Maya comes over to my side. "He's getting worse," she whispers. "He might die if we stay up here any longer."

"Right now? I thought we'd split up in the morning... spend one more night together."

"Look at him – he might be *dead* in the morning."

"...You're right," I say. "There's no sense in hanging around...it looks like I'll have to do it alone. I'll get the gear ready. You take care of Jack."

"I want to go with you," she splutters.

"It's too late in the season for you to risk it. What if a snowstorm hit and blocked you from getting back?"

"I want to go with you and not come back. Jupe, I...I want to be with you."

Her eyes are watery, ready to burst: the clouds before a storm. She's done nothing but fend off my kisses, foil my advances – and *now* she tells me?

"You can't come with me," I assert. "You've got a life here. If I make it out of this country..."

"You mean *when* you make it out," she interjects.

"...After I make it out of here and the smoke clears, we can meet up somewhere. Maybe somewhere fucking warm for a change."

"That would be nice, wouldn't it?" she says. But she doesn't believe me. It's written all over her face. "What if I just go with you to the top of the pass? I should at least get you to the top," she says "I'd feel much better if we were to go together. We've got an extra set of crampons."

We both know that if she goes to the top with me, she's not coming back. *Check those thoughts at the door, girl: your ticket is stamped return only.*

"No way in hell," I say.

"It's always the same..." she replies. "As much as I try, it's never enough."

"Maya, look at me." I hold her face in my hands. "Jack *needs* you. You're one of the few people in the world I think he actually trusts. He looks like death and can barely move right now. And what if he gets a burst of energy and discovers another bayonet in the snow? You need to go with *him*.

"Don't for a second think that I wouldn't enjoy the company," I add. "As much I would like you to come with me, you can't."

"I'll never see you again, will I?" she says. "You're going to be just another Angeline in my life...another Simon."

"Don't say that," I reply. "Shit, Maya, you could even come for a visit after I get back to the States. I'll bet you've never been to a baseball game."

"I can't say I have...can't say I'd want to, either."

"Oh, it's just cricket – with a few Yankee twists. I could show you all over Chicago. You'd love it: the Art Institute, Millennium Park... did you know Chicago was the birthplace of the skyscraper? Shit, we might even be able to get out on the water if I can steal a sailboat from the Yacht Club for a few hours. The skyline is amazing from the lake..."

She looks up at the mountains, then to me.

"If you make it over that pass, I promise to go to a baseball game. Just get over that damned pass, will you?"

"Yeah," I say. "No problem. If the weather holds I should be able to make it down in no time."

I have no fucking idea what's up there, but I've got to be strong. The more she worries, the more she'll want to come with me.

"What about Eeyore?" she asks.

"She wouldn't be any help to me up there. Besides, how the hell else are you going to get Mr Bojangles down? Funny, I made him promise to get *you* back safely...now it's up to you to get him down."

"If he gets too cheeky, I'll just push him down the next crevasse," she laughs.

Jack is hunched over Eeyore like a drunkard, coughing into his chest. Maya is cinching his pack to the saddle. I buckle the top of mine.

"What a trip, huh, kid?"

"It's not over yet. I'm only halfway there," I say.

"Some of us are closer than others. But as long as you get there in the end. And you will…you will."

I walk towards the tent, gazing back at the mountains, then stop as if frozen in a snapshot.

This was it: the mountains, the jagged rocks, the yak-skin tent flapping in the wind…*this was my dream*. Slowly, I make for the flapping door.

Then it happens. So fast…a shivering whirr.

'Ahhhhhh," groans Jack.

"Nooooo…" wails Maya.

I sprint back over to the pony. A fucking *arrow* has skewered Jack's breast.

"Would you look at that!" he grunts and gropes the shaft like a baby clutching for its mother's hand. "This is some kind of karmic retribution," he huffs. "Get my gun."

Dark-cherry sputum froths from one corner of his mouth. "Get it… *now*," he repeats.

A long shriek erupts through the mountains. A hundred yards off on a soft slope is a Tibetan nomad…*the tracker*. Dropping his bow, he flings out a tethered ball and begins spinning it above his head in huge, whispering circles.

"Soooohheee!" he screams.

It churns like the blades of a helicopter…he charges full bore at us.

"Maya, get to the tent!"

I grab her hand but she pulls away.

"Not without Jack. Help me get him off the pony!"

Blood soaks my gloves as we drop him to the ground.

"*Jesus!* Grab his other arm – hurry!"

Jack's body scrapes across the ground as we drag him to the tent.
I look back. The Tibetan drops the stone, draws a knife from his belt.

I rip the tent-flap back and hunching down to enter, we drag Jack to
the far side.

"Quick, Jupe, he's coming," cries Maya.

Where's the gun, where's the gun...*the gun...fuck!*

"Soooohheee!"

Suddenly, I fix on the ice axe propped up in the corner. I shove Maya
behind me.

The flap flies open; I swing into the light.

"Yeeaaaaaaaaahhhh!"

The axe hits hard. Maya screams. A solid hit: a home run, right in
the Tibetan's chest. His blade drops with a thud...and he stares into my
eyes in shock.

He falls to his knees, then, eyes wide, dumbstruck with miscalcu-
lation...that I was capable of such a thing. It's terrible, this thing, but I
can't stop looking at that face...that freshly killed face.

I release the axe. Jack's assailant falls back through the flap, ice
axe sticking out of him like a question mark. Maya whimpers softly in
the corner.

I turn to her.

"...Jack's dead."

"How much further?" I ask.

"Just to the top of the ridge." With our hands strapped round each of his arms, Maya and I drag the nomad up the pass. We're going to bury the two of them...bury them in the sky.

A traditional Tibetan sky burial. It was Maya's idea, but I think Jack would've liked it. Of course he would have liked it. I'm not sure how he would have felt about me taking his boots, but they aren't falling apart like mine and I've still got to get over that pass. I couldn't give a shit about the nomad, but he's Tibetan, and it is their ritual after all.

Jack never did give us a straight answer about the tracker. Someone the Managis hired to tail us out of Kathmandu? The jaded son of a fallen Tibetan chieftain Jack had crossed? Leatherface's accomplice? Blowback from the Freedom Fighter days? I guess we'll never know. Jack crossed so many paths, I don't think he was too sure, either.

Anyway, he's dead. They're both dead.

We haul the tracker's body over a hump and drag it alongside Jack's. "...Now what?"

"Now we hack them to pieces so the vultures can eat them," she says.

"Fuck that! They're already half frozen."

"If we're going to do this," she says, "we've got to do it right."

She slides Jack's machete out from under her jacket. I grab her wrist in midair.

"Goddamnit, Maya. This is totally whacked. Let's just leave him here – the vultures will take care of the rest."

"But we've got to do it right!" she screams. "Can't you see? Can't you see that this is how Jack would have wanted it? This is the way it *has to be*."

She yanks her wrist away.

"Now let me get on with it!"

"Maya..." I plead.

"Fuck off!"

She sinks the knife into Jack's shoulder.

"Maya!" I shout.

"What?"

"…We're not alone."

She whirls around, then, leaps to her feet. Twenty yards off stand two Tibetans, wrapped in heavy sheepskin jackets. They stare us down like deer hunters. It's the rest of his posse, come to finish off the job. Holding the knife out in front of her, Maya backs slowly towards me.

"Stay where you are, Jupiter," she whispers. "Don't move. Let me come to you."

She backs into my chest.

"Where's the gun?" she asks.

"…In the tent."

Spotting the dead Tibetan, one of the herdsmen turns and shouts over his shoulder, then wheels back to Maya.

"Kerang deh la kehri chige yu?"

That's it – they're going to even up the score. They're going to rip us to pieces right here and now, add us to the list. *Where's the gun*?

"What did he say?" I ask.

"I don't know; he's speaking Tibetan. I think he wants to know what we're doing up here," she replies.

"Can't you speak to them? Talk to them. Tell them it was self-defense…tell them they killed each other. Tell them we didn't mean it!"

Two more men, one with a gun, appear behind the others. Without warning, one of them marches forward and pokes their lifeless country-man with his stick. Shit, this is for real! Stowed away, slipped through airport security and huffed all the way up here for this? It can't be happening. Hey, I'm not ready to die!

They begin to talk to one another rapidly. The man with the gun rushes up and points it at Maya. She wavers. Without thinking, I jump between her and the barrel.

"*No!* Tell them it was my fault; tell them I did it! If they want to kill someone, they should kill me. *Maya, talk to them!*" I yell.

"I don't…I can't understand them!"

The herdsman swings his rifle sideways, knocking me to the ground, and pokes me in the chest with the barrel. I raise my hands in the air.

"Goddamnit, Maya, *say something*!"

"*...Nepali auunchaa?*" she whimpers.

Taken aback, they stop in their tracks. A smile erupts across the leader's face.

"*Auunchaa ni!*" he bellows.

He comes right up to my face, then. I flinch as he fingers the *dzi* around my neck. He turns it over, studying it carefully. Oh god, I realize. They want the *dzi*!

One of them flashes me a thumbs up.

"Tell them they can have it," I say. "They can have it if they let us go."

"They won't take it," says Maya. "It's yours now. It belongs with you."

Salt traders...they are salt traders. Nomads bartering salt for barley, shifting like tides among the passes – the only borders they know. They're heading south now before the winter storms seal up the passes. They weren't in with the lone nomad, whoever he was. They didn't know who he was, either. I prefer to leave it that way.

They're going to take Maya with them, get her back home. They chopped up the bodies, too. A bona fide sky burial...thought I'd never see the day.

Maya tells them my plan. They shake their heads, click their tongues like fretful mothers. There is a guard post, one says, but he's never seen it. One day if I'm quick.

They give me some *tsampa* and salted meat, tell me to hurry. Winter's coming...not much time left.

I bring my hand gently to Maya's waist.

"How's your belly holding up?"

"On the mend. I don't think the scar will ever go away, though. "

"Well, I think that you're even hotter with it."

"You're not a very good liar, you know."

I squint up at the glaring sun; against it, the silhouette of a huge bird.

"It's a vulture," says Maya. "They must have spotted the bodies. There'll be more soon."

Yaks grunt as the caravan assembles. At the front, the beasts are already beginning to tramp down the valley.

"Well," I say. "I guess this is it."

"Don't say that," replies Maya. "Don't say it with such finality."

"OK, then. I'll be looking for you on that beach."

"What?"

"The one in the picture. The picture I saw at your parents' house in Kathmandu."

"I remember…yes, I guess that would be as good a spot as any…

"So I'll see you there."

A tear hurries down her cheek; she checks it with her sleeve.

"Here." From her pocket, she pulls a braid of gold and red yarn with an intricate knot at the end, ties it round my neck. "I want you to have this…it's a good luck charm."

"Damn, girl, I've already got the *dzi*. I'm going to max out on luck if I'm not careful. I should be good for at least a half-dozen lifetimes."

"I've already taken my bit of luck from it: I got to meet you, after all." She looks away. "You just make it over that pass safely and we'll sort out the rest later.

"I got it years ago when I visited Dharamsala," she persists. "It was blessed by the Dalai Lama. I went to see him speak in Deer Park. He talked about suffering and how we will all suffer until we learn to detach ourselves from Earthly desires…

"At the end, a foreigner stood up and asked him, 'What if you can't detach yourself, what if you've given your all in trying and you simply cannot escape?' And he replied, 'You must continue to try. Even when all is against you, you must continue to try.'

"Now *you've* got to try, Jupiter. Try as hard as you can to make it over that bloody pass and get to safety... Promise me that."

"...I'll try."

She forces a smile.

"I never thought it would be this difficult," she says, swiping at a tear. "A few weeks ago, I could hardly stand you."

"Attachment is a bitch."

"But we've just got to carry on...don't we?"

"I'll never forget you, Maya."

I grab her, pull her close. I want to tuck her in my pocket and keep her. I feel her sobbing now against my chest. I bend to kiss her.

"No, Jupe...not now," she whispers. "You just get over that pass, alright?"

"When are you going to stop calling me that?"

"As soon as you're gone."

Taking my head in her hands, she lowers my forehead to her lips and kisses it.

"...I rather like you," she says.

She drops her head then, turns back towards the caravan. I can see the tears on her face. I want to cry, want to curl up in her arms and lie there forever. *Come with me, Maya: we can do this...we can do this!*

...No, we can't. That's a different script. I didn't even make the casting call.

I watch her pick her way down to the yaks, bells clanging from their necks. She doesn't look back...she shouldn't look back. That's not in the script.

I sling my pack over my back and turn towards the pass.

My crampons dig deep into the snow. Pack ice crunches under my feet like Frosted Flakes. I poke my ice axe in and out of the drift like a blind man sensing out a curb. If mom could see me now!

Maya's gone, Jack's gone…it's just me now, just me and this snow and ice, and altitude slowly sucking the life out of me. Maya came up here to help me; Jack came up here to die. And I came to run away. Looks like everything might work itself out in the end…if I make it over this pass.

I'm going to miss Maya. I wouldn't have made it without her – wouldn't have even come close. Never likely to meet another like her. Half blueblood, half rebel, with a swirl of Asia…she was the shit. Love and illusion: that's what she said her name meant, right? I couldn't have dreamed up a better girl. She was the kind you throw everything down for, the kind you could spend the rest of your life with. Did I dream her up? Her name suggests as much.

As much as she tried to hide it, Maya really cared about me. It wasn't about her dad; it wasn't even about Simon. In the end, she came all this way because she really cared. So what if it started as empathy? In the end, she threw down everything for me. I hope her father forgives her…I hope mine does, too.

And it seems I care about her. More than I'd like to admit. Shit, I just put myself between that girl and the barrel of a gun. It's as close to love as I think I've ever come – maybe as close as I'll ever get.

Damn, that sun is bearing down on me like a freight train. I can feel my face and arms starting to sizzle. I'm already down to my T-shirt and it's completely soaked. In a few more hours the sun is going to dip, the mercury will dive and everything's going to freeze harder than a steel girder. A lot of good my crampons will do me, then. They're already caking up with snow. My gators are shredded from missteps and on the brink of disintegrating.

I've got to get off this pass before it sets.

Jack…what a card. Joker's wild. He pulled through in the end, though. Awful stats but a real clutch hitter. That's what you get with old swashbucklers like him.

I wouldn't have made it without him. The river, the cave, the dog…

he saved us more than once, more times than we'll probably ever know.

I think he even saved himself at the very end. He looked so serene just before he died, like he had found what he was looking for. I wonder if he made it out of the damned wheel... Something tells me maybe he did.

Jack was ready. He'd been waiting for this for the past forty years. He just wanted someone to take along on the journey, someone to listen. All he really needed was someone who'd hear his story and understand that it wasn't his fault...that things just turned out that way.

That someone was me...and Maya. We read you, Jack, loud and clear.

If I ever get out of this mess, maybe I'll write it down. Over and out.

I can't help thinking that Gerard is here, laughing in the wind, atoms whirling with each gust. I can't help thinking that he knew where this was going all along. Laugh it up, old man, laugh it up. Maybe I'll see you on your next spin of the wheel... *'Can I buy a vowel? Three As? Is it...SAMSARA?'*

I dig the spike of the ice axe into the snow. It's getting deeper, softer now. The morning sun's taking its toll. I'm in a big tub of Rocky Road ice-cream someone forgot to put back in the freezer. An avalanche, a stray rock could take me out any step of the way. *Stop thinking, keep moving.* Why worry about things you can't control? Everything's going according to plan – though whose plan, I'm not quite sure.

I look up towards the top of the pass. Looks close, but I could be wrong... Perspective's in the eye of the beholder, right? I knock a ball of snow off my crampon with the ice axe. There's still blood on the blade.

Keep moving, stop thinking, keep moving, stop thinking.

Jack's here, too. Not hovering over me, but...inside of *me*. I can't explain it exactly. When he died, it was like he became a part of me. And a part of me became him. Shit, I even have his boots on. Took his sunglasses, too. I picked up where he left off: he never made it over that pass, but I will. He wants me to; he's telling me to. I'm just like him now, tossed into a sea of fate with little hope and less steerage…

Who knows what shore I'll wash up on next?

What's my plan? Same as it ever was. To make it over this goddamn pass, maybe force some of that *tsampa* down my throat, then melt a couple clumps of snow into water. That's about it for now. Maybe cook up some freeze-dried noodles for dinner…I really hope there's a flat spot or a cave on the other side.

Keep it simple: just take it minute by minute, hour by hour. If I go beyond that, it gets all jumbled up in my mind.

It's going to be a cold one tonight, I can assure you. I've got six packets of chow chow left, or is it five? Is there even enough gas left to cook them? Fuck it, I'm not even hungry. Got to keep moving, that's for sure – keep moving while I can. I made a promise to Maya. Promised her I'm going to make it. I'm not going to roll over and let this goddamn mountain win. It might take me, but I'm not going down without a fight. Shit, I'm almost to the top now…is that all you've got?

Stop thinking, keep moving.

Snow and sun are slowly blinding me into submission. Every time I blink, there are more spots. The wind is coming up. I should put my fleece back on but I don't want to stop. It's surreal, up here all alone, traipsing through a frozen desert at seventeen thousand feet. This is real, man, as real as it gets. You slip off a ledge, you die. You freeze, you die. You run out of food, you die. No resets on the Game Boy, no more bonus lives after 100,000 points. No spoon-fed after-school specials, soccer moms, low-carb, silicone, linoleum-clad, climate-controlled bullshit up here.

The only thing up here is rocks and ice and death. That's strange… now that I'm away from all the bullshit, that's all I can think about. *Three cheeseburgers, a Coke and a large order of fries, please. With a fake fireplace pumping fake heat out of fake logs with a fake plastic rubber-tree plant.'* But fake fires don't keep you warm, not the way real fires do…and what fuck good is a fake plant?

My leg is stiff as a board. Pain sears through me with every step, but resting is not an option. I crack open the last vial of Jack's witchdoctor oil, gulp it down…*nasty!* That oughta put hair on my back. I hope it's enough to keep infection at bay. Tastes bad enough to kill most life-forms.

Keep moving, stop thinking.

The air is strange up here. Makes you think funny thoughts. Sometimes, if I close my eyes, I can go back home, back in time. It's Thanksgiving or Christmas or a holiday with cranberry sauce and turkey in it…and everyone is smiling. Hey, even mom is happy. Dad's there, too, telling us about the year the Cubs and the White Sox almost went to the pennant. Like that will ever happen again. That's why he's telling it, because it never will happen again… because *this* will never happen again. But that's how I want to remember it.

When they took a vote on which Elvis to put on a stamp, they could pick between fat Elvis or skinny Elvis. The skinny Elvis won, right? I'm sticking with the skinny Elvis.

All these memories, all these images – I don't crave them. I don't yearn to be back around the fake fireplace, stuffing my face with a cheeseburger. They're only images; only a string of never-ending, scratchy, eight-millimeter film clips that keep spooling through my mind on a loop.Maybe I'm really getting closer to the truth, can break free from the wheel after all…but to be honest, I'd give one of my frost-bitten fingers for a cheeseburger right about now.

I open my eyes. Suddenly, I'm back: back in this cold, high death-trap, pretending I'm Sir Mallory or Hillary or Messner on the verge of summiting an unspoiled peak – and simultaneously losing my toes. I haven't felt my toes in the past three hours. That's the rub. Can't have one without the other, can you?

This life, this one life that each of us is given, any which way you go there's pain. And the further you dig, the more questions you ask, the deeper the pain. Hungry ghosts, each and every one of us.

Keep moving, stop thinking.

The straps on my pack dig deep into my shoulders. I blink my eyes again and I'm a nomad…a nomad in a yak caravan, crossing passes in a borderless land to sell my salt or barley. I pop a fistful of *tsampa* into my mouth. Still tastes like shit, even as a nomad. If I eat enough *tsampa* do I become a Khampa? I'm a smelly, frostbitten, sun-battered shell with prehistoric camping gear, some *tsampa* and seven packets of *chow chow* to his name…or is it six? A handful of *tsampa*, that's all you need. The only difference is that once I get over that pass, I'll be selling lies instead of salt. I hope they'll be buying.

How did this all begin? How will it end? In the end, you have to go back to the beginning. It never really ends, does it…things just turn out this way. We're all just stuck in this big mother of a wheel, a globe full of hamsters running round and round, going everywhere, going no-where.

I climb a step, slip back two. Sometimes my thoughts get so blur-ry – other times, they seem so clear. I can't stop thinking about that beach…the palm trees rustling. So warm, so sunny…

I'll see you there, Maya.

First published in Nepal in 2012

ISBN: 978 - 9937 - 577 - 32 - 8

Published and distributed by:

Himalayan Map House (P.) Ltd.
Basantapur, Kathmandu, Nepal
GPO Box: 20784
Phone: 977 1 4244965,4231220
Fax: 977 1 4228340
Email: maphouse@wlink.com.np
www.himalayan-maphouse.com

www.davidabramczyk.com

Design: Santosh Maharjan
        Pawan Shakya

Cover Photo: Wheel of Life
             Golden Temple, Patan
             by Dinesh Shrestha

about the author

David Abramczyk was born in Chicago, growing up in Saint Charles, Illinois. He began his education at Colorado State University studying Wildlife & Fisheries Biology.

After answering an advertisement in a newspaper, David arrived in Nepal to study Nepali language, culture and history, a decision that prompted him to dramatically change his direction in life as he become fascinated with all aspects of the Orient. Lured by quick money and adventure, he traveled to Alaska in the summer of 1990 to work on a salmon fishing boat. Over the next six years he became increasingly involved in commercial fishing.

In 1992 David transferred to University of Colorado at Boulder as a Chinese Language and Literature major. This offered the opportunity to study with an affiliated study abroad program at the University of Nanjing in Nanjing, China. He graduated with a Bachelor of Arts degree in Chinese Language and Literature from Boulder in the spring of 1995.

His knowledge of the region and his fluency in Nepali allowed David to work as a guide specializing in mountaineering, white-water rafting and kayaking. When not guiding David went exploring and mapping out relatively untouched trekking routes in the far reaches of Nepal, often alone.

David is a passionate sailor who has succeeded in two trans-Atlantic crossings and two crossings of the Pacific. He has professionally captained numerous boats in several regions of the world. David currently resides in Kathmandu, Nepal, focusing on writing and mountaineering. He is in training for a summit attempt of another 8000-meter peak this spring.

www.davidabramczyk.com